ECOLOGY IN JÜRGEN MOLTMANN'S THEOLOGY

ECOLOGY IN JÜRGEN MOLTMANN'S THEOLOGY

Celia E. Deane-Drummond

Texts and Studies in Religion
Volume 75

The Edwin Mellen Press
Lewiston•Queenston•Lampeter

Library of Congress Cataloging-in-Publication Data

This book has been registered with The Library of Congress

ISBN 0-7734-8529-5 (hard)

This is volume 75 in the continuing series
Texts & Studies in Religion
Volume 75 ISBN 0-7734-8529-5
TSR Series ISBN 0-88946-976-8

A CIP catalog record for this book is available from the British Library.

The Edwin Mellen Press
Box 450
Lewiston, New York
USA 14092-0450

The Edwin Mellen Press
Box 67
Queenston, Ontario
CANADA L0S 1L0

The Edwin Mellen Press, Ltd.
Lampeter, Ceredigion, Wales
UNITED KINGDOM SA48 8LT

Printed in the United States of America

For my parents

This work is a revised version of a thesis submitted to the University of Manchester for the degree of Doctor of Philosophy in the Faculty of Theology; 1992

Foreword

Jürgen Moltmann's ecological theology of creation is of considerable importance, not only because it is one of the most thorough and imaginative attempts to re-think the Christian understanding of creation in the context of the ecological crisis and awareness of our times, but also because it forms and integral part of his comprehensive theological project. his rejection of anthropocentric and hierarchical models of creation in favour of an ecological theology is rooted in the motifs of relationality and interconnectedness which have long characterised his eschatology, christology, pneumatology and trinitarianism. It is one of the merits of Celia Deane-Drummond's work that she situates Moltmann's God in Creation in the context of his work as a whole as well as engaging in a detailed analysis and critique of that book in particular. her work is an important contribution both to the understanding of Moltmann's theology and the development of green theology. Her own training and experience as a scientist as well as a theologian gives particular value to her critiques of Moltmann's dialogue with science and his appropriation of scientific categories for theological work. By being both appreciative and critical of his work she is able to assess its contribution to the ongoing task of the greening of theology and to point to directions in which further work in this area must go.

Richard Bauckham
Professor of New Testament Studies,
St Mary's College,
University of St. Andrews.

June 1997

CONTENTS

Acknowledgements.

I would like to thank Professor Richard Bauckham for his persistent encouragement and help throughout the period of study. Also I would like to thank Dr. Tim Bradshaw who jointly supervised this work in its early stages, and who made many constructive critical comments. I am also grateful to my friends Joyce and Patrick Thom, Sally Davies and Eva Emmanuel, all of whom offered their expertise in German language to help with the more difficult translations. I would also like to thank Edwin Mellen Press for agreeing to publish this work and Iona Williams for helpful comments. Finally I would like to thank Helen Hughes for proofreading.

July 1997.

ECOLOGY IN JÜRGEN MOLTMANN'S THEOLOGY

CHAPTER 1.

The Development of Contemporary Theologies of Creation in the Cultural Context of the West.

1. Introduction.

The rise in popularity and status of green issues must be one of the most rapid changes that we have faced in our particular cultural history in the Western world. *The Friends of the Earth*, founded in 1973, formed part of the largely middle class counter-culture to the prevailing modernist trend towards economic growth and technology. It is ironical, perhaps, that scientists have shown that even when we treat the environment as a resource within a market economy the crisis is so deep that green issues have been forced into the centre of politics.[1] A further irony is that a cultural shift towards a more pessimistic attitude to science and technology has given the Green movement public acceptance that would have been impossible even twenty years ago. Tim Beaumont points to the broadening that we find in today's politics from a narrower environmentalism to a wider ecological concern.[2] The latter includes interdependence between peoples, as well as environmental issues which serve to combine questions to do with global ecology with both nuclear issues and related questions of justice and peace.[3,4]

Once we move into global questions the underlying factors are so complex that science no longer has the power to say anything sensible even within biological boundaries. Jonathan Schell comments:

> "What is always missing from the results is the totality of the ecosphere, with its endless pathways of cause and effect, linking the biochemistry of the humblest alga and global chemical and dynamic balances into an indivisible whole. This whole is a mechanism itself, indeed it may be regarded as a single living being."[5]

He believes that our activity has become a menace to both history and biology, with a loss of both whole ecosystems and individual species and now the possible specter of human extinction, "the death of death."[6] The nuclear issue as well as the wider ecological one raises important theological questions as well as narrowly ethical ones. We need to ask ourselves if our concept of God is adequate to meet the challenge that we now understand ourselves as having the power of self-annihilation.[7]

The presupposition of the ecological movement with its stress on interdependence, is that we have become alienated from our natural environment. Jürgen Moltmann, who has a passionate concern for issues of justice and peace, alienation and oppression is now, quite understandably, attempting to incorporate more explicit ecological issues into his eschatological theology.[8] While a number of theologians have recognized the need for a theology that takes account of recent ecological concerns, the difficulty for Protestant theology is that it has largely focused on "history" rather than "nature" since the Enlightenment.[9]

The terms "history" and "nature" have ambiguous meanings. History can mean all that happened in the past, the records of these events, human responsibility or humankind's action and the results of this action. We are using the term in the present context to mean "The totality of human events in past, present and future, as governed by God and directed towards his goal."[10] The word "nature" has had historically a plurality of meanings and has at least fifteen meanings today. We will use Kaufman's definition of nature understood in terms of both the totality of processes and the context within which human activity takes place; in other words the raw material which human history transforms into culture.[11]

Kaufman believes that a historical focus to theology began prior to the Enlightenment, and is in fact endemic to the Biblical texts themselves where Israel asserted a belief in the God of history, compared with the gods of nature propagated by the pagan Canaanite cultures.[12] While it is true that Biblical theology in the Protestant tradition has focused on salvation history in the twentieth century, Santmire rejects Kaufman's thesis that the Judao-Christian tradition necessarily excludes nature as a proper basis for theology.[13] Peter Selby argues that our culture favours a biological self-understanding rather than a historical one.[14] Hence the focus of mainstream Protestant theology on history actually alienates theology from popular thought. More liberal Protestant theologians have reacted against this trend by pressing for an immanent God who is the liberator of nature.[15] The idea of immanence and liberation are not incompatible because of a novel dipolar theism introduced by Charles Hartshorne.[16] This is a modified version of panentheism where God is seen to contain the world within himself.

Process theology rejects the idea that we can trace an ecological motif back to the roots of our faith. Jerry Robbins commenting on Paul Santmire's exposition of traditional Christianity, says that "The very thin nature-affirming trajectory he traces displays the ecological bankruptcy of orthodox Western theology, rather than its utility."[17] Yet it is fair to say that the lack of interest in history shown by the theologians of Alfred Whitehead's school may make them insensitive to the message of the classics.[18] David Tracy points out that we need to indwell a classic in order to allow it to affect us in the present.[19] The appeal of a religious classic is less the violent appeal of authoritarianism than "the non-violent appeal to our minds, heart, imaginations and through them to our will."[20] He adds:

"What ultimately counts is the emergence of an analogical imagination for all those thinkers, secular and religious alike, who cannot accept either the brittleness of self-righteous ideologies masking some universal monism or the privatized sloth of an all too easy pluralism masking either a decorous defeatism or some equivocal rootlessness."[21]

We need what Johannes Metz has called a "productive non-contemporaneity," which sheds light on our present concerns.[22] Kathryn Tanner suggests that a modern interpretive framework skews traditional claims about God and the world so that Christian discourse becomes "incoherent in the hands of those theologians who intend to remain faithful to the traditional claims in reformulating them for a contemporary audience."[23] Roman Catholic and Protestant theologians have accused each other of "philosophical seduction of Christian purity."[24] She argues that we need to see modernity itself as conditioned by our own age, and at the same time view pre-modern theology as neither innocent or privileged. We agree with her thesis, which bears some resemblance to David Tracy's notion that a classic can challenge our preconceived ideas. Her approach is more analytical in that she believes we need to search for principles that regulate the construction of theological statements regardless of vocabulary or metaphysical frameworks.[25]

A trend in our more recent cultural history is that we are beginning to appreciate the value of classics especially in art and architecture.[26] Langdon Gilkey finds that our modern understanding of history is becoming less dependent on empirical data and more sensitive to the value of tradition.[27] He also foresees a potential retreat into authoritarianism as a response to our prevailing sense of insecurity and instability.[28] As much of the latter fear is bound up with a pending ecological crisis, this underlies the need for theology to take into account developments in an understanding of both nature and history. Some Biblical scholars have already recognized the need to begin to face up to biological and ecological issues, and move away from narrowly historical questions.[29,30] A key question that we hope to address in this Chapter is to analyse ways in which theological reflection on the doctrine of creation has responded in the ecological climate of our contemporary culture, and in the prevailing uncertainty that the threat of ecological collapse generates. We will focus our attention more closely on Protestant theology, asking in particular two core questions:

1. How has our understanding of God as creator been affected?

2. What is the relationship between ourselves and the natural world, as expressed in the relative significance of nature and history?

We will give a broader preview of the historical changes in cultural attitudes to nature as a way of tracing the build-up to our current ambiguous relationship with nature in terms of both alienation and ecological concern. We aim to set the contemporary theological scene within this broader context, as a way of marking points of continuity and discontinuity with past tradition. We have drawn on those theologies that have been most influential in shaping the background to Jürgen Moltmann's own position, hence we will mention the approach of two key reformers, John Calvin and Martin Luther, in the context of the changing attitudes to nature in the early modern period.

As a way of providing a background to the biological critique which will characterize our subsequent discussion, we will outline the changing climate in our attitude to nature as influenced by the rise in experimental science in the nineteenth century, giving particular mention to Charles Darwin. We find in parallel with these changes an increasing awareness of historical consciousness. The reaction against the parallel emergence of theology rooted in history was championed by Karl Barth who sought to swim "against the stream" of popular liberal Protestantism of his time by affirming once again the traditional basis for Christian theology rooted in faith in God as revealed in Jesus Christ. Overall, however, a potential weakness of his theology is that he never really took seriously enough the influence of the power and force of science in shaping our understanding of the world. Here we draw on three Catholic theologians, Teilhard de Chardin, Rahner and Küng, as examples of those who have made great efforts in this direction.

Nonetheless these positions have not really taken adequate account of the ecological pressure of contemporary culture, and here we give examples of theologians adopting process and/or feminist frameworks for their positions. In the final section we will look at the Eastern Orthodox contribution to the present debate. The latter is particularly significant amongst theologians sensitive to the increased sense of urgency for theology to be ecumenical, and insofar as this underlines the need for Christian theology to be holistic, rather than partisan, reminds us that theological reflection today has become 'ecological'. By this we mean that theology is aware of its interconnectedness and inter-relationship with other positions, in a way that would have been difficult to imagine at the time of the reformers. It also leads into our discussion of the emergence of Jürgen Moltmann's ecological doctrine of creation as found in his earlier works, and which will form the substance of the next Chapter.

2. Changing attitudes to nature in the early modern period.

(a) Martin Luther and John Calvin.

Martin Luther (1483-1546) was inclined to view the natural creation as a "concatenation of hostile energies," and under a curse following the fall of humanity. The wrath of God expresses itself in the evil which we see in the universe, which has a way of becoming "a kind of existential springboard for grace."[31] The radical separation of nature and grace in Luther's doctrine of the two kingdoms tended towards a depreciation of the material world. This aspect contrasts with Aquinas' more synthetic approach towards the realms of nature and grace. However, other aspects of Luther's theology were more affirming in their treatment of the natural world. He does insist, for example, that before the fall of humankind the creation was attractive and good.[32]

While all of nature possesses a miraculous quality and as such presents us with a "mask of God," he posits an anthropocentric view, similar in some respects to that of Aquinas, that humankind through its intellect "soars high above the earth." In this instance he rejects strongly Plato's idea that reason is given to the non-human creation.[33] The ideal state before the fall was such that humankind has no need to employ cunning or skill in its dominion over the animals.[34] We find a positive appreciation of the future redemption of all creatures in his commentary on Psalm 8.[35] Yet the overriding focus in Luther's theology is an insistence on the primacy of our justification by faith, which tends to push considerations about the created realm of nature to the periphery of his thought.

John Calvin (1509-1564) understood all knowledge of God to come from scripture. He portrays God as one whose will rules over inner and outer historical events, rather than the eternal source of being. The rule of God over the external life finds expression in his doctrine of providence, while the rule of God over our inner life finds expression in his doctrine of election.[36] This emphasis on salvation history leads to a more dynamic view of history and helps to overcome the more static view of God as one who upholds the principle of order. Our freedom lies in our willing acceptance of what is ordained by God such that all that we achieve is by an experience of *sola gratia*.[37] The natural creation becomes the theatre for God's glory, and shows us the awesome beauty of the creator.[38] Nonetheless Calvin encourages us to reach out for an active transformation of the world which weakens the more contemplative strands in his thought. In a similar fashion to Martin Luther, we find that for Calvin creation and nature tend to become pushed into the background by his overriding concern for soteriological issues.

(b) The cultural renaissance in the idea of nature.

Even while Calvin was still alive in 1554, Gomez Pereira put forward the view that animals were not so much creatures of God but machines or automata while humans differed in that they had a mind or soul. René Descartes (1596-1650) popularized this view, which was widely accepted according to Keith Thomas because it gave a Christian rationalization for the harsh treatment of animals. There were a few dissenters to this position, Henry More, for example, described it as a "murderous doctrine."[39] The increased mechanization of society gave a visible analogy for these writers. One of its more unfortunate effects was that it served to justify harsh treatment of those people who were on the margins of society, and who were treated little better than animals.[40] The underlying philosophy of nature in this period marks a development of Aristotelian ideas, and Collingwood has coined this "the renaissance" in the idea of nature.[41]

Francis Bacon (1561-1626) championed an anthropocentric vision where he perceived all of nature to be at the disposal of humankind. He insisted that scholars left their detached speculations and applied their knowledge to relieve the burdens of life. He believed that the mechanistic view of nature freed Christianity from the pagan belief which deified nature and identified God with creation. Moreover humankind's mastery over nature in the arts and sciences actually militates against some of the negative consequences of the fall. In a cultural atmosphere that was buoyant from new discoveries and international travel, Bacon viewed Utopia as within our grasp.[42]

Keith Thomas suggests that the historical period between 1500 and 1800 was crucial in setting the stage both for the development of an intense interest in the natural world along with doubts about our relationship to it in a way that has left us with our legacy of current anxiety.[43] Alongside this change in attitude to nature we find the growing development of modern historical consciousness. The static view of history more characteristic of Hellenistic thought was gradually eroded by:

(i) medieval apocalyptic where forms could be changed by divine fiat;

(ii) the criticism of inherited structures by renaissance humanism;

(iii) the challenge of the reformation to inherited medieval ecclesia;

(iv) Calvin's identification of the work of providence in historical terms;

(v) the use of the scientific method.

Gilkey considers that the rise in experimental science was the most important factor in breaking the Greek concept of changeless forms.[44] However, we might equally suggest that a change in perception of nature encouraged the emergence of empirical science. While it is difficult in this case to separate cause and effect, it seems likely that the emerging historical consciousness had an important influence on the development of the modern Darwinian view of biology nearly a century later.[45]

Immanuel Kant (1724-1804) thoroughly endorsed the mechanical view of nature championed by Descartes and Isaac Newton (1642-1727). He viewed nature as consisting of immutable, hard and dead conglomerations of moving particles.[46] Nature is the proper object of scientific knowledge and appears to us as regular and predictable, though this is not the "thing in itself."[47] This marks a shift away from the strictly mechanical view where the mechanism itself was perceived as reality. Kant's rejection of God as the proper object for our scientific study finally severed moral reason from scientific research, but in a way that still gave a value to religion within its own sphere. For Kant, God becomes a necessary postulate which serves our practical reason, and an idea that helps us understand the unity of nature. The difference between humankind and the rest of nature is our freedom, which allows us to transcend nature's deterministic quality.[48]

Paul Santmire regards Kant's philosophy as acting like an "ecological sieve" to the Lutheran and Calvinistic theologies. The soteriological focus of their theology pushed their treatment of nature to the circumference, and the latter was then lost in the post-Kantian era.[49] While this is an attractive suggestion in many respects it is only a partial one since the idea of nature shifted dramatically in the nineteenth century from the mechanical view that had underscored Kantian philosophy. The Darwinian understanding of nature left a double legacy, which we will discuss below, one aspect of which partly contributed to the final separation between science and religion. However, it is true that the Kantian approach provided the philosophical climate in which this could happen.

3. Towards the modern view of nature in the nineteenth century.

The idea of nature characteristic of the modern era is based on an analogy between the processes of the natural world studied by natural scientists and the "vicissitudes" of human affairs studied by historians.[50] The emerging historical consciousness that had begun a century earlier was based on central paradigms of process, development and change, and as applied to biology encouraged the belief that new forms could emerge. Thus in the modern view nature is no longer a closed system, and teleology becomes reintroduced.

Hegel (1770-1831) marks the transition period to the modern view of nature. He incorporated the idea of becoming or process into the primary form of logical becoming. This is not a movement in time or space, or a change of mind, but a logical movement that is part of concepts as such.[51] Unlike Plato's, the system of concepts is not static, but subject to growth. The logical becoming in the world of concepts leads to changes in the world of nature. This dynamic organism of concepts is linked with Hegel's view of God. Humankind is significant in that it is the vehicle of the mind which is the precursor to the being and becoming of the Spirit.[52] Thus Hegel's view of mind is in sharp contrast to that of Kant who believed that our mind creates nature, and requires a postulate of God for practical reason. For Hegel both nature and mind are presupposed by the Idea, and both nature and the Idea have objective reality. His philosophy is an objective idealism, while that of Kant is a subjective idealism.

Charles Darwin (1809-1882) challenged the accepted idea common amongst his contemporaries that humankind is the focal point of the created order. After the stinging critique of David Hume, natural theology had retreated from cosmology to biology as giving us evidence for the existence of God, who is a wise Designer. Hume's radical rejection of all natural theology was not recognized in his lifetime, and only gained respect after Kant had found a way of separating religious faith from science without depreciating religion. In Darwin's era natural theology was still very fashionable. William Paley (1743-1805) and other natural scientists gloried in biological science as a way of disclosing the wisdom of God. Darwin's publication of the *Origin of Species* sought to challenge this view by explaining the intricacies of nature in terms of natural causes.[53]

Darwin's theory aimed to weaken our importance in the created world, and in the period immediately after the publication of his hypothesis almost all the debate focused on this treatment of humankind as one of the animals. Some of the objections to Darwin were scientific, since he made suggestions in his thesis which were impossible to prove, though the intensity of debate depended on religious factors.[54] The real threat to Christianity seemed to many that he removed any need for God in the world. Some Christians attempted to integrate Darwin's thesis with theology by equating the sovereignty of God with natural selection.[55] An important consequence of evolutionary biology is that it encourages the breakdown of the dualism of mind and matter characteristic of Cartesian thought. On the one hand biological life was perceived to be unlike matter, while on the other hand its lack of conscious purpose was unlike mind. Collingwood believes that this marks an important shift in our philosophy of nature and comments: "it is fair to say that the conception of vital process as distinct from mechanical or chemical change has come to stay, and has revolutionized our conception of nature."[56]

Darwin's hypothesis left a double legacy in its combination of historical consciousness with biological change. Positively, it seemed to encourage a very different, more vital, concept of nature that culminated in the philosophy of Bergson, and aligned the modern view with the 'organismic' idea of nature. Yet an implicit pantheism emerges where the distinctions between God, humankind and nature become blurred through the concept of vital process. A negative consequence of its weakened sense of the importance of human beings and seeming denial of the need for God's sovereignty over nature and history encouraged writers such as Ludwig Feuerbach (1804-72) to state that our consciousness comes as a biological consequence of our brains, and religion is a rationalization for human living.

4. The significance of creation in the dialectical theology of Karl Barth.

(a) Faith in God the Creator.

Barth (1886-1968) rejected all attempts following Ritschl and Troeltsch to root theology in history, believing that this amounted to "culture Protestantism" which carried the force of "man," but not of God. The support that his teachers gave to the 1914 war policy underscored his deep mistrust of their authority to speak about genuine ethical Christian belief.[57] The starting point for Barth's doctrine of creation is an affirmation of belief in God the creator, rather than an apologetic for this position *vis-à-vis* a purely materialistic understanding of the world.[58] He presupposes that God exists in relation to creation which is both distinct from God, yet in existence as a result of God's will and action. Moreover, such assertions find their basis in faith in Christ, which can neither be demonstrated nor contested. The relationship between the creator and creation is one of free grace.[59] Heaven and earth are gifts coming from God's free creative acts, and stand in creaturely relationship with God.[60]

For Barth, a doctrine of creation emerges from the self-witness of scripture understood Christologically. In a noetic sense Jesus Christ as God and man teaches us that God, while absolute, has a partner outside himself. Moreover, Jesus Christ as man and God teaches us that humankind is never absolute, but in creaturely relationship with God. Nonetheless, the significance of Christ for creation goes beyond this noetic thesis. For Jesus Christ in an ontic sense is the Word through which God made, upholds and rules creation.[61]

(b) The unity of creation and redemption in Christ.

Barth refuses to speak of creation in isolation from salvation history, and the covenant between God and humankind. He expresses the creative work of God in trinitarian terms, with creation envisaged initially as the work of the Father, but also that of the Son as the Word, and the Holy Spirit as one who gives life to creation.[62] God's election in Christ, and through him the whole of humanity, precedes any discussion of the creation of the world *ex nihilo*. He uses the word *"saga"* to describe the account given in Genesis, in a way intended to reinforce the idea that this is not a scientific description, but an intuitive and poetic account of pre-historical reality. We only recognize the difference between saga and mythical descriptions by relating creation to covenant which finds fulfilment in Jesus Christ.[63]

While Barth describes the animals as "inferior" to humanity, their value is in their prefiguring of humankind and, as sacrifices, prefiguring the supreme sacrifice of Christ.[64] The meaning of humanity as *imago Dei* is that of a relationship of differentiation and unity. The relationship of dominion between humankind and the animals is neither one of unrestricted lordship, nor an expression of the divine image.[65] God rests on the sabbath day, not because he needs to recover, but because the creation of humankind allows him to accept his work of creation.[66]

Barth has been heavily criticized for giving his account of creation too strong an anthropological focus.[67] He does, however, make a special effort to point to the value of creation and its goodness.[68] For him both creation and redemption are joined by the work of grace. The fact of the covenant between God and his people, which finds expression in the incarnation of Christ, stresses the high value that God gives to his creation. Both covenant and creation together affirm the "Yes" of God the creator.[69] In short "where covenant is not seen in creation, or creation in covenant, affirmation that creation is benefit cannot be made."[70] This distances Christian understanding from all other faiths by showing that the covenant is the direction and intent of creation. He comes to the conclusion that creation as benefit "rests" on the "recognition that God is the Creator in Jesus Christ."[71]

The reality of creation takes its bearings from an awareness of its creatureliness. Anything that is not created by God is "unreal," and is under the divine negation. Hence "the creature is because God is its creator."[72] Creaturely existence is only known through God's self-communication in revelation, that is in Jesus Christ. Barth draws back from any suggestion that creation is somehow incomplete:

> "The only thing which can be better than creaturely existence is the goal of the covenant for which the creature is determined in and with its creation. But in the order of created existence as such there can be nothing better . . . Even its future glorification presupposes that it is already perfectly justified by the mere fact of its creation."[73]

(c) The light of creation.

Barth allows for the "luminosity" of creation, showing itself to be that which is created by God. This is quite different from divine self-revelation or divine self-disclosure. The "light" which humankind may or may not see in itself and the world is "quite other" than the light of God's self disclosure.[74] The righteousness of creation is not identical to either the "brighter" or "darker" side of creation, nor is the self-revelation of God dependent on the brightness of the created world.[75] Rather, all the joys and sorrows of creation pale into insignificance compared with the exaltation and humiliation of Christ.[76]

Barth picks up his discussion of the "lights" of creation in his doctrine of reconciliation.[77] He refrains from using the word "revelation" to describe the light of creation because of its association with natural theology, which he is quite determined to reject.[78] Yet the "lights" of creation are not "extinguished" by Christ's Light, "nor are their force and significance destroyed."[79] Thus the persistence and lights of creation rest on the faithfulness of the creator in a way which "are not extinguished by the corruption of the relationship between God and man through the sin of man."[80]

While the lights of creation are not self-revelations of God, they come from God and "they are its own lights, words and truths .... They are its own revelations ie. those of the *creatura* itself. If this expression is to be used only very sparingly it is not to be totally rejected in this sense and context."[81] Barth distinguishes clearly, then, between the saving light of Christ, who is the self-revelation of God, and the lights of the world created by God and distinct from God.

Barth resists the term "revelation" to describe the "light" of creation because he believes that no faith is required to grasp their reality, "but only an obvious and most inevitable perception" which is "only the application of the good, but invited gift of common sense."[82] At the same time the revelation of God in the incarnation is not "alien" to the creaturely world, or "another message," but the "one declaration of its Creator and Lord."[83] We can sum up Barth's understanding of the distinction between creation and Christ, yet their close interrelationship by stressing the double movement of creation and redemption:

> "The work of His creaturely grace always has in view His reconciling grace. But the converse is also true, so that he is always the Guarantor, Sustainer and Protector of His creaturely world, of the cosmos or nature, thus giving it constancy in the being with which he endowed it at Creation."[84]

(d) Subsequent developments.

While Barth attempted to establish a dialectical theology in the face of liberal Protestantism which seemed to equate God with the world, for some Protestants Barth had not gone far enough both in his acknowledgement of the authority of scripture and in his belief that theology should provide guidelines for our action in the world. The recent movement of reformation theology sought to rediscover Calvin as one who gave us more adequate guidelines for systematic theology. The traditional overarching movement of creation, fall and redemption hoped to include the whole world as that under the direct sovereign government of God. Instead of a view of revelation that becomes focused in our acceptance of faith in Christ, as in Barth, or the decision for Christ, as in Bultmann, the reformed school rooted revelation in scripture and gave it the status of objective propositional knowledge. This movement away from existential categories overcame some of the dualistic connotations of a separation of faith and knowledge that was the legacy of Kantian philosophy.

As in Barth, the covenant idea predominates, but now it is "linked explicitly" with the "fixed regularities" of creation which were established by God.[85] The motif of the kingdom of God needs to make itself felt in all areas of life, so that it moves away from the privatization of faith and is less hesitant when it comes to social action.[86] Our decision is as much the choice of service of God in the world, as an existential commitment to faith in Christ. The notion of image-bearing extends to include the stewardship of the earth, which has implications for involvement in the ecological movement.

This concern for our natural environment stems from an awareness of creation as God's gift to us, rather than any belief in the immanence of God in creation.[87] Our task is to preserve and develop the earth, and this moves Christianity into dialogue with culture rather than above, below or in paradox with culture, as defined by Richard Niebuhr.[88] The strength of this position is that it is sensitive to the interdependence of the earthly environment and provides a directive towards the rest of creation rather than a retreat into a ghetto. Its implicit danger is a tendency towards triumphalism, and a weak appreciation of the value of other theological frameworks. It offers an alternative way of overcoming the dualism of faith and nature, first recognized by Abraham Küyper and discussed by Herman Dooyeweerd, who comments that "faith is a unique function of our inner life implanted in human nature at creation."[89] Thus it moves away from the narrower identification of "sin" with "nature" in dialectical theology, and the classical division of nature and grace in Roman Catholic scholasticism.

Paul Santmire is more on the "left wing" of the reformed school, and Claude Stewart describes him as "neo-Reformed."[90] He is heavily influenced by Barth's theology, though he seeks to move beyond its concern for human salvation to a wider anthropocentric view within the classic reformed motif of the kingdom of God. His theology aims to be both biblically based and sensitive to tradition, though he believes that both need reformulating in the light of current concern. He sees a double movement in Western culture: first, towards a manipulation of nature, and second, towards an escape into the wilderness. He believes that we will overcome this schizophrenic tendency if we recapture a vision of the kingdom of God extending to all creatures. All the earth shares in the divine commonwealth. The advantage of this socio-political imagery is that it allows for a double concern for social justice and environment, though Santmire does not explore this possibility very rigorously.

Santmire's achievement is to shift awareness and concern for nature within the reformed Protestant tradition, while retaining a clear sense of the sovereignty of God and our distinct role as stewards of creation. Stewart critiques Santmire's work by pointing out that in many places he seems to show inconsistency and lack of coherence.[91] A more serious difficulty with Santmire's theology is his attempt to fit traditional reflection into his particular view of opposing currents of ecological and spiritual motifs which he traces to the ambiguity in scripture. His basic presuppositions remain undefined.

5. Recent shifts in Roman Catholic theology.

(a) Teilhard de Chardin.

Pierre Teilhard de Chardin (1881-1955) attempted a synthesis between evolutionary science and theological reflection so that Darwin's theory of evolution extended to include human society. His understanding of the relationship between God and the world is one which stresses both the immanence of God in creation and its future glory through the cosmic Christ. We will come back to details of his understanding of the relationship between God and the world in the discussion below. Our initial preliminary question is how he incorporates biological insights into his theology. While he uses Darwin's basic framework, he introduces the idea of a single axis of evolution tending towards hominization. His own "law of complexity consciousness" operates within Darwin's framework of natural selection, and is the law which governs the evolutionary axis. He calls the overall process orthogenesis, though the idea within biological science had failed to gain credibility.

The biological term *orthogenesis* meant direction in evolution regardless of external influence. For Teilhard this all-embracing category includes the successive stages of physical organization of matter, or *cosmogenesis*, the emergence of life or *biogenesis*, the development of a central nervous system or *cephalization* and finally the emergence of self-consciousness or *homogenesis*. He uses the term orthogenesis to express a teleological motif, though for him this means the specific unidirectional increase in complexification. The evolutionary process continues within society at large, so that following an expansive phase we have now entered a period of intensification so that we have reached a critical point of being aware of ourselves as evolved beings which is part of the "involution" of evolution.[92]

The final goal of orthogenesis is *Omega*, which Teilhard believes we can deduce from science, and this merges with Christian theology in its goal in the cosmic Christ. Teilhard uses evolution to provide him with a natural theology. We are required to be active participants within the evolutionary process in order to bring about the emergence of the *Omega*. This is clearly radically different from the more traditional separation of natural theology and eschatology where God breaks into our history. While Teilhard does have room for the idea of the parousia of Christ as divine intervention, for him this coincides with the *Omega* that emerges during the course of evolution. The driving force within the evolutionary process is not the neo-Darwinian law of chance and necessity, but rather a "love energy" which serves to unite the human community even to the extent of overcoming the "death barrier."[93]

Teilhard's aim was to fuse the "headless" modern humanistic ideas of progress, with the Christianity of his time that seemed for him to be detached from the world and more akin to a "head in which the blood no longer circulates at the necessary speed."[94] While he uses the concepts of evolution in a general sense, his introduction of the idea of *orthogenesis* and power of love energy puts his thought outside the possibility of empirical falsification, and so outside the realm of science. From a scientific perspective an additional weakness is that he ignores the biological fact that evolution is multidirectional rather than unidirectional, even though he claims that his ideas are scientific. From a theological perspective his vision of the cosmic Christ tends to weaken the importance of the Jesus of history. His optimistic view of humankind and lack of emphasis on human sin leaves the more general exploitative aspects of humankind's relationship with nature unresolved.

Teilhard defends himself against such criticism by arguing that science needs a soul if it is to become personal rather than impersonal, and this soul is Christ. He also refuses to separate creation, incarnation and redemption so that the Jesus of history is still significant for the cosmic Christ, rather like a "concrete germ." The incarnation serves as the link between Christ the evolver and Christ the redeemer, expressed in a concrete way through the eucharistic sacrifice. Teilhard perceived redemption more in terms of re-creation than forgiveness of sins, which reflects his stress on the cosmic rather than the juridical rôle of Christ. He introduces the concept of *pleromization* in order to keep the categories of creation, incarnation and redemption together, and he defines this as the "mystery of the creative union of the world in God."[95]

The vision of Teilhard assumes that all energy is psychic energy. The component known as tangential energy links an element with all other elements of the same order, and is that studied by science, while radial energy which draws life on towards greater complexity and centricity is that characterized by orthogenesis. Santmire believes that Teilhard's panpsychism becomes personalised in homogenesis, and this gives his theology gnostic overtones.[96] However, overall Teilhard's vision points less to a rejection of the material world, than an acceptance of it through a pervading sense of the love energy of God within the whole cosmos. He shifts the emphasis in theology of his period, which tended to stress a God who is Above, by reinforcing ideas of a God who is Ahead and Within creation. Humankind's place in the future purposes of God becomes elevated, which tends to give his theology a greater anthropocentric orientation. His apparent lack of appreciation of evil *per se* tends to encourage pantheism. Teilhard believed that he was right to downplay evil in the universe in the "interest of clarity and simplicity," but this was naive, as was his assumption that "what I have omitted could nevertheless be seen."[97] While overall his writing does allow for evil in the universe, this aspect is ignored in much subsequent interpretation.

Teilhard's work was castigated by the Roman Catholic authorities in his lifetime, but he has had a wide influence after his death, especially in liberal Protestant circles. His significance is his attempt to develop a holistic vision of the world that incorporates science and faith, though the distinction between God and the world is subtly eroded by his approach. Philip Hefner considers Teilhard's doctrine, which shows parallels with process theology, is more powerful than the theologies of hope which, he believes, seem to deny the "absolute worth" of creation.[98] He believes that Teilhard's concept of the past and present as that which serves as a basis for our future vision is the only realistic alternative. For our present discussion Teilhard's significance is that he has moved beyond the traditional categories of the ontological transcendence of God over creation, to one that in addition pictures God as the God of the future. Moreover, this future is conditioned by human action in history, which places a far greater weight on our responsibility within the world as well as a greater optimism as to our potential to achieve this end. The appearance of Christ as the culmination of this evolutionary process diminishes the value of the individual, or other species apart from humanity. Teilhard's vision was particularly vulnerable to attack in the wake of the collapse of the liberal humanistic optimism. While aspects of his thought associated with panpsychism may become popular again, his overall synthesis of technology, science and faith causes his theology to fade along with the recent disillusionment with the modernist dream.

(b) Karl Rahner and Hans Küng.

Rahner (1904-1964) combined the insights of Heidegger and Joseph Maréchal with those of Kant and Aquinas. Rather than the evolutionary method of Teilhard, or Heidegger's philosophy in Bultmann, Rahner uses instead the transcendental philosophy of Maréchal to reconcile modern culture with Christian belief in God the creator, and with an awareness of ourselves as creatures belonging to God. He rejects both biblicism and positivism in dogma, and broadens the notion of grace to include our general capacity to transcend our environment. He considers that the potential for grace is built into our beings in such a way that we can never "abandon this transcendental peculiarity."[99] Even if we reject the grace of God, which comes to all human beings like an offer, this still becomes determinative for our existence.

Rahner moves away from any dualism in the idea of nature and grace which implies that grace is added to our nature. God's intention is to give the whole of creation a supernatural end, which must have an effect on the very essence of being. This prior operation of the sphere of grace prepares us for our supernatural end which we reach in a partial sense through justification, and in a more complete sense through the beautific vision.[100] Once we accept that grace is formative for our creaturely nature, we do not need to draw a firm line between natural knowledge as perceived in creation, and revelation of God. The difference between nature and grace is of value for methodological clarity since it reminds us that grace is entirely gratuitous rather than based on our own merit. He believes that scholastic theology which posits a belief in grace added to nature was unwarranted "extrinsicism," which is "less than human" by being identified with an archaic philosophy orientated towards mechanical "physics."[101]

Rahner tackles the problem of the relationship between creation and redemption by suggesting that it is false to make a direct parallel between these categories and nature and grace. Nature and grace still remain for Rahner "distinguishable entities."[102] However, the order of redemption includes creation in the sense that the whole is related to the part, so that while they are not identical, they are not distinguishable either.

While Rahner recognizes both the interdependence and hierarchical ordering of creation, he is confident that God "wills the whole of creation for the sake of the highest being in creation."[103] The existence of creation is both "infinitely different from God," while the miracle of divine love is expressed most fully when God "takes a created reality to himself as his own in the Hypostatic Union."[104] Now from this it follows that the creation can only be healthy and whole as it is integrated into the supernatural order of grace. The natural order has an inbuilt "crying need for grace," and so is of itself always more than natural.[105] The cross reminds us that the future of creation is not utopia on earth, while the decision of God to enter our world leads us to a belief that the future of the world is already decided in terms of salvation. The future aspect of salvation gives us a mandate to work responsibly for a unity between creation and redemption which will only be realized in the future.

Rahner's theology is radical in that while he affirms the belief in the difference between the creator and creation, he overcomes the dualism implied by such a belief by a radical re-interpretation of the scholastic notion of nature and grace. The basis for overcoming this dualism has its root in the coming of Christ. However, overall Rahner's Christology stresses the incarnation, which contrasts with Barth's emphasis on divine election and soteriology. The consequence for Rahner is that all of creation is now affirmed and saved. There are similar universalistic tendencies implied in Barth's thought, though Barth clearly distinguishes the "Yes" of God towards his creation through grace, from the "No" towards sinful humanity. Barth's Protestant heritage with its focus on sinful human nature prevents him from affirming culture in the way that is possible for Rahner. Moreover, Rahner's wider vision, compared with the Christological concentration that we find in Barth, allows him to integrate the whole of creation as entering the sphere of future salvation.

Rahner's all-encompassing concept of the relation between God and the world fosters a dialogue with all branches of human life, including that of science. He is well aware of the problems of the specialization and fragmentation of science which leads to "gnoseological concupiscence."[106] This is the human awareness that through the specialization of science it is quite impossible to achieve a comprehensive view of reality. Theology differs in its focus on the "transcendence of man as such."[107] If theology became rational statements it would become unmasked by the sciences as "meaningless." Now science needs theology since it rarely considers the subjectivity of the scientist, and often fails as science to consider the unity of reality as that which is greater than the sum of the parts.   Rahner believes that a fundamental weakness in each branch of science is its tendency to monopolize other sciences, and its failure to listen to other approaches, including theology. The task of theology is to persuade science of its human nature, rather than to pretend that it can offer a material contribution.[108] In this Rahner's approach seems to be more realistic than that of Teilhard who, as we noted above, attempted a more direct synthesis between science and faith. For Rahner, our capacity for a complete knowledge or complete being is never attainable, and we are limited by our own finitude. This distinguishes God and creation, since God is pure being and pure knowing.[109]

Hans Küng(1928-), like Rahner, aims to include the secular world as a serious part of his theological discourse. In fact he believes that a theology which refuses to face scientific questions is an expression of either arrogance or ignorance.[110] He fears that traditional Catholic faith has isolated itself from the developments in science and has become trapped in the medieval scholastic view of the world. While science in a methodological sense has to leave out God, the individual scientist needs to retain an "open-mindedness towards reality as a whole."[111] Küng is closer to Rahner than Teilhard here in his claim that this is not science as such. The problem of finding a coherent unity in the whole of reality is "obviously connected with the question of God," in such a way that we are in "absolute need of a new, a modern understanding of God."[112]

We agree with Küng, and this forms the presupposition of much contemporary theology that seeks to revise our understanding of the God-world relation in a way that takes into account both the scientific perception of the world and the present ecological crisis. The success of such attempts to remain faithful to the witness of scripture, tradition and reason in developing images of God depends on presuppositions as to the relative importance of each in acting as a criterion for theological reflection. The trend towards taking account of ecological issues is not so obvious in either Rahner or Küng's theology, and reflects the particular anxiety of the period which was how to affirm belief in God the creator when Darwinian science seemed to allow us to explain the existence of the world without God. More surprising, perhaps, is Küng's relatively minor treatment of ecological themes in his latest book, *Global Responsibility*; though here he is primarily concerned with inter-religious dialogue.[113]

Küng rejects the understanding of the relationship between God and creation in anthropomorphic or rationalistic deistic categories. He prefers the panentheistic notion that God is in the world and the world is in God: he is the infinite in the finite and the absolute in the relative. Moreover, he is a living God who is active in our history. There remains an "irremovable" distance between creator and creation, divine and human; both in the ontic sense of divine nature and sinful humanity and the noetic-ethical sense of divine knowledge and human knowledge, divine revelation and human unbelief. He wishes to overcome a tendency towards deism or pantheism in the belief in God as "non-personal" or the "supreme person," preferring the idea of God as "transpersonal."[114] Like Barth, Küng believes that a positive attitude towards the world stems from faith in God the creator. The world once more becomes meaningful, as does our place in it: "believing in the creator God of the world thus means accepting with greater seriousness, greater realism and greater hope my responsibility for my fellow men and for the environment and the tasks assigned to me."[115]

He is well aware of the revolutionary significance of molecular biology within biological science and addresses the question of chance and necessity in the work of Jacques Monod (1910-1976) and Manfred Eigen. For Monod the concept of chance seems to predominate to such an extent that the world becomes meaningless, while for Elgen the world is an "inescapable necessity" coming from biological laws. This differs from the vitalism implied by the law of complexity consciousness of Teilhard de Chardin. Küng rightly resists the temptation to put God in the gaps of our biological knowledge. Rather he believes that we need to face clearly the choice between humankind in solitude where there is no God or an affirmation of the unity of all reality in God.[116] Küng wishes to redefine our concept of God as one who is both infinite yet intimately bound up with the suffering of the world. Both humankind and the environment are bound up together into God's being, so that God is not "without feeling, incapable of suffering, apathetic in regard to the vast suffering of the world and man, but a sym- pathetic, com-passionate God, who, in the future, changing everything by liberation from sin, suffering and death leads to infinite justice, to unbroken peace and to eternal life - a God of final redemption."[117]

In this way Küng has tilted the relationship of transcendence between God and creation even further towards the future, so that the power and love of God is only realized in the future. Furthermore, the idea of God as one who contains the world in himself, including a share in its suffering, marks a radical departure from the more traditional hierarchical schemes that use monarchical imagery to express the sovereignty of God over creation. As we will see later, much of his theology resonates with Moltmann's understanding of a God of the future who suffers with creation while remaining distinct from it.

6. The influence of theologies of protest against tradition.

(a) Process theology's affinity with nature.

While Hans Küng and Karl Rahner move beyond traditional Catholic formulations of God, the theologians of process take the secular view of the world with even greater seriousness. As we might expect, process theology is bolder in its willingness to re-formulate both its image of God, and the relationship between God and the world.[118] Whitehead believed that all of reality has a subjective element so that his aim was to weaken the distinction between mind and matter. He rejected the notion that cause and effect are simultaneous; rather this is an illusion known as "presentational immediacy."[119] Instead we need to understand our observations as having an objective reality or "physical pole" prior to our reception of this as empirical data.[120] Whitehead draws on the medical/biological understanding of how we perceive objects to redefine his philosophy, but at the same time introduces the idea of subjectivity into the heart of matter itself. The only difference between subject and object is a temporal one, so that objects are past events while subjects are present events.

Whitehead's philosophy gives us a completely different picture of the relationship between God and creation. Now we become fused with inanimate matter in such a way that subjectivity is felt throughout the universe, where the idea of the eternal is emergent in God's consequent nature. Thus the concept of the transcendent God only survives in a weak form in a horizontal, rather than vertical relation to the present. Henry Nelson Wieman aimed to modify Whitehead by including a larger idealistic vision, while Charles Hartshorne and other process theologians used Whitehead's philosophy and redefined it in Christian categories. A sense of the "otherness" of God comes back through a modified version of panentheism, though the transcendence of God is not understood within the traditional framework of omnipotence.

Process theology is a reaction against the dialectic theology of Barth, and insists on developing a theology that emerges from concrete rootedness in our world, as against beginning with a given faith in God the creator. The more recent process theology differs from the earlier humanistic liberalism in that it searches for more indirect and symbolic ways of expressing the meaning of our existence.[121] The grounding of process theology in empirical categories also aligns it closer to naturalism.[122]

Process theology caught the ecological mood of the 1970s and it identified readily with ecological issues more quickly than traditional theology. John Cobb promotes a theology of ecology based on a process understanding of the world.[123] While he admits that we have acute social injustice in the world, he believes that the more fundamental issue is an ecological one since it affects the survival of the entire human race. He is sharply critical of a technological attitude which, he believes, refuses to acknowledge means of production, and favours instead an ecological attitude which tries to set limits to this action.

As we might expect from the negation of the "otherness" of God in process thought, the focus of Cobb's theology is on our attitude to nature as affected by different religious perspectives.[124] Moreover, he argues that the Taoist belief in cosmic spirit did not, in practice, limit economic exploitation of the environment. Cobb thinks that St. Francis is too far removed from our civilization to give us any real guidelines for theology, and he prefers the approach of Albert Schweitzer. His aim is to encourage a love for all living beings, and in contrast to the passivity of Francis, he believes that a theology of nature "need not prevent man from continuing his scientific investigation of nature ... but it would prevent ruthless indifference to the consequences of our actions for the living environment."[125]

Cobb thinks that Whitehead's philosophy that subjectivity is at the heart of all matter is vindicated by science itself. He believes that now that we have: "excellent evidence that electromagnetic events do take account of their environment, it is reasonable to affirm that they are instances of unconscious feeling."[126] Cobb is right in insisting that we need to have a deep commitment that is no longer possible either in secular atheism or vital paganism that tends towards a thirst for escapist experiences. He recognizes that the idea of a process in the universe is too vague to warrant our commitment. However, his final conclusion seems to be that our basic commitments arise or emerge, rather than happen through choice, so that following Whitehead we become aware of dynamic life as "a creative influence that is effective in every event."[127] We can conceive of the "spirit, and belief in giver of life and love that is the basis of hope. Belief in this Spirit is belief that I am not alone ....it is because of God that it may not be too late."[128] We doubt whether this idea of the Spirit has a sufficient Christian content once it is severed from the idea of the Trinity; also it is hard to imagine how such an emergent Spirit could have any real influence in shaping both our future and that of nature, and thus giving the cosmos a real ground for hope. Moreover, Cobb makes no attempt to incorporate his Christology into a theology of nature. The difference between humankind and the rest of creation, which is presupposed in his idea of stewardship, does not seem to have a sufficient basis.

(b) Feminist theology's identification with the earth.

Rosemary Radford Ruether is a radical Catholic feminist who seeks to reinterpret traditional dogmas in the light of our current awareness of sexist attitudes, which she believes distorted previous Judao-Christian doctrines. The feminist perspective is primarily a protest against the injustice of sexual oppression which is encouraged by our previous images of God in patriarchal categories. Some feminists reject Christianity completely as hopelessly "androcentric," while more moderate feminists believe that a radical reformulation of Christianity through a demythologization of its patriarchal categories comes closer to the real truth of Christian faith.[129] Our concern here is to present examples of a more moderate position, rather than the more radical "post-Christian" view.

Ruether, like other feminists, critiques the structure of society, and calls for a replacement of the dominant patriarchal hierarchy with egalitarian structures. This includes theological reflection so that all ideas of God as one who has power over his creation need to be rejected in favour of the "Holy Spirit, who is the ground of Being of creation and the new creation."[130] Ruether believes that the dualism between spirit and matter has its roots in patriarchy, since it was this which sought to elevate consciousness and mind to a supernatural level. Eventually apocalyptic literature emerged which envisaged a radical denial of nature, so that "the patriarchal self-deception about the origin of consciousness ends logically in the destruction of the earth."[131] The structure of patriarchal consciousness is such that it denies the harmony in nature, and has its natural expression in the repression of women. We need to look to a "radical reshaping of the basic socio-economic relations and the underlying values of society" so that women play more than a "symbolic" role in the ecological crisis, but unite the "demands" of the ecological and women's movements.[132] In this way Ruether believes that unless we have liberated human relations from the false polarities of male and female, we cannot hope to find an adequate theological basis for a change in our attitude to nature.[133]

The symbol for hope of a new humanity comes from a development of Mariology. Mary, who has been used in the past for a false denial of our sexuality under images of male domination, needs to assume her right place as representative of the wholeness of humanity before the fall.[134] Moreover, Mary is a more concrete symbol of human hope, since she is human unlike the person of Jesus who is human and divine. In this way she becomes "the concrete realization of the possibility of the final glorification of the human community and the creation."[135]

Writing from a rather different, more liberal Protestant perspective Dorothee Soelle and Shirley Cloyes wish to reject any ideas of the separation of God from his creation. However, they see the divine and human interrelationship as dynamic and reciprocal, rather than emergent from creation as in process thought. They aim to recapture a sense of love for and wonder at creation, over against a more domineering attitude which they believe stems from a masculine attitude towards creation. They are anxious to replace a technological attitude, which only leads to despair, with a "passionate love for creation."[136] They also believe that the separation of our work from God's creation encourages both our alienation from nature and a retreat into religiosity. Once we become caught in this spiral we are deaf to the "cry of the earth."[137]

Ursula King believes that the distinctiveness of the women's movement is the link between politics and spirituality, and it is the sense of interrelatedness in the feminist spirituality that prevents politics becoming "partisan." The "desperate need" in our society is a vision of peace, which includes peace with nature, and as in Ruether, King aligns the ecological and women's movements: "Women believe in the power of non-violent discipline as an inner, spiritual energy which can make us experience an essential harmony between ourselves and the world around us, and lead to human reconciliation."[138]

King is concerned to reject all anthropocentric theology as unwarranted "speciesism" and prefers the Eastern belief in a bond between all creatures and the earth.[139] While she is well aware that feminist theology can become an ideology which loses its sense of historical consciousness, not all feminists would agree that it is necessary to delve into Eastern religion for an adequate understanding of the relationship between God and creation. Sallie McFague, for example, wishes to reconstruct the Christian models of God in a way that portrays God as mother to the world. Now our mistreatment of nature becomes a sin against God's body.[140] The other Judao/Christian strand that McFague develops is the portrayal of God as *Sophia* wisdom. The advantage of this image is that it brings a sense of both the transcendence and immanence of God, Jesus answering the expectation for *Sophia* wisdom.

Elizabeth Moltmann-Wendel similarly wishes to reinstate the importance of the feminine in God. She believes that there is no need to return to pagan ideas of a nature Goddess, which are exclusively for women, rather we can find parallel ideas of the feminine aspect of God in Jewish rabbinic belief about the feminine presence in *Shekinah*: "The *Shekinah* is something like the cosmic, reconciling, earthly side of God which accompanies Israel into exile whereas God has hidden himself in anger."[141] She is convinced that the feminine images of God persisted in an unwritten "subculture," even though they faded in the written tradition.[142] There is an additional latent feminine aspect to Jewish hope in the symbolism of milk and honey. Once this hidden feminine tradition is uncovered, theology learns to trust this alternative way of seeing reality. The picture of land is significant as it is all-embracing in its hospitality towards both men and women.

Moltmann-Wendel's starting hermeneutic is from the experience of interrelatedness. This includes a belief in the "deep total sociality of all things," which allows relationships to take on a "cosmological and critical ecological significance."[143] Rather than dissolving individuality the communal aspect gives room for a basic love of self that is unashamed of emotional experiences. This love leads to energetic outgoing love that is neither hierarchical nor "just brotherly and democratic," but changes all our attitudes.[144] She rejects the criticism that friendship with nature slides down a "slippery retreat into an apparent harmony with the universe," rather a sense of wholeness in ourselves provokes the pain of conflict, since the creation is not yet whole. She explains: "If I am whole, I suffer from the fact that creation is not whole, and have the right and duty to protest that the creation is no longer whole."[145]

Christopher Lasch, as cultural analyst, believes that the identification of the love of nature with femininity, and of domination over nature through technology with masculinity clouds the underlying narcissistic tendencies that are in both attitudes. He believes that the "feminine" longing for symbiosis is as psychologically regressive as the "masculine" solipsistic drive for mastery. He is particulary sharp in his critique of the use of "shopworn slogans" that have filtered into the women's movement and the environmental and peace movements.[146] His warning is that a politics of conservation must rest on a firmer philosophical foundation than the mystical adoration of nature, which only tends to loss of individuality. He advocates practical reason instead of the instrumental reason of technology or the spirituality and mysticism of feminism. The danger of feminist attitudes as far as Lasch is concerned is that they lead to a surrender of our wills through our romantic dream of symbiotic union. Instead we should face with more realism the tension that comes from the fact that while we are dependent on nature we still transcend it.

7. The Eastern Orthodox contribution to an ecumenical theology of creation.

The ecumenical movement's official organ, the World Council of Churches (WCC), has become more vocal on the implications of ecological issues over the last ten years. The idea of the "integrity of creation," first coined at the Vancouver conference in 1983, emphasized the political implications of the notion of the interdependence of the natural environment and our use or abuse of the earth's resources. Gosling sensed that ecumenical theology that focused on Christology was inadequate to meet the environmental crisis.[147] The earlier work of the WCC gave primacy to history in the relationship between nature and history. Nature is part of the prehistory of Israel, and Christ confessed as the "ultimate secret of creation."[148] The revelation of God comes through his words and deeds in history; the new world is "this world renewed" with humankind exerting a divinely appointed mastery over an "entirely subservient" nature.[149]

The WCC followed the overall trend within the theology of the late 1970s against technology and the dehumanizing effects of industrialization. The biologist Charles Birch addressed the "Faith, Science and the Future" conference at Massachusetts in 1979, using process theology as a basis for his approach. He argued that the underlying cause of injustice and ecological damage is related to the technocratic image of our Western culture, though unlike the feminists he did not link this attitude with masculinity. Birch believes that in spite of all the advances of biology since Darwin, the underlying idea of nature is still mechanistic, like pouring "new wine" into old wineskins.[150] Birch's solution to this problem is a "personal" encounter with the universe and, with this aim in mind, he is unashamed to blur the distinction between nature, humankind, and God. Like John Cobb he believes that the philosophy of Whitehead is particularly amenable to formulating a new attitude towards the world that has an ecological orientation. While God's primordial nature expresses the order within the creative energies of the world, God's consequent nature expresses the experience of joy and suffering, pain and happiness of the world.

The more recent writings of the WCC have found a way of articulating the concern for the environment through liberation theologies coming from the Third and Fourth worlds. The concern for ecological questions is of particular relevance for the indigenous peoples of the world, whose whole identity has been tied up with issues over land rights.[151] Gerhard Linn believes that the Western attitude towards land which views it as a commodity, fails to understand and appreciate the mentality of indigenous peoples. According to this view, if Christianity is to remain true to its missionary concern, it should seek to find bridges across cultures by drawing on a theology of creation and land, rather than an "unnatural" emphasis on awareness of human sinfulness.

The Malawian Harvey Sindima brings ecological issues to bear on the discussion through his understanding of human community in terms of interrelatedness. The African concept of creation reinforces our relationship with the environment, and the cultural belief in life (*moya*) remains intact as the "organising logic of the African world."[152] From this perspective our greed and obsession with the myth of progress has led to a radical disruption in the rhythm of life, and lies at the root of the ecological collapse of the environment.

As we might have expected from our earlier discussion, feminists who have contributed to the debate believe that the root cause of the ecological disaster is the oppressive attitude of men towards women. For them all language about care for the earth becomes futile without a purgation of an exploitative attitude by men towards the other half of humanity.[153] They also consider that the patriarchal attitude predominates in WCC discussions through an unfair bias given towards the views of the Orthodox church.

Ronald Preston is more critical about the overall feasibility of linking an idea as elusive as "the integrity of creation" with the prime aims of the WCC in social ethics, sexist oppression and liberation theology.[154] He wants to counter the overall swing against technology by seeing this as a loss of nerve on the part of those involved, and a failure to "take risks." Instead he proposes a greater weight be given to those documents which argue for a constructive use of technology. He is also worried about the drift towards "biocentrism" and subsequent loss of the Christian idea of unique personhood. The biblical basis for "biocentrism," or any idea of fellowship with nature, rests on "dubious exegesis" of Genesis texts. Overall Preston is highly sceptical about any ideas which might include the whole of creation in salvation. The very concept of "integrity" of creation seems to imply a static rather than dynamic view of the relationship between God and creation.

Paul Gregorios has been particularly influential in promoting an Orthodox perspective within WCC debates. He rejects the antagonism between the so-called exclusivist view of our relation with nature, which tends towards technology, and the inclusivist view of humankind as part of nature, which tends towards biocentrism.[155] Instead Gregorios wants to take the debate beyond that of our relationship in and with nature, and focus on the sphere of grace as that which is above all culture and the whole of nature. He believes that the basic separation between person and nature is not a biblical view, but comes from Indo-Hellenic thought. In the ancient Hindu *Samkhya* person and nature became separated, and he observes that this separation becomes more exaggerated in atheistic cultures where humankind replaces the idea of God.[156]

The Orthodox perspective is one which sees nature as encompassing the whole of reality, though it has never acquired divine status in Judao-Christian thought and so cannot be "desacralized." Moreover, any suggestion that we find in liberal or process theology that God is somehow incomplete without the universe fails to recognize the "non-finite" character of God. This is more than the Platonic belief in lack of boundaries, rather it gives God an "indefinable, ineffable and incomprehensible" character.[157] While we are finite created beings, we still participate in the eternity of God.

Orthodoxy draws heavily on Gregory of Nyssa's theology of God and creation. His notions of *"diastema"* and *"metousia,"* clarify the interrelationship between God and the created order.[158] Diastema refers to the unique dimension of space and time in creation, which acts between the *ousia* or being of creation and the ontologically separate Creator. There is no diastema between the Creator and the creation since the whole of creation is permanently co-present with the Creator. This limitation of space and time in the creation safeguards the distinction between God and creation. Metousia, by contrast, acts in a more positive way, and refers to the idea of participation of creation in the energeia of God. Once we realize the truth of this idea any possibility of "desacralization" is impossible since the whole of creation would cease to exist if it failed to participate in God. While diastema lies behind the idea of God's transcendence over creation, metousia expresses God's immanence in creation.

The rôle of humankind as male and female is that of mediator between God and creation. Christ is one who has broken the diastema between God and creation so that he shares the *ousia* of God. Through Christ humankind can move across the limitations of space and time into the presence of God. Our freedom is preserved in that we are given the choice of experiencing this goodness.

Gregorios draws on the perspective of Dionysius the Areopagite and Maximus the Confessor (580-662) as significant for contemporary Orthodox theology.[159] The former viewed hierarchy not as a scale of authority, but as a structured ordering of a community around the throne of God himself. The whole of the cosmos including unbelievers can participate in this community around God. Maximus developed the idea of a rhythm of reality expressed in love and response, rather than the more classical notion of subject and object. Vladimir

Solovyof (1850-1900) drew on *Sophia* wisdom as a way of expressing both the transcendence and immanence of God and creation. Gregorios' final conclusion is that we should seek to unite attitudes of mastery and mystery, but our overall shift for today should be one that seeks to surrender to rather than to exert control over the environment, coming from a deep reverence and respect for our environment.

Paul Evdokimov is more negative towards the potential of science, believing that we have now become completely deaf to the "groans" of our natural environment.[160] The problem in Western Christianity is shown up by the Eastern Christian synthesis of spiritual and material, so that we find that "nothing is more opposed to the Bible than the extended substance of Cartesian dualism." He believes that the biblical anthropocentric and geocentric perspectives become broadened through Patristic thought.

A more explicitly ecologically orientated Orthodox theology in California is bold enough to state that to "be a Christian is to be an ecologist" on the basis that all the earth belongs to the Lord.[161] We find modernity blamed for the ecological crisis so that it has caused "an unprecedented psychological and spiritual rupture of the people from its cultural and spiritual roots."[162] Vincent Rossi believes that the search for answers within ecological, economic and political realities will prove sterile, rather we need to regain our balance by a deeper appreciation of the meaning of the kingdom of God. Like other Orthodox theologians he advocates theocentrism, and he is sharply critical of the "futilities" of Heideggerian existentialism, or search within the pantheism of Spinoza, or Eastern mystic tradition.[163] Humankind's priestly rôle within creation turns stewardship, which tends towards management, into servanthood with its deep respect for creation.[164]

8. Conclusions.

We have attempted here to highlight aspects of the current cultural context as it bears on a reconstruction of an adequate theology of creation. The latter includes our understanding of the relationships between God and the world, between humankind and God and between humankind and nature. We have drawn on a range of different theological approaches so as to highlight the plurality of responses to our complex and ambiguous relationship with nature that has emerged since the early modern period. To sum up this development:

1.   In our recent history we have experienced an increasing sense of historical consciousness which moved away from a more static cosmological perception of reality. Alongside this change, though to some extent in sequel to it, we find a growing awareness of our biological rootedness in all creation encouraged by Darwin's evolutionary explanation in the *Origin of Species*. On the one hand we have an increasing awareness of ourselves as detached from nature, and having the power to explain the natural world and our own origins through science and technology, which eliminates any need to believe in God as creator. This distance from creation is encouraged still further by a self-understanding that focuses on our own history, rather than that of the natural world. While, on the other hand, we have an increasing awareness of ourselves as part of creation and participating in the ecological havoc created by the science and technology that we devised. While the legacy of the former is a loss in belief in God as creator, ourselves as creatures, and an alienation from the natural world, the legacy of the latter is an alienation from the technology we have created, and a sense of impotence and despair. The latter movement comes in the wake of the former, and is most characteristic of our culture in the last quarter of this century.

2.   Karl Barth, writing prior to the emergence of an awareness of ecological collapse, was conscious that theology had drifted too far in identifying itself with the historical consciousness of the period. As such it had become "culture Protestantism." His neo-Orthodox theology of creation did not return to the more static cosmological models, but sought to counter the movement away from faith in God as revealed in Jesus Christ. He rooted his theology firmly in biblical texts, rather than exploring wider philosophical sources. For him God as creator is a given fact that cannot be argued or debated, and knowing God as creator is only

possible through faith in Christ. His approach to the relationship between God and creation is thoroughly trinitarian and Christological, in a way which seeks to understand creation in dialogue with redemptive themes and through revelation in Christ. He has thus moved away from traditional categories of creation, fall and redemption, and reacted against any attempt to subsume theology under cultural norms in either a philosophical or scientific sense. His "No" to natural theology is more a reaction to using any means other than Christ as the grounds for reconstructing our ideas of God, rather than a negative assessment of creation *per se*. Nonetheless, Barth failed really to take our scientific analysis of the world with sufficient seriousness and rendered his approach rather too remote from our cultural context.

3.   Catholic theology, which was more resistant to incorporating our awareness of historical consciousness into its theology, retained its traditional affinity with natural theology with its more obvious affirmation of nature.[165] A historical consciousness emerged in Teilhard de Chardin's understanding of God and creation through a strong influence of ideas he discovered as a biologist in dialogue with the work of Charles Darwin. His attempt to fuse the efforts of science and theology was prophetic and visionary, combining a panpsychic view of the Spirit of God in creation with an understanding of Christ as the one who will unite both disciplines. Its theological weakness lay in an anthropocentric focus which was thoroughly over-optimistic, and seemed to make humankind bear responsibility for the evolution of the cosmos into the *Omega* in Christ. Its biological weakness was both an over-simplification of the process of evolution, and a seeming blurring of the boundary between theology and biology so that Evolution becomes almost a metaphysical category.

4.   Karl Rahner's contribution lay in a radical reinterpretation of the meaning of nature and grace in a way that helped to counter more static tendencies in scholastic theology. Like Barth, he insisted on belief in God the creator and recognized the significance of the incarnation as God's clear affirmation of

creation. Unlike Barth, both Rahner and Küng were less Christocentric and embraced culture in a way which allowed them to take account of modern developments in science and technology in their theological reflection. They did not, like Teilhard, blur the boundaries between the two disciplines. Küng's suggestion that God suffers with his creation hints at the reinterpretation of our understanding of God that is characteristic of process theology.

5.   Reformulations of traditional Protestant or Catholic theology are inadequate for theologians of process who argue for a more radical replacement of our traditional theological concepts of God, the world and humanity. While the basis for such replacement is, as we might expect, pluriform, the philosophy of A.N.Whitehead is popular amongst process theologians. Hartshorne, for example, retains a distinction between God and creation in his understanding of God's primordial nature, but this distinction is less clear in his understanding of God's consequent nature. Process theologians insist on a dynamic shaping of God by the world, hence our ecological collapse is at the same time suffered by God in a way that seems to have direct ontological consequences. We find little reference to Christ, the Trinity or the basis for hope in the future, other than a hope in the Spirit that is within ourselves and all creation.

6.   While feminist theologians offer a variety of perspectives, most trace the source of our damaged relationship with nature to patriarchal attitudes that have encouraged mastery and dominance. Through this false separation of men and women from one another we have exploited creation and disrupted our fellowship with the earth. The potential danger here is that we slide into a biocentrism that becomes incompatible with our sense of responsibility as creatures of God. The loss in the sense of the sovereignty of God is coincident with the loss in any given authority to make decisions in the face of complex questions that confront us when we have to balance anthropological humanitarian concerns with conservation issues. In other words for all the rhetoric on ecology, it remains detached from practical Christian ethics.

7.   Ecumenical theological debates through the WCC have tried to keep in view concrete issues of justice and peace alongside environmental questions. Unfortunately vague statements about the "integrity" of creation have not necessarily helped to achieve a more practical basis for decision making. Nonetheless the instinct to bring environmental issues into the arena of political questions seems valid. The Eastern Orthodox contribution here has encouraged a thoroughly theocentric perspective, rather than the "anthropocentric" or "biocentric" one characteristic of much liberal theology. The traditional understanding of the relationship between God, the world and our place in it has the strength of a classic, and is an important sounding board in assessing the chameleonic tendency characteristic of much post-enlightenment theology.[166] While it offers the stability and strength of tradition, the difficulty, perhaps, is its general lack of eschatological emphasis that can give us a basis for hope in the future for creation.

It is Jürgen Moltmann's eschatological reconstruction of theology that offers a promising approach, and it is with this in mind that we turn to the emergence of his own theology of creation.

41

End Notes

The abbreviation for End Note is n. throughout. Translations are from German original unless stated otherwise.

1. S. Cotgrave, *Catastrophe or Cornucopia: The Environment, Politics and the Future*, Chichester, John Wiley and Sons, 1982, pp. 1-12.

2. T. Beaumont, "Options for the 90's: 1. From Environmentalism to Ecology," *Modern Churchman*, 28(1), 1985, pp. 11-16.

3. D. Gosling, "Towards a Credible Ecumenical Theology of Nature," *The Ecumenical Review*, 38(3), 1986, pp. 322-331.

4. P. Selby, "Apocalyptic, Christian and Nuclear," *Modern Churchman*, 26(2), 1984, pp. 3-10.

5. J. Schell, *The Fate of the Earth*, Picador, Chaucer Press, 1982, p. 71.

6. *Ibid.*, pp. 112-119.

7. R. Bauckham, "Theology after Hiroshima," *Scottish Journal of Theology*, 38, 1989, pp. 583-601.

8. J. Moltmann, *Creating a Just Future*; translated by J. Bowden, London, SCM, 1989; hereafter referred to as CJF.

9. H.P. Santmire, "Studying the Doctrine of Creation: The Challenge," *Dialog* (USA), 21, 1982, pp. 195-200.

10. World Council of Churches, C.T. McIntire, ed., *God History and Historians*, Oxford, Oxford University Press, 1977, p. 304.

11. K.D. Kaufman, *The Theological Imagination*, Philadelphia, Westminster Press, 1981, p. 213; see also, R. Bauckham, "First Steps to a Theology of Nature," *Evangelical Quarterly*, 58(3), 1986, pp. 229-244.

12. *Ibid.*, p. 213.

13. H.P. Santmire, *The Travail of Nature*, Philadelphia, Fortress Press, 1985, pp. 6-7.

14. P. Selby, *Liberating God*, London, SPCK, 1983, pp. 76-85.

15. J.K. Robbins, "The Environment and Thinking about God," *Encounter* (USA), 48(4), 1987, pp. 401-415.

16. D. Dombrowski, "Pacifism and Hartshorne's Dipolar Theism," *Encounter* (USA), 48(4), 1987, pp. 337-350.

17. J.K. Robbins, *op. cit.* (n. 15), p. 404.

18. R.G. Collingwood, *The Idea of Nature*, Oxford, Clarendon Press, 1945, p. 176.

19. D. Tracy, *The Analogical Imagination*, New York, Crossroad,1981, p.164.

20. *Ibid.*, p. 177.

21. *Ibid.*, p. 454.

22. J.B. Metz, *"Productive Non-Contemporaneity"*; translated by A.L. Buchwalter, in, J. Habermas, ed. *Observations on the Spiritual Situation of the Age: Contemporary German Perspectives*, Cambridge, Massachusetts/London, MIT, 1984, pp. 164-177.

23. K. Tanner, *God and Creation in Christian Theology: Tyranny or Empowerment?*, Oxford, Blackwell, 1988, p. 4.

24. *Ibid.*, p. 5.

25. *Ibid.*, pp. 6-7.

26. This movement, known as post-modernism, is a reaction to the progressive idealism of modernity and technological society. See, J.F. Lyotard, *The Post-Modern Condition*, Manchester, Manchester University Press, 1984.

27. L. Gilkey, *Reaping the Whirlwind: A Christian Interpretation of History*, New York, Seabury Press, 1976, p. 84.

28. *Ibid.*, p. 86.

29. G. Wingren, *"The Doctrine of Creation; Not an Appendix, but the First Article,"* *Word and World*, 4(4), 1984, pp. 353-371.

30. P. Stuhlmacher, *"The Ecological Crisis as a Challenge for Biblical Theology,"* *Ex Auditu*, 3, 1987, pp. 1-15.

31. H.P. Santmire, *op. cit.* (n.13), p. 102.

32. M. Luther, *Volume 1, Lectures on Genesis*; translated by G.V. Schlick, in, J. Pelikan, ed., *Luther's Works*, Saint Louis, Concordia, 1988, p. 39.

33. *Ibid.*, pp. 46-47.

34. Ibid., p. 67.

35. M. Luther, *Volume 12, Selected Psalms*; translated by P. Jaroslav, in, J. Pelikan, ed., Luther's Works, Saint Louis, Concordia, 1955, p. 119.

36. L. Gilkey, *op. cit.* (n.27), p. 176.

37. *Ibid.*, pp. 177-178.

38. H.P. Santmire, *op. cit.* (n.13), p. 128.

39. K. Thomas, *Man and the Natural World: Changing Attitudes in England, 1500-1800*, London, Penguin, 1983, pp. 33-35.

40. *Ibid.*, p. 42.

41. R.G. Collingwood, *op. cit.* (n.18), pp. 6-9. The basic premise of the mechanistic view was that laws in nature were imposed from the outside and were subject to the purpose of an intelligent mind. By contrast, according to Greek natural science, the world of nature is

saturated by mind, so that nature has both a *"mind"* and *"soul"* in which individual plants and animals participate; pp. 3-4.

42. R. Hooykaas, *Religion and the Rise of Modern Science*, Edinburgh, Scottish Academic Press, 1972, pp. 78-81. This optimistic vision clouded any sense of corruption in humanity and there was a lack of awareness of the upsurge in population and little sense of the power of potential forces for change. For commentary see C.J. Glacken, *Traces on the Rhodian Shore,* Berkeley, University of California Press, 1976, p. 500.

43. K. Thomas, *op. cit.* (n.39), p. 15.

44. L. Gilkey, *op. cit.* (n.27), pp. 189-191.

45. *Ibid.*, p. 191.

46. H.P. Santmire, *op. cit* . (n.13), p. 134.

47. Ibid., see also R.G. Collingwood, *op. cit.* (n.18),p. 110.

48. H.P. Santmire, *op. cit.* (n.13), p. 135.

49. H.P. Santmire, *op. cit.* (n.9), pp. 195-200.

50. R.G. Collingwood, *op. cit.* (n.18), p. 9.

51. *Ibid.*, p. 121.

52. *Ibid.*, p. 122.

53. Y.H. Vanderpool, "Charles Darwin and Darwinism, A Naturalized World and a Brutalized Man?" in, R.A. Johnson, E. Wallwork, C. Green, H.P. Santmire and Y.H. Vanderpool, eds., *Critical Issues in Modern Religion*, Englewood Cliffs, Prentice Hall, 1973, pp. 72-113.

54. C.A. Russell, *Cross Currents: Interactions Between Science and Faith*, Leicester, IVP, 1985, pp. 159-162.

55. For example, Asa Gray, the Calvinist Professor of Natural History at Harvard, see J. Dillenberger, *Protestant Thought and Natural Science*, London, Collins, 1961, p. 228.

56. R.G. Collingwood, *op. cit.* (n.18), p. 136: Henri Bergson (1859-1941) marks the culmination of this view where reality becomes life itself. Ironically, perhaps, his reaction against empiricism and reliance on intuition is against the trend of post-enlightenment science which formed the basis for Darwin's theory of evolution. See, R.C. Solomon, *Continental Philosophy since 1750: The Rise and Fall of the Self*, Oxford, Oxford University Press, 1988, p. 108.

57. H. Hartwell, *The Theology of Karl Barth: An Introduction*, London, Duckworth, 1964, pp. 3-7. For commentary on Troeltsch's position, see R. Morgan, "Ernst Troeltsch and Dialectical Theology" in, J.P. Claydon, ed., *E. Troeltsch and the Future of Theology*, Cambridge, Cambridge University Press, 1976, pp. 32-77.

58. K. Barth, *Church Dogmatics, Volume 3/1*; translated by J.W. Edwards, O. Bussey and H. Knight; G.W. Bromiley and T.F. Torrance, eds., Edinburgh, T. and T. Clark, 1958, pp. 1-15. See also, G.W. Bromiley, *An Introduction to the Theology of Karl Barth*, Edinburgh, T.and T. Clark, 1979, pp. 109-155.

59. K. Barth, *Church Dogmatics Volume 3/1, op. cit.* (n.58), pp. 13-15.

60. *Ibid.*, pp. 15-22.

61. *Ibid.*, pp. 25-30. Barth does not develop the idea of Christ as Pantocrator to any great extent here.

62. *Ibid.*, pp. 50ff. Barth understands the event of creation to include time and it is temporality which underlies salvation history, pp. 74-76. The initial acts of God in creation did not take place in a creaturely context like other historical events and so are "non-historical" in the sense that they are prior to human and natural history, pp. 76-81.

63. *Ibid.*, pp. 81-93.

64. *Ibid.*, pp. 176-181.

65. *Ibid.*, pp. 187ff.

66. *Ibid.*, pp. 213-217.

67. Barth's comments such as: "Creation sets the stage for the story of the covenant of Grace," *ibid.*, p. 44, have been interpreted to imply a negative assessment of the value he gives to "nature" compared with human "history." See, for example, H.P. Santmire, *op. cit.* (n.9 and n.13).

68. H.P. Santmire's accusations of Barth are a little overdrawn. It is fair that his over-emphasis on Christology has tended to take away our initial focus on creation as understood in traditional theology, however Barth's intention is to give creation greater value rather than less value by interpreting it in a Christological way.

69. K. Barth, *Church Dogmatics, Volume 3/1, op. cit.* (n.58), pp. 330-333.

70. *Ibid.*, p. 334.

71. *Ibid.*, p. 342.

72. *Ibid.*, p. 345.

73. *Ibid.*, p. 366.

74. *Ibid..* p. 369.

75. *Ibid.*, p. 371. Barth separates clearly the revelation of God in Jesus Christ from either the illumination or darkness of creation. The revelation of God in Jesus Christ is an "unambiguous light," p. 372. See also under n.79, below.

76. *Ibid.*, p. 377.

77. K. Barth, *Church Dogmatics, Volume 4/3*; translated by G. Bromiley; T.F. Torrance and G. Bromiley, eds., Edinburgh, T. and T. Clark, 1961, pp. 136-164. Barth has apparently shifted from his earlier theology, which was much more negative in its tone towards creation. In this earlier theology Barth's intention was to reject E. Brunner's natural theology. See *Natural Theology*, comprising *"*Nature and Grace*"* by E. Brunner and the reply *"*No*"* by K. Barth; translated by P. Fraenkel, London, The Centenary Press, 1946, pp. 65-128.

78. K. Barth, *op. cit.* (n.77), p. 139.

79. *Ibid.*, p. 139. Barth seems to be suggesting that the lights of creation become visible in relationship with Christ, rather than mediated through humankind. He goes on to explain: "As the divine work of reconciliation does not negate the divine work of creation, nor deprive it of meaning, so it does not take from it its light and language, nor tear asunder the original connection between creaturely *esse* and creaturely *nosse."*

80. *Ibid.*, p. 139. Barth rejects any general *"*fall*"* of creation along with humankind. He draws a contrast between humankind's enlightenment by the light of God himself, which can be obscured by sin, and the lights of creation which are independent of God's self-revelation.

81. *Ibid.*, p. 140. The expression that Barth refers to in this context is use of the term revelation to describe the light of creation.

82. *Ibid.*, p. 143. Barth seems to suggest that the truth in creation is obvious, and open to rational enquiry. He does not seem to take account of the faith commitment that is part of a scientific perception of the world. See, for example, M. Polanyi, *Personal Knowledge: Towards a Post-Critical Philosophy*, London, Routledge and Kegan Paul, 1958.

83. K. Barth, *op. cit.* (n.77), p. 156. The unity of revelation in a special and general sense comes from the unity of God's purpose, even though only the former has salvific value. The lights of creation *"*serve*"* the one great Light of Christ, p. 164. Barth does not envisage any conflict between science and theology, for in Christ is the unity between God and the world. The study of science is of value in so far as it shows God to be Creator/Reconciler and Redeemer. For commentary see H. Hartwell, *op. cit.* (n.57), pp. 57-59.

84. K. Barth, *op. cit.* (n.77), p. 138. This double movement of creation to covenant, and back to creation in Barth's later theology has been somewhat overlooked by H.P. Santmire, *op. cit.* (n.9 and n.13).

85. B.J. Walsh and J.R. Middleton, *The Transforming Vision*, Downers Grove, IVP(USA), 1984, p. 50.

86. *Ibid.*, pp. 100-102. D.J. Hall has developed the symbol of *"*steward*"* in a way that seeks to challenge our relationship to the natural environment. It illustrates the shift in reformed theology towards the idea of *"*radical service*"* as part of the missionary endeavour of the

church. D.J. Hall, *The Steward: Biblical Symbol Come of Age*, New York, Friendship Press for the Commission on Stewardship, 1982, p. 39.

87. *Ibid.*, pp. 52-54. While this idea is also part of K. Barth's doctrine of creation, more practical implications tended to be smothered by his stress on humanity's election in Christ. He defined image-bearing in terms of social relationships, rather than in direct relationship to stewardship over creation which is more characteristic of the views portrayed here. For commentary on Barth see, G.A. Jonsson, *The Image of God; Genesis 1: 26-28 in a Century of Old Testament Research*; translated from Swedish by L. Svendsen, revised by M.S. Cheney, *Coniectanea Biblica*, Old Testament Series 26, Lund, Almquist and Wiksell International, 1988, pp. 65-76.

88. H.R. Niebuhr, *Christ and Culture*, New York, Harper, 1951. See also, L. Newbigin, *Foolishness to the Greeks*, London, SPCK, 1986. To some extent this marks a significant departure from Barth's position, which, according to Pannenberg, shows "a general neglect of natural and experiential evidence in theological argument." W. Pannenberg, *Christian Spirituality and Sacramental Community*, London, Darton, Longman and Todd, 1984, p. 52.

89. H. Dooyeweerd, *Roots of Western Culture: Pagan, Secular and Christian Options;* translated from Dutch by J. Kraay, Toronto, Wedge, 1979, p. 91.

90. C.Y. Stewart, *Nature in Grace: A Study in the Theology of Nature*, Macon, Mercer University Press, 1983, pp. 39-88.

91. *Ibid.*, p 86. He believes that Santmire "is coming to a threshold of a processive philosophy and theology of nature (in his eschatological emphasis *et cetera*) and to the threshold of a sacramental view of nature (in his understanding of the divine delight and the I-*Ens* relation). But in neither case does he 'pass over' and provide what his position leads us to anticipate with longing."

92. P. Teilhard de Chardin, *The Phenomenon of Man*; translated by B. Wall, London, Collins/Fontana, 1959, pp. 332-334.

93. D. Gray, *A New Creation Story*, Chambersberg, The American Teilhard Association for the Future of Man, 1979, pp. 4-5. We note here the influence of Bergson's philosophy, see n.56 above.

94. P. Teilhard de Chardin, "Christianity and Evolution: Suggestions for a New Theology," 1945 (unpublished); translated by R. Hague, in, *Christianity and Evolution*, London, Collins, 1971, pp. 173-186.

95. *Ibid.*, pp. 180-181.

96. H.P. Santmire, "Pierre Teilhard de Chardin: The Christianization of Evolution" *op. cit.*(n.53), pp. 114-140.

97. P. Teilhard de Chardin, *op. cit.* (n.92), p. 339.

98. P. Hefner, "The Future as Our Future: A Teilhardian Perspective," in, E.H. Cousins, ed., *Hope and the Future of Man*, Philadelphia, Fortress Press, 1972, pp. 15-39. Theologies of hope stress the future coming from ahead, rather than emerging from the present, as in Teilhardian/process thought. We disagree with Hefner that theologies of hope necessarily "stand against" the "absolute worth" of creation, since it is quite possible to affirm the absolute goodness of God and his creation within an eschatological understanding of God as one who comes from the future.

99. K.H. Weger, *Karl Rahner: An Introduction to his Theology*, London, Burns and Oates, 1980, p. 87.

100. K. Rahner, *Theological Investigations, Volume 1*; translated by C. Ernst, London, Darton, Longman and Todd, 1965, p. 302.

101. *Ibid.*, p. 317.

102. K. Rahner, *The Christian Commitment*; translated by C. Hastings, *Mission and Grace, Volume 1*, third edition, London, Sheed and Ward, 1970, p. 63.

103. *Ibid.*, p. 74.

104. *Ibid.*, p. 75.

105. *Ibid.*, p. 78.

106. K. Rahner, *Theological Investigations, Volume 13*; translated by D. Bourke, London, Darton, Longman and Todd, 1975, p. 95.

107. *Ibid.*, p. 96.

108. *Ibid.*, pp. 83-89.

109. P. Avis, *The Methods of Modern Theology*, Basingstoke, Marshall Pickering, 1986, pp. 104-133.

110. H. Küng, *Does God Exist?*; translated by E.Quinn, London, Collins, 1980, p. 115.

111. *Ibid.*, p. 123.

112. *Ibid.*, p. 125.

113. H. Küng, *Global Responsibility: In Search of a New World Ethic*; translated by J. Bowden, London, SCM, 1991.

114. H. Küng, *Ibid.* (n. 110), pp. 182-183; 623-633.

115. *Ibid.*, p. 642.

116. *Ibid.*, pp. 648-655. The choice between deism and panentheism may not be as well defined as Küng seems to suggest here.

117. *Ibid.*, p. 655.

118. Process theology stems from the empirical method in theology that became popular in North America in the 1920s. Alfred North Whitehead (1861-1947) combined empiricism with the organismic thought of Bergson into a comprehensive metaphysical system. See, B. Meland, "Introduction," in, B. Meland, ed., *The Future of Empirical Theology*, Chicago, University of Chicago, 1969, pp. 1-62.

119. J.B. Cobb, *A Christian Natural Theology*, London, Lutterworth, 1965, p. 31.

120. *Ibid.*, p. 34. The decision to give a sensory experience a quality, as for example the greenness of grass, introduces a novel element into the experience known as the *"mental pole."* Eternal objects become *"pure possibilities for realisation in any experience."*

121. B. Meland, *op. cit.* (n.118), p. 49.

122. H. Smith and S. Todes, "Empiricism: Scientific and Religious," *op. cit.* (n.118), pp. 129-146.

123. J.B. Cobb, *Is It Too Late?*, Bruce, Beverley Hills, 1972.

124. *Ibid.*, p. 42. He cites here the graphic example of how animism did not prevent North American Indians from adopting ecologically destructive practices. On occasions they drove "herds of buffalo over cliffs and then ate only their tongues."

125. *Ibid.*, pp. 51-52.

126. *Ibid.*, p. 111. We disagree with the link Cobb tries to make here between the sensitivity of electromagnetic events to external forces and *"unconscious feeling."*

127. *Ibid.*, p. 133.

128. *Ibid.*, p. 144.

129. For a highly influential and articulate recent contribution to post-Christian feminist literature, see, D. Hampson, *Theology and Feminism*, Oxford, Blackwell, 1990. A related issue which we will discuss further later in this thesis is the accusation that the Christian interpretation of the dominion of *"man"* over the animals in Genesis has contributed to the ecological crisis. See, L. White, "The Historic Roots of Our Ecological Crisis," *Science*, 155, 1967, pp. 1203-1207.

130. R.R. Ruether, *New Woman: New Earth*, New York, Seabury Press, 1975, p. 80.

131. *Ibid.*, p. 195. Ruether's willingness to find a causal relationship between patriarchy and a dualism of mind and matter seems overdrawn, especially as patriarchal societies existed prior to any such separation. While it is true, perhaps, that patriarchy would reinforce such dualisms, the underlying stimulus was more likely to have its origins in Plato's philosophy.

132. *Ibid.*, pp. 203-204.

133. *Ibid.*, p. 82. While liberation from sexist oppression is a natural counterpart to liberation from a tyrannical attitude to nature, Ruether's argument that feminist ideology is required as a

precursor to a revised attitude to the environment seems rather weak. She concludes: "Our final mandate is to redeem our sister the earth from her bondage to destruction, recognizing her as a partner in the creation of that new world where all things can be very good. "

134. *Ibid.*, p. 59. Ruether sees this as the deeper meaning of the Catholic doctrine of immaculate conception. While she realizes that a feminine portrayal of Jesus became necessary in Protestant circles where Mariology was rejected, she believes that Mary is "the reconciled wholeness of women and men, nature and humans, creation and God in a new heaven and a new earth. " However, Ruether does not give a proper theological basis for her assertion that Mary has the status of one who is the reconciler of nature and humans; men and women.

135. *Ibid.*, p. 56; Ruether's willingness to identify with the humanity of Mary more easily than the humanity of Christ reflects a popular implicit religious idea that Jesus' divinity somehow weakens his humanity. Her theology seems to encourage this experiential theology in a way that is not really justified according to orthodox belief.

136. D. Soelle and S. Cloyes, *To Work and to Love: A Theology of Creation*, Philadelphia, Fortress Press, 1984, p. 5. The process elements in their thought suffer from the same critical comments that we discussed above. Soelle and Cloyes include a political manifesto woven into their theology, so that social concern with sexual oppression and political ideology become incorporated into their theology. The political dimension in their theology of creation reinforces its messianic overtones, so that their starting point is a creation in need of liberation, rather than creation as a given gift of God, which is the more traditional approach. This messianic colouring to their theology of creation is a general characteristic of a feminist perspective.

137. *Ibid.*, p.110. The authors assume that only when we give nature subjectivity do we respond to her in an adequate way, as seems to be the case with process thought.

138. U. King, *Women and Spirituality*, Basingstoke, MacMillan/Education, 1989, p. 216. It is not always clear what the content of the *"vision"* which King proposes is in concrete terms.

139. *Ibid.*, p. 222.

140. S. McFague, *Models of God*, London, SCM, 1987, p. 113.

141. E. Moltmann-Wendel, *A Land Flowing with Milk and Honey*; translated by J. Bowden, London, SCM, 1986, p. 98.

142. *Ibid.*, pp. 108-109.

143. *Ibid.*, p. 138.

144. *Ibid.*, p. 148. This idea becomes highly significant in J. Moltmann's own treatment of the doctrine of creation, as we will discuss more fully later.

145. *Ibid.*, p. 160. In this she aligns herself with Ruether and other feminists who argue that the cry for liberation from sexist domination leads naturally to a cry for the liberation of the

whole earth. This close identification with the earth marks out feminist theologies of creation in general, indeed the idea of co-suffering with the earth points as much to "primitive" animistic beliefs as pantheistic ones.

146. C. Lasch, *The Minimal Self*, London, Pan/Picador, 1985, pp. 246-253.

147. D. Gosling, *op. cit.* (n.3); see also G. Limouris, ed., *Justice, Peace and the Integrity of Creation*, Geneva, WCC, 1990.

148. WCC, *op. cit.* (n.10), p. 300.

149. *Ibid.*, p. 323.

150. C. Birch, "Nature, God and Humanity in Ecological Perspective," *Christianity and Crisis*, 39, 1979, pp. 259-266.

151. G. Linn, "JPIC as a Mission Concern," *The Ecumenical Review*, 41(4), 1989, pp. 515-521.

152. H. Sindima, "Community of Life," *The Ecumenical Review*, 41(4), 1989, pp. 537-551.

153. J.C. Peck and J. Gallo, "JPIC: A Critique from a Feminist Perspective," *The Ecumenical Review*, 41(4), 1989, pp. 573-581. See also under n.133 above for critical comment on this view.

154. R. Preston, "Humanity, Nature and the Integrity of Creation," *The Ecumenical Review*, 41(4), 1989, 552-563. In spite of his scepticism a perceived link between environmental issues and questions of justice and peace is gaining in popularity, especially in the wider public sphere.

155. P. Gregorios, *The Human Presence: An Orthodox View of Nature*, Geneva, WCC, 1988, pp. 17-20. For a comparison of the inclusivist/exclusivist position see, F. Elder, *Crisis in Eden: A Religious Study of Man and Environment*, New York, Abingdon Press, 1970; also, F. Elder, "Responses to the Ecological Question; A Christian Review," *Harvard Theological Review*, 71, 1978, 318-319.

156. For an alternative Orthodox position see, J.D. Zizioulas, *Being as Communion: Studies in Personhood and the Church*, New York, St.Vladimir's Seminary Press, 1985, pp. 26-53.

157. P. Gregorios, *op. cit.* (n.155). p. 57. The difference between God and creation according to Orthodox tradition is also explained clearly in, V. Lossky, *Orthodox Theology: An Introduction;* translated by I. Kesarcardi-Watson, New York, St. Vladimir's Seminary Press, 1984, pp. 51-78.

158. *Ibid.*, pp. 58-64.

159. *Ibid.*, pp. 72-89.

160. P. Evdokimov, "Nature," *Scottish Journal of Theology*, 18, 1965, pp. 1-22.

161. V. Rossi, "The Earth is the Lord's," *Epiphany*, 6(1), 1985, pp. 3-6.

162. V. Rossi, "Theocentricism; The Cornerstone of Christian Ecology," *Epiphany*, 6(1), 1985, pp. 8-14.

163. Zizioulas draws on Heidegger's philosphy, but in a way that remains within an Orthodox framework, *op. cit.* (n.156), esp. pp. 105-108.

164. V. Rossi, *op. cit.* (n.162), p.14. His final vision is breathtaking in its comprehensiveness: "In sum the Christian theocentric position sees Man as celebrating servant, earth as mother 'married' to God the Father by everlasting covenant, all creatures great and small as children of God; and the cosmos as a vast eucharistic liturgy in which all things have their beginning and their end in Christ." See also, V. Rossi, "Christian Ecology: A Theocentric Perspective," *Epiphany*, 8, 1987, pp. 8-13.

165. O. Chadwick, *From Boussuet to Newman: The Idea of Doctrinal Development*, Cambridge, Cambridge Universitiy Press, 1957.

166. D. Tracy, *op. cit.* (n.19).

CHAPTER 2

Ecological Themes in Moltmann's Earlier Theology

1. Introduction.

So far we have tried to show how various contemporary theological scholars have responded to the need to develop an adequate theology of creation in the context of an ecologically aware, technological society. Jürgen Moltmann's own contribution to the discussion becomes explicit in his book *God in Creation*.[1]

We are directing our effort in this chapter towards uncovering the extent to which Moltmann's earlier work incorporates creation themes, in particular those concerned with ecological ideas. Christian Link seems to be of the opinion that *God in Creation* represents a new departure in Moltmann's thought, and he describes it as "a new area which up to now has not been trodden. Jürgen Moltmann becomes consciously involved in the age of the ecological crisis in his book *God in Creation*, with the contemporary universal demand for a radical rethinking at the roots of theology."[2] This radical rethink for theology includes perceiving in order to participate in creation, rather than perceiving in order to rule over creation.[3] As a consequence of this revised understanding of God is a fundamental change from transcendence to immanence.[4]

An important commentary on the development of Moltmann's doctrine of creation is the thesis by J. Niewiadomski: *Die Zweideutigkeit von Gott und Welt in J. Moltmanns Theologian.*[5] He aims to reconstruct Moltmann's "Bemühungen" towards a more Christian understanding of God. The theological task is to foster a "neue Aufklärung," which liberates us from the dependencies of the first. He explains here that: "once released, the different means of production developed their own laws, escaping human control."[6] Niewiadomski argues that Moltmann works with two models of the relationship between God and the world. The first model, which is prominent in his earlier theology, is "the radical opposition of God and reality. This is not meant to be a dualistic polarization: God, being in opposition to reality, can be seen as its unambiguous focus."[7] He claims that the radical distinction between God and the world has no systematic value after *Theologie der Hoffnung*; instead "Gott selbst wird nun als eine widersprüchliche Wirklichkeit begriffen."[8] He believes that Moltmann's use of these two models, in a logical sense, cannot be reconciled. However, he recognizes that this is not necessarily a criticism since logical clarity could be theologically sterile, while contradiction could be productive.[9]

Our aim in the present chapter is not so much to argue against Niewiadomski's reconstruction, or Link's suggestion that *God in Creation* is a radical new departure in Moltmann's theology, but to ask a different question altogether, namely, to what extent does Moltmann use ecological motifs in his earlier works? We will be addressing the important question of the logical consistency of his overall understanding of the relationship between God and creation in relation to his earlier thesis presented in *Theology of Hope* much later in this thesis. We intend to draw out implicit ecological themes in Moltmann's earlier theology, in relation to his own later explicit interpretation of the significance of the term ecology, as that which expresses both interrelatedness and indwelling.[10] We will address an additional issue compared with those raised by Niewiadomski, that is how far these themes of ecology and creation serve to interfere with or reinforce Moltmann's insistence on eschatology as the medium within which theological reflection should take place. This question leads on to the overall theological enquiry as to the future of creation, which will form the subject matter of the last section in this thesis. In the following discussion we will be drawing on works up to, but not including, *The Trinity and the Kingdom of God.*[11] The ideas of this book form the first in a series in which *God in Creation* is sequel, and are enmeshed to such an extent that we will be drawing on both sources subsequently.

2. Creation in an eschatological context.

(a) The cosmological world-view.

The ancient cosmological world-view envisaged the whole of reality as threatened by chaos. The traditional answer to this threat is in the stability of the divine monarchy, where God is portrayed in monotheistic terms. Every statement about God becomes equivalent to statements about the world and vice versa, since he is lord and creator of the world.[12] This is based on the idea of a return to the sacred origin of a lost paradise, or "myth of the eternal return," so that the real horror of history vanishes.[13] Moltmann argues that this is a false idea of God of epiphany, where "the horror of chaos is ordered and sanctified by means of the sacred festivals which celebrate the epiphany."[14] Instead we need to recognize that God's revelation comes through promise rather than epiphany.

A further challenge that Moltmann puts to the traditional understanding of God and creation is in the light of Christian experience. This is because:

> "it suggests a gap between Creator and created being (in the image of the Creator) which is not in accordance with the intimate Christian experience of God...surely the Christian doctrine of creation ought to reflect Christianity's experience of Christ and the Spirit? Theologically mystical "pantheism" is certainly not a particularly successful step in this direction, but it is at least a step."[15]

He reconciles this emerging pantheism with that of a strong rejection of "epiphany" faith in his *Theology of Hope* by seeing it in the context of the future of creation. Thus natural theology, as originally given, has its place in an eschatological perspective.[16] The vision of earlier schemes must take their place as future hopes in the light of the present suffering:

> "*Theologia naturalis* is at bottom *theologia viatorum* and *theologia viatorum* will always concern itself with the future *theologia gloriae* in the form of fragmentary sketches."[17]

The stability that we seek in the cosmological schemes of reality should be sought in the God of promise, who shows himself faithful to his promise. The identity of God is not in a transcendent "Super Ego," but in the constancy of his mercy and faithfulness, and his historic action within the horizon of his promises.[18] The extent of this horizon includes the whole of creation, so that cosmology is caught up into eschatology. Hence:

> "It might well be that once the promise becomes eschatological it breaks the bounds even of that which aetiology had hitherto considered to be creation and cosmos, with the result that the eschaton would not be a repetition of the beginning nor a return from the condition of estrangement, and the world of sin to a state of ultimate purity, but is ultimately wider than the beginning ever was. Then it would not be the case that eschatology becomes cosmological in apocalyptic and is therefore stabilized, but *vice versa*, cosmology would become eschatological and the cosmos would be taken up in terms of history into the process of the eschaton."[19]

Moltmann wishes to shake off traditional ideas that redemption means the restoration of the original creation, which is associated with the idea of creation as a closed system.[20] The historical perspective of creation is closer to the Old Testament belief that creation is "the history that precedes salvation history."[21] Once we think of creation as that which only happened in the beginning, we split apart creation and redemption, nature and supernature, in a way that "calls into question the continuity and unity of the divine creative activity itself."[22] Instead, he urges us to see creation as an open process, with an eschatological thread between initial creation (*regnum naturae*), salvation history (*regnum gratiae),* and the kingdom of glory (*regnum gloriae).*

The idea of the creation of the world *ex nihilo* is the negative background against which we can view the positive ground of creation, which comes from the freedom of God's good pleasure. The difference between the initial creation and the future creation is that the first is a creation of order in the midst of chaos, while in the future the very possibility of destruction is absent.

(b) The relationship between modern science and theology.

Once humankind understood itself as over against the world, the cosmological argument for the existence of God faded into the background. The hermeneutical context of post-enlightenment theology becomes anthropological, that is concerned with the anxiety of our existence, and now the whole is disclosed from "the potentiality of human existence for totality, and not by its furthest circumference, the world."[23]

The ontological proof of God's revelation from God himself characteristic of Karl Barth's theology seeks to move beyond the impotence of subjectivity or objectivity characteristic of the anthropological and cosmological schemes. Now God himself creates the conditions in which it is possible to hear and acknowledge him. Moltmann argues that the revelation of God either from anthropology or from ontology assumes that there is a correspondence between Word and reality, and that truth is found in such conformity and agreement. This fails to address the contradiction between Word and reality as a starting point for theological reflection. It is this contradiction or theodicy question which unites both atheists and believers.[24]

A further difficulty is that once the focus of knowledge becomes self-knowledge through an anthropological hermeneutic we become isolated from the world, so that humankind is set between "God" and "the world," which become radical alternatives. Humankind's will to power over the world in science and technology becomes close to "man's attaining to self-assurance from his works."[25] The scientific understanding of the world has served to shatter the traditional understanding of the cosmos, in the same way that historical criticism has destroyed consciousness of tradition.[26] Moltmann views the positive value of science in its rejection of the world as a self-contained cosmos or history as a universal whole.[27] However, the real problem that we face is that we have created a technological society where humankind has become "slave of his own works."[28] Today humankind finds itself surrounded by :

> "an ever denser web of his own works - social institutions, political organizations, giant industrial firms - like a new quasi-nature. The natural cosmos, which man sees through and dominates more and more, is being replaced by a new cosmos of his own objectifications, and this cosmos is increasingly hard to see through, and harder still to dominate and control."[29]

An element of "irrationality" has crept into the compulsions of civilization, so that there is a strong temptation to escape into gnostic unrealities in a way that "surrenders the real social and political world to senseless and inhuman forces."[30] The shattered ideal of peace hoped for in the scientific revolution has given way to a profound disenchantment and imprisonment since we cannot conceive of a possibly different future.[31]

The way through this dilemma is not to seek for possibilities inherent in the present, as in process thought, but to see the promise of God's future coming to us from ahead. In this way, like Abraham, we are "leaving thedwelling-placess of reality where one has peace and security and giving oneself over to the cause of history, to the way of freedom and danger, the way of disappointment and surprise, borne along and led solely by God's hope."[32]

However, Moltmann deplores any idea of the separation of theology from scientific concerns, while also rejecting the possibility of a "Christian science." Once we isolate theology from science it amounts to "self-mutilation" since we are offering "a world without salvation, a salvation without the world; and a reality without God, a God without reality."[33]

The problem of science on its own is that in its power over creation it has become powerless in knowing the direction of its future. The short-lived harmony between science and theology, which existed in the Aristotelian framework of reality, fell apart once scientific positivism replaced myth with natural law. However, science's naive belief in the correspondence between science and reality began to fade within the scientific sphere itself, so that now science becomes less certain and is, instead, "a world of possibilities."[34]

Moltmann does not reject the engagement of theology with science and philosophy, yet theology is still distinct from science in that it is "not under the categorical thought compulsions of this realm."[35] Theology must not lose the stigma of historical particularity if it is to remain *Christian* theology. Yet if it is to be true to itself as *theology* it "must relate itself to the universal, the coming of God in his kingdom."[36] The "deadly category of having," which is one of the compulsions of a technological denunciation of nature, needs to be replaced by the "category of affirmed being."[37]

He urges us to see ourselves in partnership with creation and in symbiotic relationship with it, so that just as Christ becomes a servant for us, we become servants for creation:

> "In the light of Christ's mission, Gen.1.28 will have to be interpreted in an entirely new way, not 'subdue the earth,' but 'free the earth' through fellowship with it, for according to Romans 8, the whole enslaved creation waits for the revelation of the 'glorious liberty of the children of God,' so that it itself may therefore be free."[38]

The question about the environment becomes bound up in an intimate way with the question about social justice, so that "we shall not be able to achieve social justice without justice for the natural environment, and we shall not be able to achieve justice for nature without social justice."[39]

These themes of fellowship and friendship with creation might lead to the stifling of science and technology altogether. However, Moltmann does not reject science, but sees theological and ethical questions as coming prior to scientific research rather than reflection *a posteriori*. It is the integration of science with wider concerns of society that liberates it from its "quasi-sacred" position in which experts have taken the place of priests, who in former times have closely guarded the knowledge required for power from the ignorant laity.[40] Instead, humankind has to take up the burden of responsibility that science gives, rather than leaving it for "nature," so that it is not "a question of whether to stop or rather to restrict basic research, but it is a question how to integrate scientific research and its application into the more complex system of society."[41] Hence, while the power of "nature" was blind fate, the power of scientific humankind must be seeing and open to different alternatives. Nowhere does Moltmann adequately address the problem of how we are to combine solidarity with creation and friendship with it, with the more practical use of creation in scientific research. He seems to hint that we have the balance tilted too far in the direction of manipulation and control, so that we need to recover a deeper awareness of solidarity with creation rather than mastery over it.

A further hint at the possible solution to the above dilemma comes from the difference between the environment in which animals are set which belongs to "the internal side of their instincts" compared with humanity who creates environment out of culture. Yet within this culture "there is an element and environment without which he cannot live as man, and that is hope. It is the breath of life."[42] Now it is in the context of this hope that we allow a poetic imagination to develop which anticipates the future in thought and pictures. Even though we have, through technology, become gods of nature, we remain uncreative and without imagination, so that "after three hundred years of rationalism's trend from utopia to science, the reverse way, from science to utopia, without giving up science, owns priority on today's agenda."[43] The whole world becomes an "open process" and a "great experiment," rather than a "finished house of being."[44] This is a movement towards an understanding of science in the modern sense of openness to possibility, away from the rigid structure inherent in a Cartesian framework. However, Moltmann has not yet clarified in what sense this new science can be accommodated into a more utopian framework. The priority for Moltmann is clearly not simply an open future in its widest sense, but the future of the hopeless.[45]

The possible alternatives before us are "the universal death, the nothing (*nihil)* or the home of identity of all. The world process is still undecided."[46] Now as part of the relationship between ourselves and God, he is not simply the point of our hope in heaven, but he has hope in us.[47] This seems to raise our responsibility for the future course of events, so that fulfillment of God's promises comes in the wake of our obedience. Yet Moltmann draws back from linking our future with our action in any rigid way, rather, "Here the obedience of man need not yet be understood as the efficient cause of the fulfillment, but can also be taken merely as the occasion for the fulfillment by God himself."[48]

We need to arrive at a compromise between progress and social equilibrium, without which we can expect "ecological death." The trend today must be more towards "the ancient values of joy of living and reverence for creation," so that we re-orientate our lives from "economy to ecology."[49] Moltmann realizes that political action on an international scale is required for such a change to take place and, furthermore, "if we re-orientate our societies' life values, we will find a great deal of relevance in the old, meditative, doxological forms of faith practiced by the ancient church and the monks."[50] This is not equivalent to the resignation of the epiphany religions which ignored the problem of suffering, but is "the way of life in the midst of death."[51]

Moltmann wishes to reject, then, certain aspects of our thinking that have been conditioned by a scientific view of the world. This includes the modern understanding of the world as operational rather than contemplative.

Instead, the knowledge we gain needs to become tempered by wisdom, and planning by hope.[52] The contemplation that we experience needs to be directed towards the future, rather than the "eternal presence."[53] The "I Am" of God addressed to Moses is not tied to a sacred place, but also means "I Will Be," and in this way contains the future of God.[54] While the first anticipation of the future has a form which is analogous to the concrete in history it remains "more than the restitution of the old since, through guilt and judgement, something has intervened which cannot be facilely eliminated."[55] Furthermore, unless our hope claims to be more than it was in the beginning, it ceases to be hope and becomes merely a memory. The new creation is a conquest of the "very possibility of sin" and so surpasses the ambiguity of the creation in the beginning.[56]

He argues that our future prospects of reality have to become earthed in the transformation of our historical conditions in the present. If they do not allow this they are utopian ideas that "promise more than they can keep" and the "fascination for transcendence" becomes quickly exchanged with resignation.[57] Unless we "humanize" this world by engagement with it, our own identity crisis remains unresolved.[58] The reality of suffering and evil in creation discloses a theodicy question which lurks behind both the cosmological world-view and the scientific world-view. Real Christian hope has to attack both resignation in the face of evil conditions and utopian presumption. Unless our freedom in faith includes the liberation of suffering creation it becomes other-worldly mysticism. Real hope neither dissolves history nor is swallowed up by history in a philosophy of history. Our historical future is necessarily bound up with the whole of suffering creation.

The combination of fulfillment and alienation that we experience in industrial society produces a tension that can easily trigger a flight into pantheism. The world becomes a heaven or hell, a dwelling-place or prison, in such a way that "the flower garden of irrational mysticism spreads out on the soil of rationalistic enlightenment."[59] Instead of these false alternatives we need to come to a point of acceptance of the present in spite of its unacceptability, so that "it is the critical 'Yes' response of love which goes beyond the absolute 'Yes' of shallow enthusiasm, as well as the absolute 'No' of absolute refusal."[60] Is this perspective still compatible with Moltmann's insistence that we do not become resigned to the present conditions, but work for its transformation? This does seem to be the case here since Moltmann is affirming the category of being, and a critical "Yes" does not lead to passive acceptance as long as it is in relationship with the future hope for all creation. Moltmann is really urging us to take responsibility for transformation of creation rather than exploitation or escapism. This responsibility stems from the idea of humankind created in the image of God. Humanity's uniqueness compared with the rest of creation is held in balance with its shared creatureliness with all creatures. The image of God in humankind gives "infinite freedom over against all finite things and relationships and even his own reality."[61]

Moltmann addresses the question as to how far our relationship with God in mystical adoration should influence our relationship with creation. He rejects any tendency in mysticism which allows us to love God to the exclusion of the earthly realm. Instead, true mysticism stems from the way of discipleship and resistance to oppression.[62] The only way our vision of God in the world remains free from delusion is if it is grounded in the suffering of Christ. In this way, "the person who believes that God is to be found in the God-forsakenness of the crucified Jesus, believes that he sees God everywhere in all things."[63] We need to find a balance between finding joy in creation and ethical responsibility, so that:

> "without the free play of imagination and songs of praise, the new obedience deteriorates into legalism... But without concrete obedience, which means without physical, social and political changes, the lovely songs and celebrations of freedom become empty phrases."[64]

3. Interconnectedness as a motif in Moltmann's theology.

We have hinted at this theme in the above concern for theological reflection to hold in tension the dialectic of imagination and reason, faith and hope, present and future, suffering and joy, our responsibility over creation and participation in it. The thread of interconnectedness which runs through all these themes is the eschatological perspective which forms the "medium of Christian faith, the keynote, the daybreak colours of a new expected day which bathe everything in their light."[65]

(a) The cross of the risen Christ as paradigm.

One of Moltmann's most profound experiences was the presence of God in the midst of his captivity as a prisoner of war. His faith taught him how to hope and made it impossible for him to come to terms with captivity or to give way "to the forces of annihilation in resignation or rage."[66] He admits that this experience "had a much deeper influence on me than anything that came later."[67]

His theological reflection on this experience in which he identified with the crucified and risen Christ, allowed him to see the resurrection as the "sign of God's protest against suffering."[68] Hope makes people restless and makes them suffer in solidarity with the whole of unredeemed creation. Wolfhart Pannenberg's view of reality which finds its essence in the whole course of history in such a way that the world will "one day be theophany, indirect self-revelation of God *in tote*," is rejected by Moltmann since it ignores the "cross of the present."[69] Once we start with the resurrection without the cross, our theology gives us merely another passive interpretation of the world and history. Instead we should identify with the cross and resurrection of Christ, and in this way seek to transform conditions in expectation of a divine transformation.[70]

While in *Theology of Hope* Moltmann focuses more on the resurrection of Christ it is still firmly grounded in the crucifixion. Once we move to *The*

Crucified God, we find a shift in emphasis to the cross, while retaining a sense of the future resurrection. It is the link between the cross and resurrection that gives us the reason for hope in the midst of suffering. The suffering that those who are poor and oppressed experience is in solidarity with the whole suffering creation - in this way Christ's suffering becomes universal:

> "Not only the martyrs are included in the eschatological suffering of the servant of God, but the whole creation is included in the suffering of the last days. The suffering becomes universal and destroys the all sufficiency of the cosmos, just as the eschatological joy will then resound in a 'new heaven and a new earth."[71]

The cross is a protection against enthusiastic hopes, and unless hope is born out of the cross, it becomes superstition. The concrete cross of Christ gives hope for the hopeless so that its power is more profound in the light of the resurrection event. In this sense Moltmann urges us to think of the cross as the "present form of the resurrection. We are therefore able to say that Jesus' resurrection is only indirectly, but the meaning of the cross is directly, the foundation of Christian hope for justice and life."[72]

He rejects all secondary means of mediation of the kingdom of God coming either through the church or through our faith. The more fundamental event which mediates "the eschatological rule of God and with it the new creation and redeemed existence" is the raising of the crucified Jesus.[73] The reality of evil that we suffer in this world raises the question of theodicy. The most fundamental evil is that of the oppressed, exploited, alienated and divided humanity. Their cry for freedom is also "the cry of creation which man is destroying."[74] This includes both the alienation of ourselves from our own material bodies and alienation between us and our natural environment. It is by this alienation that we have condemned ourselves to death and "the cry for liberty therefore unites humanity and nature in a single hope. They will either be destroyed by their division and enmity or will survive as partners in a new community."[75]

Moltmann insists that the cry of creation for liberation is God's own cry as well. He suffers "in nature's silent death pangs" because he loves creation. His suffering comes out of his purpose for humankind, which is for liberty, and for nature, which is "joy - as the play of his good pleasure."[76] All individual suffering becomes set against the background of God's patient suffering, as revealed in the crucified Christ. All things are living in the hope of redemption and liberation since it remains the cross of the *risen* Christ.

Salvation in history becomes the "divine opening of closed systems," which includes the faith that "non-human life systems enter into communication with one another once more."[77] God suffers through the isolation of humankind from itself, and in this suffering humankind receives the grace to become open to God, to each other and to the world. Eternal life is a life which has overcome death, and God's openness to the world, shown in Christ's suffering and death, leads to the anticipation of the universal opening of the closed world for divine life.[78] The liberation of humankind includes the liberation from the desire to exploit nature, so that there is a reciprocal relation in which nature becomes "hominized" and humankind "naturalized."[79] True salvation, then, includes turning away from the sin of the possession of nature to peace with nature.

The particularity of the cross and resurrection have cosmic significance. Hence "the cross and resurrection are then not merely *modi* in the person of Christ. Rather their dialectic is an open dialectic, which finds its resolving synthesis only in the eschaton of all things."[80] One of Moltmann's favourite texts in this discussion is Romans 8:18ff, which links the suffering of the whole of creation with the anticipation of future liberation.[81] This liberation includes at least five aspects which are all interconnected:

(i) economic justice in the face of man's exploitation.

(ii) human dignity in the face of political oppression.

(iii) human solidarity in the face of alienation and division.

(iv) peace with nature in the face of industrial destruction of the environment.

(v) hope in the face of apathy towards the whole in personal life.

All these aspects are bound up together in such an interconnected web that "today, exploitation, oppression, alienation, the destruction of nature and inner despair make up the vicious circle in which we are killing ourselves and our world."[82] The way of peace is one that breaks through these vicious circles.[83] Once we view the interconnectedness of all forms of oppression we "recognize the need for co-operation between different forms of liberation."[84] Politics and economics are interwoven both with the future of humanity and that of nature in such a way that "politics is becoming a common destiny."[85] On this basis it is understandable that Christian theology needs to become political theology.

Our understanding of liberty stems from reflection on the resurrection of the crucified Christ. Here freedom becomes less the freedom of individual choice, rather it is "the passion for the possible."[86] While the reality of freedom is in the future, it comes to us in anticipation in the present by reflecting on the resurrection of the crucified one. The difference between the freedom in faith and our experience of present unfreedom becomes "the motor and motive power for our work of realizing freedom in history."[87] Thus the freedom of God comes to earth through love and solidarity with the powerless in the cross of Christ.

(b) The interrelation between Christ and the church.

In the interrelation between Christ and the world, the church needs to become Christ's church if it is to become the true church. It is recognized by "the powers of liberation which quicken it and radiate from it and often enough by the signs of the cross which it has to bear because of its resistance."[88] The church needs to identify with the whole of suffering creation, so that "only when it freely chooses to make its own the groaning of the whole enslaved creation is the Christian community the sacrament of God's hope for the world."[89]

The relationship between Christ and the church comes through the Holy Spirit. He is the creative power of God, who makes the impossible possible and calls into existence that which does not exist. Thus, "the Spirit descends upon the talents and potentialities which an individual possesses and activates them for the kingdom of God, for the liberation of the world."[90] The true church is one that participates in the Trinitarian history of God. By this Moltmann means "it is not the church that has a mission of salvation to fulfil to the world, it is the mission of the Son and Spirit through the Father that includes the church, creating a church as it goes on its way."[91] The church, if she is to remain true to herself, shares in the fellowship of Christ's suffering and joy in the Spirit. She shares both in the "cry for freedom" and "song of thanksgiving" of those who have been liberated. Above all she participates in uniting humanity, society with creation, and creation with God in a true "fellowship of love."[92]

The theme of friendship is one that develops out of an understanding of Jesus as the true friend of those who are unlike himself such as tax collectors and sinners. His friendship is different from an ordinary understanding of friendship as the exclusive attraction of like-minded people, rather it is inclusive and public.[93] It is a friendship that springs from the overflowing joy in the kingdom of God and it is in fellowship with Christ that his disciples come to know God as friend. Within this friendship we find a deepened life of prayer so that "prayer and the hearing of prayer are the marks of a man's friendship with God and God's friendship with man."[94] Moltmann extends this idea by suggesting that the work of Christ needs to be reformulated so that it is no longer perceived in terms of sovereignty and function, but instead "can be taken to its highest point in friendship, for in his divine function as prophet, priest and king, Christ lives and acts as a friend and creates friendship."[95] The friendship of Christ is an open friendship which includes love between humankind, God and all his creatures.

Moltmann understands the whole meaning of life to be set in the context of relationships. In this way:

> "No life can be understood from its own standpoint alone. As long as it lives it exists in living relationships to other lives, and therefore in contexts of time and with perspectives of hope. It is these that constitute in the first place a living being's unique vitality, openness and capacity for communication."[96]

Hence "living hope is always connected with relationships... eschatology is always only specific as relational eschatology."[97] Eschatology becomes inclusive of all world religions, social systems and the natural environment. If the church is to become true to her task as a messianic church she needs to reformulate these relationships in anticipation of the coming kingdom of God.[98]

On a practical level, the reordering of relationships makes for dialogue with those of other denominations within the church and other religions. An ecumenical peace bears witness to the gospel of peace.[99] The unity of fellowship develops first from shared suffering under the cross of Christ.[100] Dialogue changes the atmosphere from one of hostility to the possibility of mutual participation between those of different religions.[101] This dialogue needs to include ideologies of the contemporary world and involvement in cultural, economic and political processes.[102]

The real enemy that Christianity needs to address is a paralysing apathy in the face of contemporary economic, political and ecological crises. Now faith becomes the courage to affirm life and stay in "loyalty to the earth."[103] While the church needs to assert its "passion for living," this does not mean the ecclesiasticizing of the world but the "perception of certain trends and lines of action."[104] One such trend is the realization that social justice matters more than economic growth. Such a renunciation of material gain requires "the symbiosis of people with people, nation with nation, and culture with culture."[105] The only real context for economic action is that of right relationships:

"We would therefore call symbiosis the guiding line for economic action and for our support or resistance to economic trends. It is only fellowship in respect for the unique character and needs of the natural environmental system which gives humanity and nature a chance of survival. Such symbioses in both limited and wider contexts are to be seen as corresponding to and anticipating the kingdom of God in history for it is only fellowship with the Creator in the coming kingdom that gives the coming together of men and women in the history of humanity and nature its transcendent and thus its stimulating meaning."[106]

The cultural conflicts that we face include racism, sexism and the exclusion of the handicapped. These stem from an awareness of ourselves in an ego identity based on the idea of having a particular race, sex or health. Instead our sense of self should come from the category of being which fully accepts the truth of justification by grace. All attempts at self-justification through having or achieving are superfluous; instead, human life, if it is to be fully human, is that which has "eternal value because it is loved and accepted by God."[107] The fellowship between persons that we seek is between those who are freed from an ego-identity which allows them to accept the other fully in their otherness.

(c) The relationship between the church and the future of creation.

The transformation of relationships that is an anticipation of the coming kingdom is only possible through prayer. We need to bring together the false alternatives of evangelization and humanization, interior conversion and improvement of conditions, faith in God and love for creation. Prayer and action are interrelated in such a way that self-transformation and the changing of conditions coincide.[108] Moreover, the future anticipation of the kingdom of God does not deny the reality of present suffering; instead, "the doxological anticipation of the beauty of the kingdom and active resistance to Godless and inhuman relationships in history are related to one another and reinforce one another mutually."[109] It is through prayer that we become more ready to accept pain and love more intensely than before. True worship, then, does not escape the tensions of the world by looking back to an ideal past; but by keeping focused on the promised future, the painful difference between the present and future is uncovered. True prayer remains one which seeks to join our history with that of Christ, so that "when we meditate on Christ's history and through the Spirit experience our history with Christ, we find not only ourselves but also our place and our personal tasks within God's history with the world."[110]

Hope looks not just to Christ's death and resurrection but also to his coming glory. Moreover, it is not simply a hope in a personal relationship with Christ, but also is a "substantial" hope "of his lordship, his peace and his righteousness on earth."[111] In this way we participate in the messianic history of God in Christ. The rebirth of an individual person becomes linked with the divine future of the whole of creation in such a way that it gives our own individual life "permanent significance," and "our life becomes a sign of hope for the future of the whole world."[112] Just as the destruction of nature is linked with our own self-destruction, so the rebirth of humanity in Christ is linked with the future hope for the whole of the created order. While the resurrection is the foundation for hope, Christ's *parousia* defines "hope's horizon."[113] In this way God's righteousness extends to the whole created order, so that it "provides creation as a whole with a new ground of existence and a new right for life. Hence with the coming righteousness of God we can expect also a new creation."[114] We find a similar idea expressed rather differently in *Religion, Revolution and the Future*, where the obedience of believers anticipates the resurrection not just of their own bodies, but that of the new creation. Yet this remains the work of the grace of God, since he creates the new "out of the bad, the evil and the godless."[115]

The relationship between hope and promised future remains anticipation as long as we experience contradictions in our history and that of the world. The experience of anticipation includes the whole of creation "groaning in travail."[116] The fulfillment is never the same as the promise since it comes out of the future of God and has to remain "open for moments of surprise."[117] In this we can distinguish between *futurum*, which is future based on the present possibilities, compared with *adventus*, which designates that which is coming to us.[118] The overall category of *Zukunft* which includes both *futurum/Futur* and *adventus* has the meaning of *parousia* or arrival. Once we lose confidence in the future emerging from inherent possibilities in the present, our historical continuity can only be grasped from the perspective of *Zukunft*. The double theme of future, including *futurum* and *adventus*, is similar to Moltmann's wish neither to assimilate traditional ideas in a facile way, nor to assume they are "a great garbage heap of dead facts."[119] Once we sense a future that is coming to us it becomes more appropriate to speak of **pre**volution rather than **re**volution, since now it is a "human dream turned forward."[120]

4. The indwelling of God in creation.

(a) Present and future reality.

This theme flows from the above discussion of the interrelationship between hope and promise. The theme of God's presence in the midst of suffering gives way to a sense of participation in the Trinitarian life of God himself. Yet throughout his discussion Moltmann refuses to allow his vision of the future to deny the reality of present evil conditions. His link between Christology and eschatology brings God's creative presence into the context of the suffering and the abandoned. The grace of God that emerges is not just the renewal of the original creation, but the birth of a new creation. While Moltmann describes Ernst Bloch's philosophy of hope as "magnificent," its failure to deal adequately with the reality of suffering renders his approach inadequate without a Christian reinterpretation.[121] The present suffering marks out what the future is not, and "this critical negation of the negative affords the anticipated positive the freedom to prove itself and does not define the future by means of historical prejudices.[122]

While the idea of the Trinitarian life of God is linked with the coming kingdom in a closer way after *The Trinity and the Kingdom of God*, we find hints of this perspective in Moltmann's earlier work. The new future which comes from God emerges from the relationship between the Father and Son, which Moltmann describes as "trinitarian."[125] The future is tied into the future of Christ, but not in the sense of a "spiritualizing" of humankind. Rather, there will be a totally new creation of humankind and the world.[126]

In *Theology and Joy*, Moltmann introduces a more celebratory tone where creation is seen as the expression of the goodwill of God:

> "The world as a free creation cannot be a necessary unfolding of God, nor an emanation of his being from divine fullness. When he creates something that is not God but also not nothing, this must have its ground not in itself, but in God's goodwill or pleasure. It is the realm in which God displays his glory."[127]

We find here the theme of God indwelling in his creation in an **eschatological** sense, which reaches back to include the idea of **present** indwelling in a more forceful way after Moltmann's pneumatological approach in *The Church in the Power of the Spirit*. The theme of eschatological indwelling allows him to express natural theology as that which applies to the future of creation, as, for example, in *Religion, Revolution and the Future*, where he writes:

> "The original creation was created out of the will of God. But in its future, God will dwell in it with his essence. This is to say that the new creation corresponds to the essence of God and is illuminated and transfigured by God's earthly presence. It will be a creation without the necessity of religious mediation or sacred zones. It will not be a garden of Eden, but the city of God. The first *creatio ex nihilo* will be taken up into a new *creatio ex gloria Dei*."[128]

Moltmann insists on anchoring this vision in the resurrection of the crucified Christ. By the time Moltmann writes *Experiences of God* he is careful to distinguish between the divine presence as revealed in the history of the Holy Spirit from that revealed in creation at the beginning. This is related to his notion that the gifts of the Spirit do not come *ex nihilo*, but derive from the Holy Spirit himself. Once we view the Holy Spirit as divine subject, the theme of filling present creation with eternal life by "descending on all and dwelling in them," becomes possible.[129]

The background to Moltmann's idea of God indwelling creation comes from the theme of *kabod* in the Old Testament and *doxa* in the New Testament.[130] The world becomes transfigured by the indwelling of God, and humanity is no longer just a creature of God or child of God, but "like God" and one who will "participate in God's infinite creativity."[131] In Moltmann's earlier work he is more insistent that this is a future hope, and in the present we cannot expect any more than an anticipation of what will come in the future. We are still in the "*theologia viae*," but not yet the "*theologia patriae*." Thus Christian theology remains firmly rooted in historical action and is not yet the vision of God.[132] The difference between the presence of God in history and that at the end of history is that now we find God's presence in his will, while at the end of history his presence will be a real indwelling presence. Hence, "The historical epiphanies of God, of which Israel could truly speak, were particular and transient epiphanies."[133] The concrete religious experience of God's epiphany is not **denied** by future orientation, but becomes preserved in the form of memory. In this way Moltmann suggests that "Because an ultimate future announces itself in a provisional past, hope exists in the mode of memory, and memory in the mode of hope."[134]

(b) Indwelling of the Spirit of God.

As we hinted above, once we consider the work of the Holy Spirit in the new creation, we begin to see a correspondence between "pneumatology" and what was "natural theology" in the traditional sense.[135] Provisional "doxologies" of the present show the coming future glory. The vision of God where suffering has ceased is not a denial of the cross in the midst of history, but "a perfection" of Christ's lordship. In this way Christian hope is not directed towards an "otherworldly" pantheism in which all that Christ has done to overcome the world disappears, but rather to the fact that "God will be all in all."[136]

Moltmann is clear in his discussion of ecclesiology that we can experience the new creation now, at least in part, through the power of the Holy Spirit. The rebirth of the world has already begun, though our life in the Spirit still remains "a fragment of the coming beauty of the kingdom of God" in a way that gives an individual's insignificant life an "eternal meaning."[137] A life worthy of the gospel still experiences very real tensions and this new life of the Spirit does not come from a "great harmonious ideal for life," but from the midst of the breaking points of life.[138] These tensions include that between prayer and faithfulness to the earth, meditation and political action, transcendence and solidarity.

Moltmann is influenced by the Eastern Orthodox view of the significance of the crucified and risen Lord, not just in the forgiveness of sin and alienation, but also in his "beauty and glory."[139] At every worship service we have an anticipation of the "laughter of the redeemed," and from this feast we take a memory into daily life which cannot be forgotten. Just as solidarity in suffering brings us into fellowship with the whole of creation, so "ecstatic rejoicing leads into ever deeper solidarity with the unredeemed world."[140] This springs from the emerging contrast between the foretaste of the future of creation and the reality of present evil, so that our awareness of the depth of sin becomes sensitized by experience of worship. Through the power of the Holy Spirit we are given a foretaste of coming feast.

Moltmann does not reject the place that ritual has in the ordering of the life of worship. Rather "free spontaneous and creative life, whose effect is not destructive, only becomes possible out of the security ritual confers."[141] These rituals remain creative in self-expression and playfulness in a way that challenges our modern existence that has become centred on purpose and utility. The place of ritual is not so much an escape from the chaos of reality as in former times, but a way of giving expression to our feelings of exuberance and ecstasy in worship.[142] Worship should be less an escape valve in the midst of unbearable tensions of the present, as an affirmation of existence and joy in that existence. Worship remains a messianic feast that anticipates the eternal sabbath. A feast is one that remains open for spontaneity, unlike a celebration that becomes "disturbed by unexpected events."[143] The feast is a liberating one that is "in the foreign land" and is a "fragmentary anticipation of God's free and festal world"[144]

A people that is living by the Spirit of God is an initial fulfillment of the new creation and glorification of God. The new reaches "at least in tendency, over the whole breath of creation in its present wretchedness."[145] The coming of the Spirit does not lead to a dream world that is beyond this world, but "leads ever more deeply into Christ's sufferings and earthly discipleship."[146] The way that the coming of the Spirit links us so closely in fellowship with Christ's suffering and glory comes from Moltmann's development of the doctrine of the Trinity.

(c) The Trinitarian basis for divine indwelling.

The future glorification of God in creation is such that it is bound up both with the inner Trinitarian dynamic relationship and the future of the world so that "he does not desire to be glorified without his liberated creation."[147] Moltmann distinguishes between the sending, seeking love of God which comes from the Trinitarian origin in its openness to the world from eternity, and the unifying, glorifying love of God which comes from the Trinitarian eschatological goal at the end of history. The first movement opens up the history of the Trinity for the world through the sending of the Spirit and the Son. The second movement gathers, unites and glorifies the world in God and God in the world:

> "The opening and completion correspond to one another in the openness of the triune God... At the end God has won his creation in its renewing consummation for hisdwelling-place. He comes to his glory in the joy of redeemed creation."[148]

Once we speak of glorification we remember the suffering that has been endured which, far from becoming obsolete, remains the "ground of eternal joy."[149]

While we find hints at this idea of joy in creation in earlier works such as *Theology of Hope*, the more prominent theme is that of anticipation and expectation, rather than foretaste and beginning of new creation. His original, cruciform shape of reflection on the future of creation, remains in the background in later works, as does the idea that the expectation itself brings true happiness. In this way "man can accept his whole present, and can find joy not only in its joy but also in its sorrow, happiness not only in its happiness, but also in its pain.[150]

The movement of the sending Trinity presents the world as an object of messianic activity. This brings the "action reflection" method into theological discourse. However, once we consider the movement of the glorification of the Trinity, theology becomes expressed not so much in messianic action as in doxological joy. Moltmann shifts his reflection towards the second movement in later works, though we have both threads present even in his earliest writings. The lordship of God becomes more clearly revealed once we perceive "the beauty of his grace." Faith needs the "aesthetic side" if its moral aspect is to become joyful. Moltmann also insists that unless we love God our love for our neighbour loses its spontaneity.[151]

Both themes of messianic action and glorification serve to reinforce each other. The Spirit of glorification once joined with messianic themes gives it a depth of resilience in the face of suffering, and guards against the double danger of otherworldliness or resignation. Moltmann justifies his reflection on the Trinity by insisting that such reflection is far from abstract, which means an isolation of events from time and history. Rather a Trinitarian approach helps us to see the single event within the context of history, individual experience within the whole of life, and action within its meaning for the future. Moreover, this integrating Trinitarian thinking is itself, "an element of unification in the history of God, and as being to this extent doxology."[152]

5. Conclusions.

Our study of Moltmann's writing up to *The Trinity and the Kingdom of God* has shown that he has remained true to his intention of keeping an eschatological orientation throughout his discussion of creation themes. These themes do not form the prolegomena as in the classical theology of both the reformed and catholic traditions. He rejects the idea of monarchical lordship of God over creation which is the presupposition of traditional reformed theology, as well as the cosmological understanding of the world which is inherent in much "natural" theology. After the post-Kantian era we have become trapped by a web of our own techno-scientific culture which is as threatening to us as that of purely natural forces to earlier generations.

The way through our enslavement by these vicious circles of our own making is by an awareness of the liberating power of the death and resurrection of Jesus Christ. His suffering shows us that God is involved in the whole groaning of the created order, and the pain of his passion and forsakenness by God the Father brings him into solidarity with all those who are oppressed. The Father loves the Son and loves his creation, so that he suffers through the suffering of humankind whom he created for liberty, and through the suffering of nature, that he created for his pleasure. The concrete action of God in the history of the world through Christ's life, death and resurrection prevents our future hope from becoming idle speculation or utopian vision. However, it is also a source of inspiration for our hope since it brings our history and that of the whole creation into the history of God himself. The liberating power of Christ's death and resurrection begins to heal the broken relationships between humankind and God, between ourselves and between humankind and nature.

The ambiguity that scientific truth brings to us in its potential for both good and evil can only be resolved by incorporating scientific endeavour into the wider social networks of our culture. Theology has a crucial role to play in its ethical directives for scientific research and needs to become incorporated at the beginning rather than after a problem has emerged. The temptation to retreat into otherworldly mysticism or become apathetic in resignation needs to be strongly resisted by keeping in mind our future hope. This hope is born, not so much from our scientific understanding in a rationalist sense, but from our use of the creative imagination.

Moltmann's theological reflections are infused by a pervading sense of the interconnectedness of all relationships. He includes this ecological theme both in its narrower biological sense and by implication in his discussions both of past and present reality and future hope. The new creation that we hope for is one where all these interrelationships are restored, yet it is more than a looking back to an ideal state since now the very possibility of sin no longer exists.

In looking forward to the new creation in the context of present suffering and that of the crucified Christ, the theme of Christology gives way to pneumatology, which are both set in an eschatological perspective. The Spirit of God is now not just in the sending of the Son in openness to all creation in messianic activity, but presses forward to the unification and glorification of the whole so that it becomes a fitting dwelling-place for God himself. The theme of indwelling takes on a new significance. Now the presence of God is not just through his will over history and creation, but is a real presence which overflows in doxological joy.

Without the strand of festivity the messianic search becomes moralistic and harsh. Without love for God in himself our love for our neighbour loses spontaneity. Our experience of God in the present, rather than weakening the imperative for change, actually increases its urgency. This foretaste of the divine banquet both fuels our hope and fires our missionary endeavours. We remain within the tensions of prayer and action, contemplation and political involvement, and it is within these tensions that a true mysticism is born. Once these tensions are broken our prayers can become an escapist flight from reality, or our actions a will to power and domination instead of free participation and responsibility.

The twin ecological themes of interrelationships and indwelling come together in a striking way in Moltmann's Trinitarian theology, which served as a preliminary outline to his concepts in *God in Creation*. Our next task is to trace this development in the context of his understanding of the doctrine of God.

End Notes

All books and articles are by Jürgen Moltmann unless stated otherwise. Translations are from the German text.

1. *God in Creation: An Ecological Doctrine of Creation*, translated by M. Kohl, London, SCM, 1985; hereafter referred to as GC.

2. C. Link, "Kritisches Forum, Schöpfung im messianischen Licht," *Evangelische Theologie*, 47, 1987, pp. 83-92; translation from the German original, p. 83.

3. *Ibid.*, p. 83.

4. *Ibid.*, p. 84.

5. J. Niewiadomski, *Die Zweideutigkeit von Gott und Welt in J. Moltmanns Theologien*, Innsbrucker theologische Studien 9, Innsbruck, Tyrolia, 1982.

6. *Ibid.*, p. 9.; English translation mine.

7. *Ibid.*, p. 10; English translation mine.

8. *Ibid.*, p. 10; "God himself is now seen as a contradictory reality."

9. *Ibid.*, p. 10.

10. GC, p. xii. The word *oekologie*, from the Greek οιχοζ, or house, was invented by Ernst Haeckel (1834-1919) in 1866 to refer in a loose descriptive way to the geographical location of animal and plant species. As the subject developed in the nineteenth century it included a wide range of disparate research areas from economic biology to plant and animal systematics. In the twentieth century the idea of ecological niche as a dynamic concept of interrelationships and activity of organisms connected with their energy relations replaced the more static concept of Haeckel. We also find a movement in ecological science away from an interest in a single population, to that of community ecology, or collection of species and finally systems ecology, which is an integrated web of plants, animals and physical surroundings. While ecology in the nineteenth century was more descriptive and understood itself in terms of the more static "balance of nature," by the twentieth century it had become more quantitative, reflected in the search for an explanation of ecological networks and apparent "hierarchical" food chains in terms of energy relations. For a fuller discussion see David Cox, *Charles Elton and the Emergence of Modern Ecology*, PhD thesis, 1979, Washington University, pp. 1-4; 91-100.

11. *The Trinity and the Kingdom of God*; translated by M. Kohl, London, SCM, 1985; hereafter referred to as TKG.

12. *Hope and Planning*; translated by M. Clarkson, New York, Harper and Row, 1971, pp. 5-6; hereafter referred to as HP.

13. *The Experiment Hope*; translated by M.D. Meeks, ed., London, SCM, 1975, pp. 17-18; hereafter referred to as EH.

14. *Theology of Hope: On the Ground and Implications of a Christian Eschatology*; translated by J.W. Leitch, London, SCM, 1967, p. 98; hereafter referred to as TH.

15. *Experiences of God*; translated by M. Kohl, London, SCM, 1980, p. 78; hereafter referred to as EG.

16. TH, p. 90.

17. *Ibid.*, p. 282.

18. *Ibid.*, p. 116.

19. *Ibid.*, p. 136.

20. *The Future of Creation*; translated by M. Kohl, London, SCM, 1979, pp. 116-117; hereafter referred to as FC.

21. FC, p. 118.

22. *Ibid.*, p. 119.

23. HP, p. 10.

24. *Ibid.*, pp. 15-16.

25. TH, p. 64.

26. HP, p. 57.

27. TH, p. 92.

28. "Towards the Next Step in the Dialogue," in, F. Herzog, ed., *The Future of Hope*, New York, Herder and Herder, 1970, pp. 154-164; hereafter referred to as FH.

29. FC, p. 5; for a similar treatment see *Religion, Revolution and the Future*; translated by M.D. Meeks, New York, Charles Scribner's Sons, 1969, p. 183; hereafter referred to as RRF. The quasi-religious role that science has assumed is also discussed in "Hope and the Biomedical Future of Man," in, E. Cousins, ed., *Hope and the Future of Man*, London, Teilhard Centre for the Future of Man, 1972, pp. 89-116.

30. FC, p. 7.

31. TH, p. 238. He resists the idea of a total crisis, or salvation in the future, which leads to an "unreal God." Instead through repentence and self-criticism we become aligned with God's future. For a useful summary, see, "The Future as Threat and Opportunity," in, N. Brockman and N. Piediscalzi, eds., *Contemporary Religion and Social Responsibility*, New York, Alba House, 1973, pp. 103-118.

32. EH, pp. 47-48.

33. HP, p. 204. See also, "Hope and the Biomedical Future of Man," *op. cit.* (n.29).

34. *Ibid.*, p. 210.

35. FH, p. 156.

36. *Ibid.*, p. 157.

37. RRF, p. 58.

38. FC, p. 129.

39. *Ibid.*, p. 130.

40. *Ibid.*, pp. 131-132.

41. "The Ethics of Biomedical Research and the Newer Biomedical Technologies," in, S. Blesh, ed., *Recent Progress in Biology and Medicine: Its Social and Ethical Implications*; Council for International Organizations of Medical Sciences, C.I.O.M.S., Unesco House, Paris, 1972, pp. 68-72.

42. EH, p. 21.

43. *Ibid.*, pp. 23-24.

44. *Ibid.*, p. 26.

45. *Ibid.*, p. 118.

46. *Ibid.*, p. 26.

47. *Ibid.*, p. 27.

48. TH, p. 123.

49. EH, p. 183.

50. *Ibid.*, p. 184.

51. *Ibid.*, p. 189. Moltmann urges us to resist hopelessness by focusing on the resurrection of the crucified Christ. See, for example, "The Realism of Hope: The Feast of the Resurrection and the Transformation of Present Reality," translated by G.A. Thiele, *Concordia Theological Monthly*, 40, 1969, pp. 149-155. We will be returning to this issue again below.

52. "Theology as Eschatology," in, FH, pp. 1-50.

53. *Ibid.*, p. 21.

54. EH, p. 48.

55. RRF, p. 9.

56. *Ibid.*, pp. 23-24.

57. *Ibid.*, pp. 196-197.

58. *Ibid.*, p. 266.

59. *Man: Christian Anthropology in the Conflicts of the Present*; translated by J. Sturdy, Philadelphia, Fortress Press, 1974, p. 35; hereafter referred to as M.

60. *Ibid.*, p. 35.

61. *Ibid.*, p. 108.

62. EG, p. 72.

63. *Ibid.*, p. 79.

64. *Theology and Joy*; translated by R. Ulrich, London, SCM, 1973, p. 62; hereafter referred to as TJ.

65. EG, p. 12.

66. *Ibid.*, p. 20.

67. *The Open Church: Invitation to a Messianic Lifestyle*; translated by M.D. Meeks, London, SCM, 1978, p. 97; hereafter referred to as OC.

68. EG, p. 12.

69. TH, p. 79. Pannenberg is critical of Moltmann's position and theologians of hope generally, believing that they are unjustified in making a link between the Christian tradition of eschatological promise, and revolutionary or chiliastic movements in modern history; "without establishing empirically to what degree phenomena are comparable to what the prophetic message had in mind." Further, it is a rather "careless" way of establishing analogous "relations of theological language to historical and contemporary phenomena." W. Pannenberg, *Christian Spirituality and Sacramental Community*, London, Darton, Longman and Todd, 1984, p. 52; p. 64.

70. TH, p. 84.

71. *Ibid.*, p. 137.

72. RRF, p. 53.

73. FC, p. 52. For the influence of Bonhoeffer's position on Moltmann see "The Lordship of Christ in Human Society," translated by R. Fuller, in, J. Moltmann and J. Weissbach; *Two Studies in the Theology of Bonhoeffer*, New York, Charles Scribner's Sons, 1967, pp. 19-94.

74. FC, p. 98. The theme of resurrection as liberation is scattered throughout Moltmann's works. For another example see "The Liberating Feast," translated by F. McDonagh, in, H. Schmidt and D. Power, eds., *Politics and Liturgy, Concilium*, 2(10), 1974, pp. 74-84.

75. FC, p. 98.

76. *Ibid.*, p. 98. Moltmann's concern to unite the liberation of nature with human liberation, and with God's own cry, is also outlined in, "Liberation in the Light of Hope," translated by M.D. Meeks, *Ecumenical Review*, 26, 1974, pp. 413-429.

77. FC, p. 122.

78. *Ibid.*, p. 124.

79. *The Crucified God: The Cross as the Foundation and Criticism of Christian Theology*; translated by R.A. Wilson and J. Bowden, London, SCM, 1974, p. 334; hereafter referred to as CG.

80. TH, p. 201.

81. Examples include RRF, pp. 47,65; HP, p. 49.

82. FC, p. 110.

83. EH, p. 176.

84. FC, p. 113.

85. RRF, p. 218.

86. FC, p. 103. Moltmann elaborates his understanding of the passion of Christ, as inclusive of both his suffering and commitment; for "His love is passion: passion for human beings and their worth, passion for the creation and its peace. In the depths of his suffering we perceive the greatness of his passion for us." See *The Passion for Life: A Messianic Lifestyle*; translated by M.D. Meeks, Philadelphia, Fortress Press, 1978, pp. 31ff; hereafter referred to as PL. For a summary see also, "The Passion for Life," translated by E. Leuker and R. Klein, *Currents in Theology and Mission*, 4(1), 1977, pp. 3-10.

87. RRF, p. 66.

88. FC, p. 107.

89. RRF, p. 216.

90. FC, p. 108.

91. *The Church in the Power of the Spirit: A Contribution to Messianic Ecclesiology*; translated by M. Kohl, London, SCM , 1977, p. 64; hereafter referred to as CPS.

92. *Ibid.*, p. 65. See also, "The Life Signs of the Spirit in the Fellowship Community of Christ," translated by T. Runyan, with M.D. Meeks, R.J. Hunter, J.W. Fowler, N.L. Eskine; T. Runyan, ed., in *Hope for the Church: Moltmann in Dialogue with Practical Theology*; Nashville, Abingdon, 1979, pp. 37-56.

93. OC, pp. 50-63; also CPS p. 121.

94. CPS, p. 119.

95. *Ibid.*, p. 119.

96. *Ibid.*, p. 133.

97. *Ibid.*, p. 134.

98. *Ibid.*, p. 193.

99. EH, p. 178.

100. "What Kind of Unity? The Dialogue Between the Traditions of East and West" ; in, L. Vischer, ed., *Lausanne 77: Fifty Years of Faith and Order*; Faith and Order Paper, No. 82, Geneva, WCC, 1977, pp. 38-47.

101. CPS, p. 159.

102. *Ibid.*, pp. 162-164.

103. *Ibid.*, p. 165.

104. *Ibid.*, p. 168.

105. *Ibid.*, p. 175.

106. *Ibid.*, p. 176.

107. *Ibid.*, p. 187.

108. EG, p. 2.

109. CPS, p. 190.

110. OC, p. 45; see also CPS pp. 284-287.

111. TH, p. 119.

112. EG. p. 30.

113. *Ibid.*, p. 33.

114. TH, pp. 204-205.

115. RRF, p. 12.

116. EH, p. 46.

117. *Ibid.*, p. 49.

118. *Ibid.*, p. 52; see also FC, pp. 29-31.

119. RRF, p. 29.

120. *Ibid.*, p. 32.

121. *Ibid.*, p. 17. We will discuss Moltmann's interpretation of Bloch's ideas more fully later.

122. *Ibid.*, p. 30.

123. M.D. Meeks, *Origins of the Theology of Hope*, Philadelphia, Fortress Press, 1974, p. 38.

124. RRF, p. 41.

125. FH, p. 27.

126. RRF, p. 12.

127. TJ, p. 41.

128. RRF, p. 36.

129. EG, p. 77.

130. RRF, p. 33; see also TH, p. 114.

131. RRF, p. 34.

132. *Ibid.*, p. 207.

133. *Ibid.*, p. 211.

134. *Ibid.*, p. 211.

135. HP, p. 22.

136. *Ibid.*, p. 50.

137. OC, p. 40; see also CPS, p. 279; and under section 3(c) above.

138. OC, p. 41; see also CPS, p. 282.

139. OC, p. 73.

140. *Ibid.*, p. 75.

141. CPS, p. 264.

142. *Ibid.*, p. 265.

143. *Ibid.*, pp. 272-274.

144. *Ibid.*, p. 262.

145. *Ibid.*, p. 296.

146. *Ibid.*, p. 299.

147. *Ibid.*, p. 60.

148. *Ibid.*, p. 60; see also FC, pp. 85-92.

149. CPS, p. 64.

150. TH, p. 32.

151. FC, pp. 95-96.

152. *Ibid.*, p. 96.

CHAPTER 3.

Moltmann's Ecological Doctrine of God.

1. Introduction.

Now that we have surveyed the context of the emergence of Moltmann's theology of creation, both by giving an outline of some contemporary theologies and by indicating the direction of his own ideas in his earlier work we intend to move on to a discussion of his understanding of the Trinity which forms the theoretical basis for his ecological doctrine of creation. We aim to give an exposition of Moltmann's views in this part of the thesis and as far as possible refrain from extensive critical comments until we have heard his overall position. We will engage in a full critique of the Trinitarian basis for Moltmann's doctrine of creation in Part 3.

Moltmann's doctrine of the Trinity expresses an inner ecological motif at the outset, namely that of overcoming the schism between Eastern and Western churches and between Christianity and Judaism, along with thinking that aims to be "universal and ecumenical."[1] He challenges a strongly hierarchical understanding of the relationship between God and creation as being insufficiently Trinitarian. Rather than asking how do we and the created world experience God, we should consider first, how does God experience us.

This experience is not reciprocal, as between equals, but "God experiences people in a different way from the way people experience God. He experiences them in the divine manner of his experience."[2] God's experience is related to the mystery of his passion, and this links the experience of God with the history in God, which is that of the suffering God. It is this aspect of suffering which reveals most clearly the Triune God. Real experience is not an "inward narcissism," but a giving of oneself to another through wonder and pain, coming from the difference in the other.[3] Thus as a "working assumption" Moltmann insists on a measure of reciprocity in relationship between God and the world.[4]

He rejects all thinking about God which portrays him in absolute monotheistic terms over against the world. He develops threads found in his earlier work which argue against ideas of God as supreme Substance, coming from a cosmological understanding of the world, or God as absolute Subject, based on a narrowly anthropocentric view.[5] Moltmann considers that ever "since the Renaissance" God has been portrayed "one-sidedly as 'the Almighty'" and increasingly as the Omnipotent One, who rules over the world and is transcendent over it. This has disastrous consequences since now the world could be thought of as without God in such a way that "the strict monotheism of modern Western Christianity is an essential basis for the secularization of the world and nature."[6] Moltmann uses monotheism in the sense of a tyrannical relationship between a monarchical God as absolute Subject and the world as passive Object. The alternative to this idea of God as manipulative "universal ruler in heaven" is the Christian doctrine of the Trinity.

The above has further consequences for our understanding of ourselves as rulers over the earth, and as those who have power over against nature. Such is "the language of male violation."[7] Once we view science and technology as the means through which we acquire such power its goal becomes a religious one, namely that of restoring God's image in us through the power of scientific knowledge over nature.[8] This leads into the idea of the world as work and as

machine in a way that reinforces the belief in the remote transcendence of God.
We might even go so far as to claim that "the monotheism of the transcendent
God and the mechanization of the world put an end to all ideas about God's
immanence. Atheism was the inevitable result; for the world machine must be
able to function by itself, even without God."[9]

Even in Moltmann's earlier work the link between our understanding
of God and the meaning of our lives makes it imperative that we have an
adequate understanding of who God is:

> "Theologically man's question about the meaning and the
> purpose of his life must be causally linked with God's question
> about man as his likeness, the meaning and aim of his love. If
> man is not the answer to God's question, then God cannot be the
> answer to man's question."[10]

Monotheism is offensive to Moltmann in other respects in that it
implies recognition of monarchy or theocracy, with associated subjection and
patriarchal domination. The attractive alternative in the West is atheism which
brings freedom from domination. In the East the cosmic mysticism of Chinese
and Hindu cultures with their "treasures of ancient ecological wisdom" makes
the domination and exploitation of nature through monotheism seem
"primitive."[11] He asks how can we begin to worship God as Father, Son and
Spirit when our attitude towards a sovereign God is dominated by a servile
obedience?[12] Moreover, the "first victim" of a monotheistic world-view is God.
"The God who alone is active and all-causative condemns all others to passivity
and utter dependence."[13] Such subjection now spreads to legitimize the
domination of humans over nature, man over woman, and the soul over the
body.

Moltmann proposes instead a return to Trinitarian thinking that invites
us into fellowship rather than lordship, participation rather than conquest, and
receptivity rather than production. A participatory knowledge is one

characterized by love rather than power, and wonder experienced in sharing in the life of the other.[14] Once we have developed a Trinitarian hermeneutic this

> "leads us to think in terms of relationships and community; it supersedes the subjective thinking which cannot work without the separation and isolation of its objects.. By taking panentheistic ideas from Jewish and Christian traditions we shall try to think ecologically about God, man and the world in their relationships and indwellings. In this way it is not merely the Christian doctrine of the Trinity that we are trying to work out anew, our aim is to develop and practice Trinitarian thinking as well."[15]

Once we become free from the modern anthropocentric view of the world we can begin to understand ourselves as members of the community of creation. However, this understanding presupposes an adequate "theocentric biblical world picture" and redemption from an over-evaluation of history towards an appreciation of the character of the earth which makes history possible.[16]

Moltmann traces the historical development of theologies of creation.[17] In the "first stage" the biblical traditions and ancient cosmologies "were fused," and the world was understood as "divinely ordered." The medieval theological cosmology was a "Ptolemaic" interpretation of the six days' work according to Genesis 1. In the "second stage" modern sciences have "successively freed themselves" from this ancient cosmology. Protestant theologies of creation also became detached from cosmology and amounted to a "personal belief in creation." In this way both science and faith, and the world and creation, became separated. The biblical creation narratives "were written off by historical criticism as myths."[18]

Today we have reached a "third stage" in the relationship between science and theology, born out of the tribulations of the ecological crisis. Now science has ceased to have "unquestioning faith in itself" and so some of the earlier attempts of theologians to draw dividing lines between science and faith are no longer necessary. Moltmann believes that once the scientific arrogance that dominated the nineteenth century becomes replaced by a greater humility on the part of both science and theology, mutual dialogue becomes possible. Hence he states that "theology and science will arrive together at the ecological awareness of the world" without contradicting his earlier negative statements about the scientific renaissance.[19]

Moltmann has been criticized for not taking science seriously enough in his theology of creation.[20] However, the dialogue that Moltmann seems to envisage is the shaping of scientific concerns by theological and ethical questions, rather than any specific debate over more narrowly defined scientific problems. Whether he is justified in this assumption is a matter for discussion which we will take up subsequently. With respect to the knowledge of God that we can gain from the natural world, Moltmann insists that we turn this question upside down. That is, we should allow our understanding of God to shape our knowledge of nature, so that natural theology is replaced by a theology of nature which "interprets nature in the light of the self-revelation of the creative God."[21] The basis for this approach comes from an appreciation of the way Israel shaped her understanding of creation from the special experience of God in salvation history. In this way "creation is the universal horizon of Israel's special experience of God in history."[22]

Above all an adequate understanding of creation needs to gain an eschatological perspective so that it is not limited to the question of the origin of the earth, but incorporates creation in history and creation of the end time as well. By shifting our focus towards the future, Moltmann allows the eternal kingdom, as well as historical covenant, to form the basis and "inner-ground" of creation. Hence "creation in the beginning is therefore certainly open for salvation history, but salvation history, for its part, exists for the sake of the new creation..... In this respect history is not the framework of creation, creation is the framework of history. This sets limits to the 'historization of the world.'"[23] We now arrive at a key issue in the relationship between God and the world:

"In what situation is creation if it is perceived historically in this way? This is the central question of a theology of nature. We are replying with the thesis: the time of the Christian perception of creation is the time of Jesus the Messiah. Under the presupposition of faith in Jesus the Christ the world is revealed in the messianic light as a creation that is both in bondage, and open for the future."[24]

In the traditional understanding of natural theology we have both an innate knowledge *notitia insita* and an acquired knowledge *notitia acquisita* which comes from our knowledge of nature. Both are generally accessible but are imperfect revelations of God leading to wisdom rather than salvation and blessedness. The latter can only come from the "supernatural" revelation of God in Jesus Christ, since this leads to fellowship with God. When we think in traditional categories natural revelation is the "remainder" of the perfect revelation of God that was possible in the garden of Eden and subsequently partly lost at the Fall. Moltmann insists, however, that our understanding of natural theology should be less that of education, through the questions that it encourages us to ask, or of hermeneutics, through helping us understand what we believe, but rather that of eschatology. By this he means that the place of natural theology is to serve a rôle in anticipating the knowledge of God in glory. The knowledge of creation becomes a parable of the world to come:

"In this function natural knowledge of God belongs to pneumatology: 'the light of nature' is a pre-reflection of the light of glory. This pre-reflection has the character of messianic light . . . and allows it to be perceived as true and real parable and promise of the kingdom. The distinction between 'natural theology' and 'revealed theology' is misleading. There are not two different theologies. There is only one, because God is one."[25]

Once we reach the theology of glory we arrive at a true natural theology and a perfected revealed theology, but this will only come about at the consummation of creation and history. Revealed theology is messianic and it is only in this perspective that the Christian doctrine of creation finds its basis.

Moreover, a true "natural theology" which stems from faith in God "in the history of Israel or in the history of Christ" is that which recognizes his activity everywhere in the world. This allows us to see "traces of God" in nature, indeed "the whole created world of heaven and earth is then one great promise of the coming world of God."[26]

The mystics were the first to teach us the "language of God" in nature. While Moltmann believes that this mysticism is also part of the Reformed tradition, stemming from Calvin's work, he also in some statements seems to allow for an educative rôle of natural theology, albeit in a somewhat muted form. For example: "And in fact is it not so that the non-prejudiced glance at nature and at natural history should convince us of the existence, the wisdom and the beauty of a God?"[27] This softens some of Moltmann's comments elsewhere where he rejects all natural theology as "functionless" in a scientific age.[28] Yet once we have experienced the self-revelation of God in the history of Israel's liberation and in Christ's history, we begin to see God everywhere. In this way we need natural theology less for God's sake, than for the sake of nature.

Moltmann draws on mystical knowledge as a way of approaching and experiencing the knowledge of God. Mysticism here means the general attitude which aims at receptive understanding and participation, rather than mastery or control. As we reflect on the death and resurrection of Christ, we become drawn into the history of Christ himself. Once we understand ourselves less as active subjects who recognize, but more as objects who encounter impressions from without, we become receptive to the "mystical" knowledge of the history of Christ. The vision of God's Spirit in the world becomes delusory without the cross of Christ.[29] These ideas become clarified and linked together by Moltmann's doctrine of the Trinity.

2. Tension between transcendence and immanence.

The practical consequences of an understanding of an all-powerful God in the light of the possible nuclear catastrophe, the Jewish holocaust and the ecological disaster, ends in hatred against God. Rather, we need to adjust our understanding of the "Almighty" to mean "God's fundamental love," understood as "all endurance which is his boundless ability and readiness to suffer with which he supports his creation and his likeness on earth, despite all contradictions, and as such maintains fidelity."[30] Once we understand God as the fellow-sufferer with his creation, the damage done to the earth becomes the same as the "annihilation of the living God," hence the seriousness of our crime.[31] However, God does not die with Auschwitz, or any other potential disaster, since the longing for peace and justice and "faith in the one who finally guarantees justice," puts the crimes of humanity in the light of the judgement of God.[32]

Here we find common ground with the Jewish faith struggling to express itself in the wake of the holocaust. Abraham Heschel's theology of the divine pathos is a useful expression of this belief in the covenant commitment of God through his Spirit, which allows him to share in the suffering of his people.[33] God's self remains distinct, which for Moltmann implies a self-distinction in God. Pinchas Lapide disagrees with this step in his thinking, since for him the Spirit remains eternally an emanation of God, rather than having a distinct existence.[34] Moltmann's reply hinges on his understanding of the unity of God, which he believes is not violated by the idea of self-distinction, since it is not equivalent to numerical unity. He argues that without such self-distinction true communication of God becomes difficult to understand. He draws on the Jewish writer, Franz Rosenzweig, who has developed the idea of a self-distinction in God.[35]

Both Lapide and Moltmann find their common ground in the idea of God who communicates with us through suffering. For Moltmann the unity of

God is expressed through the Holy Spirit, who unites both the Father and the Son in the self-offering of the Son on the cross. The "cleft" of the self-distinction of God on the cross allows every "cleft of sin" to be taken up and healed. At the cross we find both the love of God and his anger coming together. As we noted earlier, Moltmann's understanding of the Trinity stems from reflection on the history of God's suffering in the history of Christ. The Jewish understanding of a Messiah who heralds the redemption of the earth contrasts with the focus on the Redeemer in Christian thought. Yet Moltmann does not wish to negate this universal stance, but to take it up and develop it in his own Trinitarian theology.

While Augustine and Aquinas began with an understanding of the unity of divine substance, *De Deo Uno*, from which they derived the unity of persons, *De Deo Trino*, this, for Moltmann, leads to the first unity "forcing out" the second, so that we arrive at a "disintegration of the Trinity in abstract monotheism."[36] Instead the unity of the Triune God comes from his passion, understood both as one who suffers and one who enters life in such a way that it is ready to suffer. The love of God in this passion is also closely related to the concept of the true freedom of God, which is the "free relationship of passionate participation."[37] Once we start to speak in terms of freedom as if God need not have made such a decision we fail to understand the self-sacrifice of love that is part of the divine nature. The suffering of love does not come out of deficiency of being, as if God in some way "needed" creation, but flows from the "overabundance" of his being.[38] The endurance of a loving God in suffering allows us to view evil as the "condition of his eternal bliss because it is the presupposition of his triumph."[39]

Moltmann's critics argue that he seems to define God by our experience of suffering.[40] However, this is not strictly the case since the suffering of God is not involuntary passive suffering but active suffering coming from the overflow of his love.[41] The problem remains as to how God can deal with involuntary suffering if he has not experienced this himself. This is related to Moltmann's failure to distinguish between God's divine suffering from his human suffering in the incarnation. Yet such a tension seems necessary if we are to distinguish between God and his creation.[42] While we find Hegelian overtones in expressions such as "the power of the negative is caught up in the process of becoming of being," this is very different from the Hegelian concept of the necessity for evil in his understanding of God.[43] It is the overabundance of the love of God which refuses to avoid the pain that on its part becomes "accepted and transmuted into glory."[44] John Milbank claims that Moltmann presents the creation as a necessary, primeval suffering which must be passed through by both God and humanity, which Milbank believes is clearly a "Hegelian theme of necessary alienation."[45] Of relevance in this context is the question of the freedom of creation and the contingency of evil. On the one hand, Moltmann accepts that given the existence of evil, God suffers. But this is a rather different concept from the Hegelian idea of a necessary suffering of God. We can distinguish this again from Moltmann's idea of suffering as a necessary component in the emergence of the new creation, and into which the cosmic Spirit of God enters. This is a theme which we intend to discuss susequently.

Moltmann draws on English theology through the idea of the passibility of God, which also inspired the thought of J.K. Mozley. He also takes up C.E. Rolt's interpretation of eucharistic sacrifice with reference to the suffering of God. The Spanish mystical writings of Miguel de Unamuno also serve to deepen Moltmann's appreciation of God as one who participates in the world's evolution and suffers with those who suffer. The universal sorrow of God leads us to Christology, and from here to Trinitarian thinking. By opening himself to love the world and suffer in it, God is no "prisoner of his own history," but entirely free as he is entirely himself.[46]

The suffering of God need not imply that God changes in the same way that creation changes. Rather we need to distinguish between the relative assertion of his unchangeableness and the absolute assertion that he cannot change inwardly. By posing a suffering God Moltmann rejects the absolute assertion of the impassibility of God. In his earlier work he claimed that through the suffering of the Father in giving up his Son and the passion of the Son in God-forsakeness on the cross, we have "overcome the old dichotomy between an immanent and a functional Trinity and between the general nature of God and his inner triune nature. The functional Trinity is the immanent Trinity (Karl Rahner); the Trinity is the nature of God."[47]

Moltmann's seeming identification of the economic and immanent Trinity has provoked criticism since it seems to close the gap between creator and creation, and so to deny God's sovereignty.[48] However, after *The Crucified God*, Moltmann softens his tight linkage between the immanent Trinity and economic Trinity by allowing for an understanding of the immanent Trinity which is prior to history. The immanent Trinity for Moltmann becomes both the "Trinity in the Origin" and the "Trinity in the Glorification," while the economic Trinity is the "Trinity in the Sending." The unity that binds the "Trinity in the Origin" is a unity of divine substance, while the unity that binds the "Trinity in the Glorification" is the inclusive unity of the whole creation gathered up into the fellowship of the Father, Son and Spirit. This explains, in part, Moltmann's reluctance to use the more traditional categories of "immanent Trinity" and "economic Trinity," which have more static connotations.[49]

The common bond of love forbids a strict separation of the Trinitarian movements, so that in this way:

> "The love with which God creatively loves the world is not different from the love he himself is in eternity . . . Creation is part of the eternal love affair between Father and the Son."[50]

Moltmann insists that it is speculative to divide the work of God in salvation from his own eternal being. Such a division preserves for us a sense of liberty understood as a choice in God, yet once we allow for an equivalence of love and liberty such a dichotomy becomes unnecessary.

If we are to keep a distinction at all it is in the sense of a doxological understanding of the immanent Trinity who becomes the "object of our praise and adoration."[51] Even so we have a correspondence between the economic and immanent Trinity so that the history of God's Trinitarian relationships corresponds to the eternal interrelationships. In this way "the surrender of the Son for us on the cross has a retroactive effect on the Father and causes infinite pain."[52] In the light of the death of the risen Christ "from the foundation of the world the *opera trinitatis ad extra* correspond to the *passiones trinitatis ad intra*."[53] Just as the pain of the cross has a "retroactive effect" on the inner life of the Trinity, so too the joy of responsive love through the Spirit determines its life also.

Moltmann's more sympathetic critics are still not always convinced that his separation of the immanent and economic Trinity is adequate. O'Donnell, for example, comments that he is still "in danger of falling into a type of Hegelianism in which history is a constitutive dimension of God's self-realization."[54] Another aspect of Moltmann's thought which has not been so widely discussed is his notion of the enrichment of God through sharing in the experience of the bliss of the response of creation. This raises the question of the perfection of God rather than his freedom, both of which, but especially the latter, underlie the discussion over the possible involvement of God in the suffering of history and creation. Now while Moltmann successfully redefines God's freedom in terms of the passion of his love, which allows for a suffering God, he does not adequately redefine God's perfection.[55] Cole-Turner believes that while the idea of God's enrichment by creation is in *The Trinity and the Kingdom of God*, in *God in Creation,* "that theme is dropped entirely and

Moltmann returns to more traditional, one-sided understanding of God's relationship to the creation."[56] However, while in *God in Creation* Moltmann does not relate the idea of God's enrichment to God's perfection, his stress on the idea of God's "embodiment" as the "end" of all his works signals the intimate connection between God's future and that of creation. We will discuss this theme in more detail in a subsequent chapter.

Moltmann's understanding of God as one who is intimately bound up with the life of the world serves to express his desire to reinforce the immanence of God in the world. Israel's belief in a transcendent God grew out of a reaction to pantheistic, matriarchal and animist beliefs of the surrounding culture. Moltmann believes that an emphasis on the transcendence of God can degenerate into a monotheism which sanctions the exploitation of creation. The belief in the indwelling Spirit of God in creation which comes from the Hebrew wisdom tradition has been neglected. Once we recover this idea we can appreciate that "through the energies and potentialities of the Spirit, the creator is himself present in his creation. He does not merely confront it in his transcendence; entering into it, he is also immanent in it."[57] It is the "interplay" between God's transcendence in relation to the world and his immanence in it that marks out the "history of creation."[58] In this way the dynamics of the interrelationship between God and the world through God's transcendence and immanence takes on a distinctly relational, and so "ecological," motif. Through the interrelationships which subsist in the Spirit we begin to realize that relationships are just as primary as "things," and both "relation" and "thing" are complementary to one another.[59] Does this lead to pantheism? Moltmann rejects any suggestion that this is the case by pointing to the doctrine of the Trinity, which allows God to be present in the world without becoming merged into it.

Once we develop a sense of the Spirit of God immanent in the world the idea of causality disappears from the doctrine of creation:

"But creating the world is something different from causing it. If the Creator is himself present in his creation by virtue of the Spirit, then his relationship to creation must rather be viewed as an intricate web of unilateral, reciprocal and many-sided relationships."[60]

We can note here a shift from his earlier work, where he portrayed God as creator in more traditional categories as divine agency.[61] The starting point for a Trinitarian doctrine of creation is the "immanent tension" in God, in that he both creates the world, but at the same time enters into it. This means that:

"The God who is transcendent in relation to the world, and the God who is immanent in that world are one and the same God. So in God's creation of the world we can perceive a self-differentiation and a self-identification on God's part."[62]

3. The emergence of Trinitarian "panentheism."

In order to understand God's self-differentiation Moltmann draws on kabbalistic doctrines from the Jewish tradition, which serve to shape a modified panentheism, and the Eastern church for a doctrine of *perichoresis*, which serves to shape his understanding of the Trinity.

While in Moltmann's earlier work we find the transcendence of God expressed in terms of future hope, by the time we reach God in Creation he wishes to affirm a clear distinction between God and creation in past, present and future reality.[63] This distinction is maintained through the kabbalistic notion of *Shekinah* where we find a self-distinction in God which we mentioned above in relation to the divine "pathos." How are we to understand God as one who both experiences the world and creates it?

The doctrine of the creation of heaven and earth in the Old Testament portrayed the world as distinct from God, rather than an emanation from his being. We can distinguish between *bara*, which implies a bringing forth that is totally new, and *asah*, making, where something is given a particular character.[64] We have no human analogy for the creative work of God, so it is apt to refer to this as *creatio ex nihilo*, since it is not derivative of anything else and has no preconditions or external or internal necessity. The expression *creatio ex nihilo* serves to reinforce that the act of creation is based on the divine will. However, this is in the context not so much of an arbitrary choice, but of the love of God so that "creation is not a demonstration of his power, it is the communication of his love, which knows neither premises or preconditions, *creatio ex amore Dei.*"[65]

Once we understand the initial work of creation as coming from God who confers his goodness, and the sustaining work of creation as the communication of that goodness, this excludes any arbitrary understanding of the meaning of creation. The "making" of creation takes place through the divine Word which serves to unite both the creator and creation. Nonetheless, Moltmann denies that there is any real participation in the being of God in the initial act of creation, through his work, as medieval ontology would suggest. Instead the correspondence between God and creation is only made evident when God blesses his creation. Here we find the basis of the distinction between humankind and creation, where God finds in the essence of humankind a correspondence with himself which allows a response to the seeking love of God. Humankind prepares for the image of the Son incarnate, and so already "implies an unheard-of condescension, self-limitation and humiliation on the part of God, who is without compare."[66] This takes up the idea in *The Trinity and the Kingdom of God* where "the creation of the world and the incarnation therefore intervene deeply in the inter-Trinitarian relationships of God."[67]

The doctrine of *creatio ex nihilo* distinguishes the eternity of God from finite creation. Process thought, which rejects this doctrine, leads to a situation where "God is turned into the comprehensive ordering factor in the flux of happening."[68] Moltmann insists that we put into an eschatological perspective the alternatives of:

(i) creation as the object of divine will developed in the Reformation doctrine of decrees, and:

(ii) an understanding of creation as the emanation of divine life, expanded by Paul Tillich.

The presupposition of (i) is an understanding of God as divine subject, while that of (ii) assumes God is divine substance. While the former leads to unwarranted speculation about the freedom of God based on the freedom of choice, the latter leads to lack of distinction between God and creation. The "deeper understanding of the creative God" is a God who discloses himself through his decision, and thus the decision is part of his nature and conversely it is in his nature to express his resolve.[69]

Here we arrive at the core of Moltmann's understanding of the relationship between God and creation from his use of the kabbalistic doctrine of "self-limitation." The decision in God takes place inwardly in himself before it is expressed outwardly.[70] Further, it is necessary for God to act beyond his inner- self, since he finds bliss only in selfless love.[71] If God creates a world "outside" himself he must have made room for "finitude" in himself. Moltmann seems to be presupposing here that we need to conceive of God in a spatial sense. Even the "*Nihil*" comes into being through a deliberate act of God. Moltmann draws on the work of the Jewish writer Isaac Luria who postulated a notion of *zimzum*, which in general refers to an inner withdrawal. Once we apply this to the relationship between God and creation we find that the existence of the world "outside" God is rendered possible "by an inversion in God."[72] In this way God creates the preconditions necessary for creation and "it is the affirmative force of God's self-negation which becomes the creative force in creation and salvation."[73]

The *Nihil* "emerges" following God's inner withdrawal. Moltmann does not specify how this happens, but speculates that at this stage the *Nihil* does not contain the element of negation of creaturely being since creation does not exist yet. Instead the inner space where God is not, created by his inner withdrawal, becomes "God-forsakenness, hell" and "absolute death." God creates his creation within this "God-forsaken" space, so that creation is itself threatened by the absolute Non-Being of God the creator. Moltmann's purpose in this discussion seems to be to stress that evil powers go beyond creation itself and it is the element of Non-Being of God in the Nothingness which gives it its demonic character. Moltmann qualifies this by suggesting that the "menacing" character of the *Nihil* is acquired subsequent to the creation of created beings through their own "self-isolation" which amounts to "sin and Godlessness."

Moltmann's use of *zimzum* serves to reinforce the distance between creator and creation which becomes blurred by his other ideas such as the indwelling Spirit in creation and the correspondence between the immanent and economic Trinities. He introduces feminist thought into the Jewish kabbalistic doctrine of *zimzum* by linking the idea of "letting-be" with the idea of "inner withdrawal" and "self-humiliation."[74] The notion of letting-be is associated with the concept of ecological niche, which in its more popular form implies harmonious co-existence rather than dominance. In this way Moltmann takes a further step in the direction away from the "male" notion of God active over creation towards the "feminine" idea of passive withdrawal. For him it is this second attitude which has priority both chronologically and in a conceptual sense. The idea of creation expressed in "motherly" categories tends to weaken the disconnectedness implied by the notion of *creatio ex nihilo*. Moltmann admits that the difference between God and creation "is embraced and comprehended by the greater truth..... the truth that God is all in all."[75] As a consequence of these apparently opposing ideas Barr has accused Moltmann of inconsistency in his thinking.[76]

While the doctrine of *zimzum* seems to be necessary for Moltmann if he is to avoid either pantheism or monarchical thinking, he has become, according to Breshears, "unacceptably imaginative" or according to McPherson, "too clever" and it even appears to Walsh that he has "reinterpreted" the cross in terms of "kabbalistic cosmology."[77] A more serious criticism is whether the act of creation is really "good" if it presupposes "God-forsakenness" and "inner withdrawal."[78] Strictly speaking this "inner withdrawal" is not so much an *explanation* of the origin of evil, as McPherson seems to suggest, rather, as Cole-Turner notes, it is allowing for the *possibility* of non-being and evil.[79] While there is a biblical basis for evil forces which are beyond that directly linked with the Fall, we might question whether Moltmann is justified in defining the means through which this could happen. Nonetheless his central concern here is not so much the question of the origin of evil, as the idea of *kenosis* at the heart of God's being. McIntyre believes that Moltmann does not really have a warrant to use the kenotic idea based on Philippians 2, as this is now largely discredited in Christology today.[80] However, once we accept God who is both fully incarnate in Christ and involved in suffering love, some form of inner withdrawal becomes a necessary precondition if we are to prevent a lapse into pantheism. Moltmann insists that, like the freedom of self-giving to creation in passionate suffering, the inner withdrawal of God is an inner reflection of the love of God for the freedom of the other.

Moltmann distinguishes between the initial act of creation which is "for the Creator effortless" and the creation of salvation in human history that brings in the new creation out of God's "labour and travail."[81] Now out of this labour we find the eschatological creation of the kingdom of glory which destroys the *Nihil*. The Son exposes himself to the absolute Nothingness in such a way that God enters the "primordial space" which he himself created through his initial self-limitation.[82] Faith in God the creator is not so much the expectation of an "apocalyptic *annihilatio mundi*" as "an active anticipation of the *transformatio mundi*."[83] Christ as mediator of creation becomes its liberator. In this way "it is in looking towards his kingdom of freedom that God loves those he has created."[84] It is the Spirit who provides the divine energy for the new creation.

The idea of God making space for creation is coincident with the creation of time. Moltmann tries to find a way of thinking about God's eternity and the creature's temporality "simultaneously." He uses the idea of God's inner withdrawal as applied to time in much the same way as he uses the idea of inner withdrawal to make space for creation which we discussed above:

> "We therefore have to proceed from the assumption that it was only a self-alteration of eternity which made created time possible, and made room for it . . . In this essential resolve, God withdrew his eternity into himself in order to take time for his creation and leave his creation its own particular time."[85]

Once God has made space and time for creation the "marvel" is that the infinite God chooses to dwell in finite creation, through *Shekinah* and the incarnation. It is God the Spirit who dwells in creation, and in this way "God and the world are related to one another through the relationship of their mutual indwelling and participation: God's indwelling in the world is divine in kind; the world's indwelling God is worldly in kind."[86]

Moltmann takes up the discussion of space/time in a historical survey up to the seventeenth century. Ever since Copernicus we have become aware of the spatial "infinity" of the universe. Once we think of matter as infinite it is easy to slip into pantheism. Here Moltmann comments on Henry More's interpretation of the Jewish kabbalistic tradition which states that God is MAKOM or absolute space. More believed that once we consider space as the medium of God's omnipresence then we can distinguish between the contingent, created world, and the "eternal omnipresent God."[87] As long as we find a distinction between the endlessness of space and the infinity of God there is no danger of pantheism. Newton developed this idea by distinguishing between "absolute space," which is an attribute of the divine Being, and "relative space" which is occupied by material objects. This contrasts with Leibniz' definition of space as derived from the extension of material objects. In other words he rejected the idea of absolute space altogether. Both More's and Newton's idea of absolute space as equivalent to God's omnipresence are panentheistic. Moltmann believes that their views did not involve any idea of creation and were at fault since "this did not permit them to think of God as Creator of the world, and world as contingent creation."[88]

Moltmann rejects all forms of panentheism which tend to merge the finite world with God's infinity. Rather he insists that the idea of creation forces us to distinguish between the space of God and that of the created world. We arrive at a way of expressing this distinction through the concept of *zimzum* where God creates an inner space for creation through "divine withdrawal." To sum up:

> "In the doctrine about the world as God's creation we therefore distinguish between three things: first, the essential omnipresence of God, or absolute space; second, the space of creation in the world-presence of God conceded to it; and third, relative places, relationships and movements in the created world. The space of the world corresponds to God's world-presence, which initiates this space, limits it and interpenetrates it."[89]

Platten comments that Moltmann is "keen to steer clear of any form of panentheism by talking of a 'Trinitarian doctrine of creation.'"[90] However, it is perhaps more accurate to view Moltmann's position as one which only rejects a form of panentheism where the space of creation is equivalent to the "absolute space" of divine being, but affirms a notion of the world "in" the space created by God's inner withdrawal.[91]

4. The context of the doctrine of *perichoresis*.

The basis for Moltmann's social doctrine of the Trinity comes from reflection on the history of the relationships between Father, Son and Spirit as given in the New Testament. In the first stage of Jesus' history he is called and sent by the Father, which opens their fellowship to that of the world. The sending of the Son comes through the Spirit and in the power of the Spirit the disciples are brought into fellowship with the Son and the Father. In the second stage the Son actively chooses to surrender to the will of the Father, who gave up his Son to death on the cross. In the common sacrifice the Spirit unites the will of the Father and the Son in the God-forsakenness of the Son on the cross. In the third stage of Jesus' history the Father raises him from the dead through the Spirit and reveals him to those who believe through the Spirit. Now the Son becomes enthroned as the lord of God's kingdom, and it is in the inner unity of Father and Son that we can appreciate the Spirit as coming from both Father and Son; hence "through his resurrection the Son is evidently so near to the Father, and so much in the Father, that he participates in the sending of the Spirit out of its divine origin."[92]

The sending of the Spirit is for the renewal of heaven and earth. In faith believers become "integrated into the history of the Trinity" and "participants in the Trinitarian history of God himself."[93] During the messianic age Christ is lord, but only until the consummation of the kingdom where the Spirit becomes the Subject pointing to the Father and Son. Thus throughout the Trinitarian history of God we find: (i) that the primacy of the Father through the Spirit to the Son is in the sending, delivering up and resurrection of Christ: (ii) that the primacy of the Father through the Son to the Spirit is in the lordship of Christ and in the sending of the Spirit: (iii) that the primacy of the Spirit through the Father is in the eschatological consummation and glorification.

The idea that, in eschatological perspective, the Son and Spirit are actors introduces the idea that we can have changing patterns within the action of the Trinity. Meeks has pointed out the significance for Moltmann's theology in viewing the Spirit as a person, with an accent on the Spirit as Subject, instead of a stress on the Spirit in categories of power.[94] The emphasis here reinforces Moltmann's concern to reject monotheism which he associates with categories of power and domination, rather than social Trinitarian categories of love and participation. He puts God's Triunity prior to his lordship and it is from this

Trinity that the "rule of God" is exercised. The history of the kingdom of God has its outer aspect on earth but also "in its earthly mode within the Trinity itself."[95]

The unity of God is best thought of in terms of the mutual fellowship of the Trinity, rather than in the identity of a single subject. Moltmann does not deny the unity of divine essence, as Plantinga has suggested, but wants to put the unity of community prior to other expressions of unity.[96] Hence "The Trinitarian Persons possess in common the divine essence, and exercise in common the divine sovereignty. This means that their Trinitarian community precedes their substantial and their subjective unity *ad extra.*"[97] In this way Moltmann envisages the dynamic unity of the fellowship of the three persons having priority over both the unity of divine "nature" and the collective unity of creation with God in its eschatological consummation and glorification.[98]

Moltmann faces the danger of tritheism that his view might suggest by his distinction of subjects within the Trinity. Rahner strongly rejects the idea that three centres of activity are implied by the three persons of the Trinity because of the implicit tritheism. Moltmann insists that it is more biblical to begin with the idea of three persons and then enquire about their unity, rather than *vice versa.*[99] He maintains that our understanding of person as a free, independent individual is faulty, and for mutual love to exist there must be a "Thou" as well as an "I." Moltmann qualifies this difference by considering the inner Trinitarian relationships as expressing love between like and like. The fact that this is "not enough" for selfless love provides the incentive for the creation of the world as that which "exists because the eternal love communicates himself creatively to his other."[100] Page criticizes Moltmann's analysis of personhood, which she believes "stops at Hegel," and asks no modern "awkward" questions.[101] She is unconvinced that Moltmann has given us an adequate reason why the love between like within the Trinity "opens" God for the creation of the world.[102]

The unity between Father, Son and Spirit comes from their mutual indwelling or "*perichoresis*."[103] Drawing on the theologians of the Eastern church Moltmann understands God in terms of the eternal community of Persons who mutually interpenetrate one another and indwell each other. This manifests the "highest intensity of living which we call divine life and eternal love."[104] It is not so much a rigid pattern as "the most intense excitement and the absolute rest of the love which is the wellspring of everything that lives, the keynote of all resonances, and the source of the rhythmical dancing and vibrating worlds."[105] All relationships which are analogous to God reflect this Trinitarian *perichoresis*, and as such offer one of the foundational ideas for an ecological doctrine of creation. The brilliance of the perichoretic notion is that it "links God's threeness and oneness together without reducing one to the other."[106] The perichoretic unity is "inclusively open for all creation," so that the communal relationships of the Triune God are "a divine love story in which we are all involved together with heaven and earth."[107]

The biblical basis for a social Trinitarianism comes largely from Johannine texts. Trinitarian ideas may "sound dogmatically orthodox and very old-fashioned," but it is really a rediscovery of "the original wisdom of our own religious tradition, which has been suppressed by the modern image of God."[108] Moltmann also retains a traditional sense of the primacy of the Father as the origin of the Son and the Spirit. Olsen believes that this is a "conceptual weakness" which undermines and contradicts his social Trinitarianism.[109] Yet he draws back from any idea of a "patriarchal" God by suggesting that we view this aspect of fatherhood in "motherly" terms. God the Father "begets" the Son, while God the motherly Father gives birth to the Son. Unlike the rest of creation which comes *ex nihilo*, the Son shares in the substance of the Father. He thus allows for some primacy for the Father who "being himself without origin, is the origin of the divine persons of the Son and the Spirit."[110]

The Son does not share in the capacity of the Father to be source and origin, which would make two origins in the Triune God. Rather, the Son flows from the nature of God rather than his will and the Father loves the Son with "engendering, fatherly love," while the Son loves the Father with "responsive, self-giving love."[111] The whole of creation enters into this responsive love of the Son for the Father and in this way fulfils the joy of the Father. The generation of the Son from the Father makes us appreciate in a richer way what his fatherhood really means. As we noted earlier Moltmann believes that a monotheistic faith understood God as "heavenly Father" in a patriarchal way which associated this idea with domination and tyranny. Instead, he insists that "belief in God the Father starts from recognition of his Son, not from God's omnipotence and creation," so that the Son comes from the "womb of the Father."[112]

The Spirit who proceeds from the Father arises in a different way from the generation of the Son, though he too shares in the divine essence. The three persons "subsist" in their shared divine nature, but "exist" in their relations with one another. It is through these relationships that "they glow with perfect form through one another," their unity achieved "through the circulation of the divine life."[113] We need to distinguish between the reception of the perichoretic, relational form of the Spirit which comes from the Father and the Son, and the initial issuing of the Spirit from the Father.[114]

Overall the unity of the Trinity which comes from the perichoretic life remains uppermost in Moltmann's theology, for him: "To throw open the circulatory movement of the divine Light and the divine relationships, and to take men and women, with the whole creation, into the Life stream of the Triune God: that is the meaning of creation, reconciliation and glorification."[115] An understanding of the social aspect of the Trinity points us to the "basis" for true human community.[116] It forms the "archetype" of all relationships in creation and redemption that correspond to God.[117]

McIntyre comments that the analogy between the idea of *emperichoresis* and relationships in the world cannot be sustained since the doctrine of *perichoresis* presupposes unity of substance, or *homoousia*.[118] However, analogy does not necessitate identity, and the lack of identity is an advantage in that it safeguards the distinction between God and creation. As we note later, Moltmann draws on this difference to show how humanity bears the analogy with God more closely than the rest of creation. His prime concern is to show that the Trinity displays relationships of fellowship, rather than dominance, and that this mirrors God's relationship with the world. Nonetheless, this does raise the issue of how we are to recognize the analogical or metaphorical nature of everything we say about God, and therefore its limits.[119]

5. Trinitarian perspectives on future hope and present reality.

The hope that exists for the future of creation is in its complete penetration by the Spirit of God, as expressed in "new visions of the indwelling of God in this new world."[120] It is the completion of creation through the final peace of the sabbath which distinguishes creation from nature, for while the latter is "unremittingly fruitful," it is "the sabbath which blesses, sanctifies and reveals the world as God's creation."[121] In the sabbath rest God comes to his goal in a way that completes and crowns his creation.

Moltmann draws on the Old Testament idea of the sabbath which pointed back both to the primordial condition between God, humankind and nature, and forward to the messianic era. Israel interpreted time in terms of unique historical events. This "kairological" understanding existed alongside a belief in a "history of the promise." The latter led to the Exodus event, which in itself "determines the times which follow. It is an event that initiates history."[122] Israel's understanding of her history is through reminding herself of God's faithfulness in successive events in the past in order to awaken trust in God in the future. The prophets departed from an orientation which viewed the present as the development of the past to one which perceived the unity between present and past in the faithfulness of God, rather than in the events themselves. In this way:

> "It is true that the prophets describe God's new creation with the images of times belonging to the past, which cannot be brought back again. But they paint the new creation in incandescent colours: the new Exodus will be a festal procession, not a nocturnal flight; and there will be more splendour in the new Jerusalem than ever there was in the old."[123]

In the New Testament we find the decisive event of the death and resurrection of Jesus marking the end of the old age and the beginning of the new, and with this event "messianic time" begins. As yet universal fulfillment has not been completed, and when this happens we enter "eschatological time." In the era of messianic time the newness is not "entirely new" but "takes up the promises and experiences of Israel's hope and spreads them throughout the world."[124] The future of the new world is present in messianic time like a "daybreak" and "as yet has its own beginning, in the form of Word and faith."[125]

The relationship between past, present and future is, according to messianic faith, one that leaves behind sin, "the Law" and "death" and experiences grace, reconciliation and liberty in the present. It looks to the resurrection of the dead, the redemption of the body and eternal life. We can also distinguish between eschatological time which is determined by the fulfillment of what is promised in historical time, and is dawning now in messianic time, and "eternal time" which "will be the time of the new eternal creation in the kingdom of the divine glory."[126] In keeping with Moltmann's appreciation of the perichoretic Trinity, all modes of time are "perichoretic," and in this sense "interpenetrate one another qualitatively."[127]

A linking theme in his understanding of the present and future creation comes through his idea of heaven. The ambiguity of heaven is that it is both transcendent, yet created along with the earth. Above all, heaven is the "dwelling" of God's glory and is the environment in closest contact with God, compared with the earth which is "his less immediate environment."[128] The hope of the kingdom of God is when the kingdom of heaven comes to the earth, so that the earth is transfigured along with heaven. This idea of a dwelling-place for God was pushed into the background when God was portrayed as an active creator.

How does this view link with his earlier idea that the world is created in the space provided by the inner withdrawal in God? It seems to be related to Moltmann's wish to understand God in spatial terms. Both the incarnation of Christ and the Jewish notion of *Shekinah* show us that God chooses to make the creation his environment. It is "God the Spirit" who dwells in creation, making it his home, and in this way we can distinguish between the dwelling of the world in God, and God in the world. We can also distinguish the relationship between creator and creation and that between heaven and earth, even though Barth sought for a correlation here in hierarchical terms. Instead, Moltmann revises Barth in a more richly Trinitarian perspective, so that "heaven is the chosen dwelling place of the Father, but the chosen dwelling-place of the Son is the earth.....But then the chosen dwelling-place of the Holy Spirit must be seen in the coming direct bond between heaven and earth in the new creation."[129] Moltmann's suggestions in this context have excited criticism from Stroup where for him it seems to portray God as remaining in heaven, "where he suffers the loss of the Son on the cross and awaits the work of the Spirit, who binds heaven and earth in a new creation."[130] Nonetheless, this seems very far from Moltmann's overall intention, which is to stress the primacy of fellowship within the Trinity, even though the activity of the subject changes.

A world that is created by God is open to God, and has its foundation "outside" of itself in God himself. We can think of heaven and earth as the "undetermined" and "determined" side of this open system. The heavens are plural since they mean the creative potentialities of God, and within this realm the angels form the "potencies" of God.[131] For Moltmann, once we imagine a world without heaven it has no "qualitative transcendence" and is either more like a system closed in on itself, or one that extends into infinity. In the second case the openness of the world to the future becomes a meaningless "endless universe."[132]

Heaven and earth become more like two sides of divine creativity in love and glorification. Both are related to the history of God and are caught up in this movement:

> "In the movement of the Father's creative activity, we call heaven coelum naturae; in the movement of the Son's incarnation and ascension we call it coelum gratiae and in the movement of transfiguration through the Holy Spirit we call it coelum gloriae. As created spaces heaven and earth are caught up in this Trinitarian history of God; and it is only in this history that they will become comprehensible in all the fullness of their relationships."[133]

Heaven means the transcendent openness of all material systems from the perspective of the earth, while it means the kingdom of God's energies as his potentiality (possibilitas) and his efficacious power (potentia) from the perspective of God. The creation of the possibility of the world's reality in heaven precedes the creation of the earth. God's potentialities in heaven are not equivalent to the potentialities of the earth: hence in this sense we can understand the future in heaven as determinative for both the present and the past on earth rather than vice versa. The ontological priority is in God's potentialities in heaven, rather than those inherent in the world. Moltmann distances himself from process thought here, and answers the criticism that his theology envisages the action flowing from "historical economic reality" to "future immanent reality" in a way that is "entirely determined by the process' culminative history."[134] Olsen also believes that Moltmann characterizes the transcendence of God in exclusively future categories. However, this is much more characteristic of his earlier theology, and as we see here his approach is flexible enough to allow for a transcendence of God in the present. Heaven as an "intermediary" between God and the earth is both non-transient with respect to earthly reality, and finite with respect to God's infinity.

Moltmann is also careful to view heaven as God's potentialities and potencies, rather than heaven as God's eternal essence. Heaven is qualified through God's self-designation to be its creator. The divine potencies and potentialities in heaven are created by God as "the first world" which then makes available the potencies and potentialities of *this* earth through its creation, redemption and glorification. Once we arrive at the kingdom of glory, the created beings of this world "participate in the creative wealth of potentiality of the Creator and lover of life."[135]

In order to understand the link between reality and potentiality we need to view the realm of creative potencies as "the field of force" within which creative potentialities become realized. The realm of the created potencies is wider, surpasses that of created potentialities, and receives its energy from the creator God. All the potentialities of God are creative, and determined by the essential goodness of God the creator. The dimension of evil which negates the affirmation of life, and the redemption from evil, apply both to earthly potentialities and to heavenly potencies.[136]

The beginning of heavenly bliss comes to us already through Christ's coming. The heaven of grace present now prepares us for the heaven of glory where heaven and earth will be created anew. When "heaven opens" through the power of Christ's coming, God's energies and potentialities are made available "in order to open the life systems which are closed in on themselves, and to guide them into their newer, richer future."[137]

Moltmann insists on a doctrine of heaven that is richer than Schmaus' equation of heaven with a "symbolic term for God," or the Lutheran divinization of heaven. Once we locate heaven as God's realm it becomes cut off from the world and "it becomes difficult to go on interpreting earth as God's creation at all."[138] Further, once we identify God and heaven the modern "criticism of heaven" paves the way for atheism.

The shift in Christian thinking from heaven as the realm "above us" to that of "future kingdom" was quite understandable once God's transcendence came to be defined in future categories, rather than in terms of the spatial universe. Bloch attempted to retain the idea of heaven but reinterpreted it in atheistic categories. However, Moltmann believes this to be a "sterile" approach since this turns:

> "infinity into indefinite endlessness, and makes of the striving for fulfillment merely an 'on and on' ... Bloch's attempt to rehabilitate heaven without God shows how necessary this category is for the forecourt of the possible before the actual. . .Without God's creative potentialities for the world, worldly potentialities remain determined by present existing reality, and are totally congruent with that."[139]

Moltmann is careful to distinguish between the relative transcendence of heaven in dialectical relationship with the earth, compared with the absolute transcendence of God. God is both the transcendence of this *relative* transcendence of heaven and immanence of earth, and the immanence of this transcendence and immanence. We can understand this difference both in terms of space, as movement from heaven to earth, and in terms of time, as eschatological presence moving towards the kingdom of glory. Heaven has not yet acquired this presence of God in glory, hence "it is not only earth that requires a new creation, tormented as it is by suffering and pain and crying and death. Heaven requires a new creation too."[140] For our purposes the doctrine of heaven that Moltmann presents is significant in its ecological structure. It serves to link the immanence and transcendence of God, both in relation to space and in relation to the future. It provides a foretaste of the new creation, but is not yet the creation in glory. Once the Spirit of God completely fills the earth the dichotomy between heaven and earth will disappear and we arrive at a holistic vision without the tensions of messianic age, but also without a pantheistic fusion of the world in God.

The kingdom of glory is the indwelling of the Triune God in his whole creation through participation so that "even in the kingdom of glory the world remains God's creation and will not become God himself."[141] The sabbath is the symbol for this future hope, and as such serves to distinguish between the world as nature, subject to decay, and the world as creation. "The sabbath is God's Yes to creation without any No."[142] The work of God's creation was for the sake of the sabbath, and is the feast of both the redemption of creation and its consummation. In the sabbath God "returns to himself," but in a way that allows creation to "co-exist with himself."[143] God allows creation to act upon him, while still being present in its existence. The acts of creation point to God's transcendence, while the sabbath expresses his immanence. The work of God's creation expresses his will, while the sabbath expresses his being. In this way "the mystery of the sabbath is a profounder mystery than the mystery of the work of creation."[144] By placing greater emphasis on being rather than activity, Moltmann shows the ecological tenor of his thought. This ecological motif becomes clearer in his appreciation of the sabbath from the perspective of creation.

The search and unrest of creation is not satisfied by a world beyond, as in gnostic/mystical thought, but in God's sabbath. All creatures find their place in God, who is wholly present. The sabbath, which came from Israel's understanding of her faith, takes on cosmic dimensions and in this respect "gives Israel a special place in creation."[145] The sabbath is part of the texture of salvation history, and the "fundamental structure of creation itself," which is "defined simply by the creation story, not by any natural cycle."[146] The sanctified sabbath frees creation from striving for happiness in a rest which is "wholly present in the presence of God."[147]

While the exodus is the "elemental experience of God's history," the sabbath is the "elemental experience of God's creation."[148] The twin concepts of the sabbath as the completion of creation and the sabbath as the revelation of God's repose in creation point to the unity of creation and revelation in redemption. "God is then manifest in the whole creation, and the whole creation is the manifestation and mirror of his glory: that is the redeemed world."[149] In the future of creation God's indwelling "drives out the forces of the negative," and so banishes "fear" and the "struggle for existence."[150]

6. The dynamic involvement of the cosmic Spirit and the cosmic Christ.

(a) The cosmic Spirit.

The idea of a cosmic Spirit is a natural outcome of a belief in God's indwelling the universe through his Spirit. In this way the "evolutions and catastrophes of the universe are also the movement and experiences of the Spirit of creation."[151] The Holy Spirit is also the Spirit of the resurrection of Jesus. The power of the resurrection is the same "creative power of God, through which God communicates his energies to his creation."[152] Here we find the link between Christology and pneumatology, and the theme of the resurrection is central to his discussion of the new creation in the messianic age and in the age to come:

> "Eschatological Christology and pneumatology does in fact involve a fundamentally new interpretation of divine creative activity. It is not the protological creation of the world that is presented here. It is the eschatological creation as might be expected of testimonies belonging to the messianic era."[153]

McIntyre has criticized Moltmann for not distinguishing between the Spirit, who is at work in the initial creative activity, and the transformative power of the Holy Spirit at work in the new creation.[154] However, Moltmann does allow for this indirectly by making the Spirit's work in creation part of the movement of the "Trinity in the Sending," where the Father is the Subject. The new creation is caught up in the movement of the "Trinity in the Glorification," where the Spirit is Subject and gathers all creation to the Father through the Son.

Moltmann argues that even in the kingdom of glory where the distance between creator and creation has ended through the indwelling of the Spirit, we can distinguish between the creator and his creation. This new creation, while it is a direct manifestation of God rather than *"vestigia Dei,"* still retains a difference in essence from God himself.[155] Walsh believes that Moltmann cannot sustain the difference between God and creation in future glory, since once the space of "the *Nihil*" has been overcome there is no longer any distinction between God and creation.[156] While in some respects this seems to be a logical outcome of Moltmann's position, it does not do justice to his understanding of the ontological distinction between God and creation defined by *creatio ex nihilo*. Only if the creation is formed out of the essence of God does the distinction between God and creation become lost. The complete indwelling of creation by the Spirit allows the separation between God and creation to be lost, without losing the distinction.

Process theology rejects the concept of *creatio ex nihilo*. The latter safeguards the distinction between God and creation in the beginning, and remains important for Moltmann's theology. In process thought God's experience of the world is both reciprocal and equivalent to the world's experience of God. Moltmann recognizes a degree of reciprocity between God's experience of the world and *vice versa*, but he is careful to distinguish between them. Once God the creator fully dwells in creation the goal of the reconciliation of the world with God through Christ is realized. Hence, "All the works of God end in the presence of the Spirit."[157] The Spirit of God who acts in the new creation is the same Spirit whom the Father called upon to create the world in the beginning through the Son. The Spirit of God "emanated" from the creator and "preserves his creation against the annihilating Nothingness."[158]

The Spirit is also the one who suffers with the creation, and this suffering is related to the passionate love of the creator for his creation. "For he is the power of the love from which creation has issued and through which it is sustained."[159] Yet the Spirit is more than just this powerful love, he is also one who acts as independent Subject but in a way that points away from himself to the Son and the Father. He is the "creative Energy" and "the one who gives life to the world and allows it to participate in God's eternal life."[160] The creation is above all Trinitarian, which serves to bind God's transcendence and immanence and "exists in the Spirit, is moulded by the Son and is created by the Father."[161]

Moltmann is careful to distinguish his idea of the cosmic Spirit from animist notions by beginning with the revelation and experience of the Holy Spirit in the church of Christ. We find here a rebirth of believers, a new community, and a unique vocation for each individual. The hope which is born here extends to include hope for the whole of creation. In the "rebirth of the cosmos to glory" separated creatures become reunited and we find "direct fellowship with God of the creation united in Christ and renewed in the Spirit."[162]

The cosmic Spirit acts in nature to create new possibilities, to engender harmony in relationships, to preserve individuality and to "open" all systems of matter and life. The Spirit changes the history of creation from one of suffering to one of hope. However, lest we fall into the trap of pantheism we need to insist that "God does not manifest himself to an equal degree in everything."[163] A non-Trinitarian form of panentheism can allow for such differentiation, but this is inadequate for Moltmann since it is "not capable of linking God's immanence in the world with his transcendence in relation to it." In this case he is anxious to stress the incapacity of differentiated panentheism to *link* the transcendence and immanence of God, or, in other words, it is insufficiently *relational*. Hence the benefits of a *Trinitarian* doctrine of creation which "views creation as a dynamic web of interconnected processes. The Spirit differentiates and binds together. The Spirit preserves and leads living things and their communities beyond themselves."[164]

(b) The cosmic Christ.

Moltmann's understanding of Christ as the "ground of salvation" for the whole creation extends to include Christ as the "ground for the existence" of the whole creation.[165] The theme of the universal lordship of Christ is parallel with Israel's understanding of the eternal wisdom of God. Here we have an emergent *Sophia* Christology, which the gospel of John interprets in terms of the Logos of God. God's wisdom and his Logos become personified in Jesus. While, "Spirit Christology is also Wisdom Christology" they "express the messianic secret in different ways."[166] The advantage of these Christologies for Moltmann's theology is that they allow us to become more aware of the Trinitarian relationships. This contrasts with more binitarian Son of God Christologies.

The theme of the cosmic Christ in Ephesians and Colossians points to Christ as mediator between God and the world. Thus "heaven and earth are clasped and gathered into a whole, and in the all-embracing peace of Christ arrive at their open communication with one another."[167] The idea of the cosmic Christ also helps us to relate the kingdom of God coming in history with the "new creation."[168] We can relate these two ideas by reflection on the resurrection of Christ not just in terms of a historical act of God, but according to the natural imagery of the "rebirth of Christ from God's life-giving Spirit."[169] From the day of the resurrection and Easter appearances Christ inaugurates a "light which shines over the whole new creation."[170] Moltmann insists that "it is only a cosmic Christology which completes and perfects the existential and historical Christology."[171] Christ's redemption is inclusive so that he becomes "the universal *Shalom* of God in this world and in our history."[172] Here Moltmann more than adequately answers any criticism that he "reduces" the rôle of Son from mediator of creation to agent in consummation.[173]

Moltmann distinguishes his view of the cosmic Christ from the New Age belief in the existing "harmony of the world." Instead of the latter, cosmic Christology presupposes "disrupted harmony," yet looks to "reconciliation of all things through Christ."[174] He takes up the theme of Christ as present but hidden "Pantocrator" which Barth had suggested. For Moltmann Christ's parousia becomes the final coming forth of the Pantocrator hidden in the cosmos. While the epistemological foundation for the cosmic Christ is "the Easter appearance of the risen one" in a way that links together creation and redemption, the ontological foundation for the cosmic Christ is his death on the cross.[175] This is similar to the idea we noted earlier in the last chapter that without the death of Christ he cannot be the hope for the hopeless. Now Moltmann extends this concept to include the ontological significance of the biological death of Christ, as pointing to its inclusivity for the whole of physical creation. Hence "without these wider horizons the God of Jesus Christ would not be creator of the world, and redemption would become a Gnostic myth hostile to the body and the world."[176] In a way that echoes his treatment of the cosmic Spirit he considers that Christ mediates in creation as the "ground" of the creation of all things, the "moving power" in its evolution, and as its redeemer.[177] His understanding of Christ as the "ground" of creation is both in its protection against chaos and its existence for Christ's sake.

The fundamental unity which binds all of creation together is fellowship in God's "Wisdom, Spirit or Word." This unity is complemented by the differentiation of created beings which is reflected in the distinctive rôles of Word and Spirit in God's creative activity. The Word is more like the "song of creation" instead of "a command," which suggests servile imagery. For:

> "the Creator differentiates his creatures through his creative
> Word and joins them through his Spirit who is the sustainer
> of all his words . . . The Word specifies and differentiates
> through its efficacy, the Spirit binds and creates symmetries,
> harmonies and concord through its presence."[178]

Christ is mediator both in securing creation against chaos and in its renewal which looks to the new heaven and new earth. The rôle of Christ in the evolution of the cosmos makes no sense without his rôle as redeemer, indeed he is the "redeemer of evolution."[179] Here Christ's involvement is as one who comes from ahead and one who inaugurates the new creation. While the rôle of Christ in the evolution of the world is related to his activity in continuous creation, his rôle in the new creation is related to his coming in glory. In this double movement his activity is both distinct from, but inseparable from, that of the cosmic Spirit.

7. Conclusions.

1.   Moltmann's Trinitarian doctrine of God has a profound impact on his understanding of the relationship between God and creation. By making pneumatology the dominant strand, he encourages a thoroughly *ecological* doctrine of creation. Nonetheless the shift towards a greater focus on pneumatology which develops as Moltmann's Trinitarian theology matures, need hardly render him "guilty" of neglecting this aspect in the "first ten years" of his earlier work.[180] Moltmann's concern with the *Theology of Hope* was to write in a way relevant for this period. While his eschatological orientation has remained, it has matured into Trinitarian thinking.[181]

2.   Moltmann's primary concern in the 1980s and 1990s is to encourage a different, more *Trinitarian* approach to understanding both God and the world. His social Trinitarian doctrine, which focuses on divine *interrelationships,* links his idea of God with an ecological motif. Conversely, his concern for *ecology*, with its idea of *indwelling*, possibly encourages him to think of God in *spatial* categories. He views his primary task to be a removal of monarchical doctrines of God, and as such turns our attention away from ourselves to one which he believes is more thoroughly *theocentric* in perspective.

3.   How are we to understand God as both transcendent creator of the world, and also immanent in the world through his Spirit? First, Moltmann insists that we need to reject a monarchical "monotheistic" premise of God whose aim is a powerful tyranny over the world in favour of a loving God who decides to become creator of the world.

4.   The difference between God and his creation is best understood in terms of the Jewish kabbalistic tradition of *zimzum*, where God withdraws into himself and so creates the preconditional space and God-forsakenness for *creatio ex nihilo*. We find a modified form of panentheism emerging in Moltmann's doctrine, where the world is "in" the space created by God, and God dwells in his creation through his Spirit.

5.   The above is set in the context of the Trinity as a community of divine persons, where each indwells the other through the Eastern church's doctrine of *perichoresis*. The Son shares the essence of the Father through a "begetting" which is also a "birth" in the "womb" of God, while the Spirit shares his essence through emanation. This common source expresses a unity in the Godhead which is *subservient* to the unity of fellowship of divine persons, where each indwells the other through *perichoresis*. The "Trinity in the Origin" gives way to the "Trinity in the Sending," so that the fellowship of Father, Son and Spirit is opened up for the whole of creation.

6.   We find a similar tension, characteristic of his earlier theology, between present hope in the messianic age and eschatological glory. The new creation, which begins with the resurrection, brings something totally new. The Spirit as Subject points to the Father and the Son and gathers up all creation into the Trinitarian life.

7.   The Trinitarian theology of creation helps both to distinguish between God and creation without separating God from creation, and allows for the indwelling of God's Spirit in the universe without dissolution into pantheism.

8.   Moltmann's ecological perspective colours his view of heaven, which serves as a link between the transcendence and the immanence of God in relationship with the earth. It also allows him to conceive of a way of expressing a *spatial* dimension in God's dealing with the world, without losing the *eschatological* orientation of his theology. Heaven as well as earth will be redeemed, hence heaven reflects only the *relative* glory of the present possibility

for the earth, rather than the *ultimate* glory of the kingdom of glory where God rests from his work and dwells fully in his creation. Once this happens the sabbath has arrived, yet this sabbath has been part of both the history of creation in the beginning *and* salvation history. The doctrine of the sabbath is *ecological* in expressing the interconnectedness between creation and redemption, present hope and future glory.

9.　　　The cosmic Spirit who dwells in creation and the cosmic Christ who mediates in creation reflect the work of the Father who expresses himself through his "song" to creation. The history of creation becomes bound up with the Trinitarian history of God.

10.　　　Christ's resurrection is both the hope for the history of the world and our hope for the rebirth of all creation. His redemption has cosmic dimensions. However, we find a tension between Christ as mediator in an emerging, suffering universe, and Christ as one to whom the renewed creation looks in its future glory. This tension between present and future echoes that between the Spirit as agent in creation and the Spirit as Subject for the new creation. We arrive here at the double question of God who is both transcendent over the world in the present and future, yet is immanent in it through his Spirit indwelling in creation. Moltmann's Trinitarian doctrine is a way of interpreting this tension in terms of the changing Subject of the activity of the Trinity; however the resolution of this tension can only be expressed in eschatological categories.

11.　　　The final vision of God's sabbath is set in the context of God's initial act of self-humiliation in inner withdrawal. Without the use of *zimzum* it would be difficult for Moltmann to maintain an ontological separation of God and creation. However, since this doctrine reflects a self-limitation and self-distinction in God, it allows for a God who is in a fundamental sense feminine and ecological in orientation, rather than the more traditional idea of sovereignty and lordship.

12.   The above also reflects Moltmann's concern to keep a thoroughly *cruciform* shape to his Trinitarian theology of God and creation. It is this fundamental belief in a God who suffers that allows him to develop the doctrine of *zimzum*, rather than *vice versa*, as some critics seem to have suggested.[182] We will consider later whether Moltmann is entirely justified in bringing categories of redemption into his theology of *creatio ex nihilo*.

13.   Another area of enquiry is whether Moltmann's doctrine of God is too self-assured in its detail which fails to allow us to appreciate the mystery of the Godhead.[183] A related issue is whether Moltmann has failed to appreciate the difficulty in recognizing the limits to the analogical or metaphorical nature of everything we say about God.[184]

14.   Finally we note how Moltmann's Trinitarian doctrine of God infiltrates and colours his perspective on anthropology and the natural world. His thorough development of Trinitarian thought serves to shape his theology of creation in a way that makes it infused with *ecological* motifs. We shall turn to the way this serves to determine his anthropology in the following chapter.

End Notes

All books and articles are by Jürgen Moltmann unless stated otherwise. Translations are from the German text.

1. TKG, pp. xiv-xv. For an account of Moltmann's belief in ecumenical unity coming from a reflection on the cross of Christ see, for example, "The Expectation of His Coming," *Theology*, 88, 1985, pp. 425-428. This article hints at the Christological orientation which is dominant in Moltmann's Trinitarian doctrine.

2. *Ibid.*, p. 4.

3. *Ibid.*, p. 5.

4. *Ibid.*, p. 98.

5. *Ibid.*, pp. 10-13.

6. CJF, p. 54. Moltmann argues that after the Renaissance we find too much emphasis on the rule of God as active Subject, with the world portrayed as passive Object. For a full discussion of Moltmann's criticism of monotheism, which "obliges us to think of God without Christ and consequently of Christ without God as well;" see TKG, pp. 129-148, especially p. 131.

7. *Ibid.*, p. 55.

8. GC, p. 27. Moltmann argues for a more holistic understanding of the meaning of imago Dei based on community with creation, rather than autonomous lordship over it. Hence "Human rule is only made legitimate when it is exercised in co-operation and community with the environment and leads to life giving symbiosis between human society and the natural environment." *On Human Dignity: Political Theology and Ethics*; translated by M.D. Meeks, London, SCM , 1984, p. 27; hereafter referred to as OHD. We will be taking up this theme in more detail in the next chapter.

9. GC, p. 318. A similar idea is taken up in "The Cosmic Community: A New Ecological Concept of Reality in Science and Religion," *Ching Feng*, 29, 1986, pp. 93-105; hereafter referred to as CC. Also "The Ecological Crisis: Peace with Nature?," *Colloquium*, 20, 1988, pp. 1-11; hereafter referred to as ECPN.

10. "God's Kingdom as the Meaning of Life and of the World," translated by T. Weston, in, H. Küng and Jürgen Moltmann, eds., *Why Did God Make Me?*, *Concilium*, 108, 1977; New York, Seabury Press, 1978, pp. 97-103.

11. "The Inviting Unity of the Triune God;" translated by R. Nowell, in, C. Geffé and J.P. Jossua, eds., *Monotheism; Concilium*, 177, 1985; Edinburgh, T and T Clark, 1985, pp. 50-58.

12. "The Fellowship of the Holy Spirit: Trinitarian Pneumatology;" translated by M. Kohl; *Scottish Journal of Theology*, 37, 1984, 287- 300.

13. *Humanity in God,* joint author, E. Moltmann-Wendel; London, SCM, 1983, p.95; hereafter referred to as HG. Here Moltmann is not rejecting the idea of God as creator, but a focus on his speaking and acting which is so one-sided that he believes he "cannot be the living God. This God has become an idol, an idol of power and domination."

14. TKG, p. 9.

15. *Ibid.,* p. 19.

16. GC, pp. 31-32.

17. *Ibid.,* pp. 33-34.

18. *Ibid.,* p. 33.

19. *Ibid.,* p. 34. See previous chapter for a comment on Moltmann's wish for a re-appraisal of the scientific enterprise.

20. For example, J. Polkinghorne, "Review of *God in Creation*: Creation Without the Scientists," *Expository Times,* 97(9), 1986, p. 285; T. Peters, "A Book Worth Discussing: *God in Creation;*" *Currents in Theology of Mission,* 13(4), 1986, pp. 241-244; J. McPherson, "Life, The Universe, and Everything: Jürgen Moltmann's *God in Creation,*" *St Mark's Review,* 128, 1986, pp. 34-46.

21. GC, p. 53. Moltmann's comments here reflect a debt to Barth's Trinitarian theology, and his theology of creation. Moltmann is well aware that while Barth could not foresee the crises in relationships between ourselves and nature, his stance in his theology of creation is affirming, see, "Schöpfung, Bund und Herrlichkeit: Zur Diskussion über Karl Barths Schöpfungslehre;" *Evangelische Theologie,* 48(2), 1988, pp. 108-127; hereafter referred to as SBH.

22. *Ibid.,* p. 54.

23. *Ibid.,* p. 56; see also p. 8.

24. *Ibid.,* p. 56.

25. *Ibid.,* p. 59.

26. CJF, p. 78; see also GC, p. 64.

27. ECPN, p. 9.

28. *Theology Today: Two Contributions Towards Making Theology Present,* translated by J. Bowden, London, SCM, 1988, pp. 10-11; hereafter referred to as TT.

29. "Theology of Mystical Experience;" translated by A. Heron; *Scottish Journal of Theology,* 32(6), 1979, pp. 501-520. Moltmann is not afraid to use poetic language to express ways of understanding God and entering into the history of Christ. His linkage between these ideas and the concrete suffering of the historical Jesus, as expressed in CG, makes for a

fascinating approach to the significance of the death and resurrection of Christ. We will take up the discussion of the Christological dimension in his creation theology later.

30. "The Possible Nuclear Catastrophe and Where is God?," *Scottish Journal of Religious Studies*, 9, 1988, pp. 71-83; see also "God and the Nuclear Catastrophe," *Pacifica*, 1, 1988, pp. 157-170.

31. *Ibid.*, p. 79. Moltmann puts the stark alternative views of God as remote tyrannical ruler versus God as fellow sufferer in creation. The choice is unlikely to be as simple as this, though his style is quite deliberately provocative at this stage.

32. *Ibid.*, p. 80.

33. *Jewish Monotheism and Christian Trinitarian Doctrine: A Dialogue* by P. Lapide and J. Moltmann; translated by L. Swidler; Philadelphia, Fortress Press, 1981, p. 47.

34. *Ibid.*, p. 61.

35. "The Inviting Unity of the Triune God;" op. cit. (n. 11).

36. TKG, p. 17.

37. *Ibid.*, p. 25; see also PL for the development of the *leidend* (suffering) and *leidenschaftlich* (passionate/devoted) life of Christ to God's righteousness; especially, pp. 1-32: "His love is passion: passion for human beings and their worth, passion for creation and its peace...In the depth of his suffering we perceive the greatness of his passion for us," p. 31. Moltmann's reflections on both the inner Trinitarian relationships and that between God and creation are in the light of his reflections on the crucified and risen Christ.

38. *Ibid.*, p. 23.

39. *Ibid.*, p. 34.

40. P. Molnar, "The Function of the Immanent Trinity in the Theology of Karl Barth: Implications for Today," *Scottish Journal of Theology*, 42(3), 1989, pp. 367-399.

41. J. O'Donnell, "The Doctrine of the Trinity in Recent German Theology," *Heythrop Journal*, 23(2), 1982, pp. 153-167. The idea of God suffering in an 'active' sense seems inconsistent with the idea of suffering as an 'overflow' of love. The problem seems to be that the idea of active suffering implies choice, but for Moltmann the idea that God could turn away from his creation is impossible. He tries to resolve this difficulty by speaking of active suffering as coming from who he is, that is fundamentally a loving God, rather than suffering coming out of a need for creation in terms of deficiency. Hence Moltmann's understanding of freedom has repercussions on the meaning of 'active,' in both active suffering and his action in creating the world. Unfortunately, this does not avoid the impression that the suffering of God is somehow inevitable, even if its inevitability stems from his character as a loving God.

42. R. Cole-Turner, *God's Experience: The Trinitarian Theology of Jürgen Moltmann in Conversation with Charles Hartshorne*, PhD thesis, 1983, Princeton Theological Seminary, p. 59.

43. TKG, p. 34. Bauckham addresses the charge that Moltmann makes world history, and evil, a necessary moment in the divine process. However, he suggests that while Moltmann's trinitarian dialectic in CG is Hegelian in structure, it is not entirely Hegelian in content. Moltmann is also careful to deflect the criticism that evil is somehow necessary for the sake of good, though his more qualified statements in TKG still give the Trinity a cruciform shape, and thus "the actual sufferings of the cross are essential to who God is," R. Bauckham, *Moltmann: Messianic Theology in the Making*, Basingstoke, Marshall, Morgan and Scott, 1987, pp. 106-109.

44. TKG, p. 34.

45. J. Milbank, "The Second Difference: For a Trinitarianism Without Reserve," *Modern Theology*, 2(3), 1986, pp. 213-234, cf. p. 223; see comment under n.41 and n.43 above.

46. TKG, pp. 39-55.

47. "The 'Crucified God': A Trinitarian Theology of the Cross," translated by K. Crim, *Interpretation*, 26, 1972, pp. 278-299, cf. p. 295. By immanent Trinity we mean God as he is "in himself," and by functional or economic Trinity we mean God's "action" in the world.

48. P. Molnar, *op. cit.* (n.40).

49. R. Bauckham, "Jürgen Moltmann," in , P. Toon and J. Spiceland, eds., *One God in Trinity*, London, Bagster, 1980, pp. 111-132; R. Bauckham, *op. cit.* (n.43), pp. 92-93; 110-114.

50. TKG, p. 59.

51. *Ibid.*, p. 151.

52. *Ibid.*, p. 159; Moltmann seems to be suggesting that God is always atoning, a criticism which we will discuss more fully later.

53. *Ibid.*, p. 160.

54. J. O'Donnell, "The Trinity as Divine Community," *Gregorianum*, 69, 1988, pp. 5-34, cf. p. 20 and R. Bauckham, *op. cit.* (n.43).

55. R. Cole-Turner, *op. cit.* (n.42), p. 59.

56. R. Cole-Turner, "Review of *God in Creation*," *Zygon* (USA), 22(1), 1987, pp. 120-121.

57. GC, p. 9; see also pp. 10-13. Moltmann makes no attempt to justify his assertion that the faith of Israel was in reaction to the matriarchal, pantheistic and animist beliefs of the surrounding culture, p. 13. The influence of feminist writing, especially his wife, is likely to be significant here. See, for example, HG, p. 41 where Elizabeth Moltmann-Wendel writes "Judao-Christian religion was, from the beginning surrounded by matriarchal or semi- matriarchal

religions." Some matriarchal elements remain in the biblical texts, in, for example, the ideas of milk and honey. See, E. Moltmann-Wendel, *A Land Flowing with Milk and Honey*; translated by J. Bowden, London, SCM, 1986. Moltmann openly acknowledges the importance of the feminist critique of the canonical decisions of the church, with its bias towards male hierarchy, in, "Die Bibel und das Patriarchat: Offen Fragen zur Diskussion über 'Feministische Theologie,'" *Evangelische Theologie*, 42, 1982, pp. 480-484; hereafter referred to as BP. We intend to discuss the influence of feminist theology on Moltmann's thought in more detail later.

58. *Ibid.*, p. 206.

59. *Ibid.*, p. 11.

60. *Ibid.*, p. 14; Moltmann's move away from understanding creation in terms of causality marks a major break with Thomistic Catholic tradition. He believes that: "it is advisable to eliminate the concept of causality from the doctrine of creation," p. 14. Moltmann seems to be thinking of only efficient causation in this context. He supports this move on the basis that causality leads automatically to an overemphasis on transcendence. Nonetheless, his argument that efficient causality inevitably weakens God's immanence is not all that convincing.

61. See, for example, TJ, pp. 40-41.

62. GC, p. 15. see also CC pp. l01-103 for a parallel discussion.

63. RRF, pp. 20 ff.

64. GC, p. 73.

65. *Ibid.*, p. 76; see under n.60 above.

66. *Ibid.*, p. 78.

67. TKG, p. 117.

68. GC, p. 78.

69. *Ibid.*, p. 85.

70. TKG, p. 59.

71. *Ibid.*, p. 106.

72. GC, p. 87; see also TKG, p. 109. The idea of God having to make space for "finitude" presupposes a spatial understanding of God; an issue which we intend to take up again later.

73. *Ibid.*, p. 87. Moltmann's detailed account of the negative space in which God creates his creation leaves the impression that God allows evil to emerge. Although he rejects any notion that God creates evil, ideas such as "God's self-negation" bearing "creative force" involve him in complex speculation about different levels of negation which he makes little attempt to justify. See also, J. McPherson, *op. cit.* (n.20).

74. GC, p. 88: "In a more profound sense he 'creates' by letting-be, by making room, and by withdrawing himself. The creative making is expressed in masculine metaphors. But the creative letting-be is better brought out through motherly categories."

75. *Ibid.*, p. 89.

76. W. Barr, "Review of *God in Creation*," *Lexington Theological Quarterly* (USA), 21, 1986, pp. 60-62.

77. G. Breshears, "Creation Imaginatively Reconsidered: Review of *God in Creation*," *Journal of Psychology and Theology*, 14(4), 1986, pp. 339-351; J. McPherson, *op. cit.* (n.20); B. Walsh, "Theology of Hope and Doctrine of Creation: An Appraisal of Jürgen Moltmann," *Evangelical Quarterly*, 59(1), 1987, pp. 53-76.

78. J. Pambrun, "Review of *God in Creation* ", *Eglise et Theologie*, 17(3), 1985, pp. 412-415.

79. J. McPherson, *op. cit.* (n.20); R.Cole-Turner, *op. cit.* (n.56).

80. J. McIntyre, "Review of *God in Creation*," *Scottish Journal of Theology*, 41(2), 1988, pp. 267-273.

81. GC, p. 89.

82. *Ibid.*, p. 91. By bringing Christology into the primordial act of God's inner withdrawal Moltmann seems to be attempting to make the Jewish kabbalistic doctrines Christian. While on the one hand this could be defended on the traditional claim that the whole of the Trinity is caught up in the acts of creation, Moltmann's particular use of kenotic ideas weakens the distinction between creation, incarnation and redemption. For criticism of Moltmann's kenotic Christology see J. McIntyre, *op. cit.* (n.80). We will discuss these issues in more detail later.

83. *Ibid.*, p. 93; see also pp. 208-209.

84. TKG, p. 108.

85. GC, p. 114.

86. *Ibid.*, p. 150.

87. *Ibid.*, p. 154.

88. *Ibid.*, p. 156.

89. *Ibid.*, pp. 156-157.

90. S. Platten, "Review of *God in Creation*," *King's Theological Review*, 9(2), 1986, pp. 64-65.

91. For a critical commentary on Moltmann's panentheism, see, J. McIntyre, *op. cit.* (n.80).

92. TKG, p. 89.

93. *Ibid.*, p. 90; see also "The Trinitarian History of God," *Theology*, 78, 1975, pp. 637-646.

94. M. Meeks, "Trinitarian Theology: A Review Article," *Theology Today*, 38(4), 1982, pp. 472-477.

95. TKG, p. 95.

96. C. Plantinga, "Review of *The Trinity and the Kingdom of God*," *Calvin Theological Journal*, 18(1), 1983, pp. 105-108.

97. "The Fellowship of the Holy Spirit," *op. cit.* (n.12), p. 289.

98. R. Cole-Turner, *op. cit.* (n.42), p. 141.

99. TKG, p. 145. Moltmann has been accused of Tritheism by P. Molnar and others, see P. Molnar, "The Function of the Trinity in Moltmann's Ecological Doctrine of Creation," *Theological Studies*, 51(4), 1990, pp. 673-697. We will discuss this and other questions raised by Molnar later.

100. TKG, p. 59.

101. R. Page, "Review of *The Trinity and Kingdom of God*," *Scottish Journal of Theology*, 37, 1984, pp. 97-98.

102. TKG, p. 145.

103. *Ibid.*, p. 150.

104. GC, p. 16.

105. *Ibid.*, p. 16; we will comment on the feminist influence in Moltmann's interpretation of *perichoresis* subsequently.

106. "The Inviting Unity of the Triune God," *op. cit.* (n.11), p. 56; see also TKG, p. 175.

107. HG, p. 88.

108. ECPN, p. 4.

109. R. Olsen, "Trinity and Eschatology: The Historical Being of God in Jürgen Moltmann and Wolfhart Pannenberg," *Scottish Journal of Theology*, 36, 1983, pp. 213-227, cf. p. 226.

110. TKG, p. 164.

111. *Ibid.*, p. 167.

112. "The Motherly Father: Is Trinitarian Patripassionism Replacing Theological Patriarchalism?;" translated by G. Knowles, in, J. Metz and E. Schillebeeckx, eds., *God as Father?; Concilium*, 143, 1981, Edinburgh, T. and T. Clark, 1981, pp. 51-56, cf. p. 53.

113. TKG, pp. 175-176.

114. Here Moltmann has shifted from his earlier theology where he considered that both the Son and the Father were the source of the Spirit, FC, p. 74. Claybrook believes that this is a "drastic change of mind." Nonetheless, the Son in some sense shares in the issuing of the Spirit through his participation in the life of the Father. Moltmann's position is more a creative mediation between the Eastern and Western church's controversy over the *filioque*. It illustrates

his intention to formulate theology from an ecumenical perspective, and as such has an implicitly "ecological" basis. D. Claybrook, *The Emerging Doctrine of the Holy Spirit in the Writings of Jürgen Moltmann*; PhD thesis, 1983, The Southern Baptist Theological Seminary, p. 221.

115. TKG, p. 178.

116. GC, p. 234; we will develop this theme in the following chapter.

117. *Ibid.*, p. 258.

118. J. McIntyre, op. cit. (n.80).

119. R. Bauckham, "Jürgen Moltmann," in, D.F. Ford, ed., *The Modern Theologians: An Introduction to Christian Theology in the Twentieth Century*, Volume 1, Blackwell, Oxford, 1989, p. 308.

120. TKG, p. 104.

121. GC, p. 6; see also CFJ, pp. 84-85.

122. *Ibid.*, p. 118.

123. *Ibid.*, p. 121.

124. *Ibid.*, p. 123.

125. *Ibid.*, p. 123.

126. *Ibid.*, p. 124.

127. *Ibid.*, pp. 125-126. The idea of "perichoretic" time is somewhat confusing; we will take up this theme again in an anthropological context in the next chapter.

128. *Ibid.*, p. 149.

129. *Ibid.*, p. 161. Moltmann cites Karl Barth, *Church Dogmatics, Volume 3/3*, p. 419; see also SBH.

130. G. Stroup, "Review of *God in Creation*," *Homiletic* (USA), 11(1), 1986, pp. 21-22.

131. GC, p. 163; the idea of an "undetermined" and "determined" world has Hegelian overtones.

132. Moltmann has been heavily criticized for his "unscientific" use of the term "open system" for his own particular theological purposes. For reviews see, J. McPherson, T. Peters, *op. cit.* (n.20) and J. McIntyre, *op. cit.* (n.80). We will be raising this issue again later.

133. GC, p. 164.

134. R. Olsen, *op. cit.* (n.109), p. 219.

135. GC, p. 165.

136. We find some parallels here with the process thought of Charles Hartshorne where God acting in creation limits indeterminate possibilities within a continuous range. However, God becomes one cause among many in such a way that the "freedom" of the world is increased. For

a fuller discussion see R. Cole-Turner, *op. cit.* (n.42) pp. 223-229. Moltmann distinguishes his position from process thought by a clear insistence on *creatio ex nihilo*, which gives primacy to God's action. For a discussion of the importance of the doctrine of *creatio ex nihilo* in the early teaching of the Orthodox church against pagan philosophy, see J.D. Zizioulas "Preserving God's creation. Three Lectures on Theology and Ecology," *King's Theological Review*, Volume 12(2), 1989, pp. 41-45. While William Barr considers that Moltmann's affirmation of God's self-giving to the world which calls for and guides creation is inconsistent with his idea of the openness, movement and self-transcendence of nature which points to God, we prefer a more sympathetic interpretation; namely, that both aspects need to be held in dialectical relationship with each other. See W. Barr, *op. cit.* (n.76).

137. GC, p. 172.

138. *Ibid.*, p. 173; Moltmann seems to be exaggerating here in order to reinforce his conviction that heaven is included in a doctrine of creation.

139. *Ibid.*, pp. 180-181.

140. *Ibid.*, p. 180; Moltmann's speculations about a future redemption for heaven are somewhat unwarranted.

141. *Ibid.*, p. 184.

142. CC, pp. 97-98.

143. GC, p. 279.

144. *Ibid.*, p. 280.

145. *Ibid.*, p. 283.

146. *Ibid.*, pp. 284-285.

147. *Ibid.*, p. 286.

148. *Ibid.*, p. 287.

149. *Ibid.*, p. 288. While we might get the impression that he has shifted in his attitude to natural revelation compared with his earlier work, he is referring here to the future condition of creation, as was the case in his previous studies. He is more explicit about his intention to "keep to the rule" that Christian natural theology is a "re-recognition of God in nature, coming second to the revelation of God in Christ", translation mine, SBH, p.118.

150. *Ibid.*, p. 213.

151. *Ibid.*, p. 16; for a parallel discussion see CC, pp. 102-103. Moltmann also uses the term "cosmic spirit" to refer to the way the spirits of living beings transcend themselves. We shall confine ourselves here to a consideration of the cosmic Spirit in its broadest sense, rather than how this relates to human consciousness or the natural world, both aspects which we will take up subsequently.

152. GC, p. 67.

153. *Ibid.*, p. 65.

154. J. McIntyre, op. cit. (n.80).

155. GC, p. 64.

156. B. Walsh, op. cit. (n.77).

157. GC, p. 96.

158. *Ibid.*, p. 96.

159. *Ibid.*, p. 97.

160. *Ibid.*, p. 97.

161. *Ibid.*, p. 98.

162. *Ibid.*, p. 100; Moltmann is careful to stress in his earlier work that the new creation begins on "the underside" of society, so that a hopeless people becomes a messianic people. See previous chapter, also "The Life Signs of the Spirit in the Fellowship Community of Christ;" translated by T. Runyan, in, J. Moltmann, M.D. Meeks, R.J. Hunter, J.W. Fowler and N.L. Erskine, eds., *Hope for the Church: Moltmann in Dialogue with Practical Theology*; Nashville, Abingdon, 1979, pp. 37-56.

163. *Ibid.*, p. 103.

164. *Ibid.*, p. 103; a similar thought is expressed in ECPN where Moltmann argues for a more explicitly ecological doctrine: "The world view of the divine spirit in creation and creation in the divine spirit is the theological concept which corresponds best to the ecological doctrine of nature, which we are looking for, and need today." ECPN, p. 5.

165. GC, p. 94.

166. *The Way of Jesus Christ: Christology in Messianic Dimensions*; translated by M. Kohl, London, SCM, 1990, p. 74; hereafter referred to as WJC.

167. GC, p. 171.

168. WJC, p. 98.

169. *Ibid.*, p. 248.

170. *Ibid.*, p. 254.

171. *Ibid.*, p. 256.

172. "Peace; The Fruit of Justice;" translated by J.C. Cumming, in, H. Küng and J. Moltmann, eds., *A Council for Peace, Concilium*, 195, 1988; Edinburgh, T. and T. Clark, 1988, pp. 109-120, cf. p. 112.

173. G. Hendry, "Review of *God in Creation*," *Theology Today*, 43, 1987, pp. 576-578.

174. WJC, p. 278; Moltmann rejects the New Age belief in the determining value of the laws and rhythms of the cosmos. Christ challenges these laws, and in this way we find: "the subordination of these cosmic powers and laws to Christ's reigning sovereignty."

175. *Ibid.*, pp. 281-282.

176. *Ibid.*, p. 283.

177. *Ibid.*, p. 286.

178. *Ibid.*, p. 289.

179. *Ibid.*, p. 301.

180. D. Claybrook, *op. cit.* (n.115), p. 184.

181. Moltmann's Trinitarian doctrine is an attempt to find a balance between security, authority and belonging, versus freedom, spontaneity and community. See, "The Challenge of Religion in the '80s," in, J. Wall, 'ed., *Theologians in Transition*, New York, Crossroad, 1981, pp. 107-112. For Moltmann's critique of Germany's history of theological reflection, see, "Theology in Germany Today;" translated by A. Buchwalter, in, J. Habermas, ed., *Observations on 'The Spiritual Situation of the Age': Contemporary German Perspectives*; Cambridge, Mass./London, MIT Press, 1984, pp. 181-205.

182. B. Walsh, *op. cit.* (n.77).

183. J. Webster, "Jürgen Moltmann: Trinity and Suffering," *Evangel*, 3, 1985, pp. 4-6.

184. A similar criticism was raised by Bauckham, who notes that Moltmann has been accused of being "insufficiently aware of the necessarily analogical nature of talk about God, so that his discussion of the divine experience too often becomes unconsciously mythological;" R. Bauckham, "Jürgen Moltmann," in, D.F. Ford, ed., *The Modern Theologians: An Introduction to Christian Theology in the Twentieth Century*, Volume 1, Blackwell, Oxford, 1989, p. 308.

CHAPTER 4.

Moltmann's Ecological Anthropology.

1. Introduction.

Jürgen Moltmann's approach to theological anthropology, as we might expect, departs from more traditional, self-contained definitions of human existence. We find his earlier concern for a wider dialogue between political and theological issues subtly enlarged and transformed in the wake of the emergence of both his trinitarian doctrine of God and the current ecological climate. Themes relating to the doctrine of humanity surface throughout his discussion of *God in Creation* and as we might expect, his doctrine of God expanded in *The Trinity and the Kingdom of God* mirrors to some extent his reflections on the human condition.

Our aim in the present study is to outline the basis and orientation of Moltmann's anthropology, which by his own admission is still in its formative stages.[1] We hope to clarify both the similarities and contrasts between his more recent work and that expressed earlier in *Theology of Hope*. While we will hint at potential difficulties in his position we will reserve more critical comments until the next major section, when we will raise questions regarding his understanding of God, humankind and the natural world. While one of the strengths of Moltmann's theology is the interconnectedness between all aspects of doctrine, this lays him open to flaws which have repercussions throughout his work. Hence it becomes easier to postpone the fullest criticisms until we have heard his overall position.

We noted in the last chapter Moltmann's concern to formulate an adequate doctrine of God in the light of human suffering. Indeed it is "the open wound of life in this world," and the task of theology is to ask how we can survive with this open wound.[2] He is anxious to steer away from a narrowly defined causal link between sin and suffering, without in any way denying that the two are related. Rather, we need to expand our perspective so that it includes suffering of the innocent.[3] For Moltmann, our human experience of God begins with his experience of us, in human suffering. This suffering includes that of both the innocent and the guilty, both the oppressed and the oppressor, and the whole groaning creation. The crucified God whose love liberates creation from suffering, links our suffering with his, so that "in this sense, not only does God suffer with and for the world, liberated men and women suffer with God and for him."[4]

However, he does not seem to confine the interaction between God and creation narrowly to a treatment of human history isolated from that of the rest of creation, rather the world as a whole:

> "is the object of his will towards good; it is the counterpart of his love for freedom, and in both these things it is the fulfilment of his hope for a free response to his own goodness and love .... his world puts an impress on God too, through its reactions, its aberrations and its own initiatives."[5]

God's loving concern for the whole creation includes both creative and redemptive movements; the theme of salvation as that which extends to the whole of existence is characteristic of his earlier theology. However, redemption from suffering begins with humanity in the experience of the Holy Spirit in the lives of Christian believers. While our human bodies are the temple of the Holy Spirit, this hope extends *Shekinah* to the whole creation. [6]

We find the link between human suffering and our relationship to God clarified in Moltmann's discussion of prayer as mystical experience.[7] Our self-knowledge and knowledge of God is interconnected in the spirituality of Teresa of Avila, John Calvin and Martin Luther. Moltmann draws out the insight that our self-love deepens as we experience the love God has for us. Moltmann believes passionately that we come to awareness of ourselves through knowledge of God, yet Jesus Christ remains the mediator between these aspects of our understanding. The reality of who Jesus Christ is becomes most evident in his suffering on the cross, expressed liturgically through the eucharist. We find here hints at Moltmann's insight into the importance of Christology for an adequate anthropology. Through fellowship with Christ "non-persons become real persons and live with him in the eternal fellowship of God."[8]

2. The symbiotic character of human existence.

A primary connectedness between God and the world is expressed through the love which "communicates itself by overcoming its opposite" or "the other," and the response by "the other" to that love. Hence "creation is a fruit of God's longing for 'his other' and for that other's free response to the divine love."[9] The response of men and women to that love is related to their being God's image, so that the trinitarian love extends beyond the intertrinitarian relationships. "Does it not seek its 'image,' which is to say its response, and therefore its bliss, in men and women?"[10] Moltmannn is careful to distinguish between the "otherness" in God and "the other" in confrontation with God, as we noted earlier.

The symbiotic character of human existence expressed through the network of human relationships and between ourselves and the whole environment forms a minor key throughout Moltmann's work. By the time we reach *The Trinity and the Kingdom of God* it takes the form of pneumatological trinitarianism. His discussion of this concept in *God and Creation* widens still further and becomes clarified through his understanding of symbiosis operating at three different levels. These three core themes form the starting point of his later discussions on the meaning of *imago Dei*. Symbiosis acts at the levels of:

(a) legal and political, meaning the covenant between human beings and nature, especially the balancing of the rights of the earth and the rights of humans.

(b) medical, meaning the total human being as psychosomatic unity, which affirms our bodily nature.

(c) religious, meaning the community between humankind and the natural world in a single community of creation.[11]

Symbiotic processes are never static, but directional towards the messianic future where the indwelling of God's Spirit in humankind that we experience now in partial and provisional form, becomes complete and eternal. This future vision of glory includes the breakdown of alienation between God, humankind and nature so that the whole of creation is "at home in existence - that the relationships between God, human beings and nature lose their tension and are resolved in peace and repose."[12]

Moltmann rejects any suggestion that such symbiosis reflects the original pristine state of humankind, rather we need to distinguish between:

> "grace and glory, history and new creation, being a Christian and being perfected ... the medieval tenet has continually led to triumphalism: the glory which perfects nature is supposed already to be inherent in the grace ... and the perfection of the human condition is considered to be already integral to being a Christian."[13]

The advantage of Moltmann's eschatological perspective is that it forms a necessary link between theological dualities which are "freed from their position as mere antitheses." Hence, eschatology is necessary for a symbiotic understanding where:

> "two sides of the antithesis are understood as complementary aspects of a common process. This makes it possible to discern and define more precisely the possible reconciliation between freedom and necessity, grace and nature, covenant and creation, being a Christian and being a human being."[14]

Moltmann also links up his idea of symbiosis with space, as well as time. The cosmic Spirit is an integral part of this vision, and this Spirit is defined as "the forms of organization and modes of communication in open systems."[15] We find the cosmic Spirit operating at the level of matter, living symbioses, human beings and populations, the earth as a whole, the solar system, the Milky Way and the whole complex of galaxies in the universe. By "forms of organization" Moltmann seems to refer to both those forms in a given time through "self-assertion and integration" and those throughout time and history through "self-preservation and self-transcendence." His use of the biological terminology of Jantsch probably expresses a desire to connect the ideas of the cosmic Spirit with earthly reality. Whether he is justified in using such terms, which he makes no attempt to explain in their biological context, may be open to criticism, and we will be raising this issue again later. The theme of symbiosis is, similarly, a biological term which Moltmann uses both in the narrower biological sense and more loosely in terms of interdependence. His assertion that biological symbiosis emerged "by amalgamating open life systems" seems too vague to be very helpful.[16]

We find an example of his more loosely defined idea of symbiosis in his discussion of the spirit in humankind. In Augustinian tradition consciousness is equated with spirit, while in Thomistic tradition rationality is equated with spirit. Instead, Moltmann wishes to emphasize the hidden aspect of our unconscious as that which is **also** fully permeated by spirit, so that consciousness is simply "reflective and reflected spirit." The spirit in humans is "his inner and outward symbioses." Here we find a recurrence of the theme which we discussed above where symbiosis operates at the legal, medical and religious level. He rearranges the three themes, putting the legal level last:

(a) The spirit-soul and the spirit-body is the organizational principle of the spiritual life of the human being. Rather than a narrower definition of spirit in terms of conscious subjectivity of reason, it includes a unity and interrelationship between body and soul, an inner symbiosis.

(b) The social and cultural factors which bind together the human beings as an organized open system, again express the spirit in the mode of outward symbiosis, equivalent to Moltmann's earlier notion of symbiosis operating at the "religious" level.

(c) The interrelationship between humankind and the natural environment takes this outward symbiosis of the spirit into the whole of the environment, so that it becomes a "spiritual ecosystem."

As a natural development of (c), Moltmann weakens the overall status of humankind by placing it in the context of the whole system. While he makes vigorous attempts to support his position by defending it in terms of a rejection of a misplaced "anthropocentrism," it shows clearly a significant departure from his earlier perspective in *Theology of Hope*. In the latter we tend to find nature subsumed under a historical paradigm. Here we find rather a different attitude emerging:

> "Through the Spirit human societies as part systems are bound up with the ecosystem "earth" (*Gaia*); for human societies live in and from the recurring cycles of earth and sun, air and water, day and night, summer and winter. So human beings are participants and subsystems of the cosmic life system, and of the divine Spirit that lives in it."[17]

We find similar views expressed in his more recent articles.[18]

The basis of an adequate theological understanding of the symbiotic character of human existence expressed in the interrelationship between humankind and the environment, requires a preliminary critical analysis of the Christian tradition. Moltmann devotes considerable space to outlining the way our Western attitudes to the natural world have been shaped by the cultural influences of industrialization. A symbiosis between humankind and nature is only possible once these basic attitudes have been challenged and transformed.

Moltmann also rejects the opposite extreme, that is to take our theological bearings from modern cosmology.[19]

As we might expect from Moltmann's fervent rejection of ideas of God which portray him as dominating tyrant, he believes that human social relationships of oppression and domination stem from such a false theology, and need to be revised along with a prior revised understanding of God. The opposite of symbiosis is ecological crisis, which "brings with it social crises - crises of value and significance in human society, and a growing instability in the crises of personal life."[20] Moltmann seems to be suggesting that the ecological crisis which stems from a false understanding of God, humanity and nature, has further repercussions on the depth of the crises in the human sphere. He uses the biological analogy of "self-immunization" to express the way we deaden ourselves to facing both the seriousness and extent of the ecological crisis, or glibly assume that we can solve it by more technology. "The result is that people are becoming increasingly apathetic about the slow death of nature."[21]

While Moltmann acknowledges that science can lead to the "enhancement of living," he also believes that it is associated with our political will to achieve power. The accepted values of society shape the political context, and we can compare the thrust towards growth and progress which dominates the modern industrial world, with the emphasis on equilibrium which was characteristic of earlier civilizations. Moltmann looks to these civilizations as:

> "highly complicated systems of equilibrium, equilibrium in relationship between human beings and nature, equilibrium in the relationship between human being and human being, and equilibrium in the relationship between human beings and 'the gods.'"[22]

The Bible has been blamed for the "anthropocentric" exaltation of human beings which gives us permission to dominate the earth. Moltmann rejects any simple causal relationship since the Judao-Christian approach was many years prior to the rise in dominating attitudes characteristic of Western industrialized society. As we hinted earlier, Moltmann links the false understanding of God as one who has absolute power as his pre-eminent attribute, with the modern enlightenment understanding of humanity who "confronts nature from the outset and in principle as its ruler ... the scientific objectification of nature leads to the technological exploitation of nature by human beings."[23]

Moltmann seriously challenges the view that the Judao-Christian anthropology in Genesis underpins the modern subjugation of nature. The concept of "subduing the earth" has a much narrower context in the creation account, and is related specifically to the requirement of human beings for vegetarian food. Moreover, we can only understand what is meant by "dominion" in Genesis 1:26 once we recognize that this is linked specifically with our bearing *imago Dei*. In other words "having dominion is linked with the correspondence between human beings and God, the creator and preserver of the world - the correspondence which is meant when the human being is described as being the image of God."[24] The legitimization of the will to achieve power from a theological misinterpretation of Genesis has no foundation in the Bible. While:

> "the second creation account gives the impression that the world was created for the sake of men and women ... the logical position is a false one. Interpreting the world as God's creation means precisely not viewing it as the world of human beings, and taking possession of it accordingly ... It has to be treated according to the standards of divine righteousness, not according to the values that are bound up with human aggrandisement."[25]

While a human being as image of God gives "his special position in creation," this is only in the context of the whole creation giving glory to the creator.

We can develop an alternative attitude to creation if we engage with creatures and "participate in their life." This meditative knowledge "lets life be life and cherishes its livingness," and is "communicative knowledge as compared with dominating knowledge."[26] Theology must broaden its horizon from a narrow interpretation of creation in terms of the "existential understanding of the person," to that "which engages with the whole knowable world." Once we wake up to an awareness of "silenced and dying nature," the "primary requirement is to fit theology and the sciences ecologically into the natural surroundings which are the framework providing their conditions."[27] Thus our whole pattern of thinking becomes more open, integrating and comprehensive. Somewhat curious is Moltmann's suggestion that the symbiotic character of our relationship with the world must include an awareness of heaven as the hidden "other side of God's creation."[28] Perhaps this reinforces his understanding of ourselves as part of the creation in its broadest sense, including both heaven and earth.

3. Humankind as *imago mundi*: the world as home.

Moltmann discusses the background of our alienation from nature as a prolegomenon to the idea of the world as our home. We have already mentioned the tendency of science and technology to dissociate humankind from nature in ontological dualism. A philosophical response to this division of subject and object is to replace ontological dualism with historical dialectic. History becomes the supreme subject, and is differentiated between humanity and the natural world while seeking for a "unity within this difference."[29] German Idealism looked for a future utopia where this difference was overcome, nonetheless nature still appears as object rather than as independent subject.

A further reaction to ontological dualism was the Marxist attempt to overcome the alienation between humankind and nature through dialectical materialism. Communism is both "perfected naturalism" and "fully developed humanism." Ernst Bloch modified Marxist dialectic by incorporating

Schelling's philosophy of nature, so that nature acquired its own individual character. The significance of this development is crucial for Moltmann's position, since it is only when nature is perceived as independent from humans that it can both acquire a proper status in the future, "and only then, too, can a community between human beings and nature come into being in which both can find their 'home country.'"[30] The future of nature is that which encompasses an alliance between human beings and nature, and as such, Bloch "anticipated important ecological principles."[31] The subsequent castigation of Bloch's ideas by orthodox Marxism of this period reflects an attitude to nature which makes it subservient to human needs. The alienation between humankind and nature undergirds the practical attitude of communism which defines humankind in terms of work and productivity.

By way of contrast Moltmann insists that in addition to our concern for work, an elemental human need of equal importance is that of "habitation" or "home country." The relaxed social relationships which characterize such existence generate an equilibrium which frees us from struggle and anxiety. Human society needs to become aware of the fact that "the natural environment is just such a network of tranquilized social relationships." This does not deny possible interaction between human beings and nature, rather:

> "it is only when nature has been moulded into an environment, that it can become a home in which men and women can live and dwell. Nature is certainly capable of being a home for human beings, but only if they use it without destroying it."[32]

Moltmann hints at a practical outworking of such a symbiosis in terms of ecological horticulture and conservation.

The idea of the subjectivity of nature comes through a modern concept of the theory of open systems. While Moltmann believes that such subjectivity is well founded "on reasonable grounds," it is still flawed in its characterization of the human subject as the "great and central subject." Instead, Moltmann believes that our starting point should be different, and that we should envisage humans as "one of nature's products." By way of contrast with the earlier philosophies of history, now nature becomes the central subject. Now "the human subject must accept the fundamental subjectivity of nature; and he must continually fit his own world into the overriding cohesions of nature and its evolution."[33] This theme bears some resemblance to the *Gaia* philosophy which we mentioned in the previous section. Nonetheless, Moltmann believes that this is consistent with an understanding which begins with humankind as "the product of nature and -theologically too- as *imago mundi.*"[34] Moltmann justifies his position by claiming that this is not a "romantic" flight from responsibility so much as an awareness and rediscovery of dimensions of life which we have repressed and suppressed. It is worth asking ourselves if Moltmann's seeming elevation of the status of nature to subject tends towards a metaphysic of nature which weakens our sense of active responsibility as stewards of creation.

Nonetheless, we find other strands in Moltmann's thought which tend to correct such a progression. These strands are the affirmation of the human being as one "destined to be the eucharistic being." Human life is conscious of creation as God's creation and conscious of the presence of God as sacrament in creation. This distinguishes human beings from other living things and allows us to express the praise of all creation. Our "priestly dimension" speaks on behalf of dumb creation, who share in our eucharistic nature, but rely on humankind to voice this song of praise.[35]

Moltmann develops his idea of *imago mundi* from the Eastern Orthodox doctrine of humankind as microcosm "in which all previous creatures are to be found again, a being that can only exist in community with other created beings and which can only understand itself in that community."[36] He finds biblical support for this view in Genesis, where human beings are the last to be created, and so are dependent on all the others. The human being is "bound up with the earth" in a way that seems to lend credence to the anthropological ideas associated with the phrase "mother earth." The biblical understanding of the soul is "an animated body," but this also links humankind and animals, who are described in Genesis 1.30 as "living souls." Other links with the animal kingdom are a common dependence on plant food, a common living space on earth, and a common blessing by God given with an affirmation of fertility.[37] In some cases Moltmann seems to be straying a little too far from the original theological context, for example his seeming support from Genesis both for humankind as microcosm, and for the idea of "mother earth."[38]

Moltmann argues strongly that only when we have become aware of the similarities between humankind and animals can we appreciate the real meaning of our uniqueness, and in the light of this uniqueness understand our calling in Christ and the future of the whole cosmos. We will develop these ideas by outlining Moltmann's concept of humanity as *imago Dei* and *imago Christi*. The history of creation begins with the created world and ends with human beings, while the history of redemption begins with human beings and ends with creation. Our unique existence and calling is only discovered when we see ourselves as "belonging within the all-embracing coherence of God's history with the world, the history of creation and the history of redemption."[39] Here the idea of God's history takes precedence over the idea of nature as subject. We will raise the issue later as to whether these two strands in Moltmann's thought are compatible.

The human being's function as *imago mundi* is that of the "embodiment of all other creatures" Moltmann finds support for this view in the scientific understanding of ourselves as evolved beings. Through evolution the human being:

> "contains within itself all the simpler systems in the evolution of life, because it is out of these that the human being has been built up and proceeded ... As microcosm the human being represents the macrocosm."[40]

4. Humankind as *imago Dei* in holistic perspective.

Moltmann draws on Genesis creation accounts to outline the differences between humankind and the animals. There are three basic distinctions mentioned:

1.   The divine charge for humankind to "subdue" the earth, which means "nothing but the injunction to eat vegetable food."[41] However, he does not state explicitly that this verse encourages a return to vegetarianism. It is rather the ethical practical question of allocation of resources which means that "the transition from animal to vegetarian food is important if humankind is to survive at all."[42]

2.   We are given the task of naming the animals, which "brings animals into a community of language with human beings."[43] Moltmann's interpretation of this command serves to encourage our links with animals, and thereby weakens any sense of our rights over the animals which is found in the more traditional approach. The creation accounts do not set up a right to kill animals, and permission comes after the flood, and even then for the purposes of food "with a ban on the extermination of animal species."[44]

3.   According to the creation accounts the sociality of human beings marks us out as distinct from animals. Moltmann makes no attempt here to address the scientific discovery of sociality in other mammals, or "lower" forms of life.

Moltmann is careful to resist any suggestion that our designation as *imago Dei* is related to the above differences between humankind and animals. Rather *imago Dei*:

> "affects the whole human being, both in his community with other created things and his difference from them. As God's image human beings are God's proxy in creation, and represent him. As God's image human beings are for God himself a counterpart, in whom he desires to see himself as if in a mirror. As God's image, finally, human beings are created for the sabbath, to reflect and praise the glory of God which enters into creation, and takes up his dwelling there."[45]

He interprets the first theme of *imago Dei*, namely our rôle as God's representatives, in the light of the second two aspects. He argues strongly against any suggestion that this is a divine mandate for human domination over the creation. The idea of "dominion" comes after our designation to be the likeness of God, rather than an identification between them, as in traditional hermeneutic. While Moltmann weakens this aspect of image-bearing in order to move beyond "anthropocentric tendencies," he also insists that our stewardship only makes sense in the context of the widest human community, and the community of all creation. He wishes to express the idea of human lordship in communitarian language, and legitimate subjugation of the earth as that which is specifically related to our material need for nourishment:

> "human lordship over animals has to be distinguished from human subjection of the earth for the purposes of human nourishment, and distinguished more clearly than is the case in the traditional theological doctrine of *dominium terrae*; for this doctrine throws the two together and intermixes them, with disastrous consequences."[46]

Hence the command for stewardship, while it gives human beings responsibility to be the "authors of the further history of the earth," only makes sense once we understand ourselves as bearing the image both as whole persons, and as a community of persons. Human beings must, as God's image, "love all their fellow creatures with the Creator's love. If they do not, they are not the image of the Creator, and the lover of the living. They are his caricature."[47] Moltmann presses the case for a mutual balance between the rights of humans and the rights of nature.

We find the idea of our image-bearing related to our capacity to reflect God, developed in *The Trinity and the Kingdom of God*. Only the Son fulfils the destiny of human beings to be the image of God, so that Christ becomes the "true man."[48] Moltmann believes that the initial creation does not yet portray human beings as the true image of God, and is only fulfilled with the incarnation of Christ. He seems to suggest that our designation to be *imago Dei* is only possible after reconciliation and liberation through Christ.[49] However, the incarnation has a retroactive effect on the initial creation, so that while the creation is "open" for the appearance of God's image in Christ, the incarnation "in intention" precedes the creation of the world. Moltmann clarifies our relationship with Christ as that which shares in his image-bearing in his discussion on *imago Christi* in *God in Creation*.

As far as God is concerned, our free response to his love means that "in his work God finds, as it were, the mirror in which he recognizes his own countenance - a correspondence which resembles him."[50] The analogy is primarily that of relationship, both within the Trinity, and between God and creation. Moltmann suggests that while God relates to all his creatures, his relationship with humankind has a special quality, so that "in a certain sense God enters into the creatures whom he has designated to be his image."[51] We are not completely sure what Moltmann means here, though it seems likely that God's special relationship with humanity comes through his messianic promise of the incarnation. Thus our perception of the meaning of *imago Dei* is only clarified in "messianic light."

Moltmann distinguishes between the first two aspects of our image-bearing, namely to be (i) God's proxy in creation and (ii) a reflection of God himself through the theological concepts of image and similitude. While *imago* suggests "concrete representation" which is outward, *similitudo* implies similarity and a reflexive "inward relationship."[52] The first designation to be viceroy applies to every human being, not just royal leaders of human society. Moltmann believes that we become "one-sided" if we link the divine commission to rule exclusively with our bearing the likeness of God. Instead, our designation to be a reflection of God should come first, and only then serve to interpret our relationship with the non-human creation. Moltmann argues forcefully for a reordering of our priorities:

"Likeness to God means God's relationship to human beings first of all, and only then as a consequence of that, the human beings relationship with God. The nature of human beings springs from their relationship with God. It is this relationship which gives human nature its definition, not some characeristic or other which sets human beings apart from other living things."[53]

Moltmann reiterates the three aspects of image-bearing which we quoted above, except now he summarizes these concepts by three key phrases. Humankind is at once, (a) "God's representatives," (b) "God's counterpart on earth," and (c) "the appearance of God's splendour."[54] He notes in passing that a physical manifestation of our unique capacity to be the image of God is through the human face.

As we might have expected from Moltmann's holistic understanding of the meaning of *imago Dei*, he argues against Augustine's interpretation which identifies our image-bearing with the human soul. The root cause for this belief comes from a false prior understanding of God as the "One Being," rather than beginning with a "Trinitarian framework." He believes that Aquinas' focus on the mind and intellect for *imago Dei* is representative of a faulty elevation of the mind over the body. In both these traditional interpretations human social relationships achieve, at best, a status of *vestigia Dei* and women only achieve recognition in subordination under men. Calvin weakened this traditional dogma somewhat by including the body under the umbrella of *imago Dei* in redemption. Moltmann both challenges the traditional concept and goes beyond Calvin by insisting that the whole human being, "body, soul and spirit," bears the image of God.[55]

The logical outcome of Moltmann's argument is that our earthly sexual differentiation becomes part of our image-bearing. Here he refers to the whole community of men and women in a way that includes sexual differentiation and affirms it. He does not seem to be arguing for a "family" ideology as Leonard believes, with its implicit rejection of "celibate men and women, and of divorced people ... couples without children."[56] Instead Moltmann wishes to affirm our image-bearing as that which takes us away from individualism and isolation, and cuts across both "generations in time" and "sexes in space."[57]

The idea of *imago Dei* extending to include sexual differentiation and human communities picks up an earlier thread in Moltmann's discussion where he argues that a specific mention of bisexuality in humans in the Genesis account must have some significance, and "it is here that the real likeness to God and the uniquely human quality must lie. Sexual difference and community belong to the very image of God itself, they are not merely related to human fertility."[58] Moltmann stretches the hermeneutical significance of this text beyond its normal limits when he asks if we, as a consequence, should "think of the Creator of this human nature and condition in bisexual terms, as God and goddess at the same time."[59] He shows a tendency to overlook the historical context of this passage which is precisely to resist the fertility cults and the pagan emphasis on the goddess. We agree with Moltmann in so far as he believes that an interpretation of God as "transsexual" or "indifferent" to masculine and feminine is as fruitless a point of departure as that which identifies him with male categories. Moltmann avoids these potential pitfalls by changing tack altogether, and encouraging us to view God as Trinitarian rather than masculine, bisexual or neuter. God as Trinity affirms the differentiation which we find in our lives as men and women, without being identified with sexuality *as such*.

Thus the analogy of *perichoresis* goes beyond the bisexual image, and so avoids the potential danger of the "egoism" of the couple. His conclusions weaken some of his earlier statements which hint at the significance of bisexuality itself as part of our image-bearing. Rather, our sexual nature is only appropriated in terms of the differentiation it expresses as revealed in the life of the Trinity.

The community of human beings reflects, then, the relatedness at the heart of the Trinity, rather than the constitution of the Trinity. We noted in the last chapter that Moltmann gives some priority to the Father as source in the constitution of the Trinity. He believes that his position is not divergent from tradition, though he now takes his bearings from Eastern Orthodoxy, rather than following Augustine and Aquinas.[60]

Moltmann's understanding of our image-bearing in bodily, earthly characteristics, rather than as Gnostic spiritualization is related to his insistence that embodiment is the "end of all God's works."[61] Moltmann believes that an exaltation of the soul and denigration of body has its roots in ancient Greek thought, especially Plato who stressed the "baseness of the body" as an "insignificant casket for the soul."[62] In passing we note that Leonard views Moltmann's interpretation of Plato and Greek culture in general, as "oversimplified."[63] Moltmann interprets Descartes as one who translated the body/soul dualism in Hellenistic thought into a dichotomy of subject/object. This was followed by a subsequent spiritualization of human existence where the body becomes equated with the objective world of machines. Moltmann criticizes Barth for retaining the hierarchy between soul and body. An adequate interpretation of the Old Testament requires us to view the whole human being as the living soul.

Moltmann redefines the distinction between the soul and body so that the soul is the "core of the inner life" and the body is the "outward mental horizon."[64] Here he seems, quite deliberately, to interpret body and soul as inner and outer aspects of one whole, which are interrelated and interconnected. Furthermore, he seems to equate the conscious mind with our bodily existence rather than giving it independent status, or identifying the mind with the soul. This explains his more elusive references to "body, mind and spirit" which McIntyre believes still give insufficient primacy to the mind.[65] Barr has difficulty understanding how body and soul can be united, yet interpenetrating and so distinct.[66] Moltmann is somewhat confusing in his definitions. He seems to use "soul" in two ways: firstly in an inclusive sense to refer to our whole existence, and secondly as our core existence which is in communion with our outward bodily existence.

The designation of human likeness to God in the context of Trinitarian thought means that its future designation is to be *imago Trinitatis*. However, this makes sense only after we have reflected on Moltmann's understanding of ourselves as *imago Christi*.

5. Humankind as *imago Christi*: messianic anthropology.

The response of humankind to God is primary in our designation as *imago Dei*. However, this response is only possible through the incarnation, since it is in fellowship with the Son that humankind enters into its character as *ikon*, or image of God. The theme of *imago Christi* emerges from the messianic threads anticipated in *imago Dei*, but more specifically from the "transfigured humanity of the risen Christ."[67] The dawn of the new creation as *imago Christi* takes place through the power of the Holy Spirit, which marked by the Easter event is "always a physical experience." The main characteristic of a human community which bears the mark of Christ is that of "love that corresponds to the perichoretic unity of the triune God, as it is manifested and experienced in the history of salvation."[68]

The significance of Christ for the idea of humankind as *imago Christi* is in relationship to our vocation. Moltmann draws on the Pauline concepts developed in 2 Corinthians 4.4, where he notes that the focus is not so much on the incarnate Christ, as in *imago Dei*, but on the glory of the risen Christ.[69] Yet Christ in glory reflects back on our interpretation of *imago Dei*: "since it is through Christ that the new, true creation begins, Christ must be the mystery of creation in the beginning."[70]

The significance of the gospel is that it brings our understanding of the designation to be *imago Dei* into messianic light. Believers become *imago*

Christi through Christ, the true *imago Dei*, and by so doing anticipate their rôle as *gloria Dei* on earth. The idea of humankind bearing *imago Christi* is important for Moltmann in that it brings an eschatological component into the concept of humankind as *imago Dei*. We find, then, human beings' likeness to God referred to as "a historical process with an eschatological termination."[71] This process remains "incomplete and uncompletable" during the history of the cosmos.

Our designation to be stewards of earth, as part of *imago Dei* discussed above, is embraced by Christ's sovereignty as "the only true *dominium terrae*."[72] This rules out supremacy in any other principality or power, such as that of the state or science and technology. These forces come to their proper perspective only in the horizon of eschatological glorification in Christ.

Christ's person also shows us what our true humanity means. There are three dimensions to his personhood, summarized in *The Way of Jesus Christ:*[73] (a) **Eschatological**. Moltmann refers to the rôle of Christ as the fulfillment of Israel's longing for the Messiah, the coming Wisdom of creation, and the beginning of the new creation in the kingdom of God. In this way Christ becomes "the bearer of hope for the world" and as such is reflected in "the messianic human being."

(b) **Theological**. Christ is one who lives wholly in God, and God wholly in him. All who believe in Christ share in this unique relationship with God, and thereby become adopted as children of God.

(c) **Social**. Christ heals the wounds in society by solidarity with the sick, the forsaken and the poor. We become aware of ourselves, through Christ, as those who share in his "brotherly" and "sisterly" nature.

The bodily resurrection of Christ reminds us that our life in Christ is one that experiences a share in his death and resurrection. The significance of Christ's resurrection is that it allows us to bring into correspondence loving and dying. "Dying and death can be integrated into the loving affirmation of life if there is hope for the 'resurrection of the body.'"[74] Our identity in our relationship with God survives the transition from life to death, and "Because personal identity is found in a person's life history, it is inconceivable without somatic identity too."[75] The whole person, "body and soul" endures in the context of his *Gestalt* - a theme which we will expand in a later section.

The gathering of human beings into fellowship with the Father through Christ means that we think of ourselves as:

> "fashioned according to a single Person of the Trinity: the person of the Son. Only the Son becomes human and embodies the image for which human beings are created . . . The Son becomes human and the foundational image of God on earth. Through the Son, human beings as God's image on earth therefore acquire access to the Father. As God's image human beings are the image of the whole Trinity in that they are 'conformed' to the image of the Son: the Father creates, redeems and perfects human beings through the Spirit in the image of the Son."[76]

The above shows clearly how Moltmann's anthropological reflections are Christocentric, both in ontological and noetic terms. Our true personhood and being comes through being liberated in fellowship with Christ, and our true knowledge of God and of ourselves is only revealed in messianic light. Moltmann hesitates in aligning our personhood directly with the perichoretic personhood of Father, Son and Spirit except in a loose sense of our identity emerging in the context of symbiosis. Nonetheless, all three persons are involved in the recreation of human beings in the *imago Christi*, and it is **through** this image that we share in the life of the triune God. Moltmann's focus on the Son safeguards both the uniqueness of the Son's person compared with the Father, and the Holy Spirit, and keeps his anthropology earthed, through the unique rôle of the Son, who also "embodies the image for which human beings are created."[77]

6. The dialectic of sin and salvation.

Our self-understanding as persons made in *imago Dei* through *imago Christi* provides Moltmann with a key to the solution of the traditional dispute about whether the image of God is lost or perverted by human sinfulness. We can trace the source of such ambiguity to Romans 1.23 and Romans 4.23.[78] According to Romans 8.29 the sinner is justified through grace but glorified in the future through the path of sanctification. Yet the problem remains: namely, if sin destroys our humanity as *imago Dei*, how can we be held responsible for our sins? Alternatively, if sin just clouds our likeness to God, how can we know that we are truly sinners and as such condemned under the divine judgement?[79]

Moltmann examines two traditional answers to this problem, and then offers his own solution:

(a) The Fathers divided *imago Dei* into *imago* and *similitudo*. While *imago* reflects the being of humankind in consciousness, reason and will, and is unaffected by sin, *similitudo* reflects our moral correspondence which we can lose through disobedience. This two stage anthropology was modified by Aquinas, who believed that our reason and will was never lost, but clouded by sinfulness. The "formal" and "material" *imago Dei* of Brunner offers a similar interpretation of humankind as both at once a sinner and *imago Dei*.

(b) An alternative approach of the Reformers was to stress the centrality of justification by faith. Instead of viewing human beings as a mixture of God's image and sinfulness, as in (a), we become wholly sinners who are incapable of any worth before God through moral acts of obedience. Flacius took the extreme view that sin penetrates to the very substance of the human being. Stigel's position was more moderate, namely that sinfulness is not an essential part of our nature, but acts on human reason and will, so that they become distorted but not destroyed. Moltmann believes that we can retain an aspect of Flacius' thesis by acknowledging the power of sin in that we are all "slaves to sin," without reaching his conclusion that the *imago Dei* is totally lost, which he believes is not founded on any biblical evidence.

(c) Moltmann's understanding of the essence of *imago Dei* offers a way out of the dilemma which focuses less on our image as substance, and more on what it means in terms of relationship with God. While this sounds a promising line of enquiry, Moltmann offers a somewhat curious dialectic whereby sinfulness perverts **one side** of our relationship with God:

> "Human sin may certainly pervert human being's relationship to God, but not God's relationship to human beings.... The presence of God makes the human being undeprivably and inescapably God's image ... Even the human being who is totally inhuman, remains a human being and cannot escape his responsibility."[80]

Leonard asks: "Isn't there a touch of nominalism here?," by making humanity subjectively guilty, but without losing an objective relationship with God. He is presumably referring to nominalism as that which smacks of the Pelagian heresy.[81] However, Moltmann seems to be referring to the unconditional love of God for all humanity, rather than our salvation or lack of it through sinfulness. It is this faithful love which remains and which in some sense keeps our humanity as *imago Dei*, in spite of our turning away from God. However, it does seem difficult to imagine how overall our relationship with God is distorted in one direction but unaffected in a reciprocal direction. The concept of interrelationship itself would seem to require that a distortion in one direction would have repercussions on the relationship from God's perspective. We wonder whether Moltmann's solution to this dilemma through a bilateral understanding of a single relationship is any more helpful than the classical two stage anthropology. Nonetheless, his starting position, namely that of perceiving *imago Dei* in relational terms, is insightful.

What happens at the Fall? According to Moltmann this amounts to the domination of sin, and the designation to be God's image through God's grace alone. The image is in some way distorted into a "refractory image" and only becomes a perfected image "at the end of God's history with human beings."[82] As we noted above, Moltmann insists that through the grace of God, his relationship with humans remains, in spite of human sinfulness. The biblical support for such faithfulness comes from the account of the Flood, where God renewed his blessing even *after* the history of human wickedness:

> "It was self humiliation on God's part when he lent his divine image to a clod of earth. But how much more God lowered himself after the Flood, in the renewal of his blessing! For he now put his glory in the hands of potential evil-doers."[83]

We might ask ourselves in passing whether Moltmann's interpretation of the Flood account is exegetically correct: we find here a renewal of God's blessing, but does this lead necessarily to the conclusion that God's relationship with us is unaffected by sinfulness? Moltmann seems to equate God's blessing with his relationship with us. While this is likely in terms of God's faithful attitude to us, more seems to be implied in Moltmann's understanding of *imago Dei*.

As far as our relationship with God is concerned he shrinks from any suggestion that sin erradicates this relationship completely. His reasoning is that "evil only emerges in the light of what is good, and in the same way sin can merely pervert something which God has created, but cannot destroy it."[84] Once our lives become centred on something *other* than God, which is idolatry, this does not *destroy* our God-given relationship, but merely distorts it through channelling it in a wrong direction. We become fixed on some aspect of creation for our meaning for life, instead of the creator for whom we have been created. The image remains, but now we become *imago Satanae*, or *imago mammonis*. He makes the curious suggestion that since we have defined sin in terms of the distortion of our relationship with God, the "energies of sin" need to be redeemed as well as human creatures.[85]

Moltmann's understanding of what it means to be a sinner is characterized by our closedness towards God. We can contrast the free open fellowship which we enjoy as *imago Dei* through *imago Christi*, with a turning away from the creator in a way which "always means, in addition, being imprisoned in one's own existing being, and closed against the future."[86] Sinfulness amounts to a closedness of an "open system" and can only be freed through the vicarious sufferings of the Son. Fellowship with Christ releases us from sin, which is paralleled by a release from "closed-in-ness." Hence "if unfree, closed, introverted people are opened for this future of theirs in God, they achieve an unimagined liberty."[87]

Moltmann raises the issue of how our human freedom can become perverted. Once freedom means rule, social oppression and subjugation of the weak, it is self-centred and contrary to the true freedom which is community-centred and expressed through love. Our freedom is closely related to our openness; hence "I become truly free when I open my life for other people, and share with them, and when other people open their lives for me and share them with me."[88] Just as the *imago Dei* finds its true context in the future, so too a concept of freedom needs to include a "creative passion for the possible."[89]

The danger of closedness applies to human societies as well as individual persons. Life that is "vital, receptive and expectant" is experienced by people with open hearts and in open societies. A closed attitude is equivalent to death, both for ourselves and society. Christ's suffering is one that "opens us for his future."[90] The individual inward aspect of sin is "imprisonment" and "guilt," while the social outward aspect of sin is "tyranny and "childish dependence." Reconciliation and liberation belong together in our salvation from inward and outward aspects of sinfulness.[91] More evangelical scholars find Moltmann's understanding of sinfulness as closedness insufficient to carry the full weight of the depth and extent of human wickedness.[92] Walsh comments, more importantly perhaps, following Gilkey, that openness can be as much a menace as a possibility.[93] He suggests, in addition, that Moltmann's interpretation of sin as closedness tends to link evil with the ontological structure of creation. This is presumably because Moltmann defines sinfulness in terms of a perversion of our God-given freedom to respond to him or turn away from him. However, as we noted above, Moltmann prefers the idea of sin as that which affects, not so much the substance of our being, as our relationship with the creator. He insists that our humanness as *imago Dei* is never completely lost by sinfulness. Walsh argues that the whole concept of the Fall is weakened by Moltmann's understanding of *imago Dei* as a future event rather than a reflection of the original pristine condition.

Finally, Moltmann strongly resists the suggestion, as we noted earlier, that there is a direct causal link between suffering and sin. The rabbinical dogma of suffering as a punishment for sin forces redemption into two stages, first, the forgiveness of sin through Christ's sacrificial death, and second, the liberation from suffering and death through Christ's resurrection.[94] While Moltmann acknowledges that we can find a relationship between human sinfulness and suffering, the idea that all suffering is causally related to sin ignores the universality of human suffering. Moltmann's preoccupation with the theodicy question, especially that of innocent suffering, explains his apparent lack of detailed commentary on the more traditional categories of guilt, sinfulness and the Fall. His discussion of forgiveness becomes expressed in categories of liberation from inner imprisonment. A truly "healthy" person is one who accepts suffering, and has the strength to suffer. In this sense redemption is not deliverance from pain, or "community without conflicts."[95] This might come as a surprise in view of Moltmann's understanding of "equilibrium" in community life, which implies a *lack* of conflict. However, he seems to mean that our true peace only comes when we face up to sickness, pain and conflicts, rather than when we avoid these difficulties. Hence: "only what can stand up to both health and sickness, and ultimately to living and dying, can count as a valid definition of what it means to be human."[96]

Moltmann wants to avoid any suggestion that the handicapped are somehow less than human. Instead, "A human being - every human being - is the image of the living God. In the crucified Christ everyone can find himself again, because the crucified Christ is reflected in each and all of us, however handicapped we may be."[97] A truly human life which accepts suffering leads to a reordering of our inner and outward relationships. It also transforms our relationship to our future and to the transcendent. A truly human life is one which leads to the healing of the four dimensions of:

(a) personal confidence;

(b) social life;

(c) life history and

(d) personal significance and meaning.

In this sense our death becomes a transition to a different kind of being:

> "The human being in his embodiment is not created to end in death, he is made for the transformation through and beyond death. Hope for the resurrection of the body and a life everlasting, in redemption corresponds to the bodily creation of the human being by God, and perfects that. The hope of the resurrection is the belief in creation that gazes forward to what is ahead."[98]

7. Humankind as *gloria Dei*: future horizons.

As we might expect, the horizon of the future glorification of human beings is a vital dimension in Moltmann's anthropology. It is through the messianic path of *imago Christi* that believers become *gloria Dei* on earth.[99] As we hinted in the last section, our glorification is not an isolated elevation of "the soul," but the redemption of our whole bodily existence, which only happens after death, hence:

> "It is only the eschatological annihilation of death, the redemption of the body on a new earth and under a new heaven, which will consummate the 'becoming' process of human beings, thereby fulfilling their creaturely being."[100]

Our glorification is the natural next stage from sanctification in our messianic path with Christ. Our future glory is partly reflected in the face of believers, though what we see here is only a "fragmentary" form of future glory. This future glory, hinted at through biblical phrases such as 1 John 3.2 and 1 Corinthians 13.12, marks a difference between a *conformity* to the grace of God which we experience now, and an *entry* of the glory of God into creation in the future. Thus "the *imago per conformitatem gratiae* points beyond itself to the *imago per similitudinem gloriae*."[101]

Our designation to be *imago Dei* becomes *gloria Dei* through messianic fellowship with the Son. However, the form of this future glory "is not thoroughly determined," but is "in correspondence with the history of God's presence in the world."[102] Here we find a close correspondence in Moltmann's thought between God, who is, in some sense, still the becoming God, and humanity, who will become the mirror of this future God.

The idea of the human person as one who has his identity in the future is related to Moltmann's pneumatology. As we noted earlier the way of salvation for Moltmann is also the way of openness to God. A human spirit is not just reflective subjectivity, but the "anticipatory structure of his whole physical, mental and spiritual existence."[103] Moltmann seems, somewhat confusingly, to be using "spirit" in both an exclusive sense to refer to our spiritual dimension compared with our physical and mental existence, and an inclusive sense where all parts of ourselves are bound up in the human spirit in relation to the future. We noted a similar double meaning for "soul" in our discussion of body/soul dualism. Moltmann refers to a *perichoresis,* or interrelationship between categories of physical, mental and spiritual existence, and a unity that goes beyond these differences in a way that deliberately echoes his discussion of the Trinity. It is the unity in relationship that is primary, rather than the divisions, hence: "In the living alignment of his existence the different sides of his organism harmonize - the physical, the mental and the spiritual. The human being always realizes himself in the light of his direction. He is in that he becomes."[104]

Human reason only becomes fully rational when it is directed towards the future, so that "the essence of human reason is a kind of productive imagination."[105] Our future as anticipation here becomes much stronger in social networks, and the complementary side to our spiritual existence as anticipation is our spiritual existence as communication. We will be developing this concept further in the next section.

The way our future existence impinges on our present existence becomes clarified through Moltmann's understanding of human spirit as that which affirms life in its fullest sense, including suffering and death. In the above discussion we noted how Moltmann insists that a fully human life is one which accepts suffering, rather than one which withdraws into itself in false shame and guilt. Moltmann reiterates the theme prominent in his earlier work, that a fully loving life is one which embraces its pain. Suffering as such becomes an active energy, so that "human beings experience their mortality, not from a naked life as such, but only in life that is loved and loving."[106]

The theme of passionate love which grew in Moltmann's theological reflection of the passion of Christ, takes on a pneumatological tone. He seems to be referring to the Holy Spirit when he states:

> "It is the Spirit as love who differentiates happiness and pain, life and death so acutely. But if a person keeps back this love of life, or kills it, he will become insensitive to happiness and pain. Life and death will become a matter of indifference to him. He then becomes immortal, but he has never lived either, while on every act that affirms life, people become both alive and mortal."[107]

Moltmann describes immortality that we seek in remaining closed off from life as really a kind of death. Instead the acceptance of life, of mortality, allows us to recognize a life that is eternal. Moltmann wishes to distinguish between the pneumatology of the Old and New Testaments:

"In the Old Testament the Spirit is understood as the divine
energy of life, the creative Spirit of life. In the New
Testament the Spirit is described as the power of the
resurrection. This life-giving Spirit is experienced in this life
as unconditioned and unconditional love."[108]

Our future glory is anticipated by the Spirit of the resurrection becoming active

in us, and allowing us to experience both the joys of life and the pains of death.

Moltmann explicitly acknowledges Hegelian influence at this juncture, hence

"the life of the Spirit, says Hegel rightly, is not one that shuns death and keeps

clear of destruction. It endures its death and in death maintains its being."[109]

Moltmann's pneumatological shift in his discussion of the experience of the

passion of life aligns him more closely with Hegelian dialectic. However, his

insistence that the spiritual life is also one that is fully earthed in the material

world avoids potential esoteric idealism. We will be raising subsequently the

question of whether Moltmann's affirmation of our physical nature serves to

ground his discussion adequately.

8. The Spirit and *Gestalt* in ecological perspective.

A significant feature of Moltmann's anthropology which emerges in *God in
Creation* is his understanding of humankind in the context of *Gestalt*, which he

defines as "the configuration or total pattern of the lived life."[110] Moltmann's

understanding of the Spirit of God is one which views the Spirit as permeating

the total pattern of our existence, and this pattern as such emerges in particular

environments of persons and communities.

Gestalt is important for Moltmann's theology in that it gives him a

concept which enables him to link up the physical natural world with the future

historical horizon. *Gestalt* becomes evident in the field of interactions between

human beings and their environment. The dimensions of this field include:

"nature, in the form of the human being's genetic structure;
and in the form of the region of the world in which he is born;
the society in which he grows up; the history which moulds
his origins and conditions his future; and the sphere of

transcendence, which is represented by religion and the systems of accepted values."[111]

Gestalt is a means for describing the link between a person's individuality and his sociality, so that it can also be defined as "the form of exchange with the various environments in which a person is identifiable, and with which he can identify himself."[112] There is both an outward development of one's *Gestalt* through interaction with the outer world of other persons and nature, and an inner development through the relationship to oneself as a whole person, both conscious, and unconscious. We have already noted Moltmann's understanding of body and soul as outer and inner aspects of a single unity. Here Moltmann argues that a truly human *Gestalt* can only emerge through an exchange and interpenetration of body and soul, analogous to the perichoretic pattern of the life of the Trinity. Without such a "consensus" the pattern of equilibrium of our inner lives becomes broken. Moltmann refuses to give primacy to either the body or the soul, rather both interact and influence the other. The difference between verbal language and body language mirrors the "fragmentary unity" that is possible for *Gestalt* in human history.[113]

A further advantage of the human *Gestalt* as a way of understanding what it means to be human is that it allows us flexibility in the development of our personalities. Moltmann raises the issue of "centrations" and "decentrations" with the former meaning "convergences into a particular and determining self" which "emerge on the basis of particular concerns."[114] We can imagine such concerns shifting and changing once we view our lives as influenced by the environment. However, Moltmann believes that this does not render our concerns as capricious, rather such "centrations" remain a flexible part of our inner lives. Moltmann acknowledges a certain biological dynamic to these changes, which are "caught up in a rhythm of growth and dissolution."[115] However, he draws back from Dreizel's suggestion that this amounts to a "self-realization," since these changes happen on the basis of faithfulness to given promises to others. Hence:

> "In his promise a person commits himself, acquires a particular *Gestalt*, and makes himself someone who can be appealed to ... If he remains true to his promise he remains true to himself.... if he breaks his promise he is untrue to himself."[116]

Moltmann seems to be suggesting that while our natural constitution renders us equivocal, we need to become unequivocal through promise and faithfulness. This is not against our liberty, rather it is an identity which emerges both inwardly and outwardly as a person becomes "at one with himself." To some extent this idea counters the criticism that we encountered earlier that openness as such does not render us invulnerable to sin. A committed self is not against liberty, rather our true identity emerges when outwardly and inwardly we become "at one" with ourselves. The order in individuals is built up on a "web of conscious contacts between his organs, and their generally unconscious harmonization."[117] The order in society is built up on a network of promises and fulfillment. The theme of interconnectedness gives the idea of *Gestalt* an ecological character which, nonetheless, remains implicit in Moltmann's discussion rather than explicit.

The Spirit of God includes the human *Gestalt* in its sphere of interaction with the whole human person. The creative Spirit is one who forms the human body as spirit-body, the human soul as spirit-soul and the human *Gestalt* as spirit-*Gestalt*. Moltmann identifies the creative Spirit with the cosmic Spirit since "body, soul and their *Gestalt* can only exist in exchange with other living things in nature and in human society."[118]

Moltmann attempts to distinguish between the creative Spirit of God and the Holy Spirit, who is involved in the redemptive process:

> "The Holy Spirit is the name given to the Spirit of redemption and sanctification, that is to say, to the presence

of the redeeming and newly creating God ... 'The Holy Spirit'
does not supersede the Spirit of creation, but transforms it."[119]

McIntyre finds Moltmann's distinction between the Holy Spirit and the Spirit of
creation is "puzzling," though we note that it links up directly with ideas
expressed in *The Trinity and the Kingdom of God* where the Father is the subject
for the Spirit's action in creation, while the Holy Spirit is the subject for his
work in redemption.

The Holy Spirit transforms body, soul and *Gestalt* of the human
person, so that we become conformed to the "*Gestalt*" of Christ. Presumably
Moltmann is using this analogy in a very loose sense to mean that the inner and
outer harmony expressed in Christ's person and history becomes ours through
the Spirit. It would be impossible for us to share in the "*Gestalt*" of the
historical Christ whose environmental "field" was so different from our own.
Moltmann stresses that our whole lives become permeated by the Holy Spirit in
a way that affirms both our uniqueness and social character:

> "For though the Spirit in the person is certainly 'the common
> spirit' animating the shared life, he also gives each separate
> person his own *Gestalt* and the right to his unique
> individuality. The social character of the human being and his
> individuation are not antitheses. They are merely the two
> sides of the differentiating life-process which we call
> spirit."[120]

The above does not specifically mention the Spirit as either the creative
Spirit, or the redemptive Holy Spirit; both meanings are probably intended.
Moltmann's terminology may be deliberately vague here, though his distinction
between the creative Spirit of the Old Testament and the redemptive Holy Spirit
of the New Testament comes much later in his discussion.[121]

The transformation of our whole self: body, soul and *Gestalt* which
begins here through the power of the Holy Spirit, is marked by the transition
from life to death. Dying becomes "a transition to a different kind of being, and
a metamorphosis into a different *Gestalt*."[122] Moltmann believes that such

metamorphosis does not negate personal identity, or the history of a person which emerges in our life on earth, "so what endures is the whole person, body and soul, in the *Gestalt* that has come into being through the history of his lived life, and in which God sees him."[123]

Our historical identity and eschatological transformation are not mutually exclusive, but "two sides of the one single transition to eternal life."[124] The Spirit of the resurrection overcomes "life-hating divisions" and "necrophilic conflicts" so that our bodily nature is no longer suppressed and our soul is reintegrated into our whole life instead of becoming detached from our body. Once this happens our living *Gestalt* emerges; hence, "the new wholeness is a unity which absorbs into itself the differentiations and divisions, and heals them."[125] Our future includes all the "temporal" *Gestalt*s in a person's history, so that:

> "What is spread out and split up into its component parts in a person's lifetime comes together and coincides in eternity ... and becomes one... Each temporal *Gestalt* has the same dignity, in God's sight, and hence the same right before human beings."[126]

The above echoes an idea which Moltmann expressed earlier in *God in Creation* that human beings have a "unity of time" in the soul.[127] A more practical application of this view is that foetus, embryo and fertilized ovum cannot be "devalued" compared with a life that is already born. He even goes as far as to state that "Fundamentally speaking, human beings mutilate themselves when embryos are devalued into mere "human material," for every human being was once such an embryo in need of protection."[128] This marks a significant departure from his more apparently casual treatment of abortion in his discussion of medical bioethics some years previously.[129]

9. Humankind and nature in the horizon of the sabbath.

(a) The integration of nature into our historical existence.

The starting premise for Moltmann's reflections on nature is that our attitudes have become dangerously polarized away from a divinization of nature in ancient fertility cults, so that "the prevailing view of nature is totally godless, and the relationship of human beings to nature is a disastrous one." [130] His aim is to integrate God and nature in a way which "will draw them both into the same *vista*." As we have noted above and in the last chapter, this integration is achieved through a recognition of the cosmic Spirit in the whole of creation. We discussed the interplay between the Spirit and *Gestalt* above, and it is our experience of the Holy Spirit which gives us solidarity with the natural world:

> "So what believers experience and perceive in the Holy Spirit reveals the structure of the Spirit of creation, the human spirit, and the Spirit in the whole non-human creation; because it is to this that their experience corresponds. What believers experience in the Holy Spirit leads them into solidarity with all other created things."[131]

At this juncture we can ask ourselves what is Moltmann's understanding of the interrelationship between history and nature? In the first instance he rejects a view of history which is aligned with progress and which leads to a subsequent domination of nature.[132] Our understanding of history needs to be reformulated along the following lines:

(a) As meaningful only in the context of eschatological hope.

(b) As aware of hidden aspects of the past, which we can define as the difference between "past present" and "present past."

(c) As aware of hidden possibilities of the future, which we can define as the difference between "present future" and "future present," and "future future." The latter somewhat confusing terminology seems to indicate that the eschatological future is open-ended, compared with the historical future which emerges from history.

(d) As synchronized between all the interlaced times of history, which will lead to the alternatives of a "single humanity" or a "single catastrophe."

(e) As synchronized with the natural world, so that there is a coordination between "human historical time" and the "rhythms of natural time - the rhythms of the ecosystem earth and the biorhythms of the human body." This last harmonization is of vital significance, since "Either human history and the history of nature will arrive at a coordinated harmony, or human history will find its irrevocable end in ecological death."[133]

The modern detachment of human civilization from nature emerged in the context of a philosophy which defined our existence in terms of human hopes and purposes. Now time, defined by the clock, replaces that which is in harmony with the natural environment. Moltmann rejects history as the "fundamental symbol of the world" in the light of a world situation that has become "increasingly critical," rather than "progressively better."[134] His seeming rejection of history sits uncomfortably with his thesis in *Theology of Hope*, though he goes on to *redefine* history in a way which picks up some of his earlier theses.

Moltmann wishes to distance humankind from any absolute claim of history, whether it be based on our own individual present history or that of past tradition. His solution is a somewhat vague hope of an emergence of "a living relationalism in an intricate fabric of interconnectedness."[135] He outlines the practical outworkings of e) above in equally general terms. He recommends, for example, that we have "more systems of equilibrium," especially in the balance between progress and equilibrium which we mentioned briefly above.[136] He takes up this theme in *Creating a Just Future*.[137]

The "ecological wisdom" of ancient Chinese cultures is one which expresses the harmony of all things. This wisdom needs to be "translated" into our modern understanding of progress. Moltmann defines nature in its broadest possible category:

> "By 'nature' we mean the ecosystem of the earth, which through the atmosphere and biosphere receives and processes solar energy, and through the earth's rotation guarantees the cycles of day and night, summer and winter, rain and sunshine."[138]

He is quite insistent that he is not recommending an "arbitrary" or "romantic" return to nature, but a view that is necessary for our survival. He acknowledges the Abrahamic religions of Judaism, Christianity and Islam to be fundamentally religions of "historical existence." All these religions are "not nature religions, but religions of history, not religions of equilibrium and harmony but religions of conflict and hope."[139] The significance of the ancient Chinese wisdom is that it helps restore the balance between progress and equilibrium. However, in other contexts Moltmann makes it clear that the pantheism of these cultures is not included in his understanding, "whether in the philosophical form maintained by Spinoza, or in the mysticism of the Chinese *Tao*."[140]

A significant challenge to Moltmann's thesis is whether the idea of "equilibrium" is valid. Berry comments that the ideal of equilibrium and harmony of the natural world hardly does justice to conflict as the biological reality of existence[141] Even the idea of *Gaia*, which Moltmann refers to loosely in his discussion, tends towards equilibrium regardless of the cost in terms of loss of species. The latter raises the whole issue of the relative status of the natural world, compared with that of humankind.

(b) The status of the natural world.

While we will postpone a full discussion of the implications of Moltmann's understanding of nature, we will raise the issue here in so far as it bears on the relative status of humanity. He aims specifically to weaken an anthropological focus, which emerged in the context of history as the paradigm for theology. Instead he argues for a "cosmic theocentrism."[142]

The rights of humanity are only meaningful when "harmonized with the protective rights of the earth, and other living things, and have to become a part of these."[143] Moltmann believes human dignity is bound up with the dignity of all of God's creatures. The "fundamental" rights of nature are over and above human rights, for the sake of human survival. Moltmann does not wish to return to a "cosmocentrism" of ancient religions, which he vigorously rejected in

Theology of Hope, but believes that our anthropocentrism needs to be broadened into "the conditions for life on earth."[144] He finds biblical support for this view from reflection on the human community in the context of the whole creation, as in Psalm 104, and on an extension of the idea of the sabbath, which is given for the benefit of all God's creatures. God is in touch with all his creatures, who have "a certain subjectivity which human beings ought to respect."[145] Moreover, it is to these creatures that God can "speak his own language, through the laws of the earth and the characteristics of other creatures."[146]

Moltmann believes that evolution challenges us to reconsider the relative status of humankind. Darwin's evolutionary ideas "rocked the whole modern anthropocentric view of the world: the species human being is no more than one small link in an evolutionary sequence whose end cannot be foreseen."[147] It was this which caused such violent opposition from Christian circles. In addition Moltmann acknowledges a *real* threat of evolutionary theory once it encourages either a "materialist" or "pantheist" view of the world. He also draws back from "biomorphism, in which human conditions are supposed to be interpreted and regulated in the analogy of types of animal behaviour and forms of living."[148]

Moltmann avoids the traditional basis for the conflict between Genesis and scientific evolutionary theses, by considering the former to refer to the "miracle of existence," while the latter is the sphere of "making and ordering." Moltmann believes that evolution encourages us to see our life history as an "open process," which is compatible with his perception of the open-ended character of our existence. He balances this view with a vision of the sabbath, which is both part of our created existence and a foretaste of future glory.

(c) Reconciliation with Christ in the feast of the sabbath.

Moltmann believes that a vision for our future includes a reconciliation between God, humankind and nature in the peace of the sabbath.[149] The blessing of the sabbath is one which is in time, which "means that the sabbath blessing is universal, whereas the blessing given to one or the other creature remains particular and special to them."[150] Our self-understanding as humans made in the *imago Dei* reflects this image by resting on the sabbath. It is a foretaste of future glory, so that "though formally speaking the sabbath belongs to the cycle of human time, its nature allows it to break through the cyclical rebirth of natural time by prefiguring messianic time."[151] This insight gives the sabbath special significance, since it is a way of linking nature and history. It anticipates the future world of glory "in history."[152]

Moltmann acknowledges that the movement of redemption runs "counter to evolution."[153] Paul Fiddes criticizes Moltmann's sabbath ideal in *God in Creation*, because it seems to separate the impact of the world on God in the sabbath rest from the daily activity of the world. Hence: "It is apparently not in the works of his creatures that God comes to union and communion, but in their resting in him in workless contemplation. Yet if God truly has a desire to be glorified by his creation, as Moltmann himself insists, he will surely find satisfaction in the active response of the world, in all its work as well as worship."[154] While Fiddes finds an implicit danger here, namely that the work of creation itself is debased through the exaltation of the rôle of the creator, this is far from Moltmann's intention. The latter's particular understanding of contemplation is that it is rooted in activity, so that the sabbath rest, while being free from the restlessness of work, is not as passive as Fiddes implies. We will raise the issue of the justification of Moltmann's use of the sabbath ideal again later. Moltmann does seem to recognize a tension between the evolving universe and the recreation of the universe from "ahead," and he attempts to resolve this difficulty Christologically. *Christus evolutor* is the *Christ in his becoming*, while *Christus redemptor* is the *Christ in his coming*.[155] The cosmic Christ is the one who fills the space of all creation with the divine peace of *Shalom*, and all the time of creation with "the messianic extensity of redemption." By "extensity" he seems to refer to the whole breadth of time "to their fullest origins." Moltmann brings his discussion of the rights of all creatures into his Christological orbit:

> "The reconciliation of the whole cosmos through Christ is for the justification of all created beings who have been injured and who have lost their rights, and aims at the implementation of God's righteousness and justice, which alone secures the life and peace of creation."[156]

Christ is, then, the foundation of a community, based on law "in the cosmos as well as among God's people." His peace is the basis of reconciliation "in the depths of the human heart" and with the whole human community and whole creation. The dignity of all creatures "is conferred on them by God's love *towards* them, Christ giving of himself *for* them, and the indwelling of the Holy Spirit **in** them."[157] The latter gives a Trinitarian flavour to Moltmann's discussion of the identity of all creatures.

10. Conclusions.

We are now in a position to reach some tentative conclusions about the emergence of Moltmann's anthropology in the context of his ecological doctrine of creation.

1.   The starting point for Moltmann's understanding of a doctrine of God is in the context of the theodicy question. Just as our knowledge of self grows in relationship to our knowledge of God, through prayer, so our ability to live a fully human life is one that, like the God of the pathos, enters into the suffering both of our inner selves and outward relationships.

2.   The social Trinitarian basis for God gives us the paradigm of our human existence as that intimately connected with others, including the whole of creation. We find such symbiotic interrelationship operating at the physical, medical level of body and soul, the religious level of individuals in community, and the legal level in our covenant relationship with nature. Our basis for living should stem from communion and harmony with all of God's creation, rather than domination over it for our own benefit.

3.   In this ecological context the primary characteristic of our image-bearing comes through *imago mundi*. Here Moltmann draws on both scientific evidence for the physical continuation between the natural world and human life, and the Orthodox tradition of humanity as microcosm. However, our self-understanding is not finalized here in terms of our self-perception as the "crown of creation." Instead, our self-awareness is only possible once nature in cosmic dimensions forms the setting for our future. Until nature is appreciated as having a subjective basis independent of humans, the meaning of interrelationship remains shallow and distorted. Rather, our fundamental need for a home as well as our need for work needs to be brought into balance.

4.   Humankind created in the *imago Dei* has at least three dimensions. The idea of humankind as steward of creation is only possible if we understand creation as loved by God, rather than given to us for our own manipulation. This does not render us passive in relationship with creation, but we engage with it from a holistic perspective, rather than from one tailored to our own needs. The second dimension of *imago Dei* is that which reflects the Godhead in its Trinitarian aspect. This is not a literal equivalence, but where our social existence as men and women reflects the perichoretic life of the Trinity. It moves us away from seeing the *imago Dei* in narrowly individualistic or rationalistic terms, towards that of the *imago Dei* emerging in the context of community life. The parallel of our image-bearing with the life of the Trinity does not permit us to view God either in male categories or sexual terms, but it allows us to resist the temptation to view God as somehow over and above our earthly, sexual existence. Finally our status as *imago Dei* is also a future hope, only realized in eschatological terms where we express the glory of God in the sabbath rest.

5.   Closely related to the idea of *imago Dei* is the vision of ourselves as *imago Christi*, indeed our image-bearing becomes that of Christ through justification and sanctification once we see *imago Dei* in messianic light. Christ

in his incarnation is the full expectation and hope of *imago Dei*, while Christ in his coming is the power of the new creation which transforms us to *imago Christi*, and ultimately to *gloria Dei*. It is in Christ's person that our human identity becomes most fully present. He shares our human body, soul and *Gestalt*, which is at the same time the Son of the Father in Trinitarian fellowship. Our entry into this fellowship is through our analogy with the Son, rather than through our analogy with the whole Trinity. Yet the three persons of the Trinity are involved in transforming humans so that they become *imago Christi*. In fellowship with Christ we share in his suffering, but also in his resurrection and glory. In fellowship with Christ we find reconciliation with ourselves, with others and with the natural world.

6.   The tension between our self-understanding as frail, sinful creatures and our salvation in Christ only makes sense once we view our image-bearing in relational terms rather than through an analogy of substance. The loss of our image is not absolute, but is only related to our distorted relationship with God. God's relationship with us remains constant through his faithfulness and grace in spite of our sinfulness. Our sinfulness defined in terms of relationships is primarily that of closing ourselves off from the love of God, and one another. This closedness becomes expressed through a category of freedom which insists on power and domination instead of acknowledgement of the social network of relationships.

7.   Our future vision of ourselves as *gloria Dei* makes sense only in the context of the gathered community of all of God's creatures. This future is one that comes from God himself when he indwells fully in creation and makes it his home. The tensions of suffering creation become resolved in a future glorious *Shalom* for all creation. This abiding presence of God is anticipated in the action of the Holy Spirit in our lives and in the healing of broken relationships.

8.   The abiding Spirit of creation interpenetrates our body, soul and *Gestalt* so that all of our history is caught up in the life of God. The Holy Spirit brings a transformation of ourselves so that we achieve a harmony within, between our inner and outer consciousness of soul and body and a harmony without, in our own particular *Gestalt*.

9.   Our relationship with nature calls into question our own preoccupation with ourselves in our historical existence. Yet this does not signal a return to the cosmology of the ancient world, but an integration of ecological wisdom into our historical awareness. Indeed our own survival depends on such awareness, which embraces a recognition of the rights of nature alongside our human rights. The future vision of the world under the lordship of the cosmic Christ brings us a new hope for the future, one that does not end in despair, but a history shaped by a Christological understanding of our humanity in the context of the whole of God's creation.

End Notes.

All books and articles are by Jürgen Moltmann unless stated otherwise. Translations are from the German text.

1. GC, p. iv.

2. TKG, p. 49.

3. *Ibid.*, pp. 50-51.

4. *Ibid.*, p. 60.

5. *Ibid.*, p. 99.

6. *Ibid.*, pp. 103-104.

7. "Teresa of Avila and Martin Luther: The Turn to the Mysticism of the Cross," *Studies in Religion*, 13, 1984, pp. 265-278.

8. *Ibid.*, p. 275.

9. TKG, p. 106. Moltmann distinguishes here between "blissful love," which is the response of like being, and "creative love," which, by overcoming its opposite, has transforming power and creates life out of death. For the latter he draws on Romans 4.7. This is the reason why the divine love "presses even beyond the Trinity."

10. *Ibid.*, p. 106.

11. GC, p. 3.

12. *Ibid.*, p. 5.

13. *Ibid.*, p. 7.

14. *Ibid.*, pp. 8-9. A possible challenge to Moltmann's view is whether a symbiotic eschatological doctrine of humanity requires a rejection of perfection in the beginning.

15. *Ibid.*, p. 17.

16. *Ibid.*, p. 18.

17. *Ibid.*, p. 18.

18. CC, pp. 93-105; see also ECPN, pp. 1-11. Moltmann's free use of the *Gaia* terminology gives us the uneasy impression that he is using these ideas in an uncritical way, and absorbing them into his own position. We will raise this again later, and in the following chapter.

19. GC, p .22.

20. *Ibid.*, p. 24.

21. *Ibid.*, p. 25.

22. *Ibid.*, p. 26.

23. *Ibid.*, p. 27. This raises the controversy fuelled by Lynn White's analysis in which he concluded that Christianity's interpretation of the idea of dominion not only was responsible for

the rise in experimental science, but also was largely to blame for the ecological crisis; see, L. White, "The Historical Roots of our Ecological Crisis," *Science,* 145, 1967, pp. 1203-1207.

24. *Ibid.,* p. 29.

25. *Ibid.,* pp. 30-31.

26. *Ibid.,* p. 32.

27. *Ibid.,* p. 37.

28. *Ibid.,* p. 39.

29. *Ibid.,* p. 41.

30. *Ibid.,* p. 42. We will discuss Bloch's position and his influence on Moltmann's understanding of nature in more detail later.

31. *Ibid.,* p. 43.

32. *Ibid.,* p. 46. For a parallel discussion see, "The Alienation and Liberation of Nature," in, L. Rouner, ed., *On Nature,* Indiana, University of Notre Dame Press, 1984, pp. 133-144.

33. GC, p. 51.

34. *Ibid.,* p. 51.

35. *Ibid.,* pp. 70-71.

36. *Ibid.,* p. 186.

37. *Ibid.,* pp. 187-188.

38. Bauckham comments that Moltmann's use of creation narratives is such that he tends to "squeeze theological significance out of them in a way which is too little controlled by historical exegesis"; R. Bauckham, "Evolution and Creation: In Moltmann's Doctrine of Creation," *Epworth Review,* 15, 1988, pp. 74-81.

39. GC, p. 189.

40. *Ibid.,* p. 190. Moltmann is creatively imaginative in the way he combines Eastern Orthodox tradition with scientific theory in order to support his idea of humankind as microcosm in creation. However, it is doubtful if this is a fair use of biological concepts; and we will raise the general question as to the legitimacy of Moltmann's use of biological ideas subsequently.

41. *Ibid.,* p. 188.

42. *The Power of the Powerless;* translated by M. Kohl, London, SCM, 1983, p. 7; hereafter referred to as PP.

43. GC, p. 188.

44. PP, p.6.

45. GC, p. 188.

46. *Ibid.,* p. 224.

47. "Human Rights: The Rights of Humanity and the Rights of Nature"; translated by M. Kohl, in, H. Küng and J. Moltmann, eds., *The Ethics of World Religions and Human Rights, Concilium*, 2 ,1990, London, SCM, 1990, pp. 120-135; hereafter referred to as HR,RN.

48. TKG, pp. 116-117.

49. *Ibid.*, p. 118.

50. GC, p. 77.

51. *Ibid.*, p. 78.

52. *Ibid.*, pp. 218-219.

53. *Ibid.*, p. 220.

54. *Ibid.*, pp. 220-221.

55. *Ibid.*, pp. 235-240.

56. G. Leonard, "Moltmann on Creation," *Cross Currents*, 36(4), 1987, pp. 470-471.

57. GC, p. 241.

58. *Ibid.*, p. 223.

59. *Ibid.*, p. 223. We will discuss the influence of feminist theology on Moltmann's position in more detail later.

60. *Ibid.*, p. 242.

61. *Ibid.*, pp. 244 ff., see also ECPN.

62. *Ibid.*, p. 249. We will discuss Moltmann's use of Eastern Orthodox traditions later.

63. G. Leonard, *op. cit.* (n.56), p. 473.

64. GC, p. 257.

65. J. McIntyre, "Review of *God in Creation* by Jürgen Moltmann," *Scottish Journal of Theology*, 41(2), 1988, pp. 267-273.

66. W. Barr, "Review of Jürgen Moltmann's *God in Creation*," *Lexington Theological Quarterly*, (USA), 21, 1986, pp. 60-62.

67. TKG, pp. 121-124.

68. *Ibid.*, p. 158.

69. GC, pp. 225 ff.

70. *Ibid.*, p. 226.

71. *Ibid.*, p 227.

72. *Ibid.*, p 227.

73. WJC, p. 149.

74. *Ibid.*, pp. 260-261.

75. *Ibid.*, p. 262; see also pp. 266 ff.

76. GC, pp. 242-243.

77. *Ibid.*, p. 242.

78. *Ibid.*, p. 226.

79. *Ibid.*, p. 229.

80. *Ibid.*, p. 233.

81. G. Leonard, *op. cit.* (n.56), p. 473.

82. GC, p. 233.

83. PP, p. 4.

84. GC, p. 233.

85. *Ibid.*, p. 234.

86. TKG, p. 210.

87. *Ibid.*, p. 211.

88. *Ibid.*, p. 216.

89. *Ibid.*, p. 217.

90. PP, pp. 26-27.

91. *Ibid.*, pp. 42-43.

92. R. Cole-Turner, "Review of *God in Creation* by Jürgen Moltmann," *Zygon*, 22(1), 1987, pp. 120-122.

93. B. Walsh, "*Theology of Hope* and Doctrine of Creation: An Appraisal of Jürgen Moltmann," *Evangelical Quarterly*, 59(1), 1987, pp. 53-76. Hafstad criticizes Moltmann's seeming extension of the concept of closedness as applied to the relationship of all creation to God, and asks if it is possible to speak of nature in such anthropomorphic terms. She accurately identifies the problem here of a combination of the idea of closedness, which comes from metaphors connected with the kingdom of God, and the idea of openness, which comes from scientific theory. We will return to a discussion of Moltmann's understanding of open systems again later. K. Hafstad, "Gott in der Natur: Zur Schöpfungslehre Jürgen Moltmanns," *Evangelische Theologie*, 47, 1987, pp. 460-466.

94. TKG, pp. 49-50.

95. GC, p. 272.

96. *Ibid.*, p. 273.

97. PP, p. 149.

98. GC, p. 275.

99. *Ibid.*, p. 226.

100. *Ibid.*, p. 227.

101. *Ibid.*, p. 229.

102. *Ibid.*, p. 229.

103. *Ibid.*, p. 265.

104. *Ibid.*, p. 265.

105. *Ibid.*, p. 266.

106. *Ibid.*, p. 268.

107. *Ibid.*, p. 268.

108. *Ibid.*, p. 270.

109. *Ibid.*, p. 270.

110. *Ibid.*, p. 259.

111. *Ibid.*, p. 259.

112. *Ibid.*, p. 259.

113. *Ibid.*, pp. 260-261.

114. *Ibid.*, p. 261.

115. *Ibid.*, p. 261.

116. *Ibid.*, p. 262.

117. *Ibid.*, p. 262.

118. *Ibid.*, p. 263.

119. *Ibid.*, p. 263. For a comment on Moltmann's understanding of the Spirit see J. McIntyre, *op. cit.* (n.65). In a more recent article Moltmann insists that the creating Spirit who breathes into all creation is the Holy Spirit. The Trinitarian perichoretic unity of Father, Son and Spirit safeguards the transcendence of God, and allows an identification of the Spirit with relationship, and everything living, SBH, p. 118.

120. *Ibid.*, p. 267.

121. *Ibid.*, p. 270.

122. *Ibid.*, p. 275.

123. WJC, p. 262.

124. *Ibid.*, p. 262.

125. *Ibid.*, p. 266.

126. *Ibid.*, p. 268.

127. GC, p. 116.

128. WJC, p. 268.

129. "The Ethics of Biomedical Research and the Newer Biomedical Technologies", in, S. Blesh, ed.., *Recent Progress in Biology and Medicine*, C.I.O.M.S., Paris, Unesco House, 1972, pp. 68-72.

130. GC, p. 98.

131. *Ibid.*, p. 101.

132. *Ibid.*, p. 125.

133. *Ibid.*, p. 126.

134. *Ibid.*, p. 128.

135. *Ibid.*, p. 132.

136. *Ibid.*, p. 138.

137. CJF, pp. 87-101; see also, "In Search for an Equilibrium of 'Equilibrium' and 'Progress," *Ching Feng*, 30, 1987, pp. 5-17.

138. *Ibid.*, p. 14.

139. CJF, p. 96.

140. GC, p. 102.

141. R. Berry, "On Building the Kingdom in Our World: Review of *Creating a Just Future* by Jürgen Moltmann," *Church Times*, 10 Nov., 1979, p. 11.

142. GC, p. 139.

143. HR,RN, p. 121.

144. *Ibid.*, p. 131; see also CC for a similar treatment.

145. HR,RN, p. 131.

146. CJF, p. 74.

147. GC, p. 193.

148. *Ibid.*, p. 195.

149. *Ibid.*, p. 277.

150. *Ibid.*, p. 283; for similar themes see ECPN.

151. *Ibid.*, p. 286.

152. *Ibid.*, p. 287.

153. WJC, p. 303.

154. P. Fiddes, "Review of *God in Creation*," *Journal of Theological Studies*, 38, 1987, pp. 263-265.

155. WJC, p. 303.

156. *Ibid.*, p. 312.

157. *Ibid.*, p. 307.

CHAPTER 5

A Critical Appreciation of Moltmann's Ecological Doctrine of Creation.

Part A. Foundation in Trinitarian Theology.

1. Introduction.

We have intended Part 2 to show the emergence of Jürgen Moltmann's ecological doctrine of creation in the context of his Trinitarian framework. His priority to rethink our understanding of God in Trinitarian and pneumatological terms has helped shape his understanding of the multiple relationships between God and the world, with humankind placed in the broadest possible context of social interrelationships within the whole of creation. It is our thesis so far that the theme of interrelationships, which predominates in Moltmann's discussion, renders his thinking implicitly "ecological".

Our aim in the present chapter is to look more closely at the basis for Moltmann's insistence on a social doctrine of the Trinity and how this relates to his understanding of the relationship between God and creation. His method is thoroughly eclectic in a way that gathers up, in an imaginative way, ideas from a range of different sources and influences. We will be looking more closely at those sources which are of particular significance, and hope to show how he has transformed this material into his theological framework, which retains a Christological basis with an eschatological direction. He feels free to draw key metaphors from these sources without using their original basis in a way that may challenge us to question whether he is really engaging in true dialogue. In general, Moltmann is certainly no favourite for the specialist, and he paints his theology on a broad canvas in a way that may irritate some readers.[1] Nonetheless, those who appreciate impressionist art cannot fail to admire the sheer scope and range of his ideas, which, though they can at times leave one gasping for breath, always succeed in creating an impact and leading to further reflection. We will be trying, as far as possible, to focus on difficulties in Moltmann's theological reconstruction which affect the overall pattern, rather than dwelling on details of his approach which may be somewhat inaccurate or exaggerated.

We have divided this discussion into two parts in order to make this material more manageable. The first part, which forms the bulk of this chapter, is concerned with a critical review of Moltmann's understanding of the social Trinity according to his definition of the ecological dynamics of "interrelationships" and "indwelling". We will examine, therefore, the basis for his social doctrine of the Trinity, and whether he has succeeded in linking this doctrine with his particular ecological understanding of humankind and creation. We will show Moltmann's distinct contribution to a doctrine of the Trinity by a comparison of his social Trinitarianism with those theological positions most influential in his work, including Barth, Eastern Orthodoxy, feminist theology and Ernst Bloch's philosophy. We will also examine his ecological idea of home within God in himself drawn from *kabbalah*, with particular reference to the Jewish basis and source of this material. The changing dynamics of the relationship between God and creation as portrayed in Moltmann's theology, mark a shift in his theology which makes it more "green" than previously. It also brings his views on the dynamics of the relationship between God and creation closer to process theology, and we will assess the latter's impact and significance for the development of his thought. We will be asking how he manages to harmonize these ideas with the Old Testament witness in Genesis and his intention to engage in dialogue with biological science.

The second part of this critique, which forms the bulk of the next chapter, will assess the coherence of his method within his own concern for an eschatological theology. We will be raising questions such as: how adequate is his vision of the future of creation in the light of scientific concern?; how far does he give priority to history over nature and what is the relationship between them?; and the broader question of whether his Christological paradigm, which resurfaces in *The Way of Jesus Christ*, is adequate to offset some of the tensions that he has set up in *God in Creation*. We will be asking ourselves whether his understanding of Christology is successful as a paradigm for a truly Christian theology that is relevant in our "green" cultural climate. Overall, we hope to show lines of continuity as well as discontinuity in Moltmann's thinking. We disagree with critiques of Moltmann which have purported a:

> "Grand reversal of theological direction and sensibility, a seismic shift from a focus on history, eschatology and 'openness to the future' to one on nature, creation and respect for 'dwelling' within the present."[2]

We hope to show here that, far from causing a "seismic shift", Moltmann's thoroughly Trinitarian doctrine of creation has kept his theology broadly within its original parameters. His tendency to exaggerate in places, especially in his discussion of the *Gaia* hypothesis, gives the impression that he has reversed his thinking. However, we are more of the opinion that his method is closer to that of a dialectical approach, where philosophical exaggerations are necessary in such a way that "their emergence is essential to the final result and is in some sense 'preserved' in it."[3] We will be raising the issue later in this chapter as to whether Moltmann is justified in using ideas from *Gaia* and other more controversial hypotheses which, though "scientific", have religious undertones. He has certainly managed to confuse many of his readers about exactly where he is finding his philosophical bearings. Some have falsely depicted his understanding as being that of "a World Mother, - stripped of its mythical description and bolstered by theological and philosophical arguments, it is precisely this view of the world that Moltmann defends in this book."[4]

While Moltmann does seem to toy with the idea of "world mother", he is perhaps attempting to draw on mythological strands which strike chords with feminist theology. By this we mean theology which welcomes feminine metaphors and takes seriously early primordial images of creation. Moltmann is not alone in this view, as we shall see from our discussion of his exegesis of Old Testament texts. He is also following his mentor, Ernst Bloch, who took seriously both the women's movement and mythological ways of expressing faith.[5] Indeed, Bloch was even more forthright in his use of ideas considered by others to be heretical, preferring *kabbalah* to orthodox Judaism and incorporating Schelling's romantic understanding of nature into his Marxist historical framework.[6] While Moltmann is influenced by Bloch, it is clear that, as in his earlier *Theology of Hope*, he brings Bloch's philosophy into a thoroughly Christian understanding of the relationship between God and the world. Much of this is shaped by a Barthian attitude, although it has been denuded of most traces of monarchical overtones. Above all, the Christ mysticism of Luther's theology forms a key paradigm for Moltmann.

2. Person and subject in God, humanity and nature.

(a) Reflections in the light of Karl Barth's theology.

We showed in chapter 3 how Moltmann rejects a doctrine of the Trinity that focuses on divine unity and sovereignty in favour of one which begins with God's tri-unity and loving inter-Trinitarian relationships. Our purpose here is to show how far he has moved beyond a Barthian approach. Moltmann portrays a thoroughly social doctrine of the Trinity which understands the unity of the Triune God coming not so much from a unity of substance, or a unity in subject, as a unity of relationships. Karl Barth believed that the use of the terminology 'three persons' to describe the inner Trinitarian relationship is inadequate. It becomes, for Augustine, a *necessitas* or *consuetudo loquendi*, and as such a "really suitable term for it just does not exist."[7] In order to avoid the impression gained by three persons that three essences exist, Barth decided to replace person with three "modes of being". While Moltmann attacked Barth on this point accusing him of "modalism", it is significant that Barth, like Moltmann, understands the Godhead "in terms of their distinctive relations, and indeed their distinctive genetic relations to one another."[8]

We consider that Moltmann's view of the Trinity goes beyond that of Barth in its eschatological emphasis on the sovereignty of God in the future, which aims to counter a hierarchical understanding of the Trinity. We agree with Claybrook that the crucial difference between Barth and Moltmann is that the former roots his Trinitarian scheme in the sovereignty of God.[9] Another key difference lies in Barth's insistence on the Triunity of God coming from the idea of revelation, which tends to detach it from the concrete realization of the revelation of Jesus Christ in the New Testament. We identify with the opinion that prefers Moltmann's approach to that of either Barth or Rahner, for "one still feels with Barth and Rahner that the Trinitarian skeleton needs real flesh."[10]

Moltmann's claim to root his Trinitarian doctrine more firmly in Jesus' history led to his insistence in *The Crucified God* that the economic and immanent Trinities are identical.[11] Barth challenged Moltmann on this issue.[12] A possible misinterpretation of Moltmann's understanding of the immanent Trinity in his earlier work is raised by Olsen, who incorrectly believed it becomes "a passive product of an historical process."[13] However, we think that Moltmann's response to such criticism, which was to insist on an active and distinct immanent Trinity, was made less convincing by his detailed speculation on the pre-existent life of the immanent Trinity. One of the strengths of Moltmann's later formulations of the immanent Trinity in *The Trinity and the*

Kingdom of God is its dynamic character. It is the inner life of the Trinity which finds outward expression, as we showed in earlier chapters. Moltmann's mistake is to speak of the pre-existence of the immanent Trinity in a way that rather too easily allows him to indulge in speculation that does not seem to take adequate account of the limits to which we can use analogies to describe God.[14] Perhaps Barth is more careful in qualifying his statements, and by setting limits on what can be known of what happens in the life of the Godhead, both renders it more cautious than Moltmann's approach, yet rather more arid.[15] Moltmann's failure lies in the opposite direction, namely in speaking boldly of the inner life of the Godhead in a way which at times seems inappropriate.

Mason also compares Moltmann's approach to the Trinity with that of Barth. He notes a critical difference in their approach and affirms Barth's emphasis on a subordinate relationship between Father and Son.[16] However, we would be more sympathetic with Ford's view that Barth is unjustified in his claim that the I- Thou relation which exists in the Godhead becomes a prototype of the divine/human encounter and the male/female encounter.[17] Barth puts the subordinate relationship of God and Christ in parallel with the relationship of male and female in a way which reinforces the subordination of female to male. Barth still claims to wish to defeat tyranny of all kinds and insists that there is no essential difference between male and female as regards mutual co-operation. However, his use of analogy tends in the opposite direction, namely a reinforcement of the hierarchical structure of society. Moltmann's brilliance in this respect is that he allows for both aspects of co-operation and ordering in the interpersonal relationships of the Trinity. He claims that the inner Trinitarian relations, which are in mutual co-operation, still allow for a monarchical rôle of the Father in origin, if not in function. One of Moltmann's most significant achievements in his understanding of the Trinity is the way he has raised the profile of Trinitarian thought, but in a way which challenges the hierarchical reconstruction of Barth in favour of a thoroughly ecological and social model.

(b) Reflections in the light of Orthodoxy.

Moltmann also shows imaginative brilliance in his turn to the Eastern church to find support for his ideas. He draws on the Eastern Fathers' idea of *perichoresis* to support his social doctrine of the Trinity. Some scholars have commented on his rather haphazard treatment of details in this part of his work.[18] Moltmann may not be correct in his belief that the term *perichoresis* originally came from John of Damascus.[19] Moltmann also goes beyond traditional concepts of *perichoresis* in a way which gives the idea a more dynamic character.[20] He has correctly insisted that Eastern Orthodoxy begins with the plurality of subjects and moves to their unity, even though the Western church has interpreted *perichoresis* in a way which still gives primacy to God's unity.[21] However, the American Orthodox theologian, Havrilak, believes that while Eastern tradition supports the idea that one will and one intelligence, as aspects of God's one nature, are shared perichoretically in the Godhead, this is contra Moltmann's view which understands the reality of three distinct "wills and intellects."[22] While Havrilak is correct in noting that Moltmann's understanding of *perichoresis* goes beyond that of the Eastern church, we believe that the charge of "tritheism" in Moltmann's treatment of the doctrine of creation is quite unjustified. Moltmann's preference to let unity emerge from perichoretic movement is a more novel way of expressing the unity of God, but still sufficient to counter the charge of tritheism. Also, Moltmann acknowledges the unity of the divine nature, as we will discuss more fully below.

While we will take up a full discussion of the influence of feminist ideas on Moltmann's thought in a later section, it is worth mentioning briefly how feminist ideas are used by him to go beyond the traditional understanding of *perichoresis*. He acknowledges Patricia Wilson-Kastner's understanding of *perichoresis* as a "circle dance" which is united in a complete movement and shows the characteristics of both intense liveliness with peace in an open inviting unity.[23]

The ancient meaning of person lacked ontological content in the ancient Greek world, as against *hypostasis*, which means individual existence or nature. Later, the Cappodocian Fathers allowed a parallel treatment of the term *prosopon* with *hypostasis*. The idea of person in the Roman world was more closely identified with rôle or task. The concept of person in the Latin usage had to be deepened ontologically if it was to be applied to the doctrine of the Trinity.[24] The modern understanding of person as self-consciousness is one of the reasons why Barth is reluctant to use person as applied to the Trinity.[25]

Zizioulas' position is close to Moltmann when he claims that: "the life of God is eternal because it is personal, that is to say it is realized as an expression of free communion, as love."[26] The similarity with Moltmann's idea of person becomes reinforced still further by his suggestion that the truth and ontology of a person is eschatological in character. However, he does not go as far as Moltmann in suggesting that the ontological character of the Trinity has a future dimension. We consider that it is Moltmann's determination to put all his theological reflections into an eschatological key which marks an important difference between his position and that of Orthodoxy. However, it is of interest that in Moltmann's more recent works he seems to be coming closer to Zizioulas in his idea of the "eternal present" in God, which implies an ontology that is not so futuristic as in his earlier works.[27]

Dumitry Staniloae is another modern Orthodox theologian who insists that the divine subjectivity is not that of a single "I", rather we find internal inter-subjectivity whereby: "The Father experiences Himself as Father, but He simultaneously experiences as Father all the subjectivity of the Son. The Son is interior to Him, but as to a Father."[28] Moreover, the interior love of God is a necessary prerequisite for the love of God directed to the external world. His sense of the inward relational love of the Trinity coming to expression in outward love for the world is similar to Moltmann's position. The Spirit as Person becomes more than just the love experienced between the Father and

Son, and is necessary to prevent any "confusion" between Father and Son.[29] It is here that a difficulty in all social expressions of the inner life of the Trinity become visible: namely how far are we justified in speaking of the Spirit as a "person"? The Spirit's identity in relationship with Father and Son does not really clarify for us exactly what this personhood means. Moreover, the Spirit refuses to be categorized in any way, and remains the "faceless" person of the Trinity. Nonetheless, it is still hard for us to imagine ways of describing the identity of the Spirit without using the word "person". For all the possible problems in using such language, we are of the opinion, as we hinted above, that the Trinity can be described as three "persons".

Moltmann is rather obscure in how he imagines the inner social *perichoresis* finding practical expression in the life of the economic Trinity. We will be raising this issue again in our discussions of his Christological paradigm in the next chapter. For our present purposes we wish to point out that the social doctrine of the Trinity, in which Moltmann finds a basis for his understanding of the sociality in all creation, sits somewhat uneasily alongside his kenotic Christology, with its stress on the human person of Christ. He rejects the Orthodox Christology which speaks of the two natures of Christ in favour of a fully human understanding of the Christ's personality.[30] While this may be a necessary corrective to the docetic flavour of some of the more traditional theologies, he seems to make little attempt to clarify exactly how the person of the Son of the immanent Trinity is to be related to the person of the human Jesus. If the two are identical then he needs once more to abandon any notion of pre-existence of the Son, and once more modify his understanding of the immanent Trinity as distinct from the economic Trinity.

(c) Reflections in the light of feminist theology.

Our intention in this section is to examine how feminist ideas have helped to shape Moltmann's Trinitarian understanding of God and creation. We will postpone treatment of the influence of feminist theology which draws on process thought until we have discussed the broader influence of process theology.

Moltmann depicts the Spirit in female categories and hopes thereby to introduce the idea of feminine in God.[31] In this he goes beyond a traditional understanding of Orthodox theology, though the idea of female images having some influence on patristic theology cannot be ruled out.[32] While these influences may help soften theology that has become immunized against change by its exclusive use of male categories, we agree with Elizabeth Johnson that depicting the Holy Spirit in female terms can actually reinforce the false equation of transcendence/immanence with male/female.[33] More significantly, perhaps, once the Holy Spirit acquires a female disposition, far from acquiring a true sense of personhood, it associates the Holy Spirit with impersonal images of the female goddess characteristic of pre-Christian thought. As we noted in an earlier chapter, Moltmann draws back from an understanding of the Godhead in sexual categories, while recognizing that this is part of our human understanding of what it means to be a person. He is surely right in resisting the temptation to read back into God a literal understanding of a sexual dimension in God based on the idea of what it means for us to be in his image. However, his notion that the Trinitarian relationships are non-sexual does not seem to cohere well with his idea that the Holy Spirit, as depicted in female terms, gives value to femaleness as such.

A further development of this issue in Judaism is relevant here. Scholem has pointed out that whereas the tendency in Christian mysticism has been to describe the relationship between God and man in erotic images, that more characteristic of Jewish mysticism has been to identify the relation in the Godhead as that between I and You, the King and the Queen. He considers that the introduction of the feminine into the idea of the *Shekinah* was "one of the most important and lasting innovations of kabbalism."[34] Perhaps it is significant that this idea was also a major stumbling block for Jewish philosophers. Indeed:

"Dimly we perceive behind this mystical image the male and female gods of antiquity, anathema as they were to the pious kabbalist."[35]

We can identify with the view of Catherine La Cugna, who believes that while metaphorical theology may serve to restore the poetic and imagistic flavour lost by "scholastic" and "historicist" theologies, the opposite danger, namely that of metaphorical reductionism, is more problematic. We need to ask ourselves: Does Moltmann's view verge on metaphorical reductionism? Moltmann would agree with La Cugna, in intention at least, that Trinitarian theology should be "rooted in the mystery and death of Jesus, rather than abstractly theistic or metaphysical or linguistic."[36] The problem with Moltmann's depiction of Trinitarian inter-relations is that, while in a positive sense it is poetic and imaginative, he moves beyond his stated boundaries in a way that gives his theology a flavour which tends to alienate both traditional systematic theologians concerned with philosophical accuracy, and those, such as La Cugna, searching for more imaginative ways of depicting the doctrine of the Trinity. He begins to move into speculative theology without clarifying the limits to his use of analogical language as applied to the Trinitarian relationships, a matter which we raised earlier.

One of the main characteristics of feminist writing has been to draw our attention to the importance of our experience of God in human communities, though more especially the communities of women. Moltmann's theology shows an increasing awareness of the importance of interrelationships, and he attempts to compare the symbiotic life of human communities and that between ourselves and our natural environmnent with the Trinitarian inter-relationships. He uses the term "*perichoresis*" to imply an analogy between the two, and by doing so he combines ideas from feminist thought and Orthodoxy in a way that is thoroughly original. While Moltmann is not entirely novel in his use of the analogy of *perichoresis*, he extends the boundary of the analogy beyond the church. The idea of perichoretic relationships existing in an imperfect way amongst members of the church is part of traditional theology.[37] John McIntyre suggests that Moltmann has gone too far in extending the idea of *perichoresis* beyond the human community. However, his criticism that the way Moltmann uses this analogy fails to "leave space for the ultimate difference between God and his creation" is not really justified, since analogy does not imply identity, and in any case McIntyre seems to accept that perichoretic relations do apply to human beings.[38]

Primavesi, an eco-feminist scholar, has attacked Moltmann's theology as failing really to appreciate the fact that our relationship with the world is not simply determined by our relationship with God, but involves a choice between good and evil. Moltmann would probably argue that the latter is conditioned by the former. Nonetheless, it is difficult for those who have come to reject the Christological understanding of the revelation of God to follow Moltmann's reasoning. For "post-Christian" theology: "Creation as God's glory is at best a hollow concept to those who are reacting from within to its possible imminent destruction."[39] We believe that while these charges may be justified from a post-Christian perspective, Moltmann is sensitive to the ecological situation from within his paradigm of Christology as the criterion for Christian theology. We also disagree with the charge that his views are completely incompatible with ecology's valuation of nature for its own sake, indeed he attempts to incorporate this idea into his doctrine of creation. His failure lies in his apparent lack of perception of the difficulty in how we are to respond to creation in a practical scientific and technological culture, given the present orientation of technology, and given his insistence on nature as subject.[40]

Moltmann's affinity with feminist theology from his own perspective comes through those writers who affirm a theology of mutual relation.[41] It is quite clear, however, that he would not identify with the equation of God with the power of interrelationships. This reductionist approach is openly acknowledged by Isobel Carter-Heyward who states: "I believe that God is our power in relation to each other, all humanity, and creation itself."[42] Later this statement is qualified somewhat by a weak reference to the possibility of God acting independently of human beings.[43] She also has a stinging criticism of Moltmann's own view, believing that the emphasis is far too much on God's inner life, and not enough on humanity.[44] While it seems to us that there is an element of truth in what she says, in that Moltmann does devote rather too much attention to a detailed description of God's inner life for a theology of creation; we are in broad agreement with Moltmann's intention to re-image our understanding of God, prior to a disussion of our relationship with the world.

Our final criticism of Moltmann's social doctrine of the Trinity is his belief that this view automatically fosters harmonious human social relationships, and relationships with non-human creation. Brown argues that the links between patriarchy, the unity model of Trinitarian theology, and dominance in society are questionable from a historical perspective.[45] Maurice Wiles, similarly, insists that the correlation that Moltmann finds between the Christian doctrine of God and social and political attitudes is "very hard to determine."[46] However, while we do not dispute the dubious character of the factual evidence for close linkage between concepts of God and changes in social attitudes, we do agree with Moltmann in his insistence that religious factors are a vital ingredient in changing attitudes in society at the broadest level.

(d) Reflections in the light of Ernst Bloch's philosophy.

While we have noted that Moltmann reinforces his understanding of the social relationship within the Godhead from his Christian heritage in Barth and Orthodoxy, he aligns himself with Bloch in his understanding of the relationship between human beings and creation. Moltmann believes that P.J. Proudhon introduced the idea of mutuality into social science, but he insists that the concept of mutual help was an idea which emerged much earlier in the first Christian communities. It seems to us that this answers the criticism of Stroup that Moltmann's social and political attitudes form the basis for Moltmann's argument for a social Trinity. Rather, it is understanding ourselves in mutual relation, which has its basis in *imago Dei*, that reinforces the ideas of sociality at the socio-political level.[47]

Lønning makes some important observations on the influence of Bloch on Moltmann's theology of creation. He believes that Moltmann rejects a traditional stance of a creator God standing at the beginning of the world and supporting the political order, in favour of God as one coming to meet creation.[48] Bloch gives Moltmann a future ontology of creation, a matter which we will raise again in the next chapter. We also wish to add that Bloch's concept of sociality reinforces Moltmann's understanding of the importance of social relationships, though as we noted above, we do not believe that Moltmann uses this interpretation as the basis for his concept of a social Trinity.

Bloch's link between capitalism and the denunciation of nature in favour of a socialist politic is somewhat out-dated, and Moltmann is well aware of the potential of either capitalist or socialist systems to treat nature as a commodity. Moltmann prefers to speak more in terms which contrast the Western view of the world, which aims at economic growth and domination, with the more passive Eastern view.[49] For Bloch, the final alienation between ourselves and nature amounts to a powerful evil force, so that "this artificiality is in fact at the same time the *Negativum* emerging at the end ever more clearly in the break in the graphically physical guideline itself."[50]

Bloch believes that the potentialities of nature could be released through an alliance technology in such a way that mediates with the "co-productivity of nature". Nature is not so much ready-made, as waiting to become our home and our "building site". At the same time we have: "The real possibility of a subject of nature ...."[51]

Moltmann builds on Bloch's ideas, both in terms of his technology of alliance and his hints at the subjectivity of nature. Bloch has drawn on Bacon's

New Atlantis for his understanding of technology and whether it is feasible to conduct technology with a view to the "co-productivity" with nature seems in our opinion, to be a little fanciful. Nonetheless, we can still attempt to be less aggressive in our attitude towards nature, which has in the past been directed towards it serving our own needs. It seems to us that Moltmann goes beyond Bloch in his rejection of anthropocentric attitudes, for while Bloch wished to include nature alongside human history, he was still indebted to Marx in his stress on the value of nature as that which met human needs. Moltmann tries to introduce the idea of the value of nature quite apart from human interests, though whether he is entirely successful in this respect is an issue which we will raise again in the next chapter.

Overall we agree with Moltmann's retention of a social doctrine of the Trinity as a way of fostering a right attitude to the world. We are of the opinion that this social doctrine, when rooted in Christological theories, should serve to keep his theology from losing its moorings in the concrete social history of Christ, as well as preventing his appreciation of the subjectivity of nature straying into unwarranted equivalence of the moral value of humankind and nature in a kind of "biocentrism" characteristic of more recent radical theology. The difficulties in his understanding of the relationships between God and the world have come when he has strayed too far away from this core approach, as we shall see below in our discussion of the *kabbalah*.

3. Dialogue with Jewish mysticism: reformulated in kenotic categories?

We noted in an earlier chapter how Moltmann's use of the kabbalistic doctrine of *zimzum* was part of his deliberate effort to distinguish between God and the world, and in terms of his use of ecological language the beginning of the concept of a spatial "home" in God which has repercussions for our own need of a particular "home" in common with other living beings. Moltmann draws on the mystic Isaac Luria, interpreted through Gershom Scholem.

We will outline the kabbalists' position briefly here in order to show how Moltmann has drawn on these sources. An important distinction, that Moltmann does not raise in his discussion, is that for kabbalists the absolute Essence of God, *Ein Sof*, lies beyond any speculative or ecstatic comprehension. Moreover, any question of God's ultimate motivation for creation is, quite simply, "not a legitimate one."[52] Yet the knowable aspect of God comes through contemplation of the relationship between God and creation.

The starting point of Isaac Luria's theory is that the essence of God leaves no space for creation, which requires a divine withdrawal in God. The idea of *zimzum* originally meant contraction or concentration, but in *kabbalah* it means "withdrawal", or "retreat". Scholem's comment here is incisive:

> "Luria begins by putting a question which gives the appearance of being naturalistic, and, if you like, somewhat crude. How can there be a world if God is everywhere? If God is "all in all" how can there be things which are not God ... the solution became, in spite of the crude form which he gave it, of the highest importance in the history of later kabbalistic thought."[53]

The significance of *zimzum* for *kabbalah* was that it became a deep symbol for the Exile. For the Jewish tradition absolute homelessness "was the sinister symbol of absolute Godlessness, of utter moral and spiritual degradation."[54]

An important aspect of *zimzum* in Luria's treatment is the notion that it represents an act of judgement (*Din*) as well as an act of limitation. Before the *zimzum*, *Din* was not recognisable as such, however, the roots of *Din* remain in the space created along with a residue of divine light. For the *kabbalah*, judgement means the imposition of limits, hence "inasmuch as *tsimtsum* signifies an act of negation and limitation, it is also an act of judgement." Moreover, "the root of all evil is already latent in the act of *Tsimtsum*."[55]

For Luria the roots of *kelippot*, or "forces of evil", were in existence before the breaking of the vessels, which comes in a subsequent stage as light from *Ein Sof* flows into the primordial space created by *zimzum*.[56] The broken vessels are subject to restoration, or *tikkun*, and the rôle of humankind is "solely concerned with certain aspects of inwardness" rather than outward, cosmic processes.[57] The parallels with gnostic speculation are once again obvious here, that is the depiction of creation as a cosmic drama, a fateful crisis within the inner workings of the Godhead and a search for cosmic restoration and purging of good from evil where humanity plays a central rôle. For the kabbalists the significance of humanity is its supreme place as the perfecting agent in the structure of the cosmos. The *tikkun* was significant in drawing together kabbalistic mysticism with messianic Judaism, an appeal which finally surfaced with the Shabbatean messianic movement.[58]

The possible synthesis of messianic and mystical ideas may have been one of the reasons why Moltmann found Lurianic *kabbalah* particularly congenial. However, as is obvious from the discussion so far, he is highly selective in his use of ideas from the Lurianic system in a way that seems to ignore many of its essential characteristics, outlined briefly above. Scholem is very aware of the rootedness of Jewish mysticism in the Jewish faith itself. Indeed, he is at pains to stress that Jewish mysticism arose in a situation where its proponents sought to remain within the orthodox framework and as such did not break through the "shell of the old religious system."[59] It is only relatively recently that the idea of an abstract mystical religion has gained popularity, and Scholem doubts whether it is possible to make valid links between different mystical traditions. Jewish mysticism, in its concern to express its distinctive Jewishness, proceeds from "the belief in the Unity of God and the meaning of revelation as laid down in the Torah, the sacred law."[60] We are challenging here whether Moltmann is justified in using ideas from Jewish mystical writings, given Scholem's comment that it is not really possible to make valid links between the different mystical traditions because of their embeddedness in the orthodoxy of their particular faith.

Moltmann finds the idea of *zimzum* a convenient way of describing the concept of *kenosis*, or inner limitation of God, which is normally used in Christological debates rather than in discussions on the Trinity. In fact, he seems to replace the idea of the Exile, symbolic in Jewish kabbalistic interpretation, with the idea of the cross.[61] As such, the cross represents the ultimate self-limitation of God, which begins the first act of the Godhead prior to creation. Moltmann seems to have drifted into a conceptual difficulty here. It is far from clear how the three persons of the Trinity share in the initial *zimzum*. Indeed he prefers to speak of God in a way which seems to presuppose a Unity model rather than a Trinitarian one.[62] Does this initial limitation which reflects, for Moltmann, the *kenosis* of the Son and also of the Spirit, affect all persons equally?

A further aspect of kabbalistic thought which Moltmann uses at some length is the idea of the self-distinction in God and the exile of the *Shekinah*. The idea of a fissure in the life and actions of the Trinity is bound up with his understanding of theodicy. It is a way of explaining why the divine humiliation takes place, namely:

> "Love of freedom is the most profound reason for 'God's self-differentiation', and for 'the divine bipolarity', for 'God's self-surrender' and for the 'rift' which runs through the divine life and activity until redemption."[63]

While Moltmann uses Scholem's idea of the fissure in God to support his own interpretation of the self-distinction in God, he does not acknowledge that the context in which such a distinction took place in Jewish speculation is that of the sinfulness of Adam.[64] Indeed, Adam broke "the stream of life which flows from sphere to sphere" by setting his mind to worship *Shekinah* without recognising its union with *Sefiroth*.[65] The exile of the *Shekinah* is part of the deep bitterness of the Exile, and is a symbol of the broken state of things in the realm of divine potentialities. Luria even speaks of the letters JH being torn away from WH in the name JHWH.[66] The aim of the Torah was to lead the

Shekinah back to her master, which led to a *mythos* of God giving birth to 'himself'. Scholem describes the symbolism of humanity as "microcosmos" and God as "macro anthropos" as having "a somewhat crude texture."[67] The idea that the fall of *Shekinah* and her exile is repeated every time we sin brings into "close affinity" these ideas with those of "the Manichaeans."[68] Our criticism of Moltmann on this point is similar to that above, namely that he has ignored the context in which these ideas were formulated. The parallels between Moltmann's interpretation and that of Jewish *kabbalah* are very general indeed, and in a loose way he Christianizes the concept of the self-distinction by replacing the idea of the Exile with the cross.

Moltmann's idea of creation within God is more like female conception and gestation than male generation, with the initial withdrawal perceived as a feminine act.[69] In Jewish mysticism, however, the feminine represents "stern judgement" and thus would seem to accord well with the possibility of a Jewish idea of *zimzum* as feminine.[70] Nonetheless, the idea of judgement, as we noted earlier, is lacking in Moltmann's treatment of *zimzum*. While Moltmann's idea of "creative letting-be" at the heart of God's initial creative movement will be welcomed by feminist writers, his association of *zimzum* with *kenosis* implies a suffering in the heart of God, and so gives the inner withdrawal a tragic content.[71]

Finally, Franz Rosenzweig is also an important source for Moltmann's discussion of the divine *Shekinah*. Our criticism here is similar to the above, namely his selectivity in his use of source material. He seems to ignore Rosenzweig's key concept that it is the *Torah* that is created prior to the world and becomes "a fundamental pillar."[72] Redemption thus takes place through the relationship of the remnant to the Law, in order to unite the Holy God and his *Shekinah*. This unity can only happen in as far as *Jewish Law* is fulfilled. It is through this that the cosmic scope of these acts become apparent, so that: "The merely Jewish feeling has been transfigured into world-redemptive truth. In the innermost constriction of the Jewish heart there shines the Star of Redemption."[73]

While Moltmann uses the threads of these ideas and incorporates them into his messianic view of creation, Rosenzweig's understanding of the difference between God and creation is not akin to that of Moltmann. We will have reason to come back to this point in a later chapter; here we note that for Rosenzweig, the world "becomes", but humanity and God already "are."[74] The point we wish to make here is that the idea of a self-distinction in God, and God suffering with his people, which Moltmann incorporates into his theology have rather different connotations in the context of Rosenzweig's theological framework. While all creative writers draw on a number of different sources, and Moltmann is skilled at bringing together an exciting mix of ideas, we suggest that his lack of real appreciation of the context of many of these concepts in Jewish writing tends to weaken his claim for their views being supportive of his own position.

4. God's relationship with the world: influence of process theology?

We noted in an earlier chapter the shifts in Moltmann's theology in his understanding of the relationship between God and the world. We discussed above the way the theme of *kenosis* becomes incorporated into his understanding of the being of God prior to the creation event. We suggest that it is this priority of self-humiliation which makes Moltmann reluctant to speak in terms of divine agency, preferring to use categories of love instead. Moltmann takes up the idea of Karl Barth that freedom is "relational freedom" and as such "Trinitarian, embracing grace, thankfulness and peace."[75] However, he departs in a radical way from Barth in purging his idea of freedom from any notion of hierarchical ordering, which is an integral part of Barth's understanding of communion.[76] The love of God which Moltmann believes conditions God's freedom, is also expressed as faithfulness, hence Mason's equation of Moltmann's freedom with faithfulness.[77] We are less convinced that the common basis of both freedom and faithfulness in the love of God *necessarily* allows us to merge the two concepts. However, it is probably fair to say that Moltmann's own lack of clarity on this issue makes us anticipate such an interpretation. Mason argues that Moltmann's concept of freedom is important in distinguishing his view from that of a Hegelian necessity for suffering or dependence on history in the life of God.[78] However, we are still left with the uncertainty whether just because God has chosen to suffer in this way, this does not negate the idea that, in an ontological sense, God becomes shaped by his experience of the world. We raised this issue earlier in chapter 3. This brings Moltmann's thought in parallel with process theology in a way which becomes even more obvious in *God in Creation*.[79]

Amongst process theologians Lewis Ford has stressed the non-temporality of God in his primordial nature which gives this aspect of his being both an abstract structure and a subjective element. The divine non-temporality is capable of being related to any moment of time, while remaining independent of temporal passage. The consequent nature of the God of temporal becoming is dependent on the finite world. However, his consequent nature is grounded in an "ontologically prior non-temporal becoming that is the source of the never-ending creative advance into novelty."[80] While Moltmann agrees with process theology's insistence on the passibility of God, he does not develop the theme of God's capacity to be enriched by finite creation after *The Trinity and the Kingdom of God*. The inner suffering of God is of a different kind compared with that of humanity since he suffers not out of necessity, but only in the freedom of love.[81] Our aim here is to ask ourselves how far Moltmann's understanding of the inner Trinitarian life as a social Trinity is consistent with a God who suffers, but in a way that is distinct from human suffering. He clearly wishes to distinguish, in a way that process theology fails to do, between God and creation. Moreover, his Trinitarian formulation is a clear departure from process theology which resists a Trinitarian concept of God altogether. He redefines both suffering and freedom in God for the purpose of his discussion in a way which emphasizes the primacy of the love of God. A similar concern underlies his understanding of the social Trinitarian relationships in perichoretic categories. As we indicated earlier, the unity emerging from *perichoresis* is an open unity which desires to include the other in loving relationships.

The alignment between Jürgen Moltmann's view and that of process theology's understanding of creation encourages interpreters to see his position as undergoing a "seismic shift" from his earlier concentration on history.[82] However, while both Jürgen Moltmann and process theologians are at pains to identify with the ecological crisis, and to couch their theology in ecological language, the presuppositions of process theology and those of Moltmann are rather different. Process theologians speak of the agency of love in the world and the experience of the world in God in mutual and equivalent reciprocal relationships. Moltmann is more careful to distinguish between the world's experience of God and vice versa. In Whitehead "God and the world are for the sake of each other, and both are instruments of creativity."[83] Moreover, the links between God's primordial nature and his consequent nature are only weak in Whitehead, so that God's dependence on the world is in a general sense, rather than precisely this world. This is clearly different from Moltmann's view which insists on God's particularity and faithfulness to precisely this world, and his notion of reciprocity extending to categories of a shared suffering between God and the world, with less emphasis on divine enrichment by the world.[84]

As we will have cause to discuss more fully in the next chapter, it is in the category of the future of creation that Moltmann expresses his own disaffiliation from process thought. In addition he retains the idea of *creatio ex nihilo* in the beginning, which preserves the distinction between God and creation. The trend towards pantheism is all the more obvious in those process theologians who choose to stress God's consequent nature, such as Cobb and Hartshorne.

We are not denying that the experiential aspect of Moltmann's understanding of the God-world relationship does lend itself to a positive correlation with Hartshorne's theology.[85] In *God in Creation*, Moltmann extends the idea of the faithful suffering of God to include that of the natural world. It seems to us, however, that his insistence on bringing all of the suffering of creation into that of the crucified one is a little strained, as is his idea that the liberation of all of creation happens through identification with the resurrection of Christ. Moreover, his focus on the individual and particular history of Christ hangs rather uneasily with his appreciation of the *Gaia* hypothesis which, as we shall see below, represents an understanding of the world which envisages the whole world acting as an organism.

His struggle to fit these ideas together is part of his wider wrestling with the relative significance of nature and history, which we will discuss more fully in the next chapter. The point which we wish to stress here is that while his treatment of creation in certain respects seems to run parallel with process theology in, for example, his affirmation of the subjectivity of nature; his points of reference for such a view are different. He shares, rather, in some of the language of process theologians in showing due respect for the whole of creation, independently of its significance for ourselves.

The movement away from anthropology to a more cosmological understanding of the world in process theology is something which feminists, seeking to re-interpret their understanding of God, have welcomed as a positive shift away from categories dominated by male terminology. Mary Grey, for example, believes that process theology forms the most adequate way forward as a philosophical foundation for feminist theology.[86] Carter-Heyward is insistent on a process of mutual redemption "in the deliverance of both God and humanity from evil."[87] She insists that once we set God apart from us he becomes "useless" and "in relation to God, as in any relation, God is affected by humanity and creation, just as we are affected by God."[88] She does not know for certain if this is the God of Christianity or not, but she does believe it emerges out of experience and, in particular, we need to re-image our pictures of God, humanity and Jesus in the light of such experience. While Moltmann seems to shift closer to this position in his understanding of Christology, it is less clear that the same applies to his doctrine of creation. In *The Way of Jesus Christ*, for example, he allows for our experience of Christ in some way to act in reciprocal relationship with Jesus, as portrayed and understood in the scriptures, in informing his Christology.[89]

The criticism of Paul Fiddes of Moltmann's understanding of creation may be justified, namely how far does Moltmann's *God in Creation* really allow for the creativity in creation to emerge in a way that gives it real freedom to be itself?[90] Carter-Heyward's stress on our co-creativity may seem to place too much emphasis on our human vocation compared with the action of God, yet how far this mutual relation extends to that of creation other than humanity does not come into either her discussion or that of Moltmann's, except in a loose way by reference to Ernst Bloch's notion of the "co-productivity" of nature referred to above.[91]

Moltmann wishes to restore the dignity of all of creation by insisting on the love between God and creation, and the subjectivity of creation. He is deliberately vague as to how such subjectivity could influence the relationship between God and his creatures, though the more general notion of the value of creation as that which is good and valued of itself is one drawn from a biblical perspective.

5. Dialogue with Genesis: does the Old Testament speak?

Throughout Moltmann's *God in Creation* he has given priority to working through, in the most comprehensive way possible, an understanding of God as the creator; rather than an understanding of creation as such. This is part of his own passionate belief that until we have an adequate understanding of God, we are unable to relate to creation in a way that reflects our vocation to be in the image of God. While we agree with his basic intention, his coverage of Genesis material is rather sketchy for a systematic theology of creation. Indeed, we suggest that he tends to read into this material a Christocentric position that weakens the right the Old Testament account of creation has to speak for itself. Rather than taking up every usage of Old Testament passages in Moltmann's study which appears to be strained in exegetical terms, we shall confine ourselves to some specific examples of how he has drawn on Genesis material in shaping his doctrine of creation. We will be extending this theme further in the next chapter.

Moltmann takes up certain aspects of the creation story, for example the creation of heaven and earth, and uses this for a detailed description of the meaning of heaven for today. His extensive speculations on this issue, while they make stimulating reading, seem to be very far removed from the sketchy biblical references. In the Genesis account heaven is simply "something created." Furthermore, although heaven is intended by Moltmann to be a created reality, and so not something which is "other worldly"; he gives the impression, in the minds of most readers at least, that he is concerned for something other than this world. It is also linked closely with his understanding of future hope, as we shall see in the next chapter. However, he refuses to confine heaven to the future, in a way that makes it a realm of possibilities for now. The link with process theology's formulation at this juncture tends to encourage Moltmann in metaphysical speculation of the kind that he is anxious to criticize in earlier patristic formulations of the Trinity. Moltmann's understanding of God, unlike that of process theology, as distinctly other than creation, tends to make his speculation here all the more esoteric, detached from the more naturalistic anchorage more characteristic of process thought.

Claus Westermann describes in some detail the background to the Genesis account.[92] The alternative mythologies in the near Eastern culture were (i) creation by birth, (ii) creation after a struggle (iii) creation by activity, and

(iv) creation through the Word. While these themes find their echoes in the Old Testament, the key difference between Israel and that of the near Eastern texts, was that only in the former do we find the object of creation outside the divine. The idea that creation somehow **reveals** God is quite simply foreign to the authors of Genesis, who lived in a world where the idea of God was presupposed. The stress in Genesis is creation by the Word and by divine action.

Moltmann distinguishes between God's creative activity initially from God's subsequent "making" using the materials he has created out of nothing.[93] It is only the idea of creative "making" that can give us a model for human activity, while initial creation has no human analogy. There is some scholarly debate about whether the verb "create" has any more or less theological import than "make."[94] Another aspect of creation which Moltmann elaborates at some length contra process theology is that of *creatio ex nihilo*. He also seems to draw on the kabbalistic idea that the *nihilo* is not just an empty space, but somehow carries a negative element, and initially contains the possibility of the annihilating Nothingness.[95] This leads Moltmann on to a discussion of the kenotic character of God as Messiah in Philippians 2.[96]

While some Old Testament exegetes, such as von Rad, allow for the idea of *creatio ex nihilo* drawn implicitly from the account in Genesis, Moltmann seems to go beyond the normal hermeneutical boundaries by bringing both the idea of *kenosis* and *zimzum* into this concept. The philosophical background to *kabbalah* in the idea of creation as emanation makes the link between *zimzum* and *creatio ex nihilo* offensive to Molnar, who accuses Moltmann of emanationism.[97] We are of the opinion that Molnar's criticism is not justified because Moltmann is highly selective in his use of kabbalistic material, and would reject any idea of emanation. Nonetheless Molnar's misinterpretation is understandable because Moltmann makes little effort to show clearly how his view departs from Jewish *kabbalah*, and tends to give the impression that these sources support his own view, a matter which we criticized in our earlier discussion.

The division of plants according to their kind is the beginning of a primitive form of science, and is more advanced than other mythologies in its description of the value of creation independent of humankind.[98] Moltmann makes much of this hint in the Genesis account so that "interpreting the world as God's creation means precisely *not* viewing it as the world of human beings, and taking possession of it accordingly."[99] This contrasts with traditional Orthodoxy, which views humankind as the crown of creation. Lossky, for example, insists that Genesis 2 also reinforces this theme, in a way which elevates the place of humankind.[100] While Moltmann would endorse the theocentric approach of the Orthodox tradition, his interpretation of Genesis is such that he raises the value of non-human creation.

Moltmann is reacting against liberal Protestantism when he insists that an anthropocentric world is "unbiblical", and that the creation exists not for ourselves, but for God's glory.[101] However, this does not prevent Moltmann's discussion of *imago Dei* including the idea of stewardship by humankind over creation.[102] As we hinted in an earlier chapter, this marks a departure from Moltmann's earlier theology, where his understanding of the relationship between humankind and nature was more exclusively identified with the notion of stewardship. An example of his earlier tone is:

> "He stands in solidarity with creation, yet is set over against it through his relationship as God's counterpart. Man is thus placed in an eccentric position ....As God's image he is the 'crown of creation' when he is really 'man.'"[103]

Moltmann also seemed to have no problem with the idea of the creation as that which humanity "is to use and rule", and is more concerned that creation should not become the object of its trust, which amounts to idolatry.[104] His understanding of the biblical passages at this stage reflect his own concern for human history, where "from the beginning, Israel had an anthropocentric 'world-view', everything was created for man's sake, and man is God's representative on earth."[105] By the time we reach *God in Creation* Moltmann has shifted the focus of the culmination of the creation account from "man" to the "sabbath". We will have reason to discuss further whether he is justified in his interpretation of the significance of the sabbath in the next chapter.

The idea of image-bearing as God's representative taken up by von Rad and Moltmann is somewhat controversial. For example, scholars against this idea believe that throughout the Genesis account it is God's holiness that is stressed and, further, that the analogy between kingship and humankind is impossible for the whole species.[106] Moltmann would seem to agree with the former charge, namely that to stress that wherever humankind is, this also leads to a proclamation of God, is not really the intention of the writer. However, we believe that he is justified in keeping this as a weak theme in his anthropology, especially as the royal motif appears more clearly in other contexts in the Old Testament, such as the Psalms. There seems to be no real reason why all human beings cannot share in the royal charter.

Moltmann is also at pains to introduce a Christological future to the concept of image-bearing, in a way that still manages to affirm the dignity of human beings even after the Fall. Westermann argues that, on the basis of form-critical analysis, the overall context of Genesis 1.26-30 speaks of image-bearing in terms of an active relationship between God and humans, rather than a quality as such. Thus Moltmann's understanding of image-bearing in terms of relationship between God and humans would seem to be close to that of Westermann in this respect. What is less clear, however, is how far Moltmann is justified in bringing the Christological idea of *imago Christi* into his understanding of image-bearing, even though it may be tempting from the perspective of a deeply Christocentric faith. The problem is that once we absolutize God's saving action we are no longer in a position to see clearly what belongs to humankind as creature. We noted the same confusion/mergence of the immanent Trinity taking on redemptive categories prior to creation. A related issue is Moltmann's failure to distinguish in a clear way between the action of God's Spirit in creation and blessing from his action in redemption and recreation. While these two aspects are not independent, there is little excuse for blurring the boundaries in such a way that creation tends to collapse into salvation history, a tendency which, in intention at least, Moltmann seems most anxious to avoid. We will be developing some of these threads in a critical analysis of his Christological paradigm for creation in the next chapter.

Moltmann never really explains to what extent the Fall of humankind finds expression in concrete ways. Old Testament exegesis does suggest that our dignity as human beings is not lost at the Fall. We are in agreement with Moltmann's intention to affirm the dignity and worth of all human beings in spite of their sinfulness, as against the approach of some more conservative Protestant theological views which implied that all aspects of *imago Dei* were lost at the Fall. However, Moltmann's complex understanding of sinfulness in terms of a closed relationship with God, which seems to affect humankind's relationship with God, but not vice versa, may not be adequate. For example, in what sense does the idea of closedness convey the reality of responsibility for sinful action? The problem becomes more acute when Moltmann extends the idea of closedness to non-human creation. Kjetil Hafstad points out that it is difficult to understand Moltmann's idea of closedness in nature:

> "can the processes in nature be described in such anthromorphic terms?..And here nature can also close itself off. This begs the question whether such a way of describing it would make sense, for example, to a biologist - can nature reject evolution sinfully?"[107]

She makes the important point that Moltmann's effort to combine an idea of openness from evolutionary theory with closedness from theological concept of sin lead to a mixing of metaphors which gives confusing messages. We add that while on the one hand Moltmann's seeming extension of the idea of closedness to non-human creation seems an unwarranted application of an anthropological theological concept to nature, the extension of openness taken from evolutionary biology to the human sphere weakens the sense of the radical depth of human responsibility for sinful action. Those commentators who have reacted negatively to Moltmann's understanding of sin have tended to do so on the basis of his failure to conform to traditional concepts of the Fall, rather than asking how the hermeneutical difficulties arise in Moltmann's theology. K. Hafstad is more imaginative in her critique of Moltmann, though we doubt whether he is as optimistic about evolution as she implies, and he does allow for negative possibilities in evolution, as becomes clear in *The Way of Jesus Christ*. Moltmann's suggestion, which we will take up again later, that God's relationship to us somehow preserves our sense of responsibility, does not seem to be very convincing. We noted in the last chapter the uneasiness of many scholars on this aspect of Moltmann's theology.

Moltmann's definition of the freedom of God, as we noted above, under section 4, is couched not so much in terms of choice, as freedom for love expressed in faithfulness. Molnar objects to this understanding of God, believing that this makes him "a prisoner of love."[108] While we believe that this criticism is exaggerated, Moltmann's departure from a more traditional understanding of freedom in God as freedom of choice may partly explain Moltmann's apparent lack of development of the idea of human choice expressed as obedience which is so characteristic of Barthian theology.[109] The end result is that human sinfulness becomes down-played in a way that is resisted even by post-Christian as well as more conservative theologians.[110] In Moltmann's earlier work human sin was linked with either hopelessness or pride, the former expressing the premature anticipation of non-fulfillment and the latter expressing the premature anticipation of fulfillment. The eschatological solution to the problem of our sinfulness leaves Moltmann's anthropology open to the charge of triumphalism.[111] While Moltmann may be deliberately concentrating his efforts on the social aspect of sinfulness of human structures, especially those of dominance and oppression, he seems to fail to take sufficiently seriously the concrete nature of individual sin as it influences and feeds into those structures.

A possible modification of his position would be to develop more clearly how we discover our sinfulness as well as our image-bearing through relationship with God and with others. The purpose of Moltmann's insistence on the retention of the God-human aspect of the relationship between God and ourselves, even amidst our sinful condition, is so that we preserve a sense of our own responsibility for sin. Hence: "Even the person who is totally inhuman remains a human being and cannot escape his responsibility."[112] However, we are less convinced that a prerequisite in remaining human, and so responsible, is that God's relationship to us is unaffected. God's love towards us can remain in spite of the brokenness of the relationship. Moltmann's stress on the graciousness of God "who holds fast to his relationship to human beings in spite of their opposition" does not really do justice to the biblical theme of God's holiness and his anger towards those who deliberately choose to disobey his commands. Moltmann puts the concept of the judgement of God into eschatological categories in a way which tends to diffuse the horror of human sinfulness. While this may come from his valid concern to remove any domineering overtones which smack of unwarranted patriarchy, he needs to justify more clearly the basis for his approach from a biblical perspective.

Finally, we note that it is perhaps a little surprising that Moltmann does not make greater use of the Flood narrative in a discussion on creation which purports to deal specifically with an ecological context. In this respect we note Levenson's idea of our ground for security being not so much in creation as such, but in God's oath never to destroy the world. While Moltmann agrees with the theological primacy of the faithfulness of God towards all creation, he seems to draw the idea from Christological considerations instead of rooting it in the Noahic covenant.[113]

6. Dialogue with biology: transformation of categories?

In our final section of this chapter we shall touch on some examples of Moltmann's use of biological terms and ideas, as seen from a biologist's perspective. It is clear that one of the central metaphors that Moltmann adopts is that of *ecology*. We have been at pains to show how far his ideas have been shaped by his own understanding of the meaning of ecology as "interconnectedness" and "indwelling". Here we shall ask ourselves, not so much how he uses this metaphor, as whether he is justified in his approach from a biological perspective.

Ecology is a relatively recent science and includes a number of disparate research areas such as systematics of plants and animals, response and developmental physiology, plant and animal geography, evolutionary biology, hydrobiology, economic biology as well as more traditional ecology of plants and animals.[114] In general, the modern trend in ecology allowed three distinct areas to emerge:

(i) Population ecology, where natural selection acts on an individual or a population.

(ii) Community ecology, where natural selection acts on whole species.

(iii) Systems ecology, where selection acts on an integrated complex of plants, animals and physical surroundings.

The dogma of a "balance of nature", characteristic of the eighteenth century, shifted in favour of a dynamic interaction between the living and non-living environment. While there was a temptation to describe the pyramid structures in the ecosystem in terms of a "balance of energy", the move towards a focus on the activities of all organisms in the system, rather than the more simplistic geographical or spatial allocation, was significant. We find, then, a dynamic ordering which became conceptualized through verbal metaphors such as "food chains", "pyramid of numbers" and "niche."[115]

While Moltmann is correct in seeing ecological interrelationships as a key concept for ecology, he seems to ignore the fact that the structure of such relationships is more akin to hierarchies through pyramidical structures than the egalitarian position which he is anxious to promote. Adopting the idea of egalitarian relationships is only in the more popular sense "ecological". Moreover, the impossibility of testing out some of the interconnections which he envisages makes this concept free from any scientific and biological norms. His second idea, namely that of ecological "niche", seems to be aligned with our own psychological need for stability in a "home". This is reinforced through his development of the idea of equilibrium taken from *Tao* and Chinese philosophy. The problem with this usage of the idea of equilibrium is that this tends to ignore the fragility inherent in ecological "niche", and gives the wrong impression of stability and permanence. The Taoist belief in equilibrium does not do justice to the fragility of that equilibrium discovered by biologists. Moltmann's use of *Tao* tends to reinforce the myth that the equilibrium which exists is stable, but in practice it can be upset by a number of different factors, including that of human intervention which almost inevitably leads to some disturbance.

It is also difficult to find coherence in Moltmann's concept of an inner space in God created through the divine withdrawal, and the place for the final homecoming in the sabbath. As we noted earlier, Moltmann picks up the idea of inner withdrawal in kabbalistic thought, which amounts to a homelessness in God, an exile which can only be resolved in the future. How far can Moltmann speak in a convincing way of a future, real, "embodiment" of God when finite creation suffers from such fragile vulnerability even within its biological niche?

While biologists may not be convinced that ecological concepts can be used in a direct way to describe theological concepts, as long as Moltmann makes it clear that he is drawing on a popular understanding of ecology, then his link with Trinitarian themes is successful. The ideas of ecology which surface in popular understanding include the idea of the interrelatedness of everything to everything else, and a special home or "niche" for all living beings. The difficulty that we find is that he expresses his intention to bring together "scientific" concepts with theological ones.[116] Moltmann's theology is tailored in such a way that he incorporates evolutionary and ecological ideas into his perspective, while keeping a Christological paradigm characteristic of Barth. As we noted earlier, he goes further than Barth in removing the concept of partriarchy from his concept of God. However, Moltmann seems largely unaware of the different ideologies amongst scientists, and the strong conviction amongst green philosophers of science that ecology is a *subversive* science.[117] Here the idea of subversion is stronger than that of revolution, and implies a radical change at the foundations of political and economic faiths. He shares with Hardin the challenge to the patriarchal attitudes that have dominated religious enquiry and Western technology. Hardin is concerned to reinterpret the idea of progress in a way that is thoroughly "ecological", and Moltmann would probably also sympathize with his rejection of benevolent Providence, while refusing to accept Hardin's alternative "religion of ecology". Nonetheless, we reach an impasse at this point. Given that Moltmann affirms scientific experimentation, how can this continue when we take seriously the value of each and every creature to offer praise of the creator in a way that is independent of our human need? Fostering our sense of participation in the life of the Trinity may not simply be enough in curbing the machinery of science. Some of these issues will become clearer when we wrestle with the future of creation in Moltmann's theology in the following chapter, and how this coheres or otherwise with a biological and ecological vision.

Moltmann's use of "ecology" and "ecological" seems to have lost all moorings from concrete biological issues. Some scholars are scathing in their criticism over this issue believing that "he stresses the concept of ecology in order to catch the eye of many readers in Europe and the United States."[118] We reject this criticism, believing that Moltmann is making a sincere attempt to wrestle with an understanding of a relationship between God and the world that is in full awareness of our current ecological crisis. For popular readership his loose usage of biological terms would cause no problem, and he has shown repeatedly that he is not someone who will bend to the wishes of specialists. Nonetheless, we believe that his theology of creation would be improved as an *ecological* theology if he showed more appreciation of the biological context of creation instead of allowing himself firstly to equate the bulk of "science" with physics, and secondly to use biological images rather than to engage with biological science as such. Those biological ideas which he does use are often completely shorn of their original meaning. We have already mentioned the example of symbiosis in the last chapter.

We also note his use of more controversial "biological" ideas which carry philosophical overtones. We refer here to his use of both the *Gaia* hypothesis, and the related ideas of Jantsch in *The Self-Organizing Universe.* We have raised this issue briefly in the previous chapter. Moltmann seems to use Jantsch's terminology to describe the workings of the cosmic Spirit, that is in the ideas of (i) self-assertion and integration and (ii) self-preservation and transcendence, without really explaining in an adequate way what this means either for Jantsch or in his own understanding of the third person of the Trinity. Moltmann attempts to link these ideas with his understanding of the cosmic Spirit, but it is unclear how we are to perceive such linkage.[119] Jantsch's idea of a self-organizing universe is based on Ilya Prigogine's work on the thermodynamics of complex systems, for which he won a Nobel prize in 1976. The extension of these ideas to biological systems in Jantsch's book does not show the rigour normally expected of a scientific work. For example, he believes that self-organizing and self-regulating are characteristic of the biosphere plus atmosphere which now allows us to "overcome the dualistic split into nature and culture". Moreover, the self-transcendence which follows from the interconnectedness gives "the meaning of life. We are not the helpless subjects of evolution, we *are* evolution."[120] Jantsch seems to connect self-transcendence with evolution, and equilibrium with stagnation and death. The stability is rather a global one which comes through "autopoiesis". The creative individual reinforces fluctuations in the system so that it drives into a new system. Perhaps ironically, Jantsch also insists that the "self-reflexive mind" was one of the new directions in the evolution of the world, and God himself becomes not the creator, but "the mind of the universe."[121]

While Moltmann is careful to distance himself from Jantsch's perception of God, the mixture of science and speculation gives this book a colouring which seems to be close to the writings of Teilhard de Chardin. Such a parallel becomes even clearer in Jantsch's comment that "The God-idea does not stand above or outside of evolution as an ethical norm, but in true mysticism is placed in the unfolding and self-realization of evolution."[122] Jantsch's ideas are somewhat controversial to those more attuned to "hard" science. Moreover, his attempt to give his "biological" insights a metaphysical status is not really justified in our opinion. For those searching for a sense of meaning in a Faustian world, his visionary ideas may seem more attractive than bland materialism. Paul Hodgkin, for example, is clear that this alternative offers a reason for hope in the midst of a medical science which seems to dehumanize our existence. In addition, he makes a rather interesting link between Whitehead's views and those of Jantsch.[123]

7. Conclusions.

We are now in a position to draw some tentative conclusions as to the overall achievement of Moltmann's Trinitarian/ecological basis for his doctrine of creation. Our aim has been twofold, first to show the significance of Trinitarian themes in his formulation of his doctrine of creation; and secondly to draw out the most important sources in Moltmann's reconstruction and ask how his view coheres or otherwise with these alternative approaches. We have already discussed the first aspect in some detail in Part 2. In this section we have attempted to show his unique contribution to this aspect of theology by highlighting key differences between his position and those of Barth, Orthodoxy, feminist and process theology, as well as important non-Christian influences from Bloch, mystical Judaism and biological science. First, we wish to affirm his overall intention to counter the alienating attitudes towards creation which have predominated in our Western culture. We also give credit to the boldness of his thesis in drawing parallels between relationality in God and in creation by using the metaphor of ecology which serves to counter the dualistic tendencies in our approach to God and the world.[124]

The following summarizes our position so far:-

1.   Our comparison of Jürgen Moltmann's doctrine of the Trinity with that of Karl Barth showed how he has moved beyond that of Barth by a greater stress on the social relatedness of the Trinity as having priority over God's unity. Moltmann's position is influenced by feminist thought in his insistence on the egalitarian quality of the relationships in the Trinity, and the idea of God as mother giving birth to the world. In our opinion, his imaginative approach is a welcome alternative to more arid presentations of the Trinity, but he tends to indulge in too much speculation about the inner life of the Trinity in a way which does not seem to take account of the limits to our use of analogy in describing these relationships.

2.   Moltmann draws on the Eastern church to support his belief that the tri-unity of God is prior to his one-ness. His brilliance is in his incorporation of feminist ideas into the Eastern Orthodox idea of *perichoresis*. Our criticism is similar to that above, namely he tends to go a little too far in the direction of speculative theology which makes his own position seem less convincing. In other words it is an exciting mix of ideas, but rather over-effusive in content.

There are other areas which he could have discussed more carefully, for example the meaning of the personhood of the third person of the Trinity.

3.　　　　Moltmann's portrayal of the Spirit in female categories is partly in response to feminist theology. However, we do not consider that this is a helpful way of understanding who the Spirit is because it tends to reinforce the dualism of male/female alongside transcendence-immanence.

4.　　　　For eco-feminists Moltmann has still not gone far enough in rooting his position in the natural interrelationships of creation, as having priority over anthropological formulations of Christianity which stressed salvation history. We will be returning to this issue again in the next chapter. Here we wish to defend Moltmann against the attack of some eco-feminists, and argue that he has made a great effort to be sensitive to the ecological paradigm that is emerging in our society.

5.　　　　His retention of a Christological and eschatological vision is a welcome alternative to the creation-centred spirituality and "biocentrism" that is becoming popular in more radical feminist theology.

6.　　　　A valid criticism of Moltmann is that for a theology of creation he has given too much attention to a discussion of who God is, at the expense of explaining the value and place of humanity and non-human creation. While we believe that he is justified in his attempt to re-image God prior to searching for our place in the world, he has strayed into tangential themes such as the significance for God of the place of heaven and earth.

7.　　　　Another critical comment is that he assumes that once we have an adequate understanding of God in social Trinitarian categories then the social, political and individual relationships between ourselves and creation will follow. While we agree that our experience of God helps to shape our attitudes to the world, Moltmann seems rather naive in his belief that this can somehow change the technological, social and political structures of the Western world.

There is certainly no evidence historically that a right attitude to creation is correlated with more social views of God as Trinity.

8.   Moltmann draws on Bloch for his eschatological perspective on creation, but goes beyond Bloch in his wish to give value to nature quite apart from human interest. He takes up Bloch's idea of alliance technology, and develops his theme of the natural creation becoming our "home" through human activity. Moltmann allows Bloch's socialist views to reinforce his own conviction that egalitarian relationships were at the heart of the earliest Christian communities.

9.   Moltmann's engagement with Jewish mystical ideas is part of his struggle to re-image the creation of the world by God in non-hierarchical categories. The ecological idea of "niche" or home fits in with the Jewish idea of *zimzum* where God makes space for creation by creative "letting-be". We find a paradox here; namely that his inner withdrawal also generates a homelessness in God that foreshadows the Exile, and for Moltmann the crucified Christ.

10.   While Moltmann is imaginative in his use of Jewish *kabbalah*, we are less convinced that his Jewish neighbours will welcome the transformations that he suggests. Moltmann's intention is to engage in dialogue with his sources, but he seems to misrepresent their support for his ideas by changing the meaning of the terminology. A more fundamental difficulty is whether he is justified in thinking of God in spatial categories which is encouraged by his engagement with *kabbalah*.

11.   We find Moltmann's dialogue with process thought suffering from a similar weakness to the above: namely his use of common language gives the impression that he is in agreement with their views. We are of the opinion that he is still basically Barthian in his understanding of revelation and in his insistence on the Christological and Trinitarian basis for theology. Moltmann does seem to make more effort in showing how his views depart from process thought, which gives his own position a clearer outline. His shift to a more

panentheistic understanding of the relationship between God and the world marks a significant departure from Barth under the influence of process theology.

12.   Moltmann's determination to re-image our understanding of God in social Trinitarian categories and ourselves as social beings in fellowship with creation is reflected in his use of Old Testament material. While we agree with Moltmann's intention to find a biblical basis for his ideas, his exegesis of Old Testament passages is often rather sketchy. For example, he brings the ideas of *kenosis* from Christology and *zimzum* from Jewish *kabbalah* into his understanding of *creatio ex nihilo*, without really backing up why he is justified in making such transformations.

13.   Moltmann's understanding of anthropology through a basically relational interpretation of *imago Dei* seems to be broadly within the acceptable boundaries of the possible interpretation of the text in Genesis. We will be developing our analysis of this theme further in the next chapter. We find more problematic Moltmann's interpretation of human sinfulness as closedness, especially as he seems to extend the category of closedness to include the natural creation in a way which is rather confusing with regard to our human distinctness. Also rather unconvincing is the way he suggests that in order to retain our sense of human dignity even after the Fall, somehow our relationship with God is distorted but God's relationship with us is unchanged. His views seem to dilute the extent and pervasiveness of human sin and corruption.

14.   Moltmann's aim to draw on biological ideas is a refreshing change from the more traditional concentration on physics and mathematics in the dialogue between science and faith. However, we believe that he has not gone far enough in this direction, and he still tends to give rather superficial treatment of ideas taken from biology compared with his more lengthy discussions on space, time and cosmology. In the latter discussions he is also prone to dwell

rather too much on the historical aspects, which we will return to in the next chapter.

15.   Moltmann is not sufficiently clear that he is incorporating the popular understanding of ecology into his theological reflections. While we believe he is justified in making links between theology and ecology, in order to counter a dualism between God and creation, he needs to show more clearly that he is not engaging in true dialogue with ecology as concrete science.

16.   He also tends to confuse his ideas further by taking up more controversial pseudo-scientific ideas from Lovelock and Jantsch, and incorporating them into his understanding of the cosmic Spirit. The rôle of pneumatology in Moltmann's theology becomes clearest in his vision for the future, which will be the subject for our discussion in the following chapter.

End Notes.

All books and articles are by Jürgen Moltman unless stated otherwise. Translations are from the German text.

1.   Such criticism has beleaguered Moltmann's theology ever since *Theology of Hope*. On the latter, Van A Harvey remarks: "those who have any acquaintance with the recent literature on the philosophy of history will only find it painful reading ...mesmerized by the gross generalization and abstraction;" A. Harvey, "Secularism, Reasonable Belief and the Theology of Hope," in, FH, p. 138. Also, on *The Trinity and the Kingdom of God*, the ET editor writes "some will certainly dismiss it as speculative theology, insufficiently related to twentieth century experience and modern thought, above all it is hard to envisage the basis for authority in many of Moltmann's statements;" "Talking Points From Books," *Expository Times*, 92, 1981, pp. 289-292.

2.   W.C. French, "Returning to Creation: Moltmann's Eschatology Naturalized," *Journal of Religion*, 68, 1988, pp. 78-86, cf. p. 74.

3.   J.N. Findlay, *Hegel: A Re-Examination*, London, Allen, 1958, p. 27.

4.   D.A. Dombrowski, "Review of *God in Creation*;" *International Journal for Philosophy of Religion*, 25, 1989, pp. 127-128, cf. p. 127.

5.   E. Bloch, *The Principle of Hope*; translated by N. Plaice, S. Plaice and P. Knight, Oxford, Blackwell, 1986; for a discussion of the women's movement see, *Volume 1*, pp. 590-598; for the idea of religious mystery, *Volume 3*, pp. 1183-1302; for the idea of earth mother, *Volume 3*, p. 1152.

6.   *Ibid.*, translator's introduction, p. xxviii. They compare Bloch with Fichte and Schelling, who were "the philosophical inspiration behind German Romanticism," which is "where imagination and the world finally meet." However, unlike the subjective idealism of Schelling/Fichte, who attempted the synthesis between subjective and objective realization of the world, without allowing for development in the objective process, Bloch "insists on the bilateral development of both the subjective and the objective factors and their dialectical interaction." Moltmann is similar to Bloch in other respects: the latter's writings are an "eclectic mixture of progressive elements drawn from classical, oriental and Western philosophies." Bloch feels free to transform material from his sources: for example the idea of process from Hegel becomes an "open process at work in dialectical materialism;" Aristotle's idea of "entelechy" becomes a "theory of possibility," and Bacon's *New Atlantis* becomes part of "the historical programme for socialism," p. xxvii.

7.   K. Barth, *Church Dogmatics, Volume 1/1*; translated by G.W. Bromiley; G.W. Bromiley and T.F. Torrance, eds., second edition, Edinburgh, T and T Clark, 1975, p. 355.

8. *Ibid.*, p. 363. Molnar has accused Moltmann of tritheism, and defends Barth against Moltmann's accusation of modalism; see, P.N. Molnar, "The Function of the Trinity in Moltmann's Ecological Doctrine of Creation," *Theological Studies*, 51(4), 1990, pp. 673-697. We will return to a discussion of Molnar's views later.

9. We think that Claybrook is exaggerating when he suggests that Moltmann rejects Barth's starting point in the sovereignty of God because he believes it is "logical, but not Christian;" D.A. Claybrook, *The Emerging Doctrine of the Holy Spirit in the Writings of Jürgen Moltmann*, PhD thesis, 1983, The Southern Baptist Theological Seminary, p. 125.

10. J. O'Donnell, "The Doctrine of the Trinity in Recent German Theology," *Heythrop Journal*, 23(2), 1982, pp. 153-167, cf. p. 153.

11. CG, pp. 240 ff; Moltmann aligns himself with Karl Rahner in this matter.

12. R. Bauckham, "Jürgen Moltmann," in, P. Toon and J.D. Spiceland, eds., *One God in Trinity*, London, Bagster, 1980, p. 125. The idea of an immanent Trinity behind the economic Trinity, which Moltmann prefers to call "Trinity in the Origin" and "Trinity in the Sending," respectively, was partly in response to a letter written by K. Barth in 1965.

13. R. Olsen, "Trinity and Eschatology: The Historical Being of God in Jürgen Moltmann and Wolfhart Pannenberg," *Scottish Journal of Theology*, 36, 1983, pp. 213-227; cf. p. 221.

14. See earlier discussion of this issue in Chapter 3, also; R. Bauckham, "Jürgen Moltmann," in, D.F. Ford, ed., *The Modern Theologians: An Introduction to Christian Theology in the Twentieth Century; Volume 1*, Oxford, Blackwell, 1989, pp. 293-310.

15. K. Barth, *op. cit.* (n.7), pp. 357 ff; it is Barth's refusal to speak of the inner life of God which leads him to be wary of using the term "person" as such. He also states that "the limit of our comprehension lies in the fact that even as we comprehend these distinctions* we do not comprehend the distinctions in the divine modes of being as such," p. 372. *that is in his work as Creator, Reconciler and Redeemer.

16. G.A. Mason, *God's Freedom as Faithfulness: A Critique of Jürgen Moltmann's Social Trinitarianism*, PhD thesis, 1987, Southwestern Baptist Theological Seminary, p. 99.

17. J.C. Ford, *Toward an Anthropology of Mutuality: A Critique of Karl Barth's Doctrine of the Male-Female Order as A and B with a Comparison of the Panentheistic Theology of Jürgen Moltmann*, PhD thesis, 1984, Northwestern University, p. 11.

18. See, for example, M. Wiles, "Review of *The Trinity and the Kingdom of God*," *Journal of Theological Studies*, 33, 1982, pp. 331-335. He notes that Moltmann "wrongly ascribes to Tertullian belief in the eternal generation of the Word as Son." Moltmann's example of "orthodox dogmatic tradition" in his suggestion that the Son was begotten or born out of the

Father's womb is, according to Wiles, "odd." He refers here to TKG, pp. 64-65. See also under n.19, below.

19. Mason believes that Moltmann incorrectly attributes the first use of the term *perichoresis* with reference to the Trinity to John Damascene. It came, rather, from pseudo Cyril, who took it over from Maximus the Confessor as part of the explanation of the two natures in Christ; G. Mason, *op. cit.* (n.16), p. 123. The idea of "circuminsession" has a long history in the theology of the church. B. de Margerie believes, like Mason, that the term *perichoresis* was also used by pseudo Cyril. While the term had been used in Christology to express "*perichoresis* toward," neither pseudo Cyril nor John Damascene used the expression in this way as applied to the Trinity, rather they emphasised the idea of "*perichoresis* in." This foreshadowed Thomas' idea of *circuminsessio*, rather than *circumincessio* preferred by St. Bonaventure. Hence the way John Damascene uses *perichoresis* as applied to the Trinity lays emphasis on the mutual immanence of the Father and the Son, without a stress on active compenetration characteristic of the Christological interpretation of *perichoresis*. See, B. de. Margerie, *The Christian Trinity in History*; translated from French by E.J. Fortmann, *Studies in Historical Theology, Volume 1*, Petersham, St.Bede's Publications, 1982, pp. 182-183.

20. Moltmann's emphasis on Trinitarian dance and movement seems to take its cue from feminist theology.

21. See, for example, K. Barth, *op. cit.* (n.7), p. 370. Barth's interpretation is characteristic of the Western usage of *circuminsession*, which is "grounded on the unity of nature, the perfect numerical and transcendent unity of the divine nature."

22. G.C. Havrilak, *Eastern Christian Elements in the Christology of Karl Rahner and Jürgen Moltmann: Contemporary Trends in Catholic and Protestant Thought from an Orthodox Perspective*, PhD thesis, 1986, Fordham University, pp. 244-255. For Moltmann's interpretation of God's nature, see under n.25, below.

23. SBH, pp. 114-117.

24. J.D. Zizioulas, *Being as Communion: Studies in Personhood and the Church*, New York, St Vladimir's Seminary Press, 1985, pp. 32-40.

25. We tend to agree with Margerie, against Barth, that, as long as the idea of person is explained adequately, there is no real reason to use alternative language. "The ontological concept of person...expresses what the human mind, the human person itself perceives of its own proper reality by immediate, universal and necessary experience: it is adapted to men of all times and all places....The psychological understanding of personality is not the only modern notion of person; the ontological notion is just as modern;" Margerie, *op. cit.* (n.19), p. 220. Luther's refusal to acknowledge the distinction between person and nature in God, believing it

to be a "useless and frivolous philosophical invention," *ibid.*, pp. 200 ff., may partly explain Moltmann's reluctance to speak of the basis of God's unity in terms of the divine nature. However, as we indicated earlier, Moltmann does acknowledge one divine nature, while at the same time speaking of the unique natures of the persons of the Trinity. "They have the divine nature in common, but their particular individual nature is determined in their relationship to one another.....It is in these relationships that they are persons. Being a person in this respect means existing in relationship;" TKG, p. 172. Moltmann's acknowledgement of unity in relationships and a single divine nature counters P. Molnar's charge of tritheism; *op. cit.* (n.8).

26. J.D. Zizioulas, *op. cit.* (n.24), p. 49.

27. WJC, p. 76, Moltmann links this with Christian faith in the resurrection, pp. 215-277 and "The Day of the Lord" , pp. 326-331.

28. D. Staniloae, *Theology and the Church*; translated by R. Barringer, New York, St Vladimir's Seminary Press, 1980, p. 30.

29. *Ibid.*, pp. 93-99.

30. WJC, pp. 75, 84 ff., 149, *etc.*

31. TKG, pp. 164-165. For the background to Jürgen Moltmann's dialogue with feminism in their common rejection of patriarchy; see, BP.

32. K. Børreson, "L'Usage Patristique de Métaphores Feminines dans le Discours sur Dieu," *Revue Théologique de Louvain*, 13, 1982, pp. 205-220. A theme which deserves clarification is the difference between male/female as a biological category, and masculinity/ femininity as a cultural/gender category. Moltmann seems to hint at the latter as the basis of his perception of the Spirit as feminine, though his reluctance to speak in any way which implies dualistic thinking may explain why he has not raised this issue in his discussion.

33. E. Johnson, "The Incomprehensibility of God and the Image of God Male and Female," *Theological Studies*, 45, 1984, pp. 441-465.

34. G. Scholem, *Major Trends in Jewish Mysticism*, third edition, New York, Schocken Books, 1954, p. 229.

35. *Ibid.*, p. 225.

36. C. La Cugna, "Reconceiving the Trinity as the Mystery of Salvation," *Scottish Journal of Theology*, 38, 1985, pp. 1-23, cf. p. 16.

37. GC, pp. 258-259; "The true human community is designed to be the *imago Trinitatis*." B. de Margerie discusses the history of the analogy drawn between *perichoresis* in God and the relationships in the church. He is anxious to stress the imperfection of the human unity "in existence," compared with the perfect unity in God; see B. de Margerie, *op. cit.* (n.19), pp.180 ff.

38. J. McIntyre, "Review of *God in Creation*," *Scottish Journal of Theology*, 41(2), 1988, pp. 267-273.

39. A. Primavesi, "Review of *God in Creation*," *Heythrop Journal*, 30, 1989, 232-234. See also, A. Primavesi, "The Part for the Whole? An Eco-feminist Enquiry," *Theology*, 113, 1990, 355-362 and, A. Primavesi, *From Apocalypse to Genesis*, Tunbridge Wells, Burns and Oates, 1991.

40. His theology offers only vague guidelines in these areas, perhaps because he prefers to leave the question of detailed application to the specialists, much as Temple suggested in his theology of "middle Axioms." See, W. Temple, *Christianity in Thought and Practice*, London, SCM, 1936, pp. 69-94; also, *Nature Man and God*, London, MacMillan, 1940. Temple, like Moltmann, draws on Whitehead, and used a dialectical approach in his discussion of God's immanence in terms of the Spirit, pp. 246-270.

41. I. Carter-Heyward, *The Redemption of God: A Theology of Mutual Relation*, Lanham, University Press of America, 1982. Moltmann cites this work with approval in WJC, pp. 347; 356. See also, BP.

42. I. Carter-Heyward, *op. cit.* (n.59), p. 6.

43. *Ibid.*, pp. 16 ff., where she writes: "I am not suggesting necessarily that 'divine love' does not act independently of human experience." She argues strongly for putting the second commandment in a position of priority over the first commandment.

44. *Ibid.*, pp. 211 ff.; Appendix on "Some Christological Positions in Relation to my Own;" she is highly critical of Moltmann's depiction of God, where she believes that; "God's inner life is conceptualized as a three person cadre within which we live on a promise that some day we will be assumed fully into the divine and mysterious cadre of fellowship. What is significant is that, whereas we are in God, God is conceptualized as 'outside' of us (this is the distinction between the 'economic' and the 'inner' Trinity). One gets the feeling that it is in the latter that all that is worth while and valuable happens ....feels to me like a spectator-box to observe God in relation to God," p. 213. We believe that her accusations are exaggerated and it is even harder to level this accusation with such baldness in Moltmann's more recent WJC. While his intention has always been to ground Christology in concrete events of Jesus' life, Carter-Heyward's comments show an element of truth in his discussion of the Trinity. We will be developing this idea further in the next chapter.

45. See, for example D. Brown, *The Divine Trinity*, London, Duckworth, 1985, p. 307. The plurality Model (PM) begins with the threeness of God and works towards his unity, while the Unity Model (UM) begins with God as one and then describes his Tri-Unity.

46. M. Wiles, *op. cit.* (n.18).

47. See, SBH, p.115, footnote 9; also, G. Stroup, "Review of *The Trinity and the Kingdom of God*: A 'Christian' Doctrine of God," *Interpretation*, 37, 1983, pp. 410-412.

48. P. Lønning, "Die Schöpfungstheologie Jürgen Moltmanns - eine Norische Perspektive," *Kerygma und Dogma*, 33, 1987, 207-223.

49. E. Bloch, *op. cit.* (n.5), *Volume 2*, pp. 665 ff.

50. *Ibid.*, p. 665; by "physical guideline" Bloch refers to the way in which technology emerged in alignment with guidelines perceived in matter in a physical sense, rather than in alignment with organic or human categories. In this way technology has become detached from "real" life, and the final category is that of artificial substances where even the "physical guideline" is abandoned. Bloch's understanding is similar here in some ways to that of Martin Heidegger. Heidegger's critique of modern technology is that Being as *physis* is forgotten. "Man" needs to allow Being to be itself in a way that is different from Being as represented to "Man." The original meaning of technology is *poiesis*, or make manifest. Once we forget this, it becomes subordinate to humanity's purpose, and even the "pretence" of the objectivity of science is lost, so that nature becomes pure commodity. Like Bloch, Heidegger hoped that technology could be reformulated so that it became more aware of its foundation in *poiesis*. See, H. Alderman, "Heidegger's Critique of Science and Technology," in, M. Murray, ed., *Heidegger and Modern Philosophy, Critical Essays*, New Haven/London, Yale University Press, 1978, pp. 35-50.

51. E. Bloch, *op. cit.* (n.5), pp. 690-693; see also, GC, p. 28.

52. G. Scholem, *Kabbalah*, The New York Times Book Co/Quadrangle, 1974, p. 88-91; for a similar discussion see, G. Scholem, *op. cit.* (n.34), p.12. The kabbalistic writers wish to make clear the distinction between the living God, who has names, and *Deus absconditus*, who can only be described by metaphors. The relationship between God and the world is defined by *Sefiroth*, which is a loose term referring to different aspects of emanation, and does not share in God's essence, *Kabbalah*, p. 100. The name *Ein Sof* is impersonal, though in subsequent history it acquired some personal characteristics. As an alternative, later speculation tried to separate the impersonal *Ein Sof* from the personal *Demiurge* of scripture in a way which Scholem describes as "downright heretical," *op. cit.* (n.34), p. 12. Moltmann's seeming equation of the personal God of the Bible with *Ein Sof* is an example of the former type of transformation. The idea of a Christian *kabbalah* is not new, and there was a flowering of this movement in the seventeenth and eighteenth centuries. These writers made direct links between Adam Kadmon, who is the first being to emerge after the *zimzum*, and Jesus Christ. These correlations were largely unsuccessful in winning converts from Judaism to Christianity; see G. Scholem, *Kabbalah*, pp. 199 ff.

53.   G. Scholem, *op. cit.* (n.34), pp. 260-261. Here he notes that the idea of God abandoning a region in himself was "often felt to verge on the blasphemous." We also note that K. Barth was not adverse to the idea of God having his own "inner space." Gunton notes that, for Barth, "there must be in God a kind of spatiality, understood on the basis of becoming spatial in Christ, but apophatically." The idea of God possessing his own distinct inner space serves to stress the ontological distinction between God and the world, and has connotations of a "living space" in which God is freely God in inner trinitarian relationships. Nonetheless, we are of the opinion that however carefully qualified, as in Barth, the use of the language of space in relation to the Godhead is not very helpful, as it implies God's requirement for a particular space. For a fuller discussion of Barth's views see, C. Gunton, "Barth, The Trinity and Human Freedom," *Theology Today*, 43, 1986, pp. 316-330.

54.   G. Scholem, *op. cit.* (n.34), p. 261; see also, pp. 250 ff.

55.   *Ibid.*, p. 263; for a similar treatment see *Kabbalah, op. cit.* (n.52), p. 134.

56.   G. Scholem, *op. cit.* (n.52), p. 138. Some of the vessels were overfilled with light and thereby broke into pieces in a way which accounted for the origin of evil. Other interpretations included that the vessels were broken in order to pave the way for reward and punishment, or just simply a mishap in the life of the Godhead.

57.   *Ibid.*, pp. 138 ff. The Lurian interpretation is the "achievement of a permanent blissful state of communion between every creature and God which the *kelippot* will be unable to disrupt or prevent."

58.   *Ibid.*, p. 75.

59.   G. Scholem, *op. cit.* (n.34), p. 8.

60.   *Ibid.*, p. 10. We are challenging here, not so much whether Moltmann is justified in using *zimzum*, but whether he has really engaged in a genuine dialogue with his Jewish sources, which insist on their rootedness in the Torah and the One God. This issue was raised in a slightly different way by James McPherson who criticized Moltmann's idea of the *Nihil*, as being very different from the kabbalistic idea of Nothingness, where it is "the barrier confronting human intellectual attempts to describe and articulate *Ein Sof* and the first stage of creation." However, we dispute this interpretation of *kabbalah*. While Scholem does interpret Nothingness in *kabbalah* as the barrier confronting human intellect, he also insists on the idea that it contains an implicit "root of evil" which becomes explicit in later kabbalistic interpretation. Hence Moltmann could be justified in including a negative in his concept of *Nihil* on the basis of *kabbalah*. We agree that Moltmann does not take sufficient account of the background to kabbalistic thought, but for different reasons than those deduced by McPherson. An influence in Moltmann's treatment may have come from Karl Barth's idea of the *Nihil*.

Barth seems to use "nothingness" in an axiological sense to denote an entity that is destructive of meaning, order and value. Hendry criticizes Barth in not making it clear how a formless world, which is negated in creation, can turn into a reality which threatens both God's creation and the being of God. He also argues that Moltmann "re-states Barth's position and glosses over the difficulties." Moltmann's response to this article may partly explain his detailed wrestling with this problem, but it is doubtful if he has removed the difficulties inherent in this view, and in this respect the criticism of Hendry still stands. See, J. McPherson, "Life, the Universe and Everything: Jürgen Moltmann's *God in Creation*," *St Mark's Review*, 128, 1986, pp. 35-46; G.S. Hendry, "Nothing," *Theology Today*, 39, 1982, pp. 274-289; for Moltmann's response to Hendry see, GC pp. 74 ff.

61.　GC, pp. 91 ff.; "In the light of the cross of Christ, *creatio ex nihilo* means forgiveness of sins through Christ's suffering, justification of the godless through Christ's death, and the resurrection of the dead and eternal life through the Lordship of the Lamb."

62.　The Trinitarian interplay in the outgoing act of creation of the world implies that this initial withdrawal is a Trinitarian movement; however, Moltmann never raises the issue of how the three persons of the Trinity are involved in this inner withdrawal. His silence on this issue may stem from the difficulty of trying to match Jewish theological speculation, which presuppose God's unity, with his own stated preference to begin with God's tri-unity.

63.　TKG, pp. 28 ff. The idea of the primacy of God's freedom, even in zimzum, which Moltmann develops here, is very different from Bloch's interpretation of the kabbalistic doctrine of God's inner withdrawal, which he believes amounts to an act of imprisonment and where this imprisonment of Yahweh looks forward to "the wishful space of the end, or day of deliverance;" E. Bloch, *op. cit.* (n.5), p. 1237.

64.　TKG, p. 28.

65.　G. Scholem, *op. cit.* (n.34), p. 231; for a definition of *Sefiroth*, see n.52.

66.　*Ibid.*, p. 275.

67.　*Ibid.*, p. 269. The word "symbolism" in mystical usage is different from allegory. While the latter is defined as "the representation of an expressible something," the symbol is "an expressible representation of something which lies beyond the sphere of expression .... A hidden and inexpressible reality finds its expression in the symbol," p. 27.

68.　*Ibid.*, p. 280.

69.　GC, p. 88; "the creative letting-be is better brought out through motherly categories."

70.　G. Scholem, *op. cit.* (n.34), p. 37.

71.　The possible difficulty which emerges in this context is that Moltmann's equation of *zimzum* with *kenosis* taken from Christology, by implication hints at self-negation. This is the opposite of his intention to discourage male domination and female self-denial. While Moltmann would resist the idea that the inner withdrawal is self-negating, its association with ideas such as the *Nihil* and the suffering crucified Christ has negative connotations. Mary Bringle and other feminist writers wish to encourage an image of femaleness that is not passive and withdrawing, but active and "leaving the cocoon." In this respect, at least, Moltmann's picture of God in "motherly" categories will not be welcomed by feminists. See, M. Bringle, "Leaving the Cocoon: Moltmann's Anthropology and Feminist Theology," *Andover Newton Quarterly*, 20, 1980, pp. 153-161.

72. F. Rosenzweig, *The Star of Redemption*; translated from the second edition (1930), by W. Hallo; London, Routledge and Kegan Paul, 1970, p. 409.

73. *Ibid.*, p. 411.

74. "In the normal sequence, identity is attained on the way from within to without, from essence to appearance, from creation to revelation. This sequence must be reversed for the world as becoming. For it, identification must begin with the self-denying appearance and end with the single and wholly affirmed essence. God's soul and man's have a becoming which is from within to without, but the world's becoming is otherwise. The world is wholly self-revelation from the first, yet it is still entirely without essence;" *ibid.*, p. 219. While Rosenzweig's style is somewhat obscure, it seems that he wishes to affirm the priority of God's essence along with that of humankind in a way that aims to separate God and humanity from the world. This is very different from Moltmann's view which stresses the commonality of humanity and the rest of creation. Nevertheless, Rosenzweig is not always consistent here, and other parts of his book hint at the idea of a becoming God: "In the redemption of the world by man, of man by means of the world, God redeems himself." However, in the next sentence we find him denying any real future for the world, including humanity: both seem to be lost in the life of the Godhead: "Man and the world disappear in the redemption, but God perfects himself," p. 238. This is clearly different from Moltmann's understanding of the future, which we will discuss in more detail in the next chapter. Moltmann's correlation of the person of the Holy Spirit with the *Shekinah* is very different from Rosenzweig's understanding of the self-distinction of God within the unity of essence. Moreover, while Rosenzweig's God suffers through the *Shekinah*, this does not seem to allow for a real change within God which emerges more clearly in Moltmann's theopaschite approach.

75. K. Barth, *The Humanity of God*, London, Collins, 1961, pp. 71-72.

76. *Ibid.*, p. 71; "In God's own freedom there is encounter and communion, there is order, and consequently dominion and subordination, there is majesty and humility, absolute authority and absolute obedience, there is offer and response." While Mason has noted the dependence of

Moltmann on Barth, believing that his doctrine of freedom amounts "largely to a revision of Barth's work," in our opinion this is an overstatement in view of Barth's intention to stress the hierarchical aspect. See, G. Mason, *op. cit.* (n.16), p. 204.

77.   G. Mason, *op. cit.* (n.16), pp. 212 ff.

78.   *Ibid.*, p. 225.

79.   The parallel between Moltmann's idea of the reciprocal relationship between God and the world and process theology has been noted by a number of scholars, e.g. J. McDade, "The Trinity and the Paschal Mystery," *Heythrop Journal*, 29, 1988, pp. 175-191.

80.   W.J. Hill, "The Historicity of God," *Theological Studies*, 45, 1984, pp. 320-333, see especially p. 327.

81.   TKG, p. 56. "God demonstrates his eternal freedom through his suffering and sacrifice, through his self-giving and patience." For comment on Cole-Turner's query that this does not allow for the sharing of God's passion in the suffering of the innocent, see Chapter 3.

82.   W. French, *op. cit.* (n.2), p. 79.

83.   B. Leftow, "God and the World in Hegel and Whitehead," in, G. Lucas, ed., *Contemporary Perspectives on Systematic Philosophy*, New York, State University of New York Press, 1986, pp. 257-265; see especially p. 264.

84.   While Moltmann mentions the possibility of divine enrichment by the world in TKG, pp. 45 ff., he drops this idea in subsequent work. For a discussion see, R. Cole-Turner, *God's Experience: the Trinitarian Theology of Jürgen Moltmann in Conversation with Charles Hartshorne*, PhD thesis, 1983, Princeton Theological Seminary, pp. 39ff; also R.Cole-Turner, "Review of *God in Creation*," *Zygon*, 22(1), 1987, pp. 120-122.

85.   S. Cole-Turner, PhD thesis, *op. cit.* (n.84), for a detailed comparison between Moltmann and process thought. The contrast between Moltmann and process theology is most clearly defined in the latter's weak development of Trinitarian themes. Cobb, Griffen and Ogden do not perceive God in tripersonal terms at all, while Lewis Ford's process Trinitarianism amounts to the tri-unity of three principles in God: (a) his non-temporal creative act; (b) the outcome in his primordial nature; (c) divine experience of the world in his consequent nature. For a useful comparison between process theology and other modern approaches to the Trinity see, J. Bracken, *What are They Saying about the Trinity?*, New York, Paulist Press, 1979, pp. 28-67. A detailed comparison of the aspects of both continuity and discontinuity between Hartshorne's understanding of God and that of Barth is in C. Gunton, *Becoming and Being: The Doctrine of God in Charles Hartshorne and Karl Barth*, Oxford, Oxford University Press, 1978. Colin Gunton argues strongly for a clear difference in philosophical base between Barth and process thought. In balance it seems, in our view, that

Moltmann's basic orientation is closer to that of Barth than that of process thought, especially because he insists on a Trinitarian basis. Moltmann's free use of material from both process and Barthian theology is not acceptable to more philosophical systematic theologians who believe that he has proceeded without establishing a clear philosophical basis for such a synthesis. See D. Brown, *op. cit.* (n.45) and J. McDade, *op. cit.* (n.79). In our opinion it is still Bloch's philosophy of hope that is an implicit core to Moltmann's methodology, with an ontological basis emerging out of the idea of social relatedness and a future definition.

86.   M. Grey, "The Core of our Desire: Reimaging the Trinity," *Theology*, 113, 1990, pp. 363-372.

87.   I. Carter-Heyward, *op. cit.* (n.41), p. 2.

88.   *Ibid.*, p. 9.

89.   WJC, p. 76.

90.   P. Fiddes, "Review of *God in Creation*," *Journal of Theological Studies*, 88, 1987, 263-265.

91.   See, E. Bloch, *op. cit.* (n.5), *Volume 2*, pp. 686-690. Here he argues further that the "co-productivity of nature is required, that which Paracelsus himself had in mind when his nature already appeared to him as friendly or capable of being befriended in an utopian way 'inwardly full of remedies, full of prescriptions and one big chemist's shop,' a cosmos in which man opens up, just as the microcosm of man causes the world to come to its senses," p. 689. Moltmann refers to Bloch's idea of "co-productivity" in GC, pp. 43-45. See also Heidegger, *op. cit.* (n.50).

92.   C. Westermann, *Genesis 1-11 A Commentary*; translated by J. Scullion, London, SPCK, 1984, pp. 16-87. See also, G. von Rad, *Genesis*; translated by J. Marks, London, SCM, 1956; U. Cassuto, *Commentary on Genesis: Part 1: From Adam to Noah*; translated from Hebrew by I. Abrahams, Jerusalem, Central Press, 1961; G. Wenham, *Genesis 1-25*; D. Hubbard and G. Barker, eds., Word Biblical Commentary, Volume 1, Waco, Word Books, 1987; H.L. Ellison, "Genesis," in, F.F. Bruce, ed., second edition, *The International Bible Commentary*, Basingstoke, Marshall, Morgan and Scott, 1986, pp. 111-123; B.W. Anderson, ed., *Creation in the Old Testament*, London, SPCK, 1984; B.W. Anderson, *Creation versus Chaos*, New York, Association Press, 1967.

93.   GC, p. 73. Moltmann distinguishes between creation and making. He transforms the idea of God's resolve to create into God's creation out of love. As we noted in Chapter 3 this tends to soften the idea of divine sovereignty. It seems doubtful that the theme of God's love for creation is quite as strong, in the perception of the writer of Genesis at least, as Moltmann would have us believe. In other words Moltmann does not distinguish in an adequate way

between God's action in creation and his subsequent revelation to Israel. The two aspects are interrelated, but not merged in the Genesis account.

94. C. Westermann, *op. cit.* (n.92), p. 86. Westermann argues strongly that the verbs "create" and "make" are interchangeable in other contexts, so that there is no valid exegetical basis for their distinction. Moltmann is following von Rad in this respect, who claims that "create" designates "special and exclusive divine creativity," G. von. Rad, *op. cit.* (n.92), p. 54.

95. GC, p. 88; see also pp. 74-79; 86-87 and discussion relating to the idea of "Nothingness," n.60, above.

96. *Ibid.*, p. 89; Moltmann agrees with von Rad that the idea of *creatio ex nihilo* is implicit in the text of Genesis. Westermann is much more critical of the use of this expression at all in an exegetical sense, believing that the writers of Genesis were not concerned about where creation came from, and the causal question behind the concept of *creatio ex nihilo* is quite foreign to the text. He is strongly critical of all modern attempts to interpret Genesis in a way that allows us to follow the events of creation with our imagination believing that: "Explanations which strive after images strip the narrative of that reality which is completely beyond imagery and which is concerned with the state of the world as it is." Nonetheless, Westermann makes a controversial claim that because the idea of *creatio ex nihilo* is found in much later materials, such as 2 Maccabees 7:28, its origin is in Greek philosophy. However, such usage is atypical, and *creatio ex nihilo* in Jewish and Christian usage is usually anti-Hellenistic. In general, we believe that Moltmann is justified in having a concept of *creatio ex nihilo*, other exegetes who have used this expression include J. Calvin, J. Wellhausen, E. Konig, G. Aalders and A. Heidel. Moltmann's particular understanding of *creatio ex nihilo* in terms of kabbalistic ideas is more dubious, and in this respect Westermann's criticism of the pitfalls of modern exegesis seems to bear some relevance. See, G. von Rad, *op. cit.* (n. 92), pp. 47 ff. ; C. Westermann, *op. cit.* (n.92), pp. 108-109; 120.

97. P. Molnar, *op. cit.* (n.8).

98. D. Spanner, *Biblical Creation and the Theory of Evolution*, Exeter, Paternoster Press, 1987, pp. 59-67; C. Westermann, *op. cit.* (n.92), p. 125.

99. GC, p. 30.

100. V. Lossky, *Orthodox Theology: An Introduction*; translated by I. Kesarcodi-Watson, New York, St.Vladimir's Seminary Press, 1989, pp. 51-78.

101. GC, p. 31.

102. *Ibid.*, p. 224.

103. "Man and the Son of Man;" translated by L. Williams, J. Nelson, ed., *No Man is Alien: Essays on the Unity of Mankind*, Leiden, Brill, 1971, pp. 203-224, see p. 212.

104. *Ibid.*, p. 213.

105. *Ibid.*, p. 212. Moltmann's focus on human history puts in sharp relief Moltmann's later comments on "mother earth," which seem to have been encouraged by his dialogue with feminism, and possibly by Bloch's own interest in this idea; see E. Bloch, *op. cit.* (n.5); and GC, p. 187. Westermann acknowledges the background to the idea of the earth bringing forth in Gen. 1.12 is in the "image of mother earth," but he insists that this older definition is modified by the author of Genesis so that "it is only God's creative word that enables the earth to bring forth the plants, it cannot do so of itself," C. Westermann, *op. cit.* (n.92), p. 125. He rejects, even more firmly, the possible extrapolation of this idea to that of animals (and humankind), it: "cannot mean a direct participation of the earth in creation of the animals ... The mythical view that the earth gives birth to the animals, which occurs in a number of cosmogonies, is well in the background," pp. 141-142. In our opinion Moltmann does not make this distinction sufficiently clear, and is an example of why his work has been criticized for a lack of attention to biblical exegesis; R. Cole-Turner describes GC as "by far the least biblical of any of his major works," R. Cole-Turner, "Review of *God in Creation, Zygon*, 22(1), 1987, pp. 120-122.

106. C. Westermann, *op. cit.* (n.92), p.151. We will take up the theme of exegetical questions in the understanding of Genesis 1:26 in the next chapter. For an excellent study of the history of interpretation of *imago Dei*, see, G.A. Jønsson, *The Image of God: Genesis 1:26-28 in a Century of Old Testament Research*; translated from Swedish by L. Svendsen, M.S. Cheney, ed., *Coniectanea Biblica, Old Testament Series, 26*, T. Mettinger and M. Ottosson, eds., Lund, Almquist and Wiksell International, 1988.

107. K. Hafstad, "Gott in der Natur: Zur Schöpfungslehre Jürgen Moltmanns," *Evangelische Theologie*, 47, 1987, pp. 460-466. For other critiques of Moltmann's position, see under n.110, below.

108. P. Molnar, *op. cit.* (n.8).

109. K. Barth, *op. cit.* (n.75); where he describes human freedom as the "joy of obedience," p. 79. While Moltmann successfully counters a weakness in Barth's theology, which tends to identify God's freedom with divine election, the parallel idea of human response in obedience which we find in Barth is lost in Moltmann's anthropology.

110. B. Walsh, "Theology of Hope and Doctrine of Creation: An Appraisal of Jürgen Moltmann, *Evangelical Quarterly*, 59(1), 1987, pp. 53-76. Examples of a critical attitude towards Moltmann's discussion of sinfulness from more liberal perspectives are in R. Cole-Turner, *op. cit.* (n.84), where he states that Moltmann is "strangely optimistic" and "one simply cannot grasp the perniciousness of human evil in terms of closing ourselves to divine potentialities," p.122. A. Primavesi, similarly, believes Moltmann ignores the choice between

good and evil, A. Primavesi, "Review of *God in Creation,*" *Heythrop Journal,* 30, 1989, pp. 232-234.

111. A discussion of Moltmann's earlier position is in, G. Chapman, "Moltmann's Vision of Man," *Anglican Theological Review,* 56, 1974, pp. 310-330. Moltmann shifts the language in which he describes human sinfulness from loss of hope to loss of openness. In both cases redemption seems to be connected with liberation, either from despair or pride as in *Theology of Hope,* or from closedness, as in TKG and GC.

112. GC, p. 233. The idea of human sinfulness receives relatively scant attention in GC, occupying a mere five pages, pp. 229-234.

113. J. Levenson, *Creation and the Persistence of Evil: The Jewish Drama of Divine Omnipotence,* San Franscisco, Harper and Row, 1988, pp. 48-49; 121-127.

114. D. Cox, *Charles Elton and the Emergence of Modern Ecology,* PhD thesis, 1979, Washington University, pp. 1 ff.

115. *Ibid.*; see especially pp. 91-110, 138-40, 212-215.

116. We will be taking up this theme again in the following chapter.

117. G. Hardin, "Ecology and the Death of Providence," *Zygon,* 15(1), 1980, pp. 57-68. For an alternative position see, J. Grayson, "The Environment and Perception of Reality: A Physiologist's Point of View," *Ultimate Reality and Meaning,* 11, 1988, pp. 294-309. Moltmann seems to fail to acknowledge two philosophies of biology, or attitudes as defined as provisionalist or autonomist by Alexander Rosenberg. In summary, the provisionalists argue that anything which cannot be connected with physical theory amounts to unscientific knowledge, while the autonomists stress the limits in seeing biology in physical terms and argue that organic phenomena are in a different category. The weakness of the former view is its refusal to take seriously the advances in biology independent of physics or chemistry, while the limitation of the latter is its historical root in vitalism which gives it a weak epistemological basis. A. Rosenberg, *The Structure of Biological Science,* Cambridge, Cambridge University Press, 1985, pp. 18-25.

118. G. Terence, "Review of *God in Creation,*" *Theological Studies,* 47, 1986, pp. 527-529, see especially p. 527.

119. See GC, p. 17 for Moltmann's use of Jantsch's ideas. E. Jantsch, *The Self-Organizing Universe,* New York, Pergamon Press, 1980, p.8 ; for background discussion of the *Gaia* hypothesis see D. Sagan, and L. Margulis, "*Gaia* and Philosophy," in, L. Rouner, ed., *On Nature,* Indiana, University of Notre Dame Press, 1984, pp. 60-75. A useful definition is "*Gaia* is a theory of the atmosphere and surface sediments of the planet Earth taken as a whole. The *Gaia* hypothesis in its most general form states that the temperature and composition of the

Earth's atmosphere are actively regulated by the sum of life on the planet - the biota. The regulation of the Earth's surface by the biota and for the biota has been in continuous existence since the earliest appearance of widespread life." The temptation to turn *Gaia* into a form of philosophy has been too hard for many of its propagandists to resist. This tendency is similar to the avocation of Evolutionism soon after the success of Darwin's *Origin of Species*. Then, as now, both the ideas of evolution and that of *Gaia* are fraught with difficulties from a purely scientific perspective. It remains to be seen whether *Gaia* will receive widespread acceptance in the scientific community as the idea of evolution has since the last century. We will be taking up the discussion of the *Gaia* hypothesis again in the next chapter.

120. E. Jantsch, *op. cit.* (n.119), p. 8. The idea of self-transcendence, according to Jantsch, which we have outlined here actually seems to be at odds with Moltmann's work. Wittgenstein believed that philosophical problems arise once we allow expressions to stray outside their normal employment. For Wittgenstein knowledge amounts to power to set rules for language use; see, R. Mandel, "Heidegger and Wittgenstein: A Second Kantian Revolution," in, M. Murray, ed., *Heidegger and Modern Philosophy, op. cit.* (n.50), pp. 259-270, esp. pp. 266-268.

121. E. Jantsch, *op. cit.* (n.119), p. 18.

122. *Ibid.*, p. 308.

123. P. Hodgkin, "General Practice in the Year 2000: A Faustian Future," *British Medical Journal*, 286, 1983, pp. 944-945. He comments in this article that: "Alfred North Whitehead remarked that it is the duty of the future to almost wreck the present into which it is being born. The paradigm of self-organization gives a hard edge to this and real hope that the future might not be as dire as it often seems. Perhaps as part of a self-organizing universe we have more on our side than we think."

124. We note an alternative way of countering such dualism in Niebuhr. While this is very different from an aggressive tyrannical monotheism which Moltmann rejects, it seeks to find the glory of God within creation but starting from a basis in the unity of God rather than his triunity. See, R.H. Niebuhr, *Radical Monotheism and Western Culture*, London, Faber and Faber, 1960, pp. 49-63.

CHAPTER 6.

A Critical Appreciation of Moltmann's Ecological Doctrine of Creation.

Part B. Eschatological Horizons: Moltmann's Vision for the Future.

1. Introduction.

One of Jürgen Moltmann's major achievements has been to help shift the tone of contemporary theology into a future key. His early *Theology of Hope* reminded us that without a vision for the future our Christian witness remains static and lifeless. While we believe that his intention has always been to include "nature" along with humanity in the process of liberation, we argued in the last chapter that the shift in his interest specifically to creation itself and God as creator as well as redeemer modified his own understanding of the dynamics of the interrelationship between God and the world. This modification led to a re-expression of much of his Trinitarian theology in more explicit ecological categories. When we turn to Moltmann's understandng of the future of creation we find similar elements of continuity and discontinuity.

Our task in the present section is crucial for adequate evaluation of the significance of Moltmann's theology in the ecological crisis. To what extent does it give us a vision which encourages our attitudes to change in a way that is compatible with an orthodox understanding of Christian belief?[1] Also we will be asking: what outline can we project for the future of the natural world? How far is Moltmann's understanding dominated by anthropocentric concerns?

One of the core questions which underlies the relative significance of creation in theological discussions is its value *vis-à-vis* history. We find the same kind of problem on a broader level in the question of the interrelationship between space and time.[2] We will be taking a critical look at the way Moltmann attempts to relate history and nature and their relative importance. We hope to show that the background to some of his ideas as to the future of the world comes from Ernst Bloch's *Principle of Hope*. However, the resolution of the tension between history and nature in Moltmann's theology is couched in Christian metaphors of the sabbath and the cosmic Christ. We believe that both ideas are crucial to Moltmann's perception of the future and his attempt to come to an integrated understanding of how our history is involved in the history of the cosmos.

Our discussion will shift to one which looks at the tension between the present and future in the light of his understanding of creation in holistic terms, that is, one that does not separate material or physical reality from the mental or spiritual realms. The background to this idea is (i) the involvement of God in the world, as "embodiment"; (ii) the *Gestalt* of Christ. This raises the issue of our human distinctiveness as *imago Christi* and *gloria Dei* in relation to the rest of creation. Finally (iii) the 'transfigured' embodiment as the fulfillment of the yearning of the Spirit. All three aspects show Moltmann's concern to remain Trinitarian in his thinking about the future of creation.

As part of our assessment of Moltmann's vision we will raise the question as to how far he has taken seriously enough alternative models and/or incorporated them into his own picture. We will discuss briefly the evolutionary/scientific view, the idea of a self-organizing universe, and

Christian mysticism and Taoist philosophy. A secular critique of any future vision evaluates (i) whether it is intrinsically desirable, (ii) whether it is possible of actual achievement, and (iii) whether it is set forth in such a way that to reject it would be to court destruction.[3] We will try to assess where Moltmann goes beyond these secular boundaries, and whether he is justified for theological reasons.[4]

Moltmann has always been insistent that our language in dealing with the future must rely on evocative symbols. We will raise the issue throughout this discussion as to whether he has fallen into the trap which characterized his earlier theology in using "too many equivocal words and too few empirical references."[5] The mixed reaction to Moltmann's language use depends on our preconceived ideas about the value of language as a means of communication.[6] We hope to show that, while this particular novel use of language about the future of creation does foster inspiration and hope, he rarely develops the basis for his reconstruction in a way that is adequate scientifically, and in addition tends to stray outside generally accepted theological boundaries.

The issue of whether Moltmann really has done sufficient justice to the theme of creation in his approach, which still remains basically Christological and historical in orientation, is related to the wider question of whether his understanding of science is adequately incorporated into his theological framework. His resolution of these tensions pneumatologically emerges as a cosmic eschatological Christology which gives his theology a kerygmatic quality, even though it is highly eclectic in appearance. We hope that the analysis which follows will serve both to show the distinctive contribution of Moltmann's theology, and to hint at ways in which we can move beyond his discussion in the light of the ecological demand on our theological task.

2. The interrelationship between history and nature.

Jürgen Moltmann's treatment of the theme of creation in his earlier work was within the context of salvation history.[7] In common with many other theologians of this period he discussed the value of creation in the context of the early history of Israel outlined in the Pentateuch.[8] Reventlow considers that the shift in the theological climate towards one which takes the theme of creation more seriously came from the rising pressure of the ecological movement. The latter took up Lynn White's suggestion that Christianity is responsible for the ecological crisis through an understanding of the Genesis idea of dominion as the right to exploit the natural world.[9] While White's thesis has been largely rejected by theological academic circles, his ideas helped to shift concern from history towards creation and nature. Claus Westermann, for example, stressed the continuous act of blessing within the redemptive acts of God in history.[10] MacQuarrie proposed an organic model.[11] More recently Liedke, a student of Westermann, moved towards an incorporation of New Testament eschatology within the creation motif.[12]

Moltmann's concern to be more inclusive in his theology is not unexpected in view of the theological changes in climate. However, we suggest that many of Moltmann's ideas on the future of creation were already implicit in his earlier theology prior to any cultural changes which marked a heightened sense of awareness to ecological issues. The basis for an interrelationship between nature and history comes from Ernst Bloch's philosophy which was at least partly instrumental in shaping Moltmann's understanding of the Trinity in social categories.

(a) Background in Ernst Bloch's ontology of "Not-Yet."

According to Meeks, Bloch's philosophy is directed towards bringing nature and history into a dialectical relationship.[13] The difference between Moltmann and Bloch is that only the former distinguishes the future in terms of the Christian eschaton from the future as Utopia.[14] Moltmann shares Bloch's concern to separate the "No-Longer Conscious," which refers to past history that is forgotten or repressed, and the "Not-Yet Conscious" which comes to us from the future.[15] Bloch believed that our failure to recognize the reality of the "Not-

Yet Conscious" comes from the latter being crushed by a Platonic Ideal Memory or anamnesis.[16] The "Not-Yet Conscious" differs from fantasy in formulating the "Real-Possible," rather than the "Empty-Possible."[17] It also differs from scientific prediction, which is the "Objectively-Possible."[18] Bloch believed that Christianity is mistaken in relating the *Ultimum*, or the dialectical emergence of the whole, to the beginning or *Primum*, instead of the *Novum*.[19] We noted earlier how Moltmann similarly rejects the relationship between the *Ultimum* and *Primum*, but insists that this is a mistaken interpretation of Christianity, rather than a true Christian eschatology, which also looks to the future *Novum*.

Bloch integrated both nature and history in the horizon of the future. He viewed alliance technology as that which emerged in the dialogue between nature and history:

> "finally manifested nature lies just the same as finally manifested history in the horizon of the future, and the mediation categories of concrete technology which can well be expected in the future also run towards this horizon alone."[20]

Bloch insisted that nature is the "lasting surroundings" of humankind and was more positive than Marx in his attitude to nature; giving it a degree of "subjectivity." Nevertheless, he also qualified this idea by regarding humankind as necessary for nature's completeness: "Just as human history has not yet dawned into brightness, so nature has not yet done so through human history."[21] In this way Bloch believed that nature has a "brooding" and "incompleteness" in it which remains unfinished until humanity's involvement with it. While Moltmann takes up some of Bloch's ideas of nature as that which is "unfinished," he also moves beyond Bloch by giving nature a value in and of itself quite apart from humanity. We will discuss whether he has been entirely successful in this respect in the section below on sabbath and the cosmic Christ.

Moltmann's resolution of the tension between nature and history in his vision of the future becomes apparent in his idea of heaven, which has some parallels with Bloch's treatment.[22] Bloch distinguished between subjective hope, *qua speratur*, and *quae speratur*, which he understood as the object of hope. According to Bloch we can *only* have confidence in the former "hoping hope," not in "hoped hope." If we had a guarantee of the latter material, objective hope, then our hope would be "trivial" rather than "brave." This leads on to Bloch's idea of an "empty space" in which hope stands, which Moltmann brings into his discussion.[23] Bloch's refusal to make objective hope certain weakens the ontological content of his idea of "Not-Yet," and links it in a closer way with history. However, he also pressed towards a concept of a "dialectical leap into the New," and resisted any thought that this was "pre-ordered" "in the style of the old teleology, let alone a teleology mythologically guided from above."[24]

Moltmann distances himself from Bloch's atheistic description of heaven, believing that "a transcending without transcendence" ultimately slips into an "indefinite endlessness." Cole-Turner may be exaggerating when he claims that Moltmann's "most persuasive argument for 'heaven' is not from scripture, or tradition, but from Ernst Bloch."[25] Rather, Moltmann seems to be anxious to preserve a Christian interpretation of heaven, over against secular alternatives which try to remove the necessity for God. Moltmann's lengthy discussion on heaven in Bloch's philosophy more likely reflects his own desire to transform this philosophy into Christian categories.

The idea of heaven is also a convenient way of bringing together past and future reality, along with nature and history. Moltmann is struggling to formulate concepts which will have meaning for us in the present, while pointing to the future. The concept of heaven is a traditional idea which lends itself to such reinterpretation. However, it is probably fair to say that he has overstretched this advantage by insisting that the idea of heaven is a present as well as future concept, and by filling it with some ideas taken from process theology. His notion of heaven as a mediatory category between God and the world in space and time is ingenious, but bordering on the fantastic. Heaven bears some resemblance to his idea of *Aeon*, with the former dealing more specifically with the present and future of space, and the latter dealing with the present and future in time. In the new *Aeon* a new heaven and a new earth will emerge which, while sharing in God's eternity and omnipresence, are not identical with either. For Moltmann the idea of heaven is a convenient way of expressing his *panentheism*. We will be returning to his discussion of *Aeon* in a later section.

One of the reasons why Moltmann believes he is justified in drawing an outline of the common horizon of nature and history comes from an approach coined by Rosenzweig as "anticipatory consciousness."[26] This is an understanding of the future as anticipation, rather than extrapolation, and so has some parallels with Bloch's notions of "Not-Yet Conscious." Rosenzweig's theme in the *Star of Redemption* is that just as God, the world and humankind are represented by one triangle, so creation, revelation and redemption are represented by another. The combination forms a star, hence the title of his book, which in addition reinforces the late symbol of Judaism. Moltmann similarly shares Rosenzweig's concern to interrelate the themes of creation, revelation and redemption, but in Christian categories. Rosenzweig seeks to link creation with the past, revelation with the present and redemption with the future, and criticizes Christianity for depicting an eternity "wholly beyond time."[27] For him, Christianity allows redemption to be "swallowed back into creation, into revelation" instead of giving priority to redemption or distinguishing clearly between redemption and revelation.[28] Moltmann wants to distance himself from expressing Christianity in the way described by Rosenzweig, and through his eschatological approach comes closer to the latter's understanding of God as one who "is the Redeemer in a much stronger sense than he is Creator or Revealer."[29] Nonetheless, the significance of Rosenzweig's theology on Moltmann's perspective is more obvious in relation to his understanding of the sabbath.

(b) Nature and history through the ideal of the sabbath.

We noted in the introduction that Moltmann's own position on the meaning of creation has its background theological context in Barth's and von Rad's emphasis on salvation history. Moltmann believes that in the course of these discussions "something has been overlooked," and this is "the sabbath of the earth."[30] His intention in bringing back the idea of the sabbath is to construct a "divine ecology."[31]

Moltmann uses a combination of Jewish and biblical sources to develop his idea of the sabbath. He seems justified in using such a combination in that the bulk of biblical references come from the Old Testament. A possible query over his reconstruction, however, is whether he is similarly justified in using the sabbath ideal to express the Christian hope for the future of the cosmos. We will also explore whether linking the sabbath, which is rooted in holy time, with a future cosmic hope, underplays the concrete space of creation. Has Moltmann really corrected von Rad's focus on time and salvation history, which is his intention in developing the idea of the sabbath? It seems to amount to a broadening of this concept, rather than any more radical shift.

Von Rad draws heavily on deutero-Isaiah as a basis for his belief that the themes of creation and redemption are linked, and, more importantly, that creation is subordinate to redemption. Furthermore, he argues that Genesis is written from a soteriological perspective.[32] The history of Israel is such that the act of initial creation came to be seen as significant only in the context of this history, so that: "presumptuous as it may sound, Creation is part of the aetiology of Israel."[33] Von Rad distinguishes between God's rest after his work in creation, and the idea of God finding rest among his people, which emerges relatively late in the history of the Jewish nation. We can also distinguish God's rest from the ideal of rest for the people of God, which is linked up with the concrete human situation in all its trials and difficulties. The divine rest of Genesis 2.2 is "not at this point made normative for the rhythm of human life, but is mentioned simply as a fact in its own right."[34] Von Rad believes that we only find an interpretation of rest as eschatological hope in the New Testament, Hebrews in particular.[35]

Andreason's thorough tradition-historical investigation explores more closely the motif of the sabbath in the Old Testament. He shows that the sabbath ideal is not just related back to the seventh day of Genesis, but is linked with five other Old Testament concepts.[36] While Andreason is prepared to admit that the sabbath does provide an occasion for the "regeneration" of the earth, this is a relatively weak theme in the context of its Jewish setting. He agrees with von Rad that any link between sabbath and eschatology is in literature that is subsequent to the Old Testament period.[37]

Moltmann follows Rosenzweig in his readiness to discuss the sabbath in eschatological terms which are bound up clearly with the creation account. Rosenzweig is anxious to stress the significance of the sabbath as part of the Jewish cultic institution. It becomes "a feast of completion" and "a dream of perfection."[38] He believes that the sabbath as a festival of perfection points to the renewal of creation, and so anticipates redemption in a way which makes it "a feast of consummation."[39] The sabbath commemorates creation which acts like an "evenflow" in a way which brings stability to the "surge of joy and sorrow" of the other feasts, and in this sense the sabbath "lends reality to the year."[40]

Moltmann's treatment of the sabbath also draws on Abraham Heschel, the Jewish rabbi who speaks profoundly on the sabbath as the sanctification of time rather than space.[41] Moltmann's idea of the sabbath forms a convenient bridge between creation and history, space and time, and for him the sabbath "belongs to the fundamental structure of creation itself."[42] The sabbath is also a linking idea in his understanding of the tension between the transcendence and immanence of God. For example, "in the sabbath God joins his eternal presence to his temporal creation."[43] Just as we find Moltmann constructing the theological concept of heaven to provide a predominantly spatial link between God and creation, so his theological concept of sabbath hints at the link between God's eternity and creation's temporality. The latter link is more clearly defined in Moltmann's treatment of *Aeon*, which we will discuss later. In both concepts of heaven and sabbath the underlying tension between history and nature is resolved in a cosmic "*Shalom*," which expresses the peaceful harmony existing in a world that is reconciled to God. The sabbath in its "peace and silence" comes to reflect God's very Being, so it is at once both linked with the activity of God expressed in the acts of creation, yet more profound in meaning.[44]

Moltmann's account of the sabbath offers a fresh perspective on raising the significance of the idea for Christian reflection. We have already noted that eschatological interpretations of the sabbath are a late Jewish/Christian development, and Moltmann's imaginative portrait of the sabbath is a further step in this direction.[45] The question we raise here is whether Moltmann has drawn too much theological significance from the ideal of the sabbath in relation to the future cosmos in a way that has become rather too distant from the rootedness of this concept in the Old Testament. This criticism holds even if we allow for a more canonical approach to hermeneutics. For example, one difficulty is that the early Christian witness in Hebrews suggests that in the New Testament Christ in some sense replaces the ideal of the sabbath of the Old Testament.[46] Moltmann appears to resist replacing the sabbath ideal with Christian motifs, for example in *God in Creation* he argues that the Jewish sabbath should not be replaced by the Christian Sunday.[47] However, the links which he finds between the Jewish messianic expectation and the person of Jesus would, in practice, lead to such a replacement.[48] His discussion of the "messianic sabbath" is rather disappointing and seems to focus on the way Jesus interpreted the Old Testament laws of liberation.[49] The connection that Moltmann notes between sabbath and liberation if anything reinforces the replacement of the sabbath by Christ, who is liberator *par excellence*. While this renders his theology more traditionally orthodox in viewing the horizon of the future of creation in Christological terms rather than through the paradigm of the sabbath, it leads to a certain incoherence in his own position. If Moltmann intends the sabbath to be merely a *prolegomenon* for Christ, then he is hardly justified in making some of his bolder claims in *God in Creation* about the importance of the sabbath for the being of God, and the consummation of creation.

(c) Nature and history through the cosmic Christ.

Moltmann's earlier work looked to the redemption and liberation of the cosmos wrought through the cross and resurrection of Christ, taking Romans 8.19-22 as one of his key texts.[50] While he retains this motif, as his Trinitarian theology develops he begins to draw on the concept of the cosmic Christ using both Colossians 1.15-20, and traditional Eastern Orthodoxy. When he formulates his Christology in *The Way of Jesus Christ* we note a greater effort on his part to include nature as a whole in his discussions on soteriology in a way that is more explicit in its emphasis on ecology compared with his earlier work, *The Crucified God*. We noted previously that for Moltmann the key criterion for any theology is in its relationship with Christology. Hence the way his Christology becomes cosmic in scope to include the whole creation underpins his effort to reflect on the significance of creation. Our aim in the present discussion is to look briefly at exegetical studies of Romans 8.18-19 and Colossians 1.15-20 in the light of Moltmann's own interpretation.

Romans 8.19 speaks of "anxious watching of the creation". Further, in Romans 8.22 we read that "the creation groans together and travails together." Exegetes who tried to remove the idea of creation as cosmos by linking this expectation specifically to humanity were roundly dismissed by Sanday who argued that Paul is referring back to Genesis 3.17-19. He finds parallels in Jewish literature where the object of the appearance of the Messiah is to deliver all of creation from its ills. The idea of the "renovation" of nature comes from

Isaiah 65.17-25, and he comments that Paul is more sympathetic with nature "for its own sake" compared with Jewish writings which have a more nationalistic bias.[51]

While most contemporary exegetes would agree that the creation refers to the whole of the created order, more conservative scholars believe that the significance of Romans 8.18 ff. is to emphasize the certainty of future salvation for Christians, and "he is not concerned with creation for its own sake."[52] This is a controversial issue, since Dodd believes that our "experience of the Spirit" is "a ground of hope for the whole universe, since man cannot be isolated from the rest of nature."[53] Käsemann, similarly, steers a middle course between the view that "creation" refers to non-Christians, and the "absurd" alternative "rich speculations about plants, animals, or even spiritual powers." He believes that the term "nature" is also inappropriate since "nature plays a very small rôle for the apostle. He lays the whole stress on nature as a historical phenomenon, so that the universe is regarded as the setting of human history."[54]

Haldane, like Moltmann, seems to link the idea of future deliverance with the new heaven and a new earth, rather than a restoration to an ideal state. He remains highly cautious in his descriptions of the form of creation, except that it "shall be worthy of the Divine wisdom, although at present beyond our comprehension."[55] Cranfield equates the frustration of creation with humanity's failure, since God has decreed that "without man it should not be made perfect."[56] In other words the liberation of creation comes when humanity recognizes its true responsibility to praise God. Cranfield adds that this implies nature has "a dignity of its own," presumably because the liberation of creation comes not so much for the benefit of humankind, but for the greater praise of God.[57] The possibility hinted at by the above is that redemption is somehow necessary for the completion of creation. Forde believes that this is "treacherous" and that creation should not so much "need" Christ as "love him" in "absolute freedom and spontaneity." Such hope is qualified by a readiness to suffer, and it is through this hope of *creation itself* that we "are quite literally saved."[58]

Moltmann retains a more conservative estimate of "creation" in Romans meaning the created world, rather than an existential category, as in Forde. However, he extends the apocalyptic sufferings of Christ to include the sufferings of creation in a way that leaves us feeling a little uneasy, since it does not seem to be the requirement of this text.[59] Rimbach has argued strongly, like Moltmann, for an ecological motif in Romans 8.[60] However, he believes that the explicit context is Christological rather than messianic or apocalyptic. Moltmann combines the idea of Romans 8.18 with that of "fellowship in Christ's sufferings" drawn from Philippians 3.10, so that the whole of creation shares in a common fellowship of suffering and liberation with Christ.[61] This contrasts with Käsemann's more cautious interpretation. He believes that the participation of creation in eschatological freedom does not give us a licence to assume that this refers to a "new heaven and earth." Creation has to suffer the consequences of the Fall of humanity, and the key difference from Jewish apocalyptic is that "eschatological glory is perfected freedom."[62]

While Moltmann picks up the theme of liberation of all creation as paradigmatic for his understanding of the significance of Romans 8, his understanding of liberation is rather different from Käsemann's view that it is an anthropological concept. For Käsemann, the introduction of the idea of freedom in this text reinforces the unusually strong anthropological stance from which Paul views the *parousia*. This "exclusively anthropological angle" is expressed as "the manifestation of the children of God" in Romans 8.21. Käsemann confines the suffering which has transformative power through the Spirit in its solidarity with Christ to that of the Christian community; even though the hope engendered in this experience reaches out to all of creation.[63] While the idea of the cosmic sufferings of Christ is consistent with the notion of his cosmic lordship and reconciliation of all creation expressed in Colossians, is Moltmann justified in linking this idea of the cosmic Christ directly with the idea of the groaning of creation in Romans 8, or in reinterpreting fellowship of sufferings of Philippians 3 to include the natural world ?

We agree with Moltmann in so far as he suggests that the sufferings of creation and nature are in some sense inseparable from our own sufferings, and so part of Christ's sufferings. Yet to go beyond this borders on speculation which amounts to a "greening" of Christology that is hardly justified from biblical exegesis. If anything, it may prove a distraction since by channeling *all* the suffering of the cosmos into Christ's sufferings, we lose a sense of the sufferings of God with creation through the Holy Spirit. In other words, pneumatology could become weakened through such a strong Christological motif. This is clearly not Moltmann's intention, assuming he is still in agreement with his arguments set forth in *The Trinity and the Kingdom of God* and *God in Creation*.

Moltmann uses a traditional Eastern Orthodox interpretation of Colossians 1.15-20 to develop his cosmic Christology.[64] The idea of the cosmic Christ is a favourite paradigm among contemporary Eastern Orthodox theologians who are concerned with ecological issues.[65] Moltmann combines an interest in the cosmic Christ with the idea of Christ as the Wisdom of creation. The shift towards a renewed sense of the importance of the wisdom literature is part of a general trend within the contemporary theological scene, and is in parallel with a renewed interest in creation.[66]

Moltmann draws on the "splendid" work of the Lutheran theologian, Joseph Sittler, for his understanding of Colossians 1.15-20. Sittler was one of the pioneers in shifting the discussion among ecumenical theologians towards ecological issues.[67] He insisted that failure to acknowledge the cosmic dimensions of Christology has led to a separation of nature and grace in a way which has had disastrous environmental consequences. In other words Sittler wished to recover a lost dimension in theology, rather than the more prosaic inference that Christianity had somehow "caused" the exploitation of nature through application of the concept of human dominion over nature given in Genesis. Moltmann defends Sittler's concern to include nature within the redemptive framework of Christ's lordship, against the critics who claimed that this loses sight of personal historical salvation. Moltmann's defence seems to be quite justified in looking to cosmic Christology as the ultimate horizon towards which we express Christian faith.

Earlier twentieth century exegetes were cautious as to the possible implications of this verse. More conservative scholars, such as Lightfoot, described any attempt to make the restoration one of universal significance a "vain" speculation.[68] Schweitzer believes that the original hymn found embedded in this text is quite unique in setting forth the idea of cosmic restoration for the whole world. While we find other biblical references to the cosmic Christ, Romans 8.17-21 and Colossians 1.15-20 are unusual in their reference to *cosmic* redemption.[69] Schweitzer believes that Romans 8 connects the reconciliation of the cosmos with that of humanity in eschatological terms. It is important for our present purposes to note that Schweitzer insists that the universal overtones of the original hymn in Colossians are drastically altered by the author of the epistle. The modifications are such that: "As distinct from the whole of the hymn itself, the discussion no longer relates to the creation and reconciliation of the universe, but simply to one section of the human race instead....The theological formulation is thus completely changed."[70]

In general, there is a broad consensus among New Testament scholars that Colossians 1.15-20 has the literary form of a hymn which has been redacted by the writer of the epistle, though there is some debate about which phrases are part of the earliest hymn. There is greater divergence in opinion as to the background context for the hymn. Käsemann, for example, believes that it was originally a pre-Christian Gnostic text.[71] Other alternatives are that the hymn was set against a background of either rabbinical Judaism, or Hellenistic

Judaism.[72] O'Brien believes that a dissection of the hymn into its pre-Pauline and Pauline components is "artificial," and argues in favour of keeping the hymn as a single entity, and looking no further than Paul as the author of the hymn.[73]

The language used in the hymn hints at a possible background in Jewish wisdom literature, though the idea of wisdom as the goal of creation goes beyond the Jewish understanding.[74] Moltmann's focus on the Christological thrust of Colossians 1.15-20 is in line with Schweitzer; however he departs significantly from him in his use of these verses to include nature in redemptive categories. Schweitzer is highly critical of, for example Teilhard de Chardin or Sittler's position, and any similar views which use these verses as a basis for universal redemption. According to him their failure is in their refusal to distinguish the original hymn from its redacted version in the final letter.[75]

3. The holistic motif in the future of creation.

(a) God as embodiment.

Moltmann's idea of the future of God's relationship with the world as that of "embodiment" shows some parallels with Sittler's idea of the cosmic Christ including nature and grace discussed above. Moltmann's intention is to set forth his doctrine of creation in a way that counters dualisms between the material and spiritual realms. He also believes that historical anthropology has encouraged such dualism by speaking of the body and soul as if they were separate entities.[76] In his view the goal of all of God's works is towards "embodiment."

God as "embodiment" (i) in creation has its background in Moltmann's anthropology, where he understands the divine image as incorporating a physical bodily dimension.[77] His concern for a more holistic understanding of *imago Dei* has parallels with Vreizen's interpretation of Genesis 1.28.[78] For Moltmann, the Old Testament "thinks with the body."[79] He seems to be justified in his insistence that the idea of a separate human spirit is quite foreign to

Hebrew anthropology, where concepts such as soul, heart, flesh, etc. identify with the whole person rather than individual functions.[80] However, Moltmann seems to ignore elements in Old Testament thought which would distinguish between God, humanity and the animals in a more rigorous way. The biblical terms have a very fluid range of meanings depending on their context. *Nepeš*, for example, can mean throat, neck, desire, soul, life or person. The *Bāsār* of animals is also used for humankind but never used to describe God, unlike *Nepeš* which is very occasionally used in this way. *Bāsār* can mean flesh, body, relationship or frailty, depending on context.[81] *Rûah*, by contrast, applies to God in about a third of all cases and only occasionally to animals. Wolff describes *rûah* as a "theo-anthropological" term, which overlaps to some extent with *lêb(āb)* The latter is used more commonly for humankind, and is connected with our rationality, and only refers to God in the context of the relationship between God and humankind.[82] Once we consider God as "embodiment" in creation, what does this mean in view of the distinctive elements that we find in the Old Testament? Furthermore, it is worth noting that while Moltmann interprets *imago Dei* in holistic terms, it is never interpreted in this way by Jewish exegetes who believe that this refers to similarity of physical form.[83] Moltmann's interpretation of *imago Dei* in a Trinitarian way and as one which incorporates the idea of *imago Christi* distances his albeit canonical approach further from historical-critical exegetical studies which are now coming closer to a Jewish understanding.[84]

The idea of God as "embodiment" (ii) in reconciliation is related to Moltmann's particular kenotic Christology. Moltmann speaks of the "true humanity of God" as revealed in the incarnation.[85] He draws on Mauser who seems to suggest that humanness is taken up into the Godhead:

> "The anthropomorphic utterances of God indicated an understanding of God, that makes Yahweh so involved in human history that he takes part in the history of his people, and in so taking part lets the human *Ergehen* become his

own. On the other hand, the figure of the Prophet in Israel is presented in such a uniquely theomorphic way that at least in certain respects his human history bears witness to God in participation in the divine *Ergehen.* Thus human will and human action are seen as genuine representations of God, which for their own part, presuppose a picture of God, which makes him so much the God of humankind, *that he incorporates humanity in himself,* and thus can also be represented by humankind in human history. There is nowhere in the Old Testament where the Prophet's standing leads to a deification of man...Wholly within the bounds of his humanity he becomes the likeness of God. Humanity is thus capable in a purely human way and in purely human history, of taking the place of God, *which is only possible if God himself also adopts humanity into his divinity.*"[86]

Mauser goes on to conclude that the "inner structure" of the salvation act is completely determined by the unity of God's action and humankind's history, which echoes the Old Testament idea of "God who participates in human history and the Prophet who stands in the place of God."[87] While there is some ambiguity in the meaning of terms such as *Ergehen*, which literally means "state of health," and in *sich birgt*, which means he "incorporates," but can also mean he "shelters" or he "holds," the general train of his thought seems to be that his understanding of concrete humanity being taken up into God is more far-reaching than the more straightforward belief that God has the idea of humanity in himself. As such this seems to cohere well with Moltmann's desire to develop a fully kenotic Christology, where Jesus is God in his concrete frail human condition contra the idea of a divine and human "nature" in the person of Christ. The latter is somewhat confused by Moltmann's Trinitarian theology where he allowed for a single divine nature among the three persons of the Trinity, as well as an individual nature emerging from their interrelationships.[88] His strongly kenotic Christology moves him in the direction of a redefinition of God as one who takes human history into himself.

God as embodiment (iii) in redemption is related to the movement of the Spirit.[89] God as Spirit relates to the whole human person through *Gestalt*, which also links into the *Gestalt* of Christ, which we will discuss below. It is characteristic of Moltmann's style to extend the meaning of this term, which became a paradigm concept in psychology, for his own theological purposes. The idea of *Gestalt* in psychology is part of a search for a holistic treatment of patients, and one which aims to overcome various dualisms.[90] A good *Gestalt* is one where a "centration" provides a unifed "figure" against an empty "ground."[91] The "centration" shifts as the relationship between "ground" and "figure" changes. Moltmann seems to equate "faithfulness" with "centration" in a way that gives it a moral quality.[92] The difficulty here is that the process of transforming the meaning of *Gestalt* and related terms such as "centration" to include spiritual and future categories has not necessarily advanced our understanding of the meaning of the more traditional theological terms. In other words, he could have discussed the idea of faithfulness and liberty in a clearer way without recourse to biological categories. He seems to be trying to hold together the ideas of (a) direction and open possibility in the context of (b) an individual life and community of social relationships.[93]

(b) Creation's future in the *Gestalt* of Christ.

Moltmann's means of identification between our future and that of Christ draws on a number of different concepts including that of *Gestalt* mentioned above.[94] Moltmann's insistence that the sufferings of Christ extend to include those of the whole creation is balanced by an equal stress on the participation of the whole of creation in his resurrection. Christ's resurrection marks the beginning of the "new creation" and the end of death itself.[95] The bodily resurrection of Christ points to the holistic unity of nature and history that we can expect in the future new creation.[96] The resurrected body of Christ seems to share in God's omnipresence and eternity so that it is freed of both spatial and temporal limitations.

Our first question is whether Moltmann has provided an adequate basis for linking the past, present and future sufferings of creation with those of Christ. We have discussed the biblical ground for Moltmann's suggestion through his use of Romans 8.18 ff. above. In the present instance we are challenging the way his Christological anthropology jars unevenly with his idea of cosmic suffering of Christ. The stress on humanity becoming *imago Christi* and *gloria Dei* emphasizes the anthropological dimension of God's presence in the world which we will take up again below. It is difficult to see how the sufferings of Christ can encompass the particularity of non-human creation. In other words Moltmann has not distinguished adequately between the sufferings of human and non-human creation, and their shared unity in Christ's sufferings tends to reduce the sufferings of creation to those of humanity. This is clearly the opposite of Moltmann's aim, which is to extend Christ's sufferings into those of the created universe.[97]

The trend in Moltmann's theology towards a cosmic Christological suffering as that which marks the dawn of the new creation is understandable in view of his earlier dialectical theology of cross and resurrection, and given that he believes that the whole creation is caught up in the resurrection of Christ. Indeed, he goes further in his apocalyptic vision in his claim that without such suffering the new creation could not emerge. They are "not fortuitous sufferings. They are necessary."[98] The problem of an incipient Christomonism is clear. Moltmann is careful to identify the sufferings of Christ with the sufferings of God through the divine *Shekinah* when he speaks of the suffering of Israel.[99] It would have been more appropriate, perhaps, if he had similarly linked "creation groans together and travails together" of Romans 8.22 with the sufferings of the Spirit, especially as Moltmann understands the workings of the Spirit in holistic terms. In this way the link with the suffering and liberation in Christ becomes more indirect, so that through the Spirit the whole creation participates in both the suffering and reconciliation in Christ. This would also not involve any radical change in Moltmann's position since he already identifies the sufferings of Christ with those of the Spirit.[100] The point here is similar to one which we made in 2(c) above, namely that his earlier idea of the immanence of God in creation through the Spirit has tended to become evacuated by his theological focus on Christology.

The future of humanity directed forwards towards *imago Dei* and backwards towards *imago mundi* raises the status of humankind in the overall scheme of the future *gloria Dei*. Moltmann's primary concern is to interpret *imago Dei* in terms of interrelationships, in line with that of Karl Barth, but within an egalitarian rather than a hierarchical social framework.[101] Moltmann adopts Trible's somewhat controversial suggestion that humanity before the creation of woman was sexually undifferentiated, and an "earth creature."[102] He does not elaborate to what extent he is prepared to accept other aspects of Phyllis Trible's theological approach.[103] Moltmann's understanding of our care for the earth is one which is a consequence of *imago Dei*, rather than its meaning.[104] Moltmann extends the concept of *imago Dei* to include the concepts of *imago mundi, imago Christi* and *gloria Dei*.[105]

Moltmann is probably on safer ground in his expansion of the idea of *imago Dei* to include Christological themes compared with his inclusion of kenotic and kabbalistic ideas into his notion of *creatio ex nihilo*, which we discussed in the last chapter. However, the meaning of this concept for the future of creation is rather obscure. For example, he does not clarify how our imaging as *gloria Dei* will spread to include the future of creation. It seems that humanity is capable of entering the path towards that glorification now, yet the actual glorification remains a "future" event.[106] He suggests that death is a necessary precondition for this glorification, in a way that means we only become human in a full sense after death where we fulfil our creaturely destiny. It is only Christ who has fulfilled this task.[107] We are left wondering if non-human creation similarly shares such incompleteness, or whether it is related specifically to the reconciliation of the relationship between human and non-human creation. Moltmann never really addresses the concrete aspects of what reconciliation and redemption of creation mean. Presumably our stewardship rôle becomes unnecessary in the future since creation participates directly in God's manifested eternal presence.[108] We noted in the last section that the sabbath marks the beginning of the future of creation, and in this sabbath both God's creation and God's revelation become united.[109] The "new creation" is the "eternal sabbath."

(c) The ingathering rôle of the cosmic Spirit.

Moltmann's understanding of the rôle of the Spirit in the future creation forms a third strand in his aim to portray a holistic vision for the future, and is an important counterweight to his more strident Christological assertions discussed above. While the work of the Holy Spirit in the glorification and consummation is cosmic in scope, the basis for this hope emerges from the work of the Spirit in the church, the community and in individual vocations.[110] Moltmann takes the working of the Holy Spirit in human relationships, and applies this to the way the cosmic Spirit is operative in nature. The Spirit of God is cosmic in its work, both in the creation and evolution of the world, and in the final glorification of the cosmos. The problem in Moltmann's position remains as to how our experiences of God in the community of believers can act in any real practical way in our recognition of the work of the Spirit in creation as a whole. We found a similar problem in Moltmann's link between the sufferings of the cosmic Christ extending to include the sufferings of creation.

While Moltmann attempts to distinguish between the cosmic Christ as one who is the Evolver, and Christ the Redeemer, which we will discuss more fully below, he makes no real distinction between the work of the Spirit in creation and that in glorification.[111] It appears that the former is related to the idea of the Father as subject, while in the latter instance the Spirit is subject. However, the idea of the Spirit as the subject of glorification becomes weakened by Moltmann's strong concept of the cosmic Christ, so that while he suggests in *The Trinity and the Kingdom of God* that the Spirit looks to the Father through the Son in the glorification, in *The Way of Jesus Christ* the pneumatological accent becomes toned down and somewhat overshadowed by his cosmic Christology.

Moltmann draws his ideas on the workings of the Spirit in creation in a way which implies a kenotic self-limitation, that is a self-surrender to the history of the suffering of creation. It is the presence of the Spirit in the suffering which gives reason to hope for the new creation.[112] Moltmann's idea of kenotic pneumatology draws his understanding of the workings of the Spirit closer to that of the workings of Christ. By the time we reach *The Way of Jesus Christ* Moltmann paints a picture of the new creation as that which has passed through a vale of suffering with Christ and so entered into a new birth along with his resurrection.[113] While Moltmann seems to want to identify the work of the Spirit with that of Christ in order to avoid animist or pantheistic overtones, the only real attempt to distinguish between the work of the cosmic Christ and that of the cosmic Spirit comes from his understanding of "Word" and "Spirit" in the initial act of creation in *The Way of Jesus Christ*, where we read that the Word "specifies" while the Spirit "binds and creates symmetries." Nonetheless, the situation is still not entirely clear since a third ingredient, Wisdom, is also associated with Christ; but Moltmann makes surprisingly little use of this idea in his understanding of creation.[114]

Moltmann's interpretation of the work of the Spirit in glorification is also interwoven with his intense interest in the resurrection of Christ. He speaks of a renewed human community in the new creation in terms of a redeemed *Gestalt*, yet our renewed spiritual life is one which encompasses our whole existence. A difficulty here is similar to that raised earlier, namely whether Moltmann has given an adequate basis for extending the work of the Holy Spirit to such wide dimensions in a way that includes the inanimate as well as animate creation, given the distinctions preserved in the Old Testament. While he is justified in aiming for a holistic understanding, perhaps he goes too far in his emphasis on the all-inclusiveness of the Spirit's work. He also makes no attempt to outline a possible *Gestalt* for the animal creation, or how the Spirit could act in practical ways in the future, non-human creation. In the case of humanity he is anxious to stress that the old natural body has continuity with the new, transformed body, even through the experience of death. He rather boldly asserts that "This does not interrupt the natural laws of mortal life. It is rather that the whole quality of life is changed, and with it, of course, the laws of its mortality too."[115] Nonetheless, in the "new creation" we still seem to have human needs and dependencies, even in respect to our bodily needs, including human sexuality and our relationship with nature.[116] These ideas sit rather uneasily alongside his suggestion that mortality as well as sinfulness are overcome in the new creation, and in our view he has failed to avoid an anthropocentric focus in his discussion of the future of the cosmos.

4. Visions for the future: dialogue with Moltmann.

(a) Reflections in the light of science/evolution.

Moltmann's understanding of time in the new creation forms a novel part of his eschatological theology in comparison with the perception of time as perceived in science. Moltmann draws on Eastern Orthodoxy for a concept of *Aeon*.[117] Sasse rejects the cyclical idea of time as the meaning of *aeon*, since it confuses God and the world. For him, the future *aeon* is something "inconceivable" and is represented by "images" such as the historic image of the kingdom of God, the cosmic spatial image of the new heaven and the new earth, and the temporal image of new time.[118] Moltmann resists Sasse's suggestion that we can only describe the future of creation in purely symbolic terms and he makes the historic, spatial and temporal aspects part of a concrete hope for the future of the universe. He draws on an Eastern Orthodox understanding of *aeon* which Maximus describes as "motionless time" and refers to a realm of created existence outside the realm of time. Moltmann also agrees with Basil that the angelic world is in this non-temporal condition, but he resists the idea that we become like angels or, with Gregory of Nyssa, that "everything remains within its primordial limits" in the *aeon*.[119]

Moltmann's concept of the time, or rather the timelessness of the new *aeon*, interfaces with his idea of "interlaced" times which he discusses at length in *God in Creation*. While he finds considerable support for a more complex view of time than either simple linear or cyclical time amongst academic historians and sociobiologists, he uses the idea of "interlaced" time for his own particular purposes, namely a view of history and nature which is affected in a retrospective way by the eschatological future. The resurrection of Jesus from the dead somehow incorporates his whole life diachronically into "God's eternal moment."[120] Moltmann's bold endeavour is to combine a more teleological view of time, which he believes is most characteristic of history, with a cyclical view of time, which is most characteristic of natural rhythms, into a symbiotic whole which interfaces with the circular movements of the time of eternal life in the new *aeon*.[121] Once we reach the eternal future of the new *aeon*, time as directed towards the future becomes "transformed into the circular movements of the aeonic time of the new creation."[122] Rather strangely, perhaps, he finds it necessary to include a seemingly biological notion of rhythm within the timeless new creation; yet it is a rhythm which knows no decay, but rather the "intensity of the lived life."[123]

Throughout Moltmann's discussion we detect a failure to come to terms adequately with the reality of the future as understood in concrete historical and biological terms. While we welcome his wider vision which incorporates non-human creation, it often seems in his discussion that this aspect of the universe becomes eclipsed by his reflection on anthropology. His aim in his theological enterprise is to include scientific insight; however, his discussion on the evolution of creation seems to be pared down so that a major part is devoted to a reflection on humanity's evolution in the context of Genesis, and on early nineteenth century controversy over Darwin's hypothesis in the *Origin of Species*.[124] Moltmann's intention expressed here is to develop a synthesis between scientific theories of evolution and theories of history developed in the humanities.[125] His attempt is brave in view of the failure of social sciences to come to an evolutionary view of sociobiology that is at all adequate in scientific terms.[126] Osborn's cryptic comment that Moltmann's "attempt to formulate a 'hermeneutical' theory of evolution falls completely flat" is fairly near the mark.[127] We also agree with Osborn that Moltmann appears to lack the necessary scientific expertise to construct an adequate synthesis. While his discussion on the evolution of the cosmos could perhaps be justified in its almost exclusive reference to physical sciences, one expects a little more attention to biological ideas in his section on the evolution of life.[128]

Moltmann's notion of self-transcendence as part of the future of the universe as an open system would have been more difficult to formulate if he had paid more attention to **biological** aspects of evolution. We raise, for example, the simple basic problem of the very different life cycles of microbiological, plant and animal life, or extinct species. In what sense can vegetatively reproduced species become closed to the future? Moreover, is extinction a consequence of this? We raised a similar issue in the last chapter in our discussion of Hafstad's critique of Moltmann's concept of closedness in nature in relation to his idea of closedness as sinfulness.[129]

The idea of a universe as an "open system," which Moltmann defines in terms of openness to alteration, but then uses in a way which implies the shaping of possibilities from the future, is not really scientifically coherent. More problematic, perhaps, is his insistence that the universe is an open system, which is a breach of the working scientific hypothesis that the universe behaves as a closed system.[130] John Earman has raised the possibility of a "backward causation" as a counter to the determinism implied by the idea of causation grounded in the objective physical features of the world.[131] He bases his argument on classical electrodynamic theory.[132] However, his theory is highly controversial and the mathematical basis for his conclusions has been refuted.[133]

Moltmann acknowledges in a clearer way the potential clash between evolution and the new creation in *The Way of Jesus Christ*. Here he speaks of a "counter movement" between the way of evolution and redemption.[134] He changes Teilhard de Chardin's terminology of "involution" to a "re-volution" of evolution, so that we find in the "final eschatological cycle" a "return of all the pasts into the eternal *Aeon* of the new creation of all things."[135] Such a fantastic transformation is only possible through the power of Christ, who is both Christ the Becoming One in evolution, and Christ the Coming One in redemption. We are left wondering whether Moltmann's Christological solution to the problems is really adequate. He stretches the imagination to a point that makes it impossible to conceive of the reality of these events. As such, it could generate anxiety rather than hope.

(b) Recent trends: the self-organizing universe.

The power of the idea of a self-organizing universe lies in its sensitivity to ecological interdependence and its cosmic horizon.[136] However, not all scientists are in agreement with the idea of a self-organizing universe as accessible to scientific "proof." It becomes very difficult to assess an extrapolation of chemical thermodynamics to the highly complex system of the whole earth; we have an experimental base of one "sample" alongside numerous theoretical models. Jantsch's and Lovelock's computer simulation models might well be consistent with this view; however, a correlation is very far from stringent scientific "proof."[137] More disconcerting, perhaps, is Moltmann's adoption of the terminology of the *Gaia* hypothesis without any attempt to assess its mythological undercurrents.[138]

Stephen Toulmin believes that we must "reinstate" cosmology if we are to find a meaningful way of understanding our world.[139] He believes that we can rediscover a holistic understanding of the universe without adopting primitive science. Toulmin notes that ecology, which combines the insights of biological science with a political movement for the defense of habitats, in itself generates an "ambiguity" which we find in the notion of cosmology. By this he means that cosmology similarly straddles the fields of science, philosophy and religion.[140] While Moltmann shies away from any idea of "reinstating" cosmology, he does take up the theme of ecology, though he deals with it more on the level of a biological movement than a political one. While Moltmann is right in connecting the idea of holism with both the ecological movement and the *Gaia* hypothesis, he never really adequately faces the animist undercurrents in *Gaia*. For example, two of the propagandists of the *Gaia* hypothesis are quite ready to admit that their hypothesis "resonates strongly with the ancient magico-religious sentiment that all is one."[141]

(c) Ancient models from mystic/Taoist philosophy.

While Moltmann does not develop the theme of *Tao* philosophy to any great extent in *God in Creation*, he draws on these ideas in his later book, *Creating a Just Future*. He uses Taoist ideals as a counterweight to the attitudes generated by the scientific and technological civilization of the Western world. He does not seem to be rejecting science *per se*, but the prevailing cultural pressure towards a will to power which damages both human relationships and those with nature.[142] In his earlier work Moltmann drew on Christian mysticism as a way of countering the tendency for control of nature in a technological society.[143] By the time we reach *Creating a Just Future* he prefers the idea of the Chinese *Tao*, possibly because it is rooted in an ideal of equilibrium which is part of its understanding of the natural world.[144] The social and political aspects of Taoism may be more congenial to Moltmann's approach compared with traditional Christian nature mysticism which tended to be more individualistic.[145]

Moltmann is rather selective in his use of Taoist ideas.[146] He fails to acknowledge that the kind of equilibrium which is depicted in *Tao* is extremely passive, and looks back to the origin of all things. In this sense it is rather remarkable that Moltmann describes Taoist wisdom as having an "astonishing" parallel with the Jewish notion of the sabbath. He refers here to the texts of Lao Tzu which speak of "Returning to the Root." This is a description of what happens to living things after a process of activity and growth, whereupon they enter a phase of stillness and vacancy. This imagery, taken from observation of the natural world, does not bear all that much resemblance in our opinion to the Jewish sabbath, which by Moltmann's own admission, is a theological concept of holy time and a way of thinking which breaks free from the cycles of nature.[147] In Taoist thought humankind becomes "*Tao*'s impassive instruments, having no will or purpose of their own."[148] Moltmann's interpretation of chapter 76 in *The Tao Te Ching* as a premonition of "soft" technology is a little over-strained. Lao Tzu gives us a warning against trusting in strength, and speaks of the real strength of humility and weakness in *Tao*, seemingly analogous to the change which takes place in the body after death in rigor mortis![149] The future idea which Lao Tzu addresses in chapter 80, cited approvingly by Moltmann in its exaltation of small communities, is a lifestyle that denies all aspects of civilization.[150] The selection of ideas out of context does not really do justice to the original material.

Finally the ideal of nature as a system of equilibrium outlined in *Tao Te Ching* lacks the eschatological dimension that Moltmann wants to preserve in his theology. Hence, by definition, it becomes very difficult to conceive of such equilibrium in eschatological categories. Moltmann's earlier shift of natural theology to the future is parallel with his attempt to put the more stable ideal of equilibrium into the future. Moltmann does not seem to have appreciated in an adequate way that biological symbiosis, from which he draws out the idea of harmony and equilibrium between species, is a relatively rare occurrence.

Generally symbiotic relationships arise in order to exploit potentially hostile environments. Moltmann treats the idea of mutual harmony as if it were an underlying biological feature of the created natural world. It is also incoherent in relationship to the idea of a self-organizing universe, which relies on *"non-equilibrium"* dynamics and where a return to "equilibrium" amounts to stagnation and death.[151] Where Moltmann does acknowledge a divergence between the mystic perception of reality and that portrayed by science, he moves rather too quickly into his notion of a reconciliation through Christ, without explaining how such a reconciliation could be achieved in practical terms.[152]

5. Conclusions.

Our discussion in the present chapter has focused on the outworking of Moltmann's ecological concern in his vision for the future of the cosmos. One of the great strengths of Moltmann's theological approach is his insight into the importance of eschatology in all theological discussions. The contemporary mood in the 1990s is rather different from that of the 1970s when Moltmann formulated his *Theology of Hope*. His vision for the future of creation shows that his thinking has expanded to include changes in climate, and represents a genuine effort to re-value the world as a whole, including the non-human creation.

Moltmann's understanding of the interrelationship between nature and history has been more inclusive than acknowledged previously by other critical reviewers of his work. Its background is in Bloch's ontology of "Not-Yet," but he is careful to give this philosophy a thoroughly Christian reinterpretation. He moves more towards an understanding which examines nature for her own sake, rather than one which is directly related to human interest. His intention is to use the ideas of the sabbath and the cosmic Christ to achieve such a broad horizon.

While his sabbath idea is clever through its associations with Judaism, the link that it forms between creation/nature/space and history/time still tends to give priority to time rather than space, and history rather than nature. This is because the sabbath is rooted in the sanctification of time, and emerges in the historical institutions of Jewish religious life. An extension of the sabbath ideal into categories of eschatological and apocalyptic hope for creation is more difficult to imagine given the background usage of this term in the Old Testament. Further, while Moltmann's future sabbath is intended to be the horizon for ecological wholeness, the ideas are almost impossible to imagine and border on the fantastic rather than the visionary. It might have been more effective if he had stayed with his earlier concept of *Shalom*, that is harmonious interrelationships, instead of widening the idea in sabbatical terminology.

Moltmann's concern to make his theology thoroughly Christian has encouraged him to draw on the ancient tradition of the cosmic Christ. His understanding of Christ is one who suffers in creation so that all creation is gathered up in redemption. The dialectical themes of suffering and glory include both nature and history in a holistic vision for the future of the cosmos. While we have hints in this direction in the New Testament, Moltmann tends to speak of such events as doctrine in a way that does not always allow for alternative positions. Thus, in spite of his rhetoric on the open future, it seems that suffering is a necessary part of the transition/giving birth to new creation and new kingdom of glory. Moltmann does not seem to have taken account of the distinct kinds of suffering of different parts of the created world, or what such glorification would involve in realistic terms.

The above idea is also somewhat incongruous with the idea of a *Gestalt* of Christ which includes humanity. This idea, taken from psychotherapy, tends to treat the non-human environment in objective categories, rather than subjective ones. He also transforms the *Gestalt* insight to include spiritual categories in a way that goes beyond its original meaning and cannot really be justified from an Old Testament understanding of anthropology. While the general idea of a holistic approach is an area of common ground in his discusssion of *Gestalt*, is his engagement with psychological terms helpful? It comes over not as a "dialogue" with science, but a borrowing of language. We discussed the same issue in relation to Moltmann's usage of the term "ecology" and "symbiosis" in the previous chapters.

Moltmann's pneumatology includes the idea of the cosmic Spirit but one where the experience of the Spirit in the church acts as a criterion for discernment of the Spirit in creation. Moltmann's aim here is to avoid animist and pantheistic notions. The problem is that he does not really show us how he applies such a criterion. He discusses the work of the cosmic Spirit in terms of the detailed working out of evolutionary change in a way which would be more congenial, perhaps, to New Age mythology than to biology. He slips a little too easily into making bold claims for the activities of the cosmic Spirit in categories which are more appropriate to biological discussions, yet lacking their concrete reference. Once the latter is missing, the future hope becomes esoteric rather than visionary.

Moltmann makes bold moves to keep his theology of creation rooted in history, yet subject to a future coming from ahead, in his discussions of Christ as one who is both the Evolver and Redeemer of creation. The concrete nature of these discussions focus on suffering, those of Christ linked specially with those of creation, so that Christ suffers in the cosmos. One is left wondering if Moltmann's ideal of suffering is really sufficient to bring his theology an empirical reference. While this theme may be adequate for his consideration of the human condition, it becomes very over-stretched when he applies it to the non-human creation as well. It also has the unfortunate result of rendering his approach rather too anthropological. We are left with a soaring picture of our future as *gloria Dei*, and our transformation through death. However, while the creation is clearly there with us, it is not always clear what purpose it achieves either for itself, or for God, who is embodied in humanity. Moltmann's idea that humanity will still need the natural world in the new creation does not really address the question of the shape of the new creation itself, and how it is transformed in concrete ways.

While Moltmann's vision for the future cosmos is Trinitarian in its emphasis on God as creator, reconciler and redeemer, his focus on future redemption in Christ through the Spirit tends to weaken the value of creation in the beginning. He leaves us with the impression that not only God and humanity, but also creation in itself is somehow incomplete. Our human history is caught up with the natural world into the history of God in Christ, but in the new creation we enter a new *aeon*. Now, the circular pattern of time viewed in natural rhythm becomes imprinted into a new consciousness of youth and birth which seems to exalt life itself as the ultimate paradigm in the future *Aeon*. Is it necessary to redeem temporality in creation as well as human sinfulness?

Moltmann's worthy intention is to reconstruct theology so that it exists in relationship with science and offers a joint hermeneutic for understanding reality both now and in the future. While his theology is powerful in helping us to rethink some of our damaging attitudes to nature, it is weaker in its belief in the possibility of such an all-embracing reconstruction. Hegel had a similar intention in mind, but he seemed to be well aware of the current scientific insights of his era.[153] The wealth and breadth of current scientific knowledge makes it extremely difficult to attempt such reconstruction. While Moltmann recognizes the distinct task of Genesis *vis-à-vis* a scientific discussion of the origin of the earth, he seems to hope for a bolder synthesis in his own theological enterprise. In practice he has failed to achieve anything approaching a synthesis because of the lack of empirical references. It might have made his future vision more concrete if he had given a more thorough attention to biological concepts rather than global geophysiological quasi-mathematical ones. The idea of a self-organizing universe, which Moltmann describes as "biological," is really an application of physico-chemical theory to systems analysis. Its use of mathematical formula gives this theory a scientific gloss that may not be justified. Moltmann takes on some of Jantsch's rather tenuous exploratory science/speculation. Moltmann now stretches this concept even further by linking it with the idea of the cosmic Spirit. While this is imaginatively ingenious, it has the unfortunate result of making his theology rather too close to New Age consciousness. He would clearly not wish to identify with this position, but he fails to show adequately how his thinking differs from the New Age movement and so lends his writing too open to misinterpretation.

Finally, Moltmann's shift from more traditional mysticism of Christianity expressed through Teresa of Avila to that of kabbalistic and Taoist philosophy is not a particularly helpful shift in his spirituality, which still seems to remain Christocentric. His use of Taoist ideas seems to reinforce his own concept of ecological equilibrium. The latter is rather dubious biologically since the dynamic of biological systems is necessarily a movement down an energy gradient. The clash between mystical and philosophical/scientific ways of understanding reality is resolved in Moltmann's theology a little too readily by Christological categories.

We are left with the tension of the ideal of home which we experience both now and in the future sabbath, and the ideal of pilgrimage which is content to pass through suffering so that it can enter future glory. Moltmann selects the idea of inner harmony, but resists the idea of inactivity and speechlessness which are interwoven in Taoist thought.

End Notes.

All books and articles are by Jürgen Moltmann unless stated otherwise. Translations are from German text.

1. We mean by orthodoxy, that according to traditional Christian dogma, rather than Eastern Orthodoxy as such.

2. Hegel was well aware of the interrelationship between space and time, and his philosophy is a possible background to Moltmann's own attention to this issue. Findlay comments that for Hegel "space necessarily completes itself in time," and things in nature are in space "because space is the form of their universal externality and otherness." J.N. Findlay, *Hegel: A Re-Examination*, London, Allen, 1958, p. 274.

3. K. Cauthen, *Christian Biopolitics: A Credo and Strategy for the Future*, Nashville, Abingdon Press, 1971, p. 67.

4. Reinhold Niebuhr argues that we need illusions, as these are the transforming power of society; but they must be purged of individualism and subject to realistic criticism. For him: "The most important of these illusions is that the collective life of mankind can achieve perfect justice. It is a very valuable illusion for the moment, for justice cannot be approximated if the hope of its perfect realisation does not generate a sublime madness in the soul. The illusion is dangerous because it encourages terrible fanaticisms. It must therefore be brought under the control of reason. One can only hope that reason will not destroy it before its work is done." R. Niebuhr, *Moral Man and Immoral Society*, New York, Charles Scribner's Sons, 1960, p. 277.

5. G. Chapman, "Moltmann's Vision of Man," *Anglican Theological Review*, 56, 1974, pp. 310-330; see p. 312. Alan Race has challenged Moltmann's specific use of biblical categories such as "wisdom," "sabbath," "cosmic Christ," etc. on the basis that this language has no real status in today's society. We will be asking a slightly different question, namely whether Moltmann is justified in using such language according to theological norms. If we follow Race's critique to its logical conclusion we run the risk of reducing all theological language to common parlance in a way which fails to formulate a future vision for those struggling to find hope in the midst of the crises of our time. A. Race, "Review of *Creating a Just Future*," *Theology*, 113, 1990, pp. 355-362.

6. N. Glatzer comments on the deep distrust of language that is one of the trends in "modern times." The "scientific outlook" atomizes language into a series of "abstract nouns" so that speech is "no longer a vehicle of communication between men." Others, such as Henri Bergson rely on wordless intuition as the only adequate means through which the dynamic continuity of reality can be expressed. Process theologians argue for a shift in language towards verbs in order to express dynamic action. In short "language is the least common and least

trusted means of communication, though the term dialogue is on the lips of many." While this may be an exaggeration of our present day situation, Moltmann shares Rosenzweig's concern to develop a form of "speech thinking" rather than "abstract thinking" which was characteristic of earlier philosophy. N.N. Glatzer, "Foreword," in, F. Rosenzweig, *Star of Redemption*; translated by William Hallo, London, Routledge & Kegan Paul, 1970, p. xv.

7.   See, Chapter 2 for a discussion; similar positions to Moltmann in this respect are B.W. Anderson and W.H. Schmidt. See, for example, B.W. Anderson, "Creation and Ecology," in, B.W. Anderson, ed., *Creation in the Old Testament*, London, SPCK, 1984, pp. 152-167; W.H. Schmidt, *The Faith of the Old Testament*; translated by J. Sturdy, Oxford, Blackwell, 1983.

8.   Gerhard von Rad was very influential here; see, for example, "The Theological Problem of the Old Testament Doctrine of Creation," in, G. von Rad, *The Problems of the Hexateuch and Other Essays*; translated by E.W. Trueman-Dicken, London/Edinburgh, Oliver and Boyd, 1966, pp. 131-143; German edition 1938. Karl Barth's theology is also consistent with von Rad's subordination of creation to salvation history; see, for example, K. Barth, *Church Dogmatics; Volume 3/1*; translated by J. Edwards, O. Bussey, and H. Knight; G.W. Bromiley and T.F. Torrance, eds., Edinburgh, T. and T.Clark, 1958, pp. 42, 228 ff. A notable exception in this period was G. Lindeskog who argued for separate traditions for primordial accounts of creation and salvation history; see, G. Lindeskog, "The Theology of the Creation in the Old and New Testaments," in, A. Fridrichsen, ed., *The Root of the Vine: Essays in Biblical Theology*, London, Dacre Press, 1953, pp. 1-22. For him, the Exodus theme is elevated by equating it with the grandeur of the creation story. However, while he believes there were separate origins for the two traditions, ultimately *"ktisiology,"* or the "beginning," becomes "historicized" in the New Testament, where the work of creation becomes "an act of election;" p. 21.

9.   H. Reventlow, *Problems of Old Testament Theology in the Twentieth Century*; translated by J. Bowden, London, SCM, 1985, pp. 141-148. For a more ecologically orientated theology see also R. Dubos, *A God Within*, New York, Charles Scribner's Sons, 1972 and for Lynn White's influential essay, see, L. White, "The Historical Roots of our Ecological Crisis," *Science*, 145, 1967, pp. 1203-1207. J. Barr gives an incisive refutation of White's thesis; J. Barr, "Man and Nature, the Ecological Controversy and the Old Testament," *Bulletin of the John Rylands Library*, 55, 1972, pp. 9-32. Moltmann seems to agree with the view that White's claim that Christianity caused the exploitation of nature is false, since modern science appeared much later than Judao-Christian faith; GC, p. 26. However, he does seem to agree with one aspect of White's thesis, namely that our understanding of ourselves as ruling agents would foster a destructive attitude to the environment, GC, p. 27, footnote 11. Moltmann's own view, as we discussed earlier, comes from an insistence that it is a misapprehension of God in monarchical

terms which serves to foster an inappropriate relationship with creation. It is also worth noting briefly that the credit for Christianity as that which fosters science was brandished as an achievement by some theologians in the heyday of popular support for science; for a classic essay, see, M.B. Foster, "The Christian Doctrine of Creation and the Rise of Modern Natural Science," *Mind*, 43, 1934, pp. 446-473; 44, 1935, pp. 439-466; 45, 1936, pp. 1-27. A useful discussion of this topic is in J. MacQuarrie, "Creation and Environment," *Expository Times*, 83, 1971, pp. 4-9.

10.   C. Westermann, *Genesis 1-11: A Commentary*; translated by J. Scullion, London, SPCK, 1984. See also, C. Westermann, *Blessing in the Bible and the Life of the Church*, Philadelphia, Fortress Press, 1978. Moltmann refers to the "kairological" sense of time in Israel, drawing on De Vries; see, GC, p. 338. For a detailed discussion of the Jewish understanding of time, see, S. De Vries, *Yesterday Today and Tomorrow: Time and History in the Old Testament*, London, SPCK, 1975, pp. 40-51; 335-349. De Vries posits the contrast between "qualitative time" where historical events have revelatory significance and "quantitative time" which can be measured in a "chronological" sense, and was characteristic of (a) the royal annals in a divided kingdom; (b) the priestly writers reconstruction of primal history, and (c) apocalyptic writings. While Moltmann, like De Vries, recognizes the qualitative/kairological view of time as that which is most significant for the concept of salvation history, he does not address the issue that Jewish apocalyptic is characterized in "quantitative" terms and, according to De Vries, is "an *epoch* of its own, detached from the present and irrelevant to it," p. 342. Moltmann does distance himself from the Jewish understanding of apocalyptic as finally catastrophic, while retaining the use of apocalyptic language reinterpreted in Christological ways; see WJC, pp. 158 ff.

11.   J. MacQuarrie, *op. cit.* (n.9), p. 6.

12.   G. Liedke, *Im Bauch des Fisches: Oekologische Theology*, Stuttgart, Kreuz, 1979. An example of American treatment of ecological theology is F. Elder, *Crisis in Eden: A Religious Study of Man and Environment*, New York, Abingdon Press, 1970. See also, U. Duchrow and G. Liedke, *Shalom: A Biblical Perspective on Creation, Justice and Peace*, Geneva, WCC, 1989. Moltmann's theology bears some resemblance with Liedke's views in his attempt to put Christological eschatology in the context of an ecological understanding of creation; see, WJC, p. 378, footnote 63. Moltmann is more cautious than Liedke in taking up White's idea that a Christian concept of dominion is responsible for the ecological crisis; see n.9, above.

13.   M.D. Meeks, *Origins of the Theology of Hope*, Philadelphia, Fortress Press, 1974, p. 39.

14.   *Ibid.*, p. 117. Bloch moves beyond Marx in his understanding of the interrelationship between history and philosophy. While Marx insists that philosophy is realized in action, Bloch

still allows for metaphysical presuppositions. This allowed Bloch to develop the idea of the ontology of "Not-Yet" in a way that would have been difficult had he taken up Marx's seeming rejection of metaphysical philosophy as such. Bloch's idea of "Anticipation"(*Erwartung*) is that which is beyond the existing world, and has a genuine future which is related to the idea of "Not-Yet." For further elaboration and discussion see F. Fiorenza, "Dialectical Theology and Hope," *Heythrop Journal*, 10, 1969, pp. 26-42.

15. E. Bloch, *Principle of Hope*; translated by N. Plaice, S. Plaice and P. Knight, Oxford, Blackwell, 1986, pp. 128-130.

16. *Ibid.*, p. 140.

17. *Ibid.*, p. 144.

18. *Ibid.*, p. 196.

19. *Ibid.*, p. 202.

20. *Ibid.*, p. 690; for a discussion of alliance technology in Bloch's thought, see previous chapter.

21. *Ibid.*, p. 1353.

22. *Ibid.*, pp. 1372 ff.; for a discussion of Bloch's view of heaven, see, Chapter 3 (5), and for a further discussion in Moltmann, see, GC, pp. 178-181.

23. GC, p. 179.

24. E. Bloch, *op. cit.* (n.15), p. 1373.

25. R. Cole-Turner, "Review of *God in Creation*," *Zygon*, 22(1), 1987, pp. 120-122.

26. F. Rosenzweig, *op. cit.* (n.6), p. 219; see GC, p. 134.

27. F. Rosenzweig, *op. cit.* (n.6), p. 417.

28. *Ibid.*, p. 368.

29. *Ibid.*, p. 230. The meaning of the "stronger sense" in which God is the redeemer seems to be related to Rosenzweig's idea that "in the final analysis" God can redeem himself. This is in contrast with God's works of creation and revelation which lie "in a certain sense" behind him.

30. CJF, p. 62. Moltmann hinted at his idea of the sabbath early on in his theological development; see, Chapter 2, and Chapter 3 for a brief discussion of his view of the sabbath in later work.

31. CJF, p. 61.

32. G. von Rad, *Old Testament Theology; Volume 1*, translated by D. Stalker, Edinburgh/London, Oliver and Boyd, 1962, p. 138. He also finds a soteriological understanding of creation in Psalms 89 and 74, and for him "it is extremely likely that this soteriological understanding of creation also lies at the basis of creation stories in J. and P....in neither of these

documents of course is Jahweh's work in creation considered for its own sake: instead it is incorporated within a course of history leading to the call of Abraham and ending with Israel's entry into Palestine," p. 139.

33.   *Ibid.*, p. 138.

34.   *Ibid.*, p. 148. God's rest after creation is not a "turning away from the world," which is "folly." This rest does not have an immediate bearing on the rest towards which human living is directed, which is bound up with the Old Testament idea of "the way," for a discussion, see, G. von Rad, "There Remains Still a Rest for the People of God: An Investigation of a Biblical Conception," in, *Problems of the Hexateuch and Other Essays, op. cit.* (n.8), pp. 94-102.

35.   *Ibid.*, especially pp. 97-99.

36.   In summary these are: 1. The sabbath as social institution, which extends its regulations to the whole household; 2. The sabbath as cultic institution, that is when the human community was drawn to a "cultic site" and so "the whole creation" was thereby given an opportunity for regeneration; 3. The sabbath as law, and linked with the sabbatical commandment such as not to profane the sabbath, to keep it holy and to refrain from work; 4. The sabbath as creation, stemming from Canaanite mythology where gods attempt to achieve rest after the effort of creation. The Genesis account is not intended to imply God needed the rest in the same way as in other Near Eastern theogonies or that God's rest implies disengagement from creation; see comment from von Rad under n.34 above. And reason suggests that the divine *otiositas* becomes reinterpreted by the writer of Genesis in a way that links the work of creation with the sabbath. The word in Genesis means "cease," rather than rest after exhaustion. The creation account becomes a preparation for the sacred history of Israel in a way that makes the creation sabbath a preparation for the sabbath institution; 5. The sabbath as covenant is where sabbath "concentrates" the idea of holiness. N. Andreason, *The Old Testament Sabbath: A Tradition-Historical Investigation*; dissertation series number 7, Society of Biblical Literature, University of Montana, Missoula, USA, 1972, pp. 99-225.

37.   *Ibid.*, pp. 225 ff.

38.   F. Rosenzweig, *op. cit.* (n.6), p. 313; cited in GC, p. 280, although translated as "a dream of completion."

39.   F. Rosenzweig, *op. cit.* (n.6), p. 314.

40.   *Ibid.*, p.310.

41.   A. Heschel, *The Sabbath: Its Meaning for Modern Man*, New York, The Noonday Press, 1951, p. 19.

42.   GC, p. 284.

43.   *Ibid.*, p. 280.

44. *Ibid.*, p. 280.

45. A. Lincoln, "Sabbath Rest and Eschatology in the New Testament," in, D. Carson, ed., *From Sabbath to Lord's Day: A Biblical, Historical and Theological Investigation*, Grand Rapids, Zondervan, 1982, pp. 197-220; see also N. Andreason, *op. cit.* (n.36). A discussion of the significance of the sabbath commandment in the decalogue, in a canonical context, is in, B.S. Childs, *Old Testament Theology in a Canonical Context*, London, SCM, 1985, pp. 70-72.

46. A. Lincoln, *op. cit.* (n.45), pp. 201-209; 215. Commentators on Hebrews 4.9-10 tend to make the sabbath rest hoped for apply to the people of God, and not to creation *per se*; see, for example, P. Hughes, *A Commentary on the Epistle to the Hebrews*, Grand Rapids, Erdmans, 1977. Perhaps it is a little surprising that Moltmann does not discuss Hebrews in his consideration of the sabbath and its meaning for the future of creation; it may be difficult for him to interpret this text in an inclusive way, which is his clear intention in his overall perception of the meaning of the sabbath.

47. GC, pp. 290-296.

48. WJC, pp. 21-37; it is true, however, that Moltmann retains the idea of the ultimate glorification in sabbatical terms, but this theme is much weaker than in his earlier work: "God only arrives at his rest in the sabbath of the new creation..... The goal is soteriological, but at the same time it is doxological through and through," pp. 182-183.

49. *Ibid.*, pp. 119-122.

50. For comment on Moltmann's use of Romans 8:18 in his earlier theology, see Chapter 2(3).

51. W. Sanday, *The Epistle to the Romans*, Edinburgh, T. and T.Clark, 1907, p. 207; for a historical comment on the exegesis of this text in the period 1500-1800; see, K. Thomas, *Man and the Natural World: Changing Attitudes in England: 1500-1800*, London, Penguin, 1983, pp. 139 ff. Even in this period there was considerable disagreement as to the extent to which this text implied an inclusive salvation for the non-human creation.

52. C.K. Barrett, *The Epistle to the Romans*, H. Chadwick, ed., *Black's New Testament Commentary*, London, Black, 1957, p. 165.

53. C.H. Dodd, *The Epistle of Paul to the Romans*, J. Moffatt, ed., London, Hodder and Stoughton, 1932, p. 134.

54. E. Käsemann, *A Commentary on Romans*; translated by G.W. Bromiley, ed., London, SCM, 1980, pp. 232-233. He qualifies the stress that Paul makes on human history by drawing attention to the importance of its cosmic setting, and he argues that, in balance, the emphasis today in the exegesis of this passage should be put on the non-human creation.

55. R. Haldane, *An Exposition of the Epistle to the Romans*, McLean MacDonald, 1958, pp. 371-374.

56. C. Cranfield, *Romans: A Shorter Commentary*, Edinburgh, T. and T. Clark, 1985, p. 196.

57. *Ibid.*, p. 198.

58. G. Forde, "Romans 8.18-27," *Interpretation*, 38, 1984, pp. 281-285; Forde re-defines creation, not as a general term for "nature," but as a theological category, a "perception of the world and existence opened up by faith," p. 281.

59. See, WJC, pp. 151-160; Christ: "suffered as the Head and Wisdom of the whole creation, and died for the new creation of all things," the "fellowship of Christ's sufferings is experienced by.... the whole sighing non-human creation," p. 155; "the message of the human and non-human creation which is dying of injustice and violence is its collective martyrdom" p. 157; "The cosmic sufferings of this ecological end-time also become 'sufferings of Christ'," p. 159; for further comment on Romans 8.18-19, see, p.170.

60. J. Rimbach, "'All Creation Groans': Theology/Ecology in St. Paul," *Asia Journal of Theology (Singapore)*, 1, 1987, pp. 379-391; see esp. pp. 386-387.

61. WJC, p. 159.

62. E. Käsemann, *op. cit.* (n.54), pp. 233-234.

63. *Ibid.*, p. 234; it is worth citing Käsemann in full here: "By allowing Christians to suffer with Christ, the Spirit brings about the transforming of the old creation into an expectancy of glorification and an initial participation in this. Hope, then reaches beyond believers to creation as a whole....Since Paul understands eschatological freedom as salvation in a cosmic dimension, he here singularly describes the event of the *parousia* from the standpoint of anthropology. He could not say the world was on the way to Christ, even though he regarded Christ as the designated Cosmocrator, and orientated world history to him. He was concerned to show, however, that within the world, in remarkable connection with the ecstatic events during Christian worship, and by contrast in the community which suffers with Christ, eschatological freedom as salvation for all creation appears in outline." Moltmann also locates the beginning of the new creation firmly in the Christian community. However, he is far bolder than Käsemann in using hints from exegetical textual criticism to shape his understanding of the future salvation for all creation. For example, he links the suffering and liberation of creation to Christ's death and resurrection without always going via the sinfulness and reconciliation of humanity.

64. WJC, pp. 274 ff.; for a summary of Moltmann's views see Chapter 3(6).

65. See, for example, P. Gregorios, *The Human Presence: An Orthodox View of Nature*, Geneva, WCC, 1978; also, "Jesus Christ: The Life of the World," in, G. Tsetsis, ed., *Orthodox*

Thought, Geneva, WCC, 1983, pp. 77-88; and, V. Rossi, "Christian Ecology is Cosmic Christology," *Epiphany*, 8, 1988, pp. 52-62.

66.   For extensive bibliography on wisdom literature see, H. Reventlow, *op. cit.* (n.9), pp. 168-172; and for a review, see, J. Harvey, "Wisdom Literature and Biblical Theology," *Biblical Theology Bulletin*, 1, 1971, pp. 308-319; Moltmann hints at the paradigm shift in theology which has arisen in the aftermath of pending ecological collapse, WJC, p. 274.

67.   For a discussion of J. Sittler in Moltmann, see, WJC pp. 275ff.; see also, J. Sittler, *Essays On Nature and Grace*, Philadelphia, Fortress Press, 1972; J. Sittler, "A Theology for Earth," *The Christian Scholar*, 37, 1954, 367-374. Paul Santmire also acknowledges Sittler's contribution; H. Santmire, *The Travail of Nature*, Philadelphia, Fortress Press, 1985. The exegetical question focuses around what τα παντα means; which we will return to again below. The most anthropocentric exegetes are sceptical about whether this term can be extended to include the non-human creation; see N. Kehl, *Der Christushymnus in Kolosserbrief*, Stuttgart Verlag, 1985, p. 25.

68.   J. Lightfoot, *St. Paul's Epistles to the Colossians and to Philemon*, London, MacMillan, 1875, pp. 224-225.

69.   By hymn we mean a broad category which includes dogmatic, liturgical or doxological material. E. Schweitzer, *The Letter to the Colossians: A Commentary*; translated by A. Chester, London, SPCK, 1982, p. 81; see also, R.P. Martin, *Colossians: The Church's Lord and the Christians Liberty*, Exeter, Paternoster Press, 1972, pp. 40-49.

70.   In Schweitzer's reconstruction the author of Colossians adds; "thrones and dominions or principalities" to 1.16, "the church" and "that in everything he may be pre-eminent" to 1.18, and "making peace by the blood of the cross" to 1.20. This addition is significant in the present context as Schweitzer considers that there is an important distinction between "making peace," which is in the final text, and "reconciliation" in the original hymn. O'Brien is less convinced that such a distinction is possible, or that Schweitzer's reconstruction is necessarily valid. E. Schweitzer, *op. cit.* (n.69), 82-84; P.T. O'Brien, *Colossians, Philemon*, D. Hubbard and G. Barker, eds., *Word Biblical Commentary, 44*, Waco, Word Books, 1982, pp. 34-35.

71.   E. Käsemann, "A Primitive Christian Baptismal Liturgy," in, *Essays on New Testament Themes*; translated by W. Montague, *Studies in Biblical Theology, 41*, London, SCM, 1964, pp. 149-168; "creation and new creation are invariably linked together in the myth of the Archetypal Man, who is also Redeemer," p.154. Käsemann argues that in the redacted version of the hymn there was a shift from cosmology to eschatology, "Because it stands within forgiveness, it is a new creation, the cosmic powers have nothing more to say to it, to give to it, or to ask of it," p. 168. O'Brien finds Käsemann's thesis "unconvincing," as he believes that the

message of the New Testament is unlikely to become clearer by reflection on a "gnostic redemption saga;" *op. cit.* (n.70), pp. 38-39.

72.　For a survey of these positions, see, R.P. Martin, *op. cit.* (n.69), pp. 40 ff. W.D. Davies is a strong exponent of the hypothesis that the background to the letter is in rabbinical Judaism, drawing on the parallels between the hymn, Proverbs 1 and Genesis 1 with wisdom literature. Schweitzer is influential in promoting the idea of a background in Hellenistic Judaism. He believes that the writer of the letter corrected the theology of the original Hellenistic hymn, and by so doing the author stressed that it is humankind, but not nature, that is reconciled. E. Schweitzer, *op. cit.* (n.69), pp. 82 ff.

73.　P.T. O'Brien, *op. cit.* (n.70), pp. 41-42; he asks, "is it impossible to imagine that Paul is using a hymn which he had earlier composed?"

74.　For the Jewish understanding of wisdom, see, R.P. Martin, *op. cit.* (n.69), p. 58.

75.　E. Schweitzer, *op. cit.* (n.69), pp. 261-273.

76.　GC, p. 244.

77.　*Ibid.*, p. 245.

78.　For an outline of Vreizen's position see G. Jønsson, *The Image of God: Genesis 1.26-28 in a Century of Old Testament Research*; translated by L. Svendsen, revised by M.S. Cheney; *Coniectanea Biblica, Old Testament Series, 26*, T. Mettinger and M. Ottosson, eds., Lund, Almqvist and Wiksell International, 1988, pp. 118-125.

79.　GC, p. 256.

80.　H. Wolff, *Anthropology of the Old Testament*; translated by M. Kohl, London, SCM, 1974, pp. 7-8.

81.　*Ibid.*, pp. 26-30; *nepeš* applies to God in only 3% of all cases.

82.　*Ibid.*, p. 32; *Rûah* can mean wind (eg. Genesis 1.2), breath (eg. Genesis 7.22), vital powers (eg. Ezekiel ll.5), spirit or feelings. *Lêb(āb)* or "reasonable man," can mean heart, feelings, will, wish, reason or the "heart" of God depending on context. *Lêb* only applies to animals on five occasions, pp. 40 ff.

83.　Examples of Jewish scholars are Moshe Weinfeld and Michael Klein; for a discussion, see, G. Jønsson, *op. cit.* (n.78), p. 176; also, A. Altmann, "*Homo Imago Dei* in Jewish and Christian Theology," *Journal of Religion*, 48, 1968, pp. 235-259.

84.　*Ibid.*, p. 235; it is a matter of debate whether a more historical exegetical approach to Old Testament studies should set the boundaries for a canonical approach to hermeneutics. Moltmann seems to go beyond the normal boundaries of a canonical approach to an interpretation of *imago Dei*; see, for example, B.S. Childs, *op. cit.* (n.45), pp. 97-99; also, pp.

189-182. For Moltmann's interpretation of *imago Dei* in terms of *imago Christi* see Chapter 4; we will be discussing this issue further below.

85. TKG, p. 118.

86. U. Mauser, *Gottesbild und Menschwerdung*, Tübingen, J. Mohr, P. Siebeck, 1971, p. 187; English translation mine.

87. *Ibid.*, p. 187.

88. We raised this issue in the previous chapter; for Moltmann's definition of the divine nature, see; CG, pp. 227-235; TKG, pp. 120; 172 ; WJC, pp. 50-55.

89. GC, p. 246.

90. See, F. Perls, R. Hefferline and P. Goodman, *Gestalt-Therapy: Excitement and Growth in the Human Personality*, London, Souvenir Press, 1951, pp. 56 ff.; 239 ff. and 411 ff. The dualisms refer to that between: body/mind; self/world; subject/object; infantile/mature; biological/cultural; poetry/prose; spontaneous/deliberate; personal/social; love/aggression; unconscious/conscious. Moltmann draws on this source, with the caveat that he is not making a dogma out of *Gestalt* therapy itself, GC, p. 353, footnote 40. D. Bonhoeffer speaks of becoming conformed to Christ by acceptance of suffering. The *"Gestalt,"* or "form" of Jesus Christ takes "form" in humankind, while "the longing of the Incarnate to take form in all men is as yet unsatisfied." Moltmann seems to be linking the psychological idea of *Gestalt* with Bonhoeffer's idea of the *Gestalt* of Christ. For Bonhoeffer Christ's *Gestalt* is both concrete and that which is "the same at all times and in all places." In this sense Moltmann can speak of the acquisition of Christ's *Gestalt* by all humanity, though it amounts to a transformation of the meaning of *Gestalt* in its psychological context. See D. Bonhoeffer, E. Bethge, ed., *Ethics*, London, SCM Press, 1955, pp. 62-68.

91. F.S. Perls, *et. al.*, *op. cit.* (n.90), pp. 56 ff.; the "ground" refers in a loose way to the environmental influences, and the "figure" to the individual.

92. GC, pp. 261-262; see also, Chapter 4 (3) and Chapter 4 (4).

93. *Ibid.*, pp. 264-266.

94. See comment on the *Gestalt* of Christ under n.90, above; also Chapter 4(4).

95. Moltmann interprets the death of Christ as the death on behalf of all living creatures; WJC, pp. 169; 258 ff.; he insists that mortality is in itself in need of redemption. He speaks, for example, of "the redemption of enslaved creation from the fate of transience," WJC, p. 251. These suggestions are somewhat incongruous both (i) with his idea that human death "does not interrupt the natural laws of mortal life; it is rather that the whole quality of mortal life is changed - and with it, of course, the laws of its mortality too;" WJC, p. 250, and (ii) with the

practical reality of what such lack of transience would mean in the non-human world, especially amongst the luxuriant vegetative growth of the plant and microbiological kingdoms.

96. See Section 2, above, for a discussion of the cosmic Christ in relation to the future of nature and history. Moltmann believes that "The raised body of Christ therefore acts as an embodied promise for the whole creation," WJC, p. 258.

97. WJC, p. 155; see also under n.95 above; the sufferings of Christ are universal because they are a suffering with the cosmos; WJC, p. 362, footnote 7. Moltmann wants Christology to be broadened into cosmic suffering, rather than the opposite telescoping of cosmic suffering into that of Christ. The latter is the theological concept of E. Peterson. Moltmann reinforces the suggestion of Christ suffering in creation with the idea of the fellowship of Christ suffering with creation, where once again it is Christ's sufferings extended outwards. Instead of identifying our suffering and that of creation with that of Christ, Christ moves out to identify with the whole suffering creation.

98. WJC, p. 153. Moltmann's insistence on the necessity for suffering in the apocalyptic horizon of the new creation brings him more in line with Hegelian philosophy. It is hard to avoid the impression that the idea of "fruitful" suffering somehow justifies it; O'Collins, comments on TKG; "one wonders whether the risen Christ and those who share in his resurrection will ever be rid of suffering, even in their risen state." Moltmann resists such asuggestion, with suffering confined to the birth of the new creation; see G. O'Collins, "Christ's Resurrection as Mystery of Love," *Heythrop Journal*, 25, 1984, pp. 39-50, see p. 48.

99. WJC, p. 168; see also, Chapter 3(2) and Chapter 5(3).

100. *Ibid.*, p. 93.

101. Claus Westermann also expresses the idea of *imago Dei* in relational terms; for a discussion, see, G. Jønsson, *op. cit.* (n.78), pp. 61-76; 223-224.

102. Phyllis Trible's idea of Adam is complicated by her interpretation of *ha adam* as a two stage process. In the first stage, prior to the arrival of woman, *adam* is an 'earth-born' human being. Once woman is created *adam* refers to the male gender, and together they express the "image of God." Moltmann takes up Trible's suggestion that Adam is a reference to an "earthly creature," GC, p. 187, and also integrates Trible's belief that sexuality is part of the meaning of *imago Dei.* He believes that in sexuality "the real likeness to God and the uniquely human quality must lie," GC, p. 222. P. Trible, *God and the Rhetoric of Sexuality*, Philadelphia, Fortress Press, 1978, pp. 10-21; 80-95.

103. Moltmann does not seem to have taken account of Trible's particular hermeneutical stance, which is "rhetorical criticism" which welcomes the unique, intuition, guess and surprise; P. Trible, *ibid.*, p. 10. Childs rejects Trible's suggestion that there is a direct relation between

the creation of *adam* in Gen 1.26 and the creation of sexuality in Genesis 2 from a literary perspective. He argues that the term *adam* is not used in a different way after the creation of woman, and in the Masoretic text Adam is a proper name. He believes that it is possible to stay within normal hermeneutical rules without implying any subordination of women. The latter comes from an overemphasis on Genesis 2 at the expense of Genesis 1.26. He insists that the opposite danger is an egalitarian ideology which sees both sexes in the same "rôles, goals and capacities." B.S. Childs, *op. cit.* (n.45), pp. 189-192. For further critique of Trible's position see, P. Bird, "Male and Female He Created Them: Genesis 1:27 in the Context of the Priestly Account of Creation," *Harvard Theological Review*, 74(2), 1981, pp. 129-159. While Moltmann mentions the latter critique, GC, p. 349, footnote 13, he does not take up the criticism. For general discussion of feminist theological contribution to the debate see G. Jønsson *op. cit.* (n.78), pp. 178-188.

104. Jønsson notes the overall consensus within Old Testament scholarship towards a functional interpretation of *imago Dei*, especially since the 1960s. He believes that one of the factors which caused this shift from an understanding that was based more in ontological terms was the pressure of the ecological movement. Broadly speaking the functional interpretation views *imago Dei* as related to humanity's stewardship of the earth. Moltmann incorporates this idea as one component in his understanding of the meaning of *imago Dei*, while agreeing with Wildberger and Jacob that there is a distinction between the essence of the image and its consequences; GC, pp. 224-225; G. Jønsson, *op. cit.* (n.78), pp. 219-223.

105. C. Jønsson, *op. cit.* (n.78), p.224; see also J. Barr, "The Image of God in Genesis - A Study in Terminology," *Bulletin of the John Rylands Library*, 51, 1968, pp. 11-26. Barr has re-examined his understanding of the meaning of the divine image in the wake of the ecological crisis, and strongly resisted White's suggestion that the Christian idea of dominion is responsible for the crisis; J. Barr, "Man and Nature: The Ecological Controversy and the Old Testament," *op. cit.* (n.9).

106. GC, pp. 226-227; also Chapter 4(7).

107. GC, p. 227.

108. *Ibid.*, p. 277; see earlier under n.95, above and also later, under n.115.

109. *Ibid.*, p. 288; see earlier section for critique of Moltmann's use of sabbath.

110. *Ibid.*, pp. 99-100; see also Chapter 3(6).

111. Moltmann insists that the Spirit of God in creation is the Holy Spirit; and that there is no danger of pantheism if we think in trinitarian terms; see discussion in last chapter, also SBH.

112. GC, pp. 101-103.

113. WJC, pp. 153-155.

114. *Ibid.*, p. 289; for reference to wisdom literature, see n.66.

115. WJC, p. 250. Moltmann believes that creation is delivered from transience, but he does not elaborate what this means in concrete terms; see under n.95, above. Moltmann's sources for these ideas are obscure, and one suspects that they are an imaginative guess. While it might be helpful to think theologically of the kind of future which we can expect after death, he may be in danger of alienating his readers who have a more scientific understanding of the world, which we will discuss more fully below.

116. *Ibid.*, p. 262.

117. Moltmann's idea of *Aeon* is more prominent in his most recent works; see WJC, pp. 158; 330-331.

118. H. Sasse, "Αιων" G. Kittel, ed.; translated by G.W. Bromiley; *Theological Dictionary of the New Testament*, Grand Rapids, Erdmans, 1964, pp. 199-209.

119. For an outline of the Eastern Orthodox view on *Aeon*, see, V. Lossky, *The Mystical Theology of the Eastern Church*, London, Clarke, 1957, pp. 101-103. Gregory of Nyssa takes his bearings for the new creation from the primordial beginning, which contrasts with Moltmann's own view of a new creation emerging in an open future. Unlike Basil, Moltmann does not equate humanity's future existence with that of the angels, since he insists that in the future our relationship with creation is retained, as is our bodily/sexual existence. He makes little attempt to justify such claims, except in so far as they are consistent with his holistic understanding of redemption; see WJC, pp. 262 ff.

120. WJC, p. 76; the resurrection is a revelation "ahead of time" in our own present history, p. 219.

121. GC, pp. 138-139; compare with WJC, pp. 330-331.

122. WJC, p. 331.

123. *Ibid.*, p. 331. The idea of "life" as the core of our future goal fits in with the more recent suggestion of Kenneth Cauthen in his vision for the future. It also has echoes in Albert Schweitzer's interpretation. See K. Cauthen, *op. cit.* (n.3), p. 143; A. Schweitzer, C. Campion, ed., *Out of My Life and Thought*, New York, New American Library, 1953, p. 188.

124. GC, pp. 185-190, on humankind as *imago mundi*; pp. 190-197 on evolution/creation debate.

125. *Ibid.*, pp. 198-206. Moltmann is overly ambitious here since he tries to achieve such a synthesis in less than ten pages. The rest of the chapter on the evolution of creation is devoted to a discussion of a reformulation of traditional doctrines of creation in the beginning, continuous creation and consummation of creation. This is not so much a "synthesis" with scientific theory

as reformulation in eschatological categories using the idea of open systems; see n.130, below for critical comment.

126. For a discussion of sociobiology's use of the idea of evolution, see, S. Gould "Biological Potentiality *vs* Biological Determinism;" *Ever Since Darwin*, Harmonsworth, Penguin/Pelican, 1980, pp. 251-260.

127. L. Osborn, "Review of God in Creation," *Themelios*, 12(1), 1986, pp. 30-31.

128. GC, pp. 198-206.

129. See, GC, p. 100; also, K. Hafstad, "Gott in der Natur: Zur Schöpfungslehre Jürgen Moltmanns," *Evangelische Theologie*, 47, 1987, pp. 460-466; and discussion in previous chapter.

130. GC, pp. 203-205; FC, pp. 115-130 for an earlier treatment. The validity of Moltmann's idea of an open system in scientific terms has been challenged by a number of reviewers; including McPherson and Peters. Ted Peters, for example, comments "we need to caution him regarding a serious pitfall in logic if he claims a scientific warrant for applying the term "open system" to the creation as a whole. What we need is a theology of creation....which is open to patterns of reconceptualization on the basis of serious dialogue with the current frontiers of scientific research." He also criticizes Moltmann's scant reference to Barbour, Peacocke, Torrance and other theologians working on the frontier of science-faith interface. However, this issue is not quite as simple as it appears at first sight. McPherson refers to Peacocke's *Creation and the World of Science*, but Peacocke quotes Moltmann where he refers to open systems in several places, apparently with approval, see, pp. 80; 210; 337; 344. The problem seems to be that our solar system and galaxy has a horizon fixed by the impossibility of observing distant galaxies, so in a strict sense it is not "isolated" - the term Peacocke prefers to "closed." However, for working scientists the universe is *ipso facto* "isolated," and thus obeys the second law of thermodynamics, tending to move towards thermodynamic equilibrium, that is a state of maximum entropy, *Creation and the World of Science*, p. 326, footnote 20. Nonetheless, Peacocke elsewhere comments that scientists are not justified in assuming that the second law of thermodynamics "inevitably" applies to the universe as a whole, which would predict ultimate extinction of the whole universe. While he seems to accept the scientific prediction of the "death" of the earth, he refuses to accept that "this will happen to the whole universe;" *Science and the Christian Experiment*, p. 198. This might be small comfort, perhaps, as far as the future of this earth is concerned; even though we are many millions of years away from this projected event. See, Paul Davies, *The Runaway Universe*, pp. 162-165. While we agree that Moltmann has transformed the category of "open system" from its origin in physical sciences, this is quite consistent with his own theological style. The question is whether this is a misleading

transformation. Moltmann's own contribution to the theology of creation is, by his own admission, not as specialized in terms of scientific acumen as accounts given, for example, in I. Barbour, *Issues in Science and Religion*. To take on the whole scientific milieu is a task that would be quite impossible in view of the wealth of scientific terms, *etc*. However, we do agree that a greater awareness of the original meaning of language in a scientific context would help prevent the kind of alienation expressed by John Polkinghorne in his review of *God in Creation*. In scientific parlance a system is "closed" or "isolated" if its thermodynamic life is self-contained, and where the law of increasing entropy applies. A system is "open" if it has different possibilities of alteration; its future behaviour has not been determined by its previous behaviour; it can communicate with other systems and its final condition is different from its initial state. While Moltmann was seemingly aware of this definition in FC, p. 190, footnote 14, he discards any scientific rootedness by treating both the earth and the universe automatically as an open system; GC pp. 204-206. More worrying, perhaps, from a theological point of view, is that in spite of his rhetoric on "open systems" it appears that suffering is **necessary** for the emergence of the new creation; in other words, if suffering is necessary, what does openness mean? The idea that suffering is a prerequisite for the new creation seems to imply that the true potential for openness happens after the process of suffering and death, and that the openness of the new creation is somehow different from the openness of the initial creation. K. Hafstad raised this issue in relation to the problem of understanding what openness and closedness means for the natural world; she asks, does closedness mean a sinful rejection of evolution? While we are less sure that Moltmann correlates openness with evolution in the way she implies, the problem remains as to how to interpret what this means theologically. Hence, a radical open system seems to apply to the new creation and new earth, which tends to separate the metaphor from its original context in the concrete reality of creation, which is not presumably Moltmann's intention. K. Hafstad offers another insightful critique, namely that Moltmann derives the idea of open systems originally from science, but he mixes this with the theological category of closedness, taken from metaphors associated with the kingdom of God, an issue which we mentioned in the last chapter. I. Barbour, *Issues in Science and Religion*, London, SCM, 1986, pp. 81-97; 365-385; T. Peters, "A Book Worth Discussing," *Current Theology of Mission*, 13(4), 1986, pp. 241-244; J. McPherson, "Life, The Universe and Everything: Jürgen Moltmann's Doctrine of Creation," *St Mark's Review*, 128, 1986, pp. 34-46; J.Polkinghorne, "Creation Without the Scientists: Review of *God in Creation*," *Expository Times*, 97(9), 1986, p. 285; A. Peacocke, *Creation and the World of Science*, Oxford, Clarendon, 1979; A. Peacocke, *Science and the Christian Experiment*, London, Oxford

University Press, 1971; P. Davies, *The Runaway Universe*, London, Dent, 1978; K. Hafstad, *op. cit.* (n.129).

131. J. Earman, "Causation a Matter of Life and Death," *Journal of Philosophy*, 73, 1976, pp. 5-25.

132. *Ibid.*, p. 13. Earman uses the Lorentz-Diroc equation of motion for relativistic charged particles. The integro-differential equation predicts a "pre-acceleration" effect, such that if a sharp impulsive force acts on a particle at time r, then the particle will begin to accelerate before r.

133. A. Gränbaum and I. Janis, "Is There Backward Causation in Classical Electrodynamics?," *Journal of Philosophy*, 74, 1977, 475-482.

134. WJC, 302-303.

135. *Ibid.*, p. 303.

136. .Jantsch bases his idea of the self-organizing universe on a consideration of I. Prigogine's study of thermodynamics of complex systems, which won her the Nobel prize for chemistry in 1976. We note in passing that Jantsch's hypothesis depends on the dynamic system moving down an entropy gradient, that is one which is in a non-equilibrium state. A self-organizing system also requires the system to be open to the flux of matter and energy and to be non-linear in flux-force relationships. "Under these conditions steady states belonging to a finite neighbourhood of the state of thermodynamic equilibrium are asymptotically stable. Beyond a critical distance from equilibrium they may become unstable;" A. Peacocke, *An Introduction to the Physical Chemistry of Biological Organization*, Oxford, Clarendon Press, 1989, p. 62. Hence while there is global "stability" it presupposes non-equilibrium dynamics. Jantsch has called this "autopoiesis," and for him: "Equilibrium is the equivalent of stagnation and death." These ideas jar rather unevenly with Moltmann's ideal of equilibrium which he loosely associates with the more passive Taoist ideal "equilibrium," which we will discuss in more detail later; see under n.144. The issue we wish to raise here is that Moltmann has not distinguished *between* thermodynamic "equilibrium," which is only possible in "closed" systems and amounts to maximum entropy/death *and* steady-state conditions characteristic of the "equilibrium" of complex eco-system, *and* the ideal of harmony and "equilibrium" in Taoist thought. A biological or ecological steady-state depends on maximum diversity of species, so that interference by humankind which in any way reduces this species' diversity automatically weakens the possibility of "equilibrium." Moltmann is not seemingly aware of this biological insight in his treatment of the so-called "equilibrium" between ourselves and other creatures. See also, A. Peacocke, *Creation and the World of Science, op. cit.* (n.130), p. 260; E. Jantsch, *The Self-Organizing Universe*, New York, Pergamon Press, 1980.

137. Moltmann makes no reference to Polanyi's idea of personal knowledge in science, and the way science arrives at its claims for the truth. Karl Popper's classic theory on deductive science is modified by Polanyi's acknowledgment of human commitment in science. K.Popper, *The Logic of Scientific Discovery*, London, Hutchinson, 1956; M. Polanyi, *Personal Knowledge*, London, Routledge & Kegan Paul, 1958.

138. J. Lovelock admits that "the idea that the earth is alive is at the outer bounds of scientific credibility," p. 3; and while his first book was a "pencil sketch that tried to catch a view of the earth from a different perspective....second book is a statement of *Gaia* theory; the basis of a new and unified view of the Earth and life sciences...I have called the science of *Gaia* geophysiology," p. 11. In some other statements an implicit mythos comes through; for example, his belief that *Gaia* is "a total planetary being," p.19; and in a final chapter on "God and *Gaia*" he raises the question of whether the religious attachment to Mary is a reaction to the concept of a remote God, in which case: "What if Mary is another name for *Gaia*?....She is of this Universe and, conceivably, a part of God. On earth she is the source of life everlasting, and is alive now; she gave birth to humankind and we are part of her," p.206; which reminds us that "In ancient times belief in a living Earth and in a living cosmos was the same thing," p. 209. Further, if humans stand in the way of *Gaia*, "we shall be eliminated with as little pity as would be shown by the microbrain of an intercontinental ballistic nuclear missile in full flight to its target," p. 212. J.E. Lovelock, *The Ages of Gaia: A Biography of our Living Earth*, Oxford, Oxford University Press, 1988; see also his earlier work, *Gaia: A New Look at Life on Earth*, Oxford, Oxford University Press, 1979, second edition, 1987.

139. S. Toulmin, "Cosmology as Science and as Religion," in, L. Rouner, ed., *On Nature*, Indiana, University of Notre Dame Press, 1984, pp. 27-41. Toulmin acknowledges that he is moving against more recent theological trends to remove the cosmological world-view under the influence of Bultmann's theology of "demythologizing."

140. *Ibid.*, p. 28.

141. D. Sagan and L. Margulis, "*Gaia* and Philosophy," in, L. Rouner, ed., *On Nature*, Indiana, University of Notre Dame Press, 1984, p. 60.

142. Duchrow and Liedke, for example, have been more strident in their condemnation of science and technology, believing that the very possibility of neutral science is a "myth," so that the conduct of experiments always leads to violence against nature; *op. cit.* (n.12), pp. 65-66.

143. For Moltmann's understanding of mysticism in relation to science, see, Chapter 2(1); see also F. Capra, who insists that holism is part of the "New Physics" and who draws almost exclusively on Eastern mysticism. F. Capra, *The Tao of Physics*, London, Wildwood House, 1975; F. Capra, *The Turning Point*, London, Wildwood House, 1982.

144. Moltmann's perception of the Taoist ideal of equilibrium comes from reflection on the natural world, in this case the "ricefield." "The rice field resists both the capitalist principle of competition and individualism;" CJF, p. 89.

145. Moltmann makes little reference to nature mysticism of early Christian saints. For a discussion of Francis of Assisi's views see, R. Sorrell, *St. Francis of Assisi and Nature: Tradition and Innovation in Western Christian Attitudes Toward the Environment;* Oxford, Oxford University Press, 1988. A possible explanation is that Moltmann's particular mystical theology bears the mark of *crux Christi,* though this would not necessarily exclude an extension into nature mysticism, as is the case for St. Francis himself.

146. Moltmann compares the Jewish sabbath ideal with Taoist understanding of perfection, in GC, p. 321, footnote 5.

147. For a discussion of the meaning of divine rest, see, G. von Rad, *op. cit.* (n.34).

148. Lao Tzu, *The Tao Te Ching, Part 1,* in, J. Legge, ed., *The Texts of Taoism,* New York, Dover Publications, 1962, p. 60.

149. CJF, p. 100; compare Chapter 76, Lao Tzu, *The Tao Te Ching, Ibid.,* p. 118; the dead body becomes hard, while a living body remains "soft."

150. CJF, p. 101; compare Chapter 80, *ibid.,* p. 122, which is called "Standing Alone," and we are recommended to return to a use of knotted characters instead of writing, coarse food, plain clothes and poor dwellings!

151. For Jantsch's concept of equilibrium as death, E. Jantsch, *op. cit.* (n.136), p. 10. Moltmann is not alone in using the idea of symbiosis in a loose way to imply interdependence. However, he extends this idea further for his own purposes. See, for example, E. Ashby, *Reconciling Man With the Environment,* Oxford, Oxford University Press, 1978, pp. 84-85.

152. An example would be Moltmann's reconciliation of Christ the Evolver with Christ the Redeemer.

153. J. Findlay, *op. cit.* (n.2), p. 346.

CHAPTER 7

Conclusions: Towards a Green Theology of Creation.

1. Introduction: Moltmann's hope for creation.

In our previous chapter we examined the basis and outline of Moltmann's holistic vision for the future. It is one of his brilliant achievements that he has looked behind the immediate ecological crisis as such, to the anxiety that pervades human attitudes to our environment. He roots the cause of much of this anxiety to our failure to have an adequate understanding of God as the loving creator, and as one who promises a future of fellowship with both humankind and creation. His concern to portray theology of creation in eschatological categories is singularly relevant for a culture which is fearful of what the future may hold for the cosmos.

So far we have been concerned to show how Moltmann has shifted in his theology towards a more consciously ecological approach, with much of this "greenness" already implicit in his earlier work. The themes of interconnectedness and indwelling, which by his own admission represent paradigms for an ecological doctrine, are already emergent in his social Trinitarian understanding and his appreciation of homecoming drawn from Bloch's philosophy of hope. He draws together catholic and Protestant insights by taking up chords of natural theology, and putting them in the future key.[1] Our aim in the present chapter is to give a brief summary of the most significant aspects of Moltmann's theology of creation, and then offer a brief critique of his overall position in the light of a concern to develop a green theology. By the latter we mean one that is thoroughly aware of ecological issues, but within the framework of theological concerns.

2. Re-imaging God, humankind and nature.

(a) Re-imaging God as social Trinity.

As we have hinted above, one of Moltmann's aims is to reach out to the root cause of our problem in relating to creation, which he believes stems from our misconception of God. Instead of thinking about God exclusively in categories of power, and as one who exerts tyranny over humankind and creation, we need to re-image him as one who loves creation, and who exists in Trinitarian social fellowship. God as Trinity does not begin with the category of "oneness," since Moltmann believes that this leads to an incipient abstractness in our understanding of God.[2] Instead, God as Trinity exists in perichoretic fellowship with each person retaining a distinct existence. The unity of the Trinity flows from the quality of the interrelationship where each person indwells in the others.

It is this interconnectedness and indwelling at the heart of the social life of the Trinity that gives Moltmann the means to speak about God as Trinity in ecological language. Nonetheless, he takes the idea of interconnectedness beyond that of traditional Eastern Orthodoxy by bringing in feminist insights to his understanding of the meaning of these interrelationships. He also takes the idea of indwelling beyond the traditional view by using the Jewish kabbalistic doctrine of *zimzum*, where God withdraws into himself to make space for his creation.

Our experience of God is matched by God's experience of creation, and though this experience is not equivalent, it is reciprocal. This theme moves the idea of the social Trinity beyond itself into the dynamics of the interrelationship between God and the world. Here Moltmann comes close to some aspects of process theology; though his insistence that God creates the world *ex nihilo*, and that the future of creation emerges from God's future rather than creation itself, distinguishes his view from process thought.

The theme of *kenosis* within the life of the social Trinity marks this life in a particularly Christological way. Moltmann resists the Hegelian idea of suffering as a requirement of the life of the Trinity, though the trend of his thought has Hegelian overtones. His attempt to bring the self-emptying of Christ on the cross into the initial act of divine withdrawal tends to confuse the categories of creation and redemption. The theme of the divine pathos is an important one for Moltmann, who backs up his ideas by drawing on a number of Jewish writers.[3] Moltmann is anxious to re-image God, as one who is not impassible, but who shares in our suffering, and whose experience of suffering reaches right into the heart of the social Trinity.

Alongside this theme of the social Trinity participating in the suffering of the world, we find the parallel theme of all creation and history participating in the life and glory of the Godhead. The image of the sabbath is one which extends to the future, and only in the future is the glory of God manifest through the shared participatory life of all creation.

(b) Re-imaging humankind as interdependent community.

Moltmann is not content just to leave us with a new picture of God in social terms. He develops his anthropology along similar lines, though he tends to weave this aspect of his theology into his discussion of other themes. His discussion of humankind shows significant shifts compared with his earlier work. While his writing in the 1970s tended to focus on the historical aspects of our existence, the theme of history in *God in Creation*, has become part of a more creation-centred framework. Earlier he discussed the relationship between "man" and nature in terms of stewardship, but later this theme is incorporated into his concern to stress the solidarity between humankind and creation in a way which is sensitive to feminist developments in theology. However, even in his earlier work he stressed the importance of our environment, and to some extent he brings back the theme of creation caught up in a historical Christological framework in his more recent *The Way of Jesus Christ*. Nonetheless, as we shall discuss more fully below, his Christology has also shifted in a way which incorporates biological themes.

Moltmann interprets both the early chapters of Genesis and the *imago Dei* in ways which stress human identification with creation in all its earthiness and material aspects. Our rôle as *imago mundi* precedes our future vocation to become *gloria Dei* through *imago Christi*.

Alongside this emphasis on the earthiness of human existence we find Moltmann drawing on the perichoretic life of the Trinity as analogous to our life in human communities. This life is marked by the experience of the Holy Spirit in Christian identification with the death and resurrection of Jesus. In this way Moltmann looks both to the immanent Trinity as a source of inspiration for human community life, and to the economic Trinity which reminds us of the death and resurrection of Jesus in history.[4]

The social life of the human community is marked by love and fellowship with the oppressed. This category is broad enough to include those whom we have tended to reject in our society, such as the handicapped or socially isolated groups, as well as the natural creation itself. Moltmann believes that our attitude towards creation should be that of love and friendship, instead of antagonism and management. Moltmann aligns himself with feminist thought, both in its rejection of hierarchical structures and its identification with the earth. Our rôle as stewards of creation only makes sense in this context of love and care for creation, which reflects the loving attitude of our creator.

(c) Re-imaging nature in solidarity with Christ.

Moltmann's discussion of the natural world dwells not so much on an appreciation of nature *as such*, but rather on how it relates to God and humankind. He is, however, thoroughly convinced of creation's value independent of humans. For him this value comes from God's love for creation, which finds expression in the extension of Christ's solidarity to include nature and humankind. God as cosmic Spirit pervades every aspect of earthly creation in a way which refuses to separate the spiritual from the material. God as cosmic Spirit moves beyond a simple holism of body and mind in a way which includes all aspects of communication at every conceivable level of reality. In a similar way, God as cosmic Christ shares in the suffering of every mortal creature, and becomes the liberator of enslaved creation. Christ in his cosmic rôle reaches out to all the groaning and suffering of creation in a way which allows it to participate in his death and resurrection. The pain is a necessary part of the birth pangs in the emergence of the new creation.

While Moltmann stresses the love of God for his creation which tends to draw out the rôle of the Father as subject, in *The Way of Jesus Christ* the rôle of the cosmic Christ comes into the foreground. The death and resurrection of Jesus also mark the beginning of the task of the Spirit as subject of the glorification of the cosmos. The cosmic Christ and the cosmic Spirit have complementary rôles in redemption and glorification. However, it is only in solidarity with Christ that the Spirit's rôle in glorification becomes possible, for the latter emerges in the context of the participation of all creation in Christ's death and resurrection.

Hence the life of all the cosmos is caught up into Christ's history and that of humanity. Moltmann also uses the sabbath motif to link creation and history, space and time. The glorious sabbath reflects the time of the new *aeon*, where linear historical time and biological cyclical time somehow become caught up into the eternal life of God. The theme of participation in God's life safeguards the distinction between God and creation in future creation.

3. Towards a green theology of creation.

(a) God, ecologically reconsidered.

One of Moltmann's achievements has been to encourage us to reconsider who God is in the light of the ecological awareness of our culture. He is brilliant in his subtle interweaving of themes taken from green issues into his own perception of God as social Trinity. However, he may have gone rather too far in his own speculative theology; especially in his discussions of the immanent Trinity. We find his portrayal of the immanent Trinity in spatial categories through his use of the Jewish idea of *zimzum* unconvincing. He does not appear to have recognized the difficulty in discerning the limits to the appropriateness of language in drawing analogies between God and creation.

The above concentration on re-imaging God means that overall Moltmann has not really gone far enough in his discussions of both humankind and nature. Hence, while his theology of creation is a step in the direction towards a green theology, it is only a first step.

(b) Creation, Christologically re-considered.

Moltmann's often unspoken agenda is a reliance on Christ Mysticism at the heart of his spirituality. It is natural, then, for him to extend the significance of the cross and resurrection of Christ into the orbit of creation in a way which allows Christ to become creation's hope for the future. The symbol of hope which is engendered by the resurrection neatly dovetails with biological images of new birth and spring festivals. However, Moltmann's Christology refuses to leave us content with a biological concept of time, since the resurrection points to the new *aeon* where creation is no longer subject to mortality. The new birth in Christ is one of dynamic participation in the life of the Trinity.

While these images taken from the history of Christ have certain advantages in broadening soteriology beyond a narrowly human horizon, they also carry some disadvantages. It becomes, for example, increasingly difficult for us as human beings to identify with Christ in cosmic solidarity with all the suffering of groaning creation. While it might encourage us to become more sensitive to nature's pain, it could also have a different effect, namely to alienate us from the person of Christ. This is the opposite of Moltmann's intention, which has been to emphasize the earthly humanity of Christ in his concrete existence. Behind this difficulty is Moltmann's failure to tackle the relationship between the person of Jesus in his human existence, and the person of the Son in Trinitarian fellowship. In what sense, for example, can the human sufferings of Jesus reach out into his divine sufferings in his rôle as the cosmic Christ? Moltmann seems to indicate that the divine sufferings are equivalent to Jesus' human sufferings, but this becomes rather difficult to imagine in purely anthropological terms.

The idea of the sufferings of the Spirit of God through the groaning creation is rather underdeveloped in Moltmann's theology, especially in his later works such as *The Way of Jesus Christ*. We suggest that Moltmann's tendency to relate the sufferings of Christ to the issue of mortality in creation without going via pneumatology is an unhelpful shift in his position. He is surely right, however, in not assuming that all the sufferings of creation are somehow a direct consequence of the fall of humankind. The latter view would interpret the redemption of humankind as the only necessary precondition for the restoration of cosmic order. Moltmann not only resists this view, he also insists that the new creation is radical in its newness and not simply a re-creation as in the beginning. While Moltmann is bold in his attempt to envisage cosmic redemption, he is not always justified in giving details as to what this might mean for the biological world.

The above raises the question of how far has Moltmann really engaged with the concrete reality of creation? The images of, for example, sabbath peace, participation of the whole of life in the Trinitarian life of God, sound visionary, but are they fully convincing? Again Moltmann strays a little too far into speculation in his explicit descriptions of the way humans and creation will share in the glory of God.

(c) Integrating science and theology, nature and history.

Moltmann's basic intention of bringing together science and theology, nature and history is a worthy one and makes for an excitingly original combination of ideas and concepts. He is more successful in his attempt to bring together nature and history than in his effort to integrate science and theology. His failure to do justice to the latter is partly related to his apparent lack of real appreciation of the momentous difficulty of such a task. For example, he does not seem to be sufficiently aware of the immense restructuring of science which would have to be done if the ecological sensitivity to creation was followed through in its practical consequences. It really is not that easy to practice scientific research when the theme of friendship with all creation and Taoist equilibrium with nature comes to the surface of our consciousness. Moltmann tends, rather too glibly, to resolve potential difficulties Christologically. He suggests, for example, that Christ could somehow re-volve evolution in a way which echoes Teilhard de Chardin's ideas, but which remains rather unconvincing.

While we believe that Moltmann is right in giving theology the task of making scientific enterprise more aware of its ethical consequences, he may have alienated scientists by not seeming to take sufficient notice of the way science works in practice. His use of biological analogies, such as symbiosis and *Gestalt*, may give the appearance of dialogue with science, but is too far removed from their biological rootedness to convince biologically-minded readers of its relevance. Hence, while his approach sounds adequate for a more popular audience, and encourages an eclectic appreciation of the world, it may not influence those who are in positions of power in science and technology. Moltmann's intention to be in dialogue with science does not really work as far as many scientists are concerned, because he has transformed the meaning of scientific concepts.[5]

Moltmann also uses more controversial ideas which are on the borders of science and mythology. We have in mind in this context the *Gaia* hypothesis and Jantsch's notion of a self-organizing universe. While Moltmann is instructive in his recognition of the increasing popularity of these ideas, he has not adequately distanced himself from their presuppositions.[6] He also seems relatively unaware of the clash between the traditional understanding of the purpose of science, and that presented by geophysiology. The latter's stress on the planet as a whole reduces the place of humankind to just one strand in the biotic life. While Moltmann would wish to distance himself from such views, he does not do this sufficiently clearly, and so leaves himself open to attack from those who identify his position with that of Lovelock and his colleagues.

The above raises another important issue, namely how far does Moltmann draw history into the orbit of nature or vice versa? Overall we are of the opinion that his focus on both eschatology and Christology tends to let history have priority over nature, but not in the way that it has in the past, which has tended to be a focus on history to the exclusion of nature. However, a difficulty in Moltmann's theology arises as a result of his explicit use of kenotic Christology. The latter brings redemptive themes into creation at the beginning in a way which tends to confuse the two and tends to weaken the value of creation *as such*. While Moltmann's intention has always been to affirm creation as beloved of God, its Christological categorization, as we examined above, puts the focus back on anthropology and history. Are we left with a choice of either understanding Christ in cosmic terms, which weakens his reality in our historical life, or understanding creation in redemptive Christological terms, which weakens its value as creation as distinct from history? Both problems stem from Moltmann's failure to face up to the concrete nature of scientific and material existence, in spite of his rhetoric on God as "embodiment."

4. Conclusions.

Moltmann's theology of creation painted in ecological terms is an inspirational beginning towards a green theology. He always challenges and provokes discussion, and the sheer diversity of his use of different ideas is admirable, if at times a little overwhelming. His achievement is in the direction of integration and synthesis, which makes his theology thoroughly ecological in an implicit sense. This is perhaps more successful than his more explicit use of ecological terms in his theological discussions. The latter are important in helping to shift our attitudes to creation, and in overcoming false dualisms between material and spiritual, private and public existence. However, he has not always been sufficiently aware either of the concrete biological aspects of reality, or of the theological problems which are raised by using particular analogies to describe God. Hence, while he says rather too little about creation itself, he says rather too much about God.

Another significant contribution of Moltmann's theology is in his drawing together themes from diverse theological traditions as, for example, in Eastern Orthodoxy and feminism, process theology and Barthian dialectics. Moltmann has done a great service to feminist thought in bringing some of its more important insights into the mainstream of theological discussion. This is a vital corrective to other tendencies in feminist theology which seem to be either drifting towards a rejection of Christianity as irredeemably patriarchal, or an identification of radical feminism with the kingdom of God. Moltmann's concern to broaden strands of theology which might otherwise become narcissistic and ideological also applies to his attempt to rehabilitate Barthian thought in the context of a more appreciative stance towards culture. He carefully resists the opposite tendency towards relativism which we find in much process theology.

Overall we believe that Moltmann's imaginative brilliance is an important corrective to the more sterile approach characteristic of much traditional theology in the past. His intention to bring imagination into the sphere of reason sometimes gives way to a taste for speculation which takes him too far from concrete issues. However, Moltmann's theology of creation, in its explicit attempt to stay in touch with green issues, is an important first step.

Like most great theologians, his thought should serve to stimulate further fruitful dialogue, and above all help us to change our attitudes to both God and his creation. It is only then that we shall be in a position to think clearly about the multi-faceted relationships between God, humanity and nature. If a green theology is to have a message for this ecologically damaged fragile earth, it has to include Moltmann's concept of hope in God, who through Christ makes all things new.

End Notes

1.　By allowing for "natural theology" in the future he recognizes the catholic affirmation of creation in and of itself as a means through which the glory of God is revealed. However, his stance is still characteristic of Barthian thought in his insistence that such reflection only makes sense in the context of faith in Christ. By putting "natural theology" in eschatological terms he avoids the controversy over the place of creation as given to reveal the creator.

2.　Moltmann describes this view in terms of "abstract monotheism." He believes that an emphasis on God's unity distances God from creation since it begins with an understanding of God in abstract terms. Instead, if we begin with the history of Jesus, this leads to an emphasis on the tri-unity which is more biblical, and therefore more "orthodox."

3.　F. Rosenzweig is particularly influential here. A clear summary of Moltmann's debate with Jewish concepts of the divine pathos is in J. Moltmann and P. Lapide, *Jewish Monotheism and Christian Trinitarian Doctrine: A Dialogue*; translated by L. Swidler, Philadelphia, Fortress Press, 1981.

4.　It is important for Moltmann to stress that while the immanent and economic Trinities are distinct, they are inseparable. In his earlier work he stressed their inseparableness, while more recently he has been concerned to draw out their distinctness. As we will discuss below he does not always clarify in what sense the persons of the immanent Trinity relate to the persons of the economic Trinity. This is particularly obvious in his discussion of the person of the Son, whose personhood as Jesus is fully human through his kenotic Christology.

5.　Hence John Polkinghorne's cryptic comment that Moltmann's *God in Creation* is "Creation without the Scientists." J. Polkinghorne, "Review of *God in Creation*," *Expository Times*, 97 (9), 1986, p 285.

6.　While these theories claim authority from science, by their own admission they are still at the borders of accepted scientific dogma. While Moltmann no doubt is attracted to ideas which sound new and exciting, he may not have appreciated the risks involved in taking up a scientific theory that has become particularly fashionable outside the established scientific community. We discussed the scientific difficulties of establishing this theory in the previous chapter. We also raised the difficulty that there is a magnetism to this theory which encourages a reversion to a more Platonic understanding of the earth which encompasses the idea of a "world soul."

Bibliography

A. Jürgen Moltmann's Works.

1. Abbreviations used.

BP, *Die Bibel und das Patriachat.*

CC, *The Cosmic Community.*

CG, *The Crucified God.*

CJF, *Creating a Just Future.*

CPS, *The Church in the Power of the Spirit.*

ECPN, *The Ecological Crisis: Peace with Nature.*

EG, *Experiences of God.*

EH, *The Experiment Hope.*

FC, *The Future of Creation.*

FH, *The Future of Hope*, F. Herzog, ed.

GC, *God in Creation.*

HG, *Humanity in God*, with E. Moltmann-Wendel.

HP, *Hope and Planning.*

HR,HN, *Human Rights: The Rights of Nature.*

M, *Man.*

OC, *The Open Church.*

OHD, *On Human Dignity.*

PL, *The Passion for Life.*

PP, *The Power of the Powerless.*

RRF, *Religion, Revolution and the Future.*

SBH, *Schöpfung, Bund und Herrlichkeit.*

TH, *Theology of Hope.*

TJ, *Theology and Joy.*

TKG, *The Trinity and the Kingdom of God.*

TT, *Theology Today.*

WJC, *The Way of Jesus Christ.*

2. Primary Sources.

Books and articles are given in alphabetical order, and translated from the
German text.

"Christliche Hoffnung: Messianisch oder transzendent?." *Münchener
Theologische Zeitschrift*, 33, 1982, pp. 241-260.

Creating a Just Future. Translated by J. Bowden. London, SCM,1989.

"Creation and Redemption." Translated by W. McKinney, ed. *Creation Christ
and Culture: Studies in Honour of T.F. Torrance.* Edinburgh, T and T
Clark, 1976, pp. 119-134.

"Die Bibel und das Patriarchat: offene Fragen zur Diskussion über
'Feminiskische Theologie'." *Evangelische Theologie*, 42, 1982, pp. 480-
484.

Experiences of God. Translated by M. Kohl. London, SCM, 1980.

"God and the Nuclear Catastrophe." *Pacifica*, 1, 1988, pp. 157-170.

God: His and Hers. Joint author, E. Moltmann-Wendel. Translated by John
Bowden. London, SCM, 1991.

God in Creation: An Ecological Doctrine of Creation. Translated by M. Kohl.
London, SCM, 1985.

"God's Kingdom as the Meaning of Life and of the World." Translated by T. Weston. In, H. Küng and J. Moltmann, eds. *Why did God Make Me? Concilium*, 108, 1977. New York, Seabury Press, 1978, pp. 97-103.

"Has Modern Society any Future?" Translated by M. Kohl. In, The Foundation, ed. *On the Threshold of the Third Millenium. Concilium*, 1, 1990. London, SCM, 1990, pp. 54-65.

Hope and Planning. Translated by M. Clarkson. New York, Harper and Row, 1971.

"Hope and the Biomedical Future of Man." In, E.W. Cousins, ed. *Hope and the Future of Man*. London, Teilhard Centre for the Future of Man, 1972, pp. 89-116.

Humanity in God. Joint author, E. Moltmann-Wendel. London, SCM, 1983.

"Human Rights: The Rights of Humanity and the Rights of Nature." Translated by M. Kohl. In, H. Küng and J. Moltmann, eds. *The Ethics of World Religions and Human Rights. Concilium*, 2, 1990. London, SCM, 1990, pp. 120-135.

"Ich glaube an Gott den Vater: Patriarchalische oder nichtpatriarchalische Rede von Gott?" *Evangelische Theologie*, 43, 1983, pp. 397-415.

"In Search for an Equilibrium of 'Equilibrium' and 'Progress'." *Ching Feng*, 30, 1987, pp. 5-17.

Jewish Monotheism and Christian Trinitarian Doctrine: A Dialogue. Joint author, P. Lapide. Translated by L. Swidler. Philadelphia, Fortress Press, 1981.

"Liberation in the Light of Hope." Translated by M.D. Meeks. *Ecumenical Review*, 26, 1974, 413-429.

"Man and the Son of Man." Translated by Mrs Williams. In, J. Robert, ed. *No Man is Alien: Essays on the Unity of Mankind*. Leiden, Brill, 1971.

Man: Christian Anthropology in the Conflicts of the Present. Translated by J. Sturdy. Philadelphia, Fortress Press, 1974.

310

"Messianic Hope. 2. In Christianity." Translated by F. McDonagh. H. Küng and
W. Jasper, eds. *Ecumenism: Christians and Jews. Concilium*, 8(10), 1974.
London, Concilium, 1974, pp. 155-161.

On Human Dignity: Political Theology and Ethics. Translated by M.D. Meeks.
London, SCM, 1974.

"Peace: The Fruit of Justice." Translated by J. Cumming. In, H. Küng and J.
Moltmann, eds. *A Council for Peace. Concilium*, 195, 1988. Edinburgh, T
and T Clark, 1988, pp. 109-120.

Religion, Revolution and the Future. Translated by M.D. Meeks. New York,
Charles Scribner's Sons, 1969.

"Schöpfung, Bund und Herrlichkeit: Zur Diskussion über Karl Barths
Schöpfungslehre." *Evangelische Theologie*, 48(2), 1988, pp. 108-127.

"Teresa of Avila and Martin Luther: The Turn to the Mysticism of the Cross."
Studies in Religion, 13, 1984, pp. 265-278.

"The Alienation and Liberation of Nature." In, L. Rouner, ed. *On Nature*,
Indiana, University of Notre Dame Press, 1984, pp. 133- 144.

"The Challenge of Religion in the '80s." In, J. Wall, ed. *Theologians in
Transition.* New York, Crossroad, 1981, pp. 107-112.

*The Church in the Power of the Spirit: A Contribution to Messianic
Ecclesiology.* Translated by M. Kohl. London, SCM, 1977.

"The Confession of Jesus Christ: A Biblical Theological Consideration."
Translated by D. Smith. H. Küng and J. Moltmann, eds. *An Ecumenical
Confession of Faith? Concilium*, 118, 1978. New York, Seabury Press,
1978, pp. 13-19.

"The Cosmic Community: A New Ecological Concept of Reality in Science and
Religion." *Ching Feng*, 29, 1986, pp. 93-105.

"The 'Crucified God': A Trinitarian Theology of the Cross." Translated by K.
Crim. *Interpretation*, 26, 1972, pp. 278-299.

The Crucified God. The Cross as the Foundation and Criticism of Christian Theology. Translated by R.A. Wilson and J. Bowden. London, SCM, 1974.

"The Diaconal Church in the Context of the Kingdom of God." Translated by T. Runyan. J. Moltmann, M. Meeks, R. Hunter, J. Fowler and N. Erskine, eds. *Hope for the Church: Moltmann in Dialogue with Practical Theology.* Nashville, Abingdon, 1979, pp. 21-36.

"The Ecological Crisis: Peace with Nature?" *Colloquium*, 20, 1988, pp. 1-11.

"The Ecumenical Church under the Cross," *Theology Digest*, 24, 1976, pp. 380-389.

"The Ethics of Biomedical Research and the Newer Biomedical Technologies." In, S. Blesh, ed. *Recent Progress in Biology and Medicine: Its Social and Ethical Implications.* Council for International Organizations of Medical Sciences, Paris, UNESCO House, 1972, pp. 68-72.

"The Expectation of His Coming." *Theology*, 88, 1985, pp. 425-428.

The Experiment Hope. Translated by M.D.Meeks. London, SCM, 1975.

"The Fellowship of the Holy Spirit: Trinitarian Pneumatology." Translated by M. Kohl. *Scottish Journal of Theology*, 37, 1984, pp. 287-300.

"The Future as Threat and Opportunity." In, N. Brockman and N. Piediscalzi, eds. *Contemporary Religion and Social Responsibility.* New York, Alba House, 1973, pp. 103-117.

The Future of Creation. Translated by M. Kohl. London, SCM, 1979.

"The Inviting Unity of the Triune God." Translated by R. Nowell. In, C. Geffé and J. Jossua, eds. *Monotheism. Concilium*, 177, 1985. Edinburgh, T. and T.Clark, 1985, pp. 50-58.

"The Liberating Feast." Translated by F. McDonagh. H. Schmidt and D. Power, eds. *Politics and Liturgy. Concilium*, 2(10), 1984, London, Concilium, 1984, pp. 74-84.

"The Life Signs of the Spirit in the Fellowship Community of Christ." Translated by T. Runyan. In, J. Moltmann, M.D. Meeks, R.J. Hunter, J.W. Fowler and N.L. Erskine, eds. *Hope for the Church. Moltmann in Dialogue with Practical Theology*. Nashville, Abingdon, 1979, pp. 37-56.

"The Lordship of Christ and Human Society." In, J. Moltmann and J. Weissbach, joint authors. *Two Studies in the Theology of Bonhoeffer*. New York, Charles Scribner's Sons, 1967, pp. 19-94.

"The Motherly Father: Is Trinitarian Patripassionism Replacing Theological Patriarchalism?" Translated by G. Knowles. In, J. Metz and E. Schillebeeckx, eds. *God as Father? Concilium*, 143, 1981. Edinburgh, T. and T. Clark, 1981, pp. 51-56.

"The Passion for Life." Translated by E.Leuker and R. Klein. *Currents in Theology and Mission*, 4(1), 1977, pp. 3-10.

The Passion for Life. Translated by M.D. Meeks. Philadelphia, Fortress Press, 1978.

"The Realism of Hope: The Feast of the Resurrection and the Transformation of Present Reality." Translated by G.Thiele. *Concordia Theological Monthly*, 40, 1969, pp. 149-155.

Theology and Joy. Translated by R.Ulrich. London, SCM, 1973.

"Theology as Eschatology." In, F. Herzog, ed. *The Future of Hope*. New York, Herder and Herder, 1970.

"Theology in Germany Today." Translated by A.L. Buchwalter. In, J. Habermas, ed. *Observations on 'The Spiritual Situation of the Age': Contemporary German Perspectives*. Cambridge, Mass/London, MIT Press, 1984, pp. 181-205.

Theology of Hope: On the Ground and Implications of a Christian Eschatology. Translated by J.W. Leitch. London, SCM, 1967.

"Theology of Mystical Experience." Translated by A. Heron. *Scottish Journal of Theology*, 32(6), 1979, pp. 501-520.

Theology Today. Translated by J.Bowden. London, SCM, 1988.

The Open Church: Invitation to a Messianic Lifestyle. Translated by M.D. Meeks. London, SCM, 1978.

The Passion for Life: A Messianic Lifestyle. Translated by M.D. Meeks. Philadelphia, Fortress Press, 1978.

"The Possible Nuclear Catastrophe and Where is God?" *Scottish Journal of Religious Studies*, 9, 1988, pp. 71-83.

The Power of the Powerless. Translated by M. Kohl. London, SCM, 1983.

"The Trinitarian History of God." *Theology*, 78, 1975, pp. 637-646.

The Trinity and the Kingdom of God. Translated by M. Kohl. London, SCM, 1985.

The Way of Jesus Christ: Christology in Messianic Dimensions. Translated by M. Kohl. London, SCM, 1990.

"Towards the Next Step in the Dialogue." In, F. Herzog, ed. *The Future of Hope*. New York, Herder and Herder, 1970, pp. 154-164.

"What kind of Unity? The Dialogue Between the Traditions of East and West." In, *Lausanne 77: Fifty Years of Faith and Order, Faith and Order Paper, No 82*, Geneva, WCC, 1977, pp. 38-47.

B. Secondary Literature.

For Bible quotations the NIV translation was used, see also under A. Marshall below.

Abbott, D. *Divine Participation and Eschatology in the Theodicies of Paul Tillich and Jürgen Moltmann*. PhD thesis, 1987, University of Virginia.

Attfield, D. "Can God be Crucified? A Discussion of Jürgen Moltmann." *Scottish Journal of Theology*, 30, 1977, pp. 45-57.

Barr, W. "Review of '*God in Creation*'." *Lexington Theological Quarterly* (USA), 21, 1986, pp. 60-62.

Bauckham, R. "Bibliography: Jürgen Moltmann." *Modern Churchman*, 28, 1986, pp. 55-60.

_____ "Evolution and Creation in Moltmann's Doctrine of Creation." *Epworth Review*, 15, 1988, pp. 74-81.

_____ "Jürgen Moltmann." In, P. Toon and J.D. Spiceland, eds. *One God in Trinity*. London, Bagster, 1980, pp. 111-132.

_____ "Jürgen Moltmann." In, D.F. Ford, ed. *The Modern Theologians: An Introduction to Christian Theology in the Twentieth Century, Volume 1*. Oxford, Blackwell, 1989, pp. 293-310.

_____ "Moltmann's Eschatology of the Cross." *Scottish Journal of Theology*, 30, 1977, pp. 301-311.

_____ *Moltmann: Messianic Theology in the Making*. Basingstoke, Marshall, Morgan and Scott, 1987.

_____ "Moltmann's *Theology of Hope* Revisited." *Scottish Journal of Theology*, 42, 1989, pp. 199-214.

_____ "Theodicy from Ivan Karamazov to Moltmann." *Modern Theology*, 4, 1987, pp. 83-97.

Berry, R. "On Building the Kingdom in Our World: Review of *Creating a Just Future*." *Church Times*, 10 Nov., 1979, p. 11.

Braaten, C. "A Trinitarian Theology of the Cross." *Journal of Religion*, 56, 1976, pp. 113-121.

Breshears, G. "Creation Imaginatively Reconsidered: Review of *God in Creation*." *Journal of Psychology and Theology*, 14(4), 1986, pp. 337-351.

Bringle, M. "Leaving the Cocoon: Moltmann's Anthropology and Feminist Theology." *Andover Newton Quarterly*, 20, 1980, pp. 153-161.

Capps, W.H. *Hope Against Hope: Moltmann to Merton in One Theological Decade*. Philadelphia, Fortress Press, 1976.

_____ "Jürgen Moltmann: Theological Proversions." In, *Time Invades the Cathedral: Tensions in the School of Hope*. Philadelphia, Fortress Press, 1972, pp. 41-61.

Chapman, G. "Hope and the Ethics of Formation: Moltmann as Interpreter of Bonhoeffer." *Studies in Religion*, 12, 1983, pp. 449-460.

_____ "Moltmann's Vision of Man." *Anglican Theological Review*, 56, 1974, 310-330.

Claybrook, D. *The Emerging Doctrine of the Holy Spirit in the Writings of Jürgen Moltmann*. PhD thesis, 1983, The Southern Baptist Theological Seminary.

Cole-Turner, R. *God's Experience: The Trinitarian Theology of Jürgen Moltmann in Conversation with Charles Hartshorne*. PhD thesis, 1983, Princetown Theological Seminary.

_____ "Review of *God in Creation*." *Zygon* (USA), 22(1), 1987, pp. 120-121.

Dombrowski, D. "Review of *God in Creation*." *International Journal for Philosophy of Religion*, 25, 1989, pp. 127-128.

Editorial, "Talking Points From Books." *Expository Times*, 92, 1981, pp. 289-292.

Ford, J. *Towards an Anthropology of Mutuality: A Critique of Karl Barth's Doctrine of the Male-Female Order as A and B with a Comparison of the Panentheistic Theology of Jürgen Moltmann*. PhD thesis, 1984, Northwestern University.

Fiddes, P. "Review of *God in Creation*." *Journal of Theological Studies*, 38, 1987, pp. 263-265.

French, W. "Returning to Creation: Moltmann's Eschatology Naturalized." *Journal of Religion*, 68, 1988, pp. 78-86.

Gibbelini, R. *La Theologia di Jürgen Moltmann*. Brescia, Queriniana, 1975.

Hafstad, K. "*Gott in der Natur*: Zur Schäpfungslehre Jürgen Moltmanns." *Evangelische Theologie*, 47, 1987, pp. 460-466.

Havrilak, G. *Eastern Christian Elements in the Christology of Karl Rahner and Jürgen Moltmann: Contemporary Trends in Catholic and Protestant Thought from an Orthodox Perspective*. PhD thesis, 1986, Fordham University.

Hendry, G. "Review of *God in Creation*." *Theology Today*, 43, 1987, pp. 576-578.

King, A. *The Question of "Person" and "Subject" in Trinitarian Theology: Moltmann's Challenge to Rahner and its Implications*. PhD thesis, 1987, Fordham University.

Leonard, G. "Moltmann on Creation." *Cross Currents*, 36(4), 1987, pp. 470-471.

Link, C. "Kritisches Forum, Schäpfung im Messianischen Licht." *Evangelische Theologie*, 47, 1987, 83-92.

Lønning, P. "Die Schöpfungstheologie Jürgen Moltmanns - eine Nordische Perspektive." *Kerygma and Dogma*, 33, 1987, pp. 207- 223.

MacQuarrie, J. "Today's Word for Today: Jürgen Moltmann." *Expository Times*, 92, 1980, pp. 4-7.

Marshall, A., *The NASB-NIV Parallel New Testament in Greek and English*, with an interlinear translation, Zondervan Publishing House, Grand Rapids, 1986.

Mason, G. *God's Freedom as Faithfulness: A Critique of Jürgen Moltmann's Social Trinitarianism*. PhD thesis, 1987, Southwestern Baptist Theological Seminary.

McDade, J. "The Trinity and the Paschal Mystery." *Heythrop Journal*, 29, 1988, pp. 175-191.

McIntyre, J. "Review of *God in Creation*." *Scottish Journal of Theology*, 41(2), 1988, pp. 267-273.

McPherson, J. "Life, the Universe and Everything: Jürgen Moltmann's *God in Creation.*" *St Mark's Review*, 128, 1986, pp. 34-46.

Meeks, M.D. *Origins of the Theology of Hope.* Philadelphia, Fortress Press, 1974.

_____ "Trinitarian Theology: A Review Article." *Theology Today*, 38(4), 1982, pp. 472-477.

Migliori, D. "Biblical Eschatology and Political Hermeneutics." *Theology Today*, 26, 1969/70, pp. 116-132.

Molnar, P. "The Function of the Trinity in Moltmann's Ecological Doctrine of Creation." *Theological Studies*, 51(4), 1990, pp. 673-697.

Morse, C. *The Logic of Promise in Moltmann's Theology.* Philadelphia, Fortress Press, 1979.

Newlands, G. "Review of *The Way of Jesus Christ.*" *Expository Times*, 102(2), 1990, p. 56.

Niewiadomski, J. *Die Zweideutigkeit von Gott und Welt in J. Moltmanns Theologien.* Innsbrucker Theologische Studien 9, Innsbruck, Tyrolia, 1982.

O'Donnell, J. "The Doctrine of the Trinity in Recent German Theology." *Heythrop Journal*, 23(2), 1982, pp. 153-167.

_____ "The Trinity as Divine Community." *Gregorianum*, 69, 1988, pp. 5-34.

_____ *Trinity and Temporality.* Oxford, Oxford University Press, 1983.

Olsen, R. "Trinity and Eschatology: The Historical Being of God in Jürgen Moltmann and Wolfhart Pannenberg." *Scottish Journal of Theology*, 36, 1983, pp. 213-227.

Osborn, L. "Review of *God in Creation.*" *Themelios*, 12(1), 1986, pp. 30-31.

Page, R. "Review of *The Trinity and the Kingdom of God.*" *Scottish Journal of Theology*, 37, 1984, pp. 97-98.

Pambrun, J. "Review of *God in Creation*." *Eglise et Theologie*, 17(3), 1985, pp. 412-415.

Peters, T. "A Book Worth Discussing: *God in Creation*." *Currents in Theology of Mission*, 13(4), 1986, pp. 241-244.

Plantinga, C. "Review of *The Trinity and the Kingdom of God*." *Calvin Theological Journal*, 18(1), 1983, pp. 105-108.

Platten, S. "Review of *God in Creation*." *King's Theological Review*, 9(2), 1986, pp. 64-65.

Polkinghorne, J. "Creation Without the Scientists: Review of *God in Creation*." *Expository Times*, 97(9), 1986, p. 285.

Primavesi, A. "Review of *God in Creation*." *Heythrop Journal*, 30, 1989, pp. 232-234.

Race, A. "Review of *Creating a Just Future*." *Theology*, 113, 1990, pp. 355-362.

Schuurman, D. "Creation, Eschaton and Ethics: An Analysis of Theology and Ethics in Jürgen Moltmann." *Calvin Theological Journal*, 22(1), 1987, pp. 42-67.

Stroup, G. "Review of *God in Creation*." *Homiletic* (USA), 11(1), 1986, pp. 21-22.

_____ "Review of *The Trinity and the Kingdom of God*: A 'Christian' Doctrine of God." *Interpretation*, 37, 1983, pp. 410-412.

Terence, G. "Review of *God in Creation*," *Theological Studies*, 47, 1986, pp. 527-529.

Timm, H. "Evangelische Weltweisheit: Zur der äkotheologischen Apokalyptik." *Zeitschrift für Theologie und Kirche*, 84(3), 1987, pp. 340-370.

Vandergoot, H. "Review of *The Future of Creation* by J. Moltmann." *Calvin Theological Journal*, 15(2), 1980, pp. 284-289.

Walker, T. "Review of *God in Creation* by J. Moltmann." *Interpretation*, 41(1), 1987, p. 218.

Walsh, B. "*Theology of Hope* and Doctrine of Creation: An Appraisal of Jürgen Moltmann." *Evangelical Quaraterly*, 59(1), 1987, pp. 53-76.

Webster, J. "Jürgen Moltmann: Trinity and Suffering." *Evangel*, 3, 1985, pp. 4-6.

Wiles, M. "Review of *The Trinity and the Kingdom God*." *Journal of Theological Studies*, 33, 1982, pp. 331-335.

C. Other Works.

Altmann, A. "*Homo Imago Dei* in Jewish and Christian Theology." *Journal of Religion*, 48, 1968, pp. 235-259.

Anderson, B. Ed. *Creation in the Old Testament*. London, SPCK, 1984.

_____ *Creation versus Chaos*. New York, Association Press, 1967.

Andreason, N. *The Old Testament Sabbath: A Tradition-Historical Investigation*. Dissertation Series 7, Society of Biblical Literature, Missoula, University of Montana, 1972.

Armstrong, E. *St Francis: Nature Mystic. The Derivation and Significance of Nature Stories in the Franciscan Legend*. Berkeley, University of California, 1973.

Ashby, E. *Reconciling Man with the Environment*. Oxford, Oxford University Press, 1978.

Attfield, R. *The Ethics of Environmental Concern*. Oxford, Blackwell, 1983.

Avis, P. *The Methods of Modern Theology*. Basingstoke, Marshall Pickering, 1986.

Barnley, G. "The Future of Creation: The Central Challenge for Theologians." *Word and World*, 4(4), 1984, pp. 422-429.

Barbour, I.G. *Earth Might be Fair: Reflections on Ethics, Religion and Ecology*. Englewood Cliffs, Prentice Hall, 1972.

_____ *Issues in Science and Religion*. London, SCM, 1966.

Barbour, I. *Myths, Models and Paradigms: The Nature of Scientific and Religious Language*. London, SCM, 1974.

Barr, J. "The Image of God in Genesis: A Study in Terminology." *Bulletin of the John Rylands Library*, 51, 1968, pp. 11-26.

_____ "Man and Nature; The Ecological Controversy and the Old Testament." *Bulletin of the John Rylands Library*, 55, 1972, pp. 9-32.

Barrett, C.K. *The Epistle to the Romans*. H. Chadwick, ed. London, Black, 1957.

Barth, K. *Church Dogmatics, Volume 1/1*. Translated by G.W. Bromiley. G.W. Bromiley and T.F. Torrance, eds. Second edition. Edinburgh, T and T Clark, 1975.

_____ *Church Dogmatics, Volume 3/1*. Translated by J.W. Edwards, O. Bussey and H. Knight: G.W. Bromiley and T.F. Torrance, eds. Edinburgh, T and T Clark, 1958.

_____ *Church Dogmatics, Volume 4/3*. Translated by G.W.Bromiley; T.F. Torrance and G.W. Bromiley, eds. Edinburgh, T and T Clark, 1961.

_____ *The Humanity of God*. London, Collins, 1961.

_____ "No." Translated by P. Fraenkel, in, *Natural Theology*. London, The Centenary Press, 1946.

Bauckham, R. "First Steps to a Theology of Nature." *Evangelical Quarterly,* 58(3), 1986, pp. 229-244.

_____."The Genesis Flood and the Nuclear Holocaust." *Churchman,* 99(2), 1985, pp. 146-155.

_____."Theology after Hiroshima." *Scottish Journal of Theology*, 38, 1989, pp. 583-601.

Beaumont, T. "Options for the 90's: 1. From Environmentalism to Ecology." *Modern Churchman*, 28(1), 1985, pp. 11-16.

Bethge, E. *Dietrich Bonhoeffer: Theologian, Christian, Contemporary*. London, Collins, 1970.

Birch, C. "Nature, God and Humanity in Ecological Perspective." *Christianity and Crisis*, 39, 1979, pp. 259-266.

Bird, P. "'Male and Female He Created Them': Genesis 1.27 in the Context of the Priestly Account of Creation." *Harvard Theological Review*, 74(2), 1981, pp. 129-159.

Black, J. *The Dominion of Man*. Edinburgh, T and T Clark, 1970.

Bloch, E. *The Principle of Hope*. Translated by N. Plaice, S. Plaice and P. Knight. Oxford, Blackwell, 1986.

Bonhoeffer, D. *Creation and Fall*. Translated by J. Fletcher. London, SCM, 1959.

_____ *Ethics*. Translated by N. Horton-Smith. E. Bethge, ed. London, SCM, 1955.

Børreson, K. "L'Usage Patristique de Metaphores Feminines dans le Discours sur Dieu." *Revue Théologique de Louvain*, 13, 1982, pp. 205-220.

Braaten, C. *The Future of God. The Revolutionary Dynamics of Hope*. New York, Harper and Row, 1969.

Bracken, J. *What Are They Saying About the Trinity?* New York, Paulist Press, 1979.

Bromiley, G.W. *An Introduction to the Theology of Karl Barth*, Edinburgh, T and T Clark, 1979.

Brown, D. *The Divine Trinity*. London, Duckworth, 1985.

_____ "Trinitarian Personhood and Individuality." In, R.J. Feenstra and C. Plantinga, eds. *Trinity, Incarnation and Atonement*. Library of Religious Philosophy, Volume 1. Indiana, University of Notre Dame Press, 1989, pp. 48-78.

Brunner, E. *Christian Doctrine of Creation and Redemption, Volume 2, Dogmatics*. Translated by O. Wyon. London, Lutterworth Press, 1952.

Caird, E. *Hegel*. Reprinted from 1883 edition. New York, AMS Press, 1972.

Capra, F. *The Tao of Physics*. London, Wildwood House, 1975.

_____ *The Turning Point*. London, Wildwood House, 1982.

Carson, D. Ed. *From Sabbath to Lord's Day. A Biblical, Historical and Theological Investigation*. Grand Rapids, Zondervan, 1982.

Carter-Heyward, I. *The Redemption of God: A Theology of Mutual Relation*. Lanham, University Press of America, 1982.

Cassuto, U. *Commentary on Genesis: Part 1; From Adam to Noah*. Translated from the Hebrew by I. Abrahams. Jerusalem, Central Press, 1961.

Chadwick, O. *From Boussuet to Newman. The Idea of Doctrinal Development*. Cambridge, Cambridge University Press, 1957.

Childs, B.S. *Old Testament Theology in a Canonical Context*. London, SCM, 1985.

Church Assembly 1 General Synod Report. *Our Responsibility for the Living Environment*. London, Church House Press, 1986.

Clark, S. "Christian Responsibility for the Environment." *Modern Churchman*, 28(2), 1986, pp. 24-31.

Cobb, J.B. *A Christian Natural Theology*. London, Lutterworth Press, 1965.

_____ *Is It Too Late?* Bruce, Beverley Hills, 1972.

Collingwood, R.G. *The Idea of Nature*. Oxford, Clarendon Press, 1945.

Cotgrave, S. *Catastrophe or Cornucopia: The Environment, Politics and the Future*. Chichester, John Wiley and Sons, 1982.

Cousins, E.H, ed. *Hope and the Future of Man*. Philadelphia, Fortress Press, 1972.

Cox, D. *Charles Elton and the Emergence of Modern Ecology*. Ph.D thesis, 1979, Washington University.

Cranfield, C.E.B. *Romans: A Shorter Commentary*. Edinburgh, T and T Clark, 1985.

Davies, P. *The Runaway Universe*. London, Dent, 1978.

Dawkins, R. *The Blind Watchmaker*. London, Longman, 1986.

De Margerie, B. *The Christian Trinity in History.* Translated from French by E.J. Fortmann. Studies in Historical Theology, Volume 1. Petersham, St. Bede's Publications, 1982.

De Vries, S. *The Achievements of Biblical Religion.* Lanham, University Press of America, 1983.

_____ *Yesterday, Today and Tomorrow: Time and History in the Old Testament.* London, SPCK, 1975.

Dillenberger, J. *Protestant Thought and Natural Science.* London, Collins, 1961.

Dodd, C.H. *The Epistle of Paul to the Romans.* J. Moffatt, ed. London, Hodder and Stoughton, 1932.

Dombrowski, D.D. "Pacifism and Hartshorne's Dipolar Theism." *Encounter* (USA), 48(4), 1987, pp. 337-350.

Dooyeweerd, H. *Roots of our Western Culture: Pagan, Secular and Christian Options.* Translated from Dutch by J. Kraay. Toronto, Wedge, 1979.

Dubos, R. *A God Within.* New York, Charles Scribner's Sons, 1972.

Duchrow, U. and Liedke, G. *Shalom: A Biblical Perspective on Creation, Justice and Peace.* Geneva, WCC, 1989.

Earman, J. "Causation : A Matter of Life and Death." *Journal of Philosophy*, 73, 1976, 5-25.

Ellison, H.L. "Genesis." In, F.F. Bruce, ed., second edition. *The International Bible Commentary.* Basingstoke, Marshall, Morgan and Scott, 1986, pp. 111-123.

Elder, F. *Crisis in Eden: A Religious Study of Man and Environment.* New York, Abingdon, 1970.

_____ "Responses to the Ecological Queston: A Christian Review." *Harvard Theological Review*, 71, 1978, 319-319.

Evdokimov, P. "Nature." *Scottish Journal of Theology*, 18, 1965, pp. 1-22.

Findlay, J. *Hegel: A Re-Examination.* London, Allen, 1958.

Fiorenzia, F. "Dialectical Theology and Hope, 111." *Heythrop Journal*, 10, 1969, pp. 26-42.

Forde, G. "Romans 8.18-27." *Interpretation*, 38, 1984, pp. 281-285.

Foster, M. "The Christian Doctrine of Creation and the Rise of Modern Natural Science 1." *Mind*, 43, 1934, pp. 446-473.

_____ "The Christian Doctrine of Creation and the Rise of Modern Natural Science 2." *Mind*, 44, 1935, pp. 439-466.

_____ "The Christian Doctrine of Creation and the Rise of Modern Natural Science 3." *Mind*, 45, 1936, pp. 1-27.

Fox, M. *Original Blessing*. Santa Fe, Bear and Company, 1983.

_____ *The Coming of the Cosmic Christ*. San Francisco, Harper and Row, 1988.

Fridrichsen, A, ed. *The Root of the Vine: Essays in Biblical Theology*. London, Dacre Press, 1953.

Frye, N. *Creation and Recreation*. Toronto, University of Toronto Press, 1980.

Gabathuler, H. *Jesus Christus - Haupt der Kirche - Haupt der Welt: Der Christus Hymnus Colosser 1: 15-20 in der theologischen Forschung der letzten 130 Jahre*. Zurich, Zwingh Verlag, 1965.

George, R, ed. *Contemporary Perspectives on Systematic Philosophy*. New York, State University of New York Press, 1986.

Gilkey, L. *Reaping the Whirlwind: A Christian Interpretation of History*. New York, Seabury Press, 1976.

Glacken, C.J. *Traces on the Rhodian Shore*. Berkeley, University of California Press, 1976.

Gosling, D. "Towards a Credible Ecumenical Theology of Nature." *The Ecumenical Review*, 38(3), 1986, pp. 322-331.

Gould, S.L. *Ever Since Darwin*. Harmsworth, Penguin/Pelican, 1980.

Gränbaum, A. and Janis, A. "Is There Backward Causation In Classical Electrodynamics." *Journal of Philosophy*, 74, 1977, pp. 475-482.

Gray, D. *A New Creation Story*. Chambersberg, The American Teilhard Association for the Future of Man, 1979.

Grey, M. "The Core of Our Desire: Re-Imaging the Trinity." *Theology*, 113, 1990, pp. 363-372.

Grayson, J. "The Environment and Perception of Reality: A Physiologist Point of View." *Ultimate Reality and Meaning*, 11, 1988, pp. 294-309.

Greene, J. *Science, Ideology and World View*. Berkeley, University of California Press, 1981.

Gregorios, P. *The Human Presence: An Orthodox View of Nature*. Geneva, WCC, 1978.

Gunton, C. *Becoming and Being: The Doctrine of God in Charles Hartshorne and Karl Barth*. Oxford, Oxford University Press, 1978.

_____ "Barth: The Trinity and Human Freedom." *Theology Today*, 43, 1986, pp. 316-330.

_____ *Enlightenment and Alienation*. Basingstoke, Marshall, Morgan and Scott, 1985.

Gustafson, J. *Ethics from a Theocentric Perspective*. Chicago, University of Chicago, 1981.

Habermas, J, ed. *Observations on the Spiritual Situation of the Age: Contemporary German Perspectives*. Cambridge/Massachusetts, London, MIT, 1984.

Haldane, R. *An Exposition of the Epistle to the Romans*. McLean, MacDonald, 1958.

Hall, D.J. *The Steward:A Biblical Symbol Come of Age*. New York, Friendship Press for Commission on Stewardship, 1982.

Hampson, D. *Theology and Feminism*. Oxford, Blackwell, 1990.

Hardin, G. "Ecology and the Death of Providence." *Zygon* (USA), 15(1), 1980, pp. 57-68.

Hartshorne, C. *The Divine Relativity*. New Haven, Yale University Press, 1948.

Hartwell, H. *The Theology of Karl Barth: An Introduction.* London, Duckworth, 1984.

Harvey, J. "Wisdom Literature and Biblical Theology." *Biblical Theology Bulletin*, 1, 1971, pp. 308-319.

Hegel, G. *The Phenomenology of Mind.* Translated by J. Baillie. New York, Harper and Row, 1967.

Hendry, G. "Nothing." *Theology Today*, 39, 1982, pp. 274-289.

Herzog, F, ed. *The Future of Hope.* New York, Herder and Herder, 1970.

Heschel, A. *The Sabbath: Its Meaning for Modern Man.* New York, Noonday Press, 1951.

Hiers, R. "Ecology, Biblical Theology and Methodology: Biblical Perspectives on the Environment." *Zygon*, 19, 1984, pp. 43-59.

Hill, W. "The Historicity of God." *Theological Studies*, 45, 1984, pp. 320-333.

_____ *The Three Personed God: The Trinity as Mystery of Salvation.* Washington, The Catholic University of America Press, 1982.

Hockel, A. *Christus der Erstgeborene: Zur Geschichte der Exegese von Kol 1.15.* Düsseldorf, Verlag, 1963.

Hodgkin, P. "General Practice in the Year 2000: A Faustian Future." *British Medical Journal*, 286, 1983, pp. 944-945.

Hooykaas, R. *Religion and the Rise of Modern Science.* Edinburgh, Scottish Academic Press, 1972.

Horne, B. *A World to Gain.* London, Darton, Longman & Todd, 1983.

Hughes, P. *A Commentary on the Epistle to the Hebrews.* Grand Rapids, Erdmans, 1977.

Innes, K. "Bibliography: Christian Attitudes to the Environment and Human Responsibility for it." *Modern Churchman*, 29(4), 1987, pp. 32-36.

Jantsch, E. *The Self-Organizing Universe.* New York, Pergamon Press, 1980.

Johnson, E. "The Incomprehensibility of God and the Image of God, Male and Female." *Theological Studies*, 45, 1984, pp. 441-465.

Johnson, R.A, Wallwork, E, Green C, Santmire, H.P, Vanderpool, Y.H, eds. *Critical Issues in Modern Religion*. Englewood Cliffs, Prentice Hall, 1973.

Jønsson, G.A. *The Image of God: Genesis 1.26-28 in a Century of Old Testament Research*. Translated from Swedish by L. Svendsen; revised by M.S. Cheney. T. Mettinger and M. Ottosson, eds. Coniectanea Biblica, Old Testament Series 26, Lund, Almquist and Wiksell International, 1988.

Käsemann, E. *A Commentary on Romans*. Translated by G.W. Bromiley, ed. London, SCM, 1980.

_____ "A Primitive Baptismal Liturgy." In, *Essays on New Testament Themes*. Translated by W. Montague. *Studies in Biblical Theology*, 41. London, SCM, 1964, pp. 149-168.

Kaufmann, G.D. *The Theological Imagination*. Philadelphia, Westminster Press, 1981.

Kehl, N. *Der Christushymnus in Kolosserbrief*. Katholisches Bibelwerk, Stuttgart, Verlag, 1967.

Kenway, I. *Rationality, Judgement and Certainty: A Study of the Significance of John Henry Newman's Account of Imagination and Reason in Religious Faith*. Ph.D thesis, 1986, University of Bristol.

King, U. *Women and Spirituality*. Basingstoke, MacMillan Education, 1989.

Kittel, G, ed. *Theological Dictionary of the New Testament*. Grand Rapids, Erdmans, 1964.

Küng, H. *Does God Exist?* Translated by E. Quinn. London, Collins, 1980.

_____ *Global Responsibility: In Search of a New World Ethic*. Translated by J. Bowden. London, SCM, 1991.

_____ *On Being a Christian*. Translated by E. Quinn. London, Collins, 1978.

Ladriere, J. *Language and Belief*. Translated by G. Barden. Dublin, Gill and MacMillan, 1972.

Lähnemann, J. *Der Kolosserbrief: Koposition, Situation und Argumentation.* Gütersloher Verlagshaus, 1971.

Lasch, C. *The Minimal Self.* London, Pan/Picador, 1985.

La Cugna, C. "Reconceiving the Trinity as Mystery of Salvation." *Scottish Journal of Theology*, 38, 1985, pp. 1-23.

Leftow, B. "God and the World in Hegel and Whitehead." In, G.Lucas, ed. *Contemporary Perspectives on Systematic Philosophy.* New York, State University of New York Press, 1986, pp. 257-265.

Levenson, J. *Creation and the Persistence of Evil: The Jewish Drama of Divine Omnipotence.* San Fransisco, Harper and Row, 1988.

Liedke, G. Im Bauch des Fisches: Ockologische Theologie. Stuttgart, Kreuz, 1979.

Lightfoot, J. *St Paul's Epistles to the Colossians and to Philemon.* London, MacMillan, 1875.

Limouris, G, ed. *Justice, Peace and the Integrity of Creation.* Geneva, WCC, 1990.

Linn, G. "JPIC as a Mission Concern." *The Ecumenical Review*, 41(4), 1989, pp. 515-521.

Lohse, E. "Christologie und Ethik im Kolosserbrief." In, *Apophoreta: Festschrift für E. Haenchen.* Berlin, 1964, pp. 156-168.

_____ "Pauline Theology in the Letter to the Colossians." *New Testament Studies*, 15, 1969, pp. 211-220.

Lossky, V. *Orthodox Theology: An Introduction.* Translated by I. Kesarcodi-Watson. New York, St Vladimir's Seminary Press, 1989.

_____ *The Mystical Theology of the Eastern Church.* London, Clarke, 1957.

Lovelock, J. *Gaia: A New Look at Life on Earth.* Second edition, Oxford, Oxford University Press, 1987.

_____ *The Ages of Gaia: A Biography of Our Living Earth.* L. Thomas, ed. Oxford, Oxford University Press, 1988.

Lowen, A. *Bioenergetics,* London, Penguin, 1976.

Luther, M. *Volume 1, Lectures on Genesis.* Translated by G.V. Schlick, in, J. Pelikan, ed., *Luther's Works.* Saint Louis, Concordia, 1988.

_____ *Volume 12, Selected Psalms.* Translated by P. Jaroslav, J. Pelikan, ed., *Luther's Works.* Saint Louis, Concordia, 1955.

Lyotard, J.F. *The Post-Modern Condition.* Manchester, Manchester University Press, 1984.

Mackey, J. *The Christian Experience of God as Trinity.* London, SCM, 1983.

MacQuarrie, J. "Creation and Environment." *Expository Times,* 88, 1971, pp. 4-9.

_____ *Thinking About God.* London, SCM, 1975.

Martin, R. *Colossians: The Church's Lord and the Christian's Liberty.* Exeter, Paternoster, 1972.

Mauser, R. *Gottesbild und Menschwerdung.* Tübingen, Mohr/Siebeck, 1971.

Mayr, E. *The Growth of Biological Thought.* Boston, Harvard University Press, 1982.

McCoy, J. "Towards a Theology of Nature." *Encounter,* 46, 1985, pp. 213-228.

McDonagh, S. *To Care for the Earth: A Call to a New Theology.* London, Chapman, 1986.

McFague, S. *Models of God.* London, SCM, 1987.

McIntire, C.T, ed. *God History and Historians.* Oxford, Oxford University Press, 1977.

McIntyre, J. "The Theological Dimension of Ecological Problems." *Scottish Journal of Religious Studies,* 2, 1981, pp. 83-96.

McPherson, J. "Towards an Ecological Theology." *Expository Times,* 97(8), 1986, pp. 236-240.

Meland, B, ed. *The Future of Empirical Theology.* Chicago, University of Chicago, 1969.

Milbank, J. "The Second Difference: For a Trinitarianism Without Reserve." *Modern Theology*, 2(3), 1986, pp. 213-234.

Molnar, P. "The Function of the Immanent Trinity in the Theology of Karl Barth: Implications for Today." *Scottish Journal of Theology*, 42(3), 1989, pp. 367-399.

Moltmann-Wendel, E. *A Land Flowing with Milk and Honey.* Translated by J. Bowden. London, SCM, 1986.

_____ *Liberty, Equality and Sisterhood: On the Emancipation of Women in Church and Society.* Translated by R. Gritsch. Philadelphia, Fortress Press, 1978.

Montifiore, H. *Man and Nature.* London, Collins, 1975.

Morgan, R. "Ernst Troelsch and Dialectical Theology." In, J.P. Claydon, ed. *E. Troelsch and the Future of Theology.* Cambridge, Cambridge University Press, 1976.

Moule, C. *Man and Nature in the New Testament: Some Reflections on Biblical Theology.* Philadelphia, Fortress Press, 1967.

Murray, M, ed. *Heidegger and Modern Philosophy: Critical Essays.* New Haven, Yale University Press, 1978.

Newbigin, L. *Foolishness to the Greeks.* London, SPCK, 1986.

Niebuhr, H.R. *Christ and Culture*: New York, Harper, 1951.

_____ *Radical Monotheism and Western Culture.* London, Faber and Faber, 1960.

_____ *Moral Man and Immoral Society.* New York, Charles Scribner's Sons, 1960.

Oakley, F. "Christian Theology and Newtonian Science." *Church History,* 30, 1961, pp. 433-457.

O'Brien, P.T. *Colossians; Philemon.* D. Hubbard and G. Barker, eds. Word Biblical Commentary, 44. Waco, Word Books, 1982.

O'Collins, G. "Christ's Resurrection as Mystery of Love." *Heythrop Journal,* 25, 1984, pp. 39-50.

Pannenberg, W. *Anthropology in Theological Perspective.* Edinburgh, T and T Clark, 1985.

_____ *Christian Spirituality and Sacramental Community.* London, Darton, Longman and Todd, 1984.

_____ "The Doctrine of Creation and Modern Science." *East Asia Journal of Theology,* 4(1), 1986, pp. 33-46.

_____*Theology and the Philosophy of Science.* London, Darton, Longman and Todd, 1976.

Passmore, J. *Man's Responsibility for Nature.* London, Duckworth, 1974.

Peacocke, A.R. *An Introduction to the Physical Chemistry of Biological Organization.* Oxford, Clarendon Press, 1989.

_____ *Creation and the World of Science.* Oxford, Clarendon, 1979.

_____ *God and the New Biology.* London, Dent, 1986.

_____ *Science and the Christian Experiment.* London, Oxford University Press, 1971.

Peck, J.C. and Gallo, J. "JPIC: A Critique from a Feminist Perspective." *The Ecumenical Review,* 41(4), 1989, pp. 573-581.

Perkins, P. "God in the New Testament: Preliminary Soundings." *Theology Today,* 42, 1985, pp. 332-341.

Perls, F.S., Hefferline, R.F. and Goodman, P. *Gestalt-Therapy: Excitement and Growth in the Human Personality.* London, Souvenir Press, 1951.

Polanyi, M. *Personal Knowledge: Towards a Post-Critical Philosophy.* London, Routledge & Kegan Paul, 1958.

Popper, K.R. *The Logic of Scientific Discovery.* London, Hutchinson, 1956.

Preston, R. "Humanity, Nature and the Integrity of Creation." *The Ecumenical Review*, 41(4), 1989, pp. 552-563.

Primavesi, A. "The Part for the Whole? An Eco-Feminist Enquiry." *Theology*, 113, 1990, pp. 355-362.

_____ *From Apocalypse to Genesis*. Tunbridge Wells, Burns and Oates, 1991.

Rahner, K. *The Christian Commitment. Mission and Grace, Volume 1. Third Edition*. London, Sheed and Ward, 1970.

_____ *Theological Investigation, Volume 1*. Translated by C. Ernst. London, Darton, Longman and Todd, 1965.

_____ *Theological Investigations, Volume 13*. Translated by D. Bourke. London, Darton, Longman and Todd, 1975.

Ramsay, A. *F.D. Maurice and the Conflicts of Modern Theology*. Cambridge, Cambridge University Press, 1951.

Reventlow, H. *Problems of Old Testament Theology in the Twentieth Century*. Translated by J. Bowden. London, SCM, 1985.

Rimbach, J. "All Creation Groans.' Theology/Ecology in St. Paul." *Asia Journal of Theology* (Singapore), 1, 1987, pp. 379-391.

Robbins, J.K. "The Environment and Thinking about God." *Encounter* (USA), 48(4), 1987, pp. 401-415.

Rosenberg, A. *The Structure of Biological Science*. Cambridge, Cambridge University Press, 1985.

Rosenzweig, F. *The Star of Redemption*. Translated by W. Hallo from 1930 edition. London, Routledge/Kegan Paul, 1970.

Rossi, V. "Christian Ecology: A Theocentric Perspective." *Epiphany*, 8, 1987, pp. 8-13.

_____ "Christian Ecology is Cosmic Christology." *Epiphany*, 8, 1988, pp. 52-62.

_____ "The Earth is the Lord's." Epiphany, 6(1), 1985, pp. 3-6.

_____ "Theocentrism: The Cornerstone of Christian Ecology." *Epiphany*, 6(1), 1985, pp. 8-14.

Rouner, L, ed. *On Nature*. Indiana, University of Notre Dame Press, 1984.

Ruether, R.R. *New Woman: New Earth*. New York, Seabury Press, 1975.

Russell, C.A. *Cross Currents: Interactions between Science and Faith*. Leicester, IVP, 1985.

Rust, E. *Nature and Man in Biblical Thought*. London, Lutterworth Press, 1953.

Sanday, W. *The Epistle to the Romans*. Edinburgh, T and T Clark, 1907.

Santmire, H. *Brother Earth: Nature, God and Ecology in Time of Crisis*. Camden, Nelson, 1970.

_____ "Studying the Doctrine of Creation: The Challenge." *Dialog* (USA), 21, 1982, pp. 195-200.

_____ "The Future of the Cosmos and the Renewal of the Church's Life with Nature." *Word and World*, 4(4), 1984, pp. 410-421.

_____ *The Travail of Nature*. Philadelphia, Fortress Press, 1985.

Schell, J. *The Fate of the Earth*. Picador, Chaucer Press, 1982.

Schmidt, W. *The Faith of the Old Testament*. Translated by J. Sturdy. Oxford, Blackwell, 1983.

Scholem, G. *Kabbalah*. New York, Times/Quadrangle, 1974.

_____ *Major Trends in Jewish Mysticism*. Third edition. New York, Schocken, 1954.

Schweitzer, A. *Out of My Life and Thought*. C.T. Campion, ed. New York, New American Library, 1953.

Schweitzer, E. *The Letter to the Colossians: A Commentary*. Translated by A. Chester. London, SPCK, 1982.

Selby, P. *Liberating God*. London, SPCK, 1983.

_____ "Apocalyptic: Christian and Nuclear." *Modern Churchman*, 26(2), 1984, pp. 3-10.

Sindima, H. "Community of Life." *The Ecumenical Review*, 41(4), 1989, pp. 537-551.

Sittler, J. "A Theology for Earth." *The Christian Scholar*, 37, 1954, pp. 367-374.

_____ *Essays on Nature and Grace*. Philadelphia, Fortress Press, 1972.

Soelle, D. and Cloyes, S. *To Work and To Love: A Theology of Creation*. Philadelphia, Fortress Press, 1984.

Solomon, R.C. *Continental Philosophy Since 1750: The Rise and Fall of the Self*. Oxford, Oxford University Press, 1988.

Sorrell, R.D. *St Francis of Assisi and Nature*. Oxford, Oxford University Press, 1988.

Spanner, D. *Biblical Creation and the Theory of Evolution*. Exeter, Paternoster Press, 1987.

Spring, D and Spring, E. *Ecology and Religion in History*. London, Harper and Row, 1974.

Staniloae, D. *Theology and the Church*. Translated by R. Barringer. New York, St Vladimir's Seminary Press, 1980.

Stewart, C.Y. *Nature in Grace: A Study in the Theology of Nature*. Macon, Mercer University Press, 1983.

Stuhlmacher, P. "The Ecological Crisis as a Challenge for Biblical Theology." *Ex Auditu*, 3, 1987, pp. 1-15.

Tanner, K. *God and Creation in Christian Theology: Tyranny or Empowerment?* Oxford, Blackwell, 1988.

Teilhard de Chardin, P. "Christianity and Evolution: Suggestions for a New Theology" (1945). Translated by R. Hague. In, *Christianity and Evolution*. London, Collins 1971.

_____ *The Phenomenon of Man*. Translated by B. Wall. London, Collins/Fontana, 1959.

Temple, W. *Christianity in Thought and Practice*. London, SCM, 1936.

_____ *Nature, Man and God.* London, MacMillan, 1940.

Thomas, K. *Man and the Natural World: Changing Attitudes in England, 1500 - 1800.* London, Penguin, 1983.

Toulmin, S, Hepburn, R and MacIntyre, A, eds. *Metaphysical Beliefs.* London SCM, 1957.

Tracy, D. *The Analogical Imagination.* New York, Crossroad, 1981.

Trible, P. *God and the Rhetoric of Sexuality.* Philadelphia, Fortress Press, 1978.

Tsetsis, G, ed. *Orthodox Thought,* Geneva, WCC, 1983.

Tzu, L. *The Tao Te Ching. Part 1.* In, J. Legge, ed. *The Texts of Taoism.* New York, Dover, 1962.

Von Rad, G. *Genesis: A Commentary.* Translated by J. Marks. London, SCM, 1956.

_____ *Old Testament Theology, Volume 1.* Translated by D. Stalker. Edinburgh, Oliver and Boyd, 1962.

_____ *The Problems of the Hexateuch and Other Essays.* Translated by E. Trueman-Dicken. London, Oliver and Boyd, 1966.

Walsh, B.J. and Middleton, J.R. *The Transforming Vision.* Downer's Grove, IVP (USA), 1984.

Weger, K.H. *Karl Rahner: An Introduction to his Theology.* London, Burns and Oates, 1980.

Wenham, G. *Genesis 1-25.* D. Hubbard and G. Barber, eds. Word Biblical Commentary, 1. Waco, Word Books, 1987.

Westermann, C. *Blessing in the Bible and the Life of the Church.* Philadelphia, Fortress Press, 1978.

_____ *Genesis 1-11: A Commentary.* Translated by J. Scullion. London, SPCK, 1984.

White, L. "The Historical Roots of our Ecological Crisis." *Science,* 145, 1967, pp. 1203-1207.

Williams, G. "Christian Attitudes to Nature." *Christian Scholar's Review*, 2(1), 1971, pp. 3-35.

Williams, J. "Yahweh, Women and the Trinity." *Theology Today*, 32(3), 1975, pp. 234-242.

Wingen, G. "The Doctrine of Creation: Not an Appendix, But the First Article." *Word and World*, 4(4), 1984, pp. 353-371.

Wolff, H.W. *Anthropology of the Old Testament*. Translated by M. Kohl. London, SCM, 1974.

Zizioulas, J.D. *Being as Communion: Studies in Personhood and the Church*. New York, St Vladimir's Seminary Press, 1985.

_____ "Preserving God's Creation. Three Lectures on Theology and Ecology." *King's Theological Review*, Volume 12(2), 1989, pp. 41-45.

Index

TEXTS AND STUDIES IN RELIGION

48. Alexander Sándor Unghváry, **The Hungarian Protestant Reformation in the Sixteenth Century Under the Ottoman Impact: Essays and Profiles**
49. Daniel B. Clendenin and W. David Buschart (eds.), **Scholarship, Sacraments and Service: Historical Studies in Protestant Tradition,** *Essays in Honor of Bard Thompson*
50. Randle Manwaring, **A Study of Hymn-Writing and Hymn-Singing in the Christian Church**
51. John R. Schneider, **Philip Melanchthon's Rhetorical Construal of Biblical Authority: Oratio Sacra**
52. John R. Eastman (ed.), **Aegidius Romanus,** *De Renunciatione Pape*
53. J.A. Loubser, **A Critical Review of Racial Theology in South Africa: The Apartheid Bible**
54. Henri Heyer, **Guillaume Farel: An Introduction to His Theology**, Blair Reynolds (trans.)
55. James E. Biechler and H. Lawrence Bond (ed.), **Nicholas of Cusa on Interreligious Harmony: Text, Concordance and Translation of** *De Pace Fidei*
56. Michael Azkoul, **The Influence of Augustine of Hippo on the Orthodox Church**
57. James C. Dolan, **The** *Tractatus Super Psalmum Vicesimum* **of Richard Rolle of Hampole**
58. William P. Frost, **Following Joseph Campbell's Lead in the Search for Jesus' Father**
59. Frederick Hale, **Norwegian Religious Pluralism: A Trans-Atlantic Comparison**
60. Frank H. Wallis, **Popular Anti-Catholicism in Mid-Victorian Britain**
61. Blair Reynolds, **The Relationship of Calvin to Process Theology as Seen Through His Sermons**
62. Philip G. Kreyenbroek, **Yezidism - Its Background, Observances and Textual Tradition**
63. Michael Azkoul, **St. Gregory of Nyssa and the Tradition of the Fathers**
64. John Fulton and Peter Gee (eds.), **Religion in Contemporary Europe**
65. Robert J. Forman, **Augustine and the Making of a Christian Literature: Classical Tradition and Augustinian Aesthetics**
66. Ann Matheson, **Theories of Rhetoric in the 18th-Century Scottish Sermon**
67. Raoul Mortley, **The Idea of Universal History From Hellenistic Philosophy to Early Christian Historiography**
68. Oliver Logan, **The Venetian Upper Clergy in the 16th and 17th Centuries**
69. Anthony Blasi, **A Sociology of Johannine Christianity**